Making Fiscal Policy in Japan

Economic Effects and Institutional Settings

HIROMITSU ISHI

OXFORD

UNIVERSITY PRESS

OXFORD
UNIVERSITY PRESS

Great Clarendon Street, Oxford OX2 6DP
Oxford University Press is a department of the University of Oxford.
It furthers the University's objective of excellence in research, scholarship,
and education by publishing worldwide in

Oxford New York

Athens Auckland Bangkok Bogotá Buenos Aires Calcutta
Cape Town Chennai Dar es Salaam Delhi Florence Hong Kong Istanbul
Karachi Kuala Lumpur Madrid Melbourne Mexico City Mumbai
Nairobi Paris São Paulo Shanghai Singapore Taipei Tokyo Toronto Warsaw

and associated companies in Berlin Ibadan

Oxford is a registered trade mark of Oxford University Press
in the UK and certain other countries

Published in the United States
by Oxford University Press Inc., New York

British Library Cataloguing in Publication Data

Data available

Library of Congress Cataloging in Publication Data

Ishi, Hiromitsu, 1937–
Making fiscal policy in Japan : economic effects and institutional settings / Hiromitsu Ishi.
p. cm.
Includes bibliographical references and index.
1. Fiscal policy—Japan. 2. Japan—Economic policy. I. Title.
HJ1391.I828 2000   336.3'0952—dc21   00–044605

ISBN 0–19–924071–X

1 3 5 7 9 10 8 6 4 2

Typeset by Graphicraft Limited, Hong Kong
Printed in Great Britain
on acid-free paper by
Biddles Ltd.,
Guildford & King's Lynn

For Mamiko

Contents

Preface

The Japanese economy, which has developed notably through the effects of defeat at the end of the Second World War, occupational reforms, post-war rapid growth, followed by a more moderate growth pattern and subsequently the recent bubble phenomenon, provides very interesting material for in-depth study, particularly for outsiders. It is widely believed that the Japanese government has played a significant role in developing the economy throughout the post-war period. At first sight the interaction between economic growth and the government looks to be closely linked, and is apparently self-evident. However, analysis of this interaction is no easy task.

Reflecting the long-standing interest in the success story of Japan's economic growth, a large amount of literature on the Japanese economy already exists and, indeed, is available in English. It seems to me, however, that there is relatively little material available in English on government policies, and in particular on fiscal policy. A number of titles relevant to monetary policy and financial markets in Japan have been published in English, reflecting more academic interest in the subject. In contrast, there is, as yet, no one book exploring from an academic point of view the actual influence of fiscal policy on the post-war growth of Japan which is aimed specifically at foreign readers. Europeans, Americans, Asians and others who seek to understand Japanese fiscal policy will experience great difficulty accessing reliable literature in English. The aim of this book is to help fill this gap.

In general, this book is non-technical and is written not only for public finance specialists but also for non-academics, such as bureaucrats, businessmen and so on. Furthermore, it is intended to be of help to general readers who are interested in Japanese economic policy and history. Instead of relying on sophisticated theoretical and econometric models, the discussion in this book is developed in terms of what general insights are to be derived or what lessons are to be learned from this course of study. Potentially this book could be appropriate as a textbook for a Japanese economy course at university level. In fact, a substantial part of the book comprises material written to support a lecture course on the Japanese economy, given at Carlton College in the USA, the University of New South Wales in Australia and Bocconi University in Italy. In addition, the book also contains manuscripts prepared for public lectures given by the author in various parts of the world, as well as a number of papers presented at international conferences.

I am grateful to a number of colleagues and associates and to various circumstances which have combined to assist me in the writing of this book. I have been fortunate to be a member of the Fiscal System Commission and the Post-war Fiscal History Project at the Japanese Ministry of Finance for more than twenty years. Work on other related government committees has also stimulated the discussion. These valuable experiences have had a major influence on my ideas about the making of fiscal policy in the post-war period and have enabled me to access the resources needed to pursue my research. In particular, staff at the Research Division, the Budget Bureau, at the Japanese Ministry of Finance, have greatly assisted me by providing the necessary data.

My deep thanks ought to be expressed to Professor Hugh T. Patrick at Columbia University for writing the foreword in this book. Moreover, I have accumulated many debts to overseas friends who have assisted me in the writing of such a book in English. Following the publication of my previous book, *The Japanese Tax System* (2nd edn, 1993), I would like to acknowledge the warm-hearted support of Andrew Schuller at Oxford University Press. I wish to express my indebtedness to Director Arthur Stockwin and Jenny Corbett at the Nissan Institute of Japanese Studies at Oxford University, who very kindly provided me with office space on more than one occasion.

As usual, I am greatly indebted to Hiroko Sugimoto at Hitotsubashi University for her sincere aid in the production of the manuscript. George Samu at the University of Toronto helped me in editing the drafts in English and I would like to thank him very much.

H. I.
Tokyo

Foreword

Understanding the post-war performance and structure of the Japanese economy, and the government's macroeconomic policies shaping this performance, is of great importance to us all. After all, despite its current difficulties, next to the USA, Japan has the world's largest and most technologically advanced economy. Perhaps equally important, it provides a range of experiences directly relevant to policy-making elsewhere, and that experience has its remarkable elements—most positive but some negative.

Professor Ishi, in this very useful study of fiscal policy-making in post-war Japan, appropriately takes such a broad, comprehensive approach. A distinguished specialist on Japanese tax and budget policy, the essential components of public finance, the author effectively combines academic expertise and policy insight based on having served for many years on various Ministry of Finance commissions and study groups. This book is designed for those who want to understand the role and performance of fiscal policy as an integral component of macroeconomic policy, and the attendant effects on the economy's growth. Within this framework, the author then traces and analyses the basic features of Japanese fiscal policy as the economy evolved over time, and considers the institutional features and policy objectives which shaped the budget process. The discussion is straightforward and not highly technical; this book is appropriately designed for the more general reader, not just the technical specialist on public finance.

The author divides the post-war economy into three periods: the high growth era to the mid-1970's oil crisis; the moderate growth period from 1975 to 1990, when the stock and real estate bubbles burst; and the current slow growth, poor performance period of the 1990s.

For many, the high growth period is particularly interesting; it provides probably the most relevant 'lessons' for developing markets and transforming socialist economies. Since private business investment and consumption generated high aggregate demand, in retrospect, macroeconomic policy had the relatively easy task of containing demand. As Professor Ishi well analyses, it was during this period that the balanced budget policy objective became so well-entrenched at the Ministry of Finance. Parenthetically, when I arrived in Japan in 1957 for dissertation research, I suffered a huge shock to see Japanese macroeconomic policy seemingly floating the textbook of Keynesian economics I had been learning, and yet doing so well. It took some time for me to understand the dynamics of follower country, private sector-based, rapid growth.

However, due to lack of domestic demand the balanced budget policy was sharply breached during 1975–1979 and again in 1991–1996, and Keynesian pump-priming fiscal deficits increased rapidly and in large amounts. Such episodes have invariably heightened the tension between the proponents in other ministries of such short-run demand stimulus measures and the longer-run budget deficit reduction policies always advocated by the Ministry of Finance. Ishi nicely discusses this, and cautiously tends toward the anti-Keynesian position. In large part the trade-off between stimulus and restraint (budget deficit reduction) is a matter of timing: when the economic recovery is sufficiently private demand driven, then government stimulus is no longer necessary. (This is a large part of the story of the US government's success, finally in the 1990s, of reducing its budget deficit.)

A further virtue of this book is its nice treatment of a number of specific public finance topics and issues in the second and third Parts: the author clearly explains the complex Japanese budget system, which confusingly consists of separate budgets, each quite independent and with different functions. There is a good chapter on the evolving shares of government expenditures by functional category, with special consideration of health, welfare, and education, and the special interest pressures affecting public works allocations. The chapter on the Fiscal Investment and Loan Program (FILP), about which so little has been written in English, is especially useful. So too is the chapter on ageing and the social security system, probably Japan's most difficult future public finance issue.

In addition to its clear exposition of these and related major themes, the book contains valuable nuggets of policy insights as well as detailed institutional and empirical information. I commend it to the reader.

Hugh T. Patrick
Columbia University

List of Figures

List of Tables

List of Abbreviations

AFF	Agriculture, Forestry and Fisheries Finance Corporation
BIS	Bank for International Settlements
BOJ	The Bank of Japan
CPI	Consumer Price Index
DBJ	Development Bank of Japan
DIC	Deposit Insurance Corporation
EHI	Employees' Health Insurance
EIBJ	Export–Import Bank of Japan
EP	Employees' Pension
EPA	Economic Planning Agency
ESB	Environment Sanitation Business Financing Corporation
ESC	Economic Strategic Council
EMSFS	Emergency Measure to Stabilize Financial System
EROA	Economic Rehabilitation in Occupied Area
FIL	Fiscal Investment and Loan agencies
FILP	Fiscal Investment and Loan Programme
FRC	Financial Revitalization Committee
FRRL	Financial Revitalization Related Law
GARIOA	Government and Relief in Occupied Area
GATT	General Agreement on Tariffs and Trade
HL	Housing Loan Corporation
HTD	Hokkaido–Tohoku Development Corporation
IBJ	Industrial Bank of Japan
IISA	Industrial Investment Special Account
JBIC	Japan Bank for International Cooperation
JDB	Japan Development Bank
JBIC	Japan Bank for International Cooperation
JR	Japan Railway
JNR	Japanese National Railroad
JT	Japan Tobacco Inc
LDP	Liberal Democratic Party (the current ruling political party)
LTCB	Long-term Credit Bank
MAA	Mutual Aid Associations
MAFF	Ministry of Agriculture, Forestry and Fishery
MCF	Medical Care Facilities Financing Corporation
MITI	Ministry of International Trade and Industry
MOC	Ministry of Construction
MOF	Ministry of Finance
MOFA	Ministry of Foreign Affairs
MOHA	Ministry of Home Affairs
MOHW	Ministry of Health and Welfare

MOPT	Ministry of Posts and Telecommunications
MOT	Ministry of Transportation
NCB	Nippon Credit Bank
NHI	National Health Insurance
NI	National Income
NLA	National Land Agency
NTA	National Tax Administration
NTT	Nippon Telegraph and Telephone
ODA	Official Development Aid
ODF	Okinawa Development Finance Corporation
OECF	Overseas Economic Corporation Fund
PF	People's Credit Insurance Corporation
RCB	Resolution and Collection Bank
RCO	Resolution and Collection Organization
RFB	Reconstruction Finance Bank
RPI	Retail Price Index
SBC	Small Business Credit Insurance Corporation
SBF	Small Business Finance Corporation
SCAP	Supreme Commander for the Allied Powers
SII	Structural Impediments Initiatives
STM	Special Temporary Management
VAT	Value-added tax
WPI	Wholesale Price Index
WTO	World Trade Organisation

Introduction

The most remarkable feature of Japan's post-war economic performance was the rapid surge of economic growth from a state of devastation and defeat in the Second World War. Particular attention should be paid to the 1950s and 1960s. This period is often referred to as an 'economic miracle' and continues to attract worldwide attention. In the process of rapid growth, Japan succeeded in catching up with the Western powers by the late 1960s, reaching the forefront of major industrialized countries in the 1980s. Since such a remarkable record of economic growth is unparalleled in history, many relevant lessons may be gleaned by other countries from the 'Japanese model'.

However, a new era has emerged for Japan since the early 1970s. In particular, the first oil shock, caused by the oil embargo of the Arab countries, was an epoch-making incident in that Japan's weakness became evident along with its vulnerability as a very resource-poor country. Thereafter, Japan has undergone a sea of changes and has faced significant problems requiring solution through the 1980s. These changes were induced by a drastic slowdown of economic growth due to two oil shocks, the occurrence of a large current-account surplus, the sharp rise of fiscal deficits and the inevitable deregulation of financial markets. However, its damage was successfully overcome by the cooperation of private businesses and the government. After overcoming the initial hardship of the 1970s, Japan emerged before the world as an economic superpower in the 1980s. Indeed, Japan's economy achieved great success in its overall performance until the late 1980s and attained the highest rate of economic growth among major industrial countries with no serious problems of unemployment or inflation.

From the late 1980s Japan induced a 'bubble economy', and after the collapse of the 'bubble', Japan's economy suffered from recession or depression for almost ten years. In some sense, recession as a result of the collapsing bubble might be stressed as Japan's second hardship in the post-war period, next to the oil shock. There are a number of people, in and out of Japan, who believe that Japan's era is over and that its economy has been substantially weakened, deteriorating in its fundamental and potential capability. They see Japan's economy as having lost the brilliant buoyancy it has showed in the past.

It is often pointed out that the government has played a vital role in promoting economic growth by intervening in the market-based activity of post-war Japan. Japan's institutions may have been rather unique in terms of economic performance, and they have certainly been instrumental in bringing about an exceptional pattern of economic growth. Generally speaking, government policies performed well in encouraging rapid economic growth in collaboration with private sector activities. This good performance ensued at least until the mid-1970s. For instance, fiscal policy

was keeping the budget of the national government balanced until 1965, never generating an inflationary impetus caused by fiscal deficits. This neutral budgetary stance
was very important in establishing a sound policy framework that had not been seen
in any other countries. In addition, tax policy was centred on the annual reduction of
tax revenues, refunding the benefits of growth to the private sector to a large extent,
thus helping to restrain the scale of government intervention and encourage the
efficient performance of both the public sector and the market economy.

In a word, we can say that fiscal policy played a relatively passive role in the process
of rapid economic growth, rather than taking initiatives to promote it directly using
fiscal instruments.

In contrast, monetary policy has played a more positive role in accommodating
macroeconomic fundamentals in the Japanese economy. In the earlier post-war period,
the monetary authority kept mainly to a low-interest policy to encourage private
investment, which at the same time was reinforced by favourable government loans.
To combat overheated situations, tight monetary policy was opportunely and tactic-
ally triggered to calm down the inflationary pressures and to stop a reduction in foreign reserves. Overall, it is widely acknowledged that fiscal and monetary policies were
well-matched with the brisk economic activity of the private sector until the 1970s.
Since then, however, the successful performance of fiscal and monetary policies has
slowed down to a considerable extent, mainly reflecting both the occurrence of a large
fiscal deficit and the far-reaching deregulation of financial markets.

Greater emphasis should be placed on the role of government intervention in the
market, for example in the form of administrative guidance, regulation or selective
protectionism as an industrial policy, when assessing the past performance of government policies in the process of economic growth. Apart from the adoption of fiscal
and monetary policies, the Japanese government successfully intervened in the markets through the unconventional policy instrument of administrative guidance. The
Miti's policy is a typical and well-known case. It is generally acknowledged that a
market-based growth strategy might not best serve a number of developing economies
whose markets were not well developed in the past. Incipient markets need to develop
in a proper manner and the government should intervene to guide market development, correcting market failures. This is what was seen in the Japanese example during the earlier post-war period. Perhaps such a 'Japanese model' would help to develop
policy issues among Asian countries and countries in a transitional phase from a
centrally-planned economy. In fact, government intervention has figured prominently
in many countries of East Asia, such as Korea, which have so far succeeded in achieving better economic performance than other countries with a market-based strategy.
What is evident from these experiences is that priority should be given to government
intervention, at least in the earlier stages of a nascent market economy, than macroeconomic policies. In the process, we may witness a productive, not a distortive,
government intervention.

Needless to say, attention should also be paid to the less favourable aspect of the
success of the growth process in post-war Japan. The recent experience of the Japanese

economy after the collapse of the 'bubble economy' in the early 1990s offers certain negative lessons regarding the pitfalls of both an inefficient public sector and regulated markets which have been steadily fostered throughout the post-war period. It is widely believed that policy measures and institutions remained intact long after their original goal had been completed in the economy. Entrenched policy stances are likely to take on a life of their own once they are embarked upon, reflecting mainly both strong vested interest groups and the persistent resistance of bureaucracy to a reformist approach. At present, government intervention and tight regulation are beginning to work against each other in their attempt to achieve better economic performance in the market.

The growth process of post-war Japan after the end of the Second World War seems to contain special policy implications and is therefore an interesting case study as a 'Japanese model'. The following two points are worth noting. First of all, the Japanese experience during the earlier post-war period must be of great heuristic value and interest to East Asian countries as their economies have successfully taken off from an underdeveloped stage to achieve annual growth rates of over 10 per cent. Similar to Japan's earlier post-war years, many have dubbed this recent phenomenon in the East Asian region 'an Asian miracle'. Interestingly enough, Japan had achieved economic growth from the mid-1950s until 1973 at a rate comparable to that of the East Asian economies in the 1990s. What is more, during the period under consideration, the Japanese economy encountered the same problems that some East Asian economies experienced later, towards the end of the 1990s, such as overheating, a shortage of foreign reserves and so on, and the government had to tackle the difficult task of engineering a 'soft-landing' (see, for instance, Ito 1996).

Second, Japan's model has occasionally been explored in conjunction with the transitional process of remodelling the failed centrally-planned economies into market economies. In particular, Japan's experience may be relevant to the monumental task of reforming the former Soviet and East European countries. Moreover, it is generally thought that the Japanese experience of transforming its war-controlled economy might provide a model for the introduction of market-based economies in those countries. Perhaps a variety of socioeconomic reforms during the occupation period of 1945–52 would be worth noting as preconditions to subsequent economic growth in Japan.

Obviously, the positive contribution of the 'Japanese model' can be derived from the past experience of occupation and rapid economic growth era. However, the less favourable example of Japan's recent experience, as described above, must equally provide valuable lessons to many other countries.

The basic aim of this book is to argue systematically the role of government, particularly through fiscal policy in the post-war growth process of Japan. How has the government made fiscal policy in post-war Japan? When we refer to the role of government in connection with growth-oriented policies, it sounds as if it has been a very positive role, but this is not necessarily true. Generally speaking, the government has traditionally taken a rather passive or inactive stance in guiding economic activities as a whole, a phenomenon which is somewhat unique to Japan. In particular, fiscal policy has not been employed intentionally to initiate the economy through deliberate expenditure and tax policies but instead it has tended to take action passively in support of the private economy which was self-activated. A more powerful weapon has been the direct control of government intervention and administrative guidance through the policy instruments of the public sector. To conclude, it may be said that it is a market-enhancing approach which has traditionally been adopted by the government, rather than the stronger strategy of government intervention.

Discussion of the major issues in this book are divided into three parts, each with four or five chapters. Part I provides an overview of post-war economic performance and a preliminary consideration of the policy environment, covering the whole post-war period from 1945 to today. Chapter 1 begins with an examination of occupational policies and reforms as the preconditions of post-war economic growth. In Chapter 2, the process of rapid economic growth and its effects are investigated to highlight the success story of the 'Japanese model' in the 1950s and 1960s. Chapter 3 sheds light on structural changes moving Japan towards a new dimension after the first oil shock in 1973 and explains the arrival of Japan in the international community. Chapter 4 describes the emergence of the bubble economy which occurred in the late 1980s and its aftermath.

In Part II the main topics of this book are explored as fiscal policy responses. These studies constitute the primary part of the book. Chapter 5 explains the basic framework of budgets and the budgetary process in Japan which are indispensable in analysing the government's fiscal activities. Chapter 6 considers fundamental strategies of fiscal authority, based upon the traditional principle of budget orthodoxy in which deficit reduction has been persistently given the first priority in fiscal management. In Chapter 7, an empirical study is undertaken to look at unique aspects of the balanced budget policy for 1953–1965. Chapter 8, using statistical procedures, focuses on how financial resources for budgeting were automatically generated in a growing economy.

Part III is devoted to an analysis of specific policy issues in the public sector. Several important issues are addressed in each chapter. Chapter 9 begins with an investigation of the past trend of public expenditure in relation to human resource development. Chapter 10 discusses the most important problem for Japan to face in the twenty-first century; that is, an ageing population and its effect on the social security system, focusing on institutional settings with statistical evidence. In Chapter 11 an empirical analysis is undertaken to clarify the effects of tax incentives for export promotion. The Fiscal Loan and Investment Program has played a unique role in operating fiscal management as an off-budget activity, and this is studied in detail in Chapter 12. Chapter 13 deals with certain aspects of local public finance in view of intergovernmental grant policy. Lastly, certain remarks are added to conclude the arguments put forward in the thirteen chapters.

Observing the past trend of Japan's economy and fiscal policy up to the present time, it can be seen that both of them have reached a turning point in their search for a better direction. The economy has remained inactive for a long time since the collapse of the bubble boom, and shows no signs of any strong momentum for growth. In order to revitalize the Japanese economy, it should be structurally rebuilt to encourage the market-based activities more aggressively. Similarly, the accumulation of fiscal deficits has interfered with government fiscal performance in various ways and structural fiscal reforms are definitely needed to restore sound public finance. At the end of the 1990s the Hashimoto cabinet was tackling a grandiose reform package concentrating on six areas in which to reconstruct the socioeconomic structure of Japan towards the twenty-first century, encompassing economic, administrative, fiscal, financial, social security, and educational reforms. Needless to say, of these fiscal reform is given the highest priority. To our regret, we cannot proceed further with our study of this topic at present, because the structural reform movement has been postponed until the full recovery of the Japanese economy by the Obuti and Mori cabinet, and it is still too early to appraise it effectively.

Part I
Overview: The Policy Environment

1

The Preconditions for Post-war Economic Growth

No doubt, one of the most salient features of Japan's post-war economic performance was the rapid surge of economic growth from a state of devastation and defeat at the end of the Second World War. This transition is often referred to as an 'economic miracle' and continues to attract worldwide attention. In fact, Japan succeeded in catching up with the Western economic powers by the late 1960s, and it has continued to grow, coming to the forefront of major industrialized countries in the 1980s. Since Japan's remarkable economic growth is unparalleled in history, many relevant lessons can be gleaned by other countries.

The government has played an important role in the process of economic growth throughout the post-war period with relative success. In leading the economy to achieve a better performance, its role has occasionally altered depending upon the changing dimensions of the Japanese economy. In order to clarify this success story, and before embarking on the main arguments, we must seek the preconditions, if any, of post-war economic growth. In this chapter, particular attention is paid to a specific period, 1945–1955, in which a variety of occupational reforms were successfully attempted by the occupation authorities to establish the fundamental base of economic reconstruction and subsequent growth.

The basic aim of this study is to explore the general background of the defeat, subsequent reforms and economic reconstruction in relation to micro- and macro-economic policies attempted by the government during the occupation period.

THE DEFEAT AND OCCUPATION POLICIES

The Rise of the Phoenix from the Ashes
Japan was utterly defeated in the Second World War, and the economy was completely destroyed beyond any hope of recovery. As a result of American bombing around the end of the war, its industries were at a standstill, and its infrastructure was virtually demolished. In August 1945, when the Second World War was over, no one could ever imagine that Japan would attain the position of second industrial power in the world by the late 1960s. At that time, most of its major cities were crushed and lay in rubble, with their inhabitants scattered throughout the country.

However, Japan arose from this hopelessly depressed state of the immediate post-war period and eventually joined the top group of industrial nations in terms of per

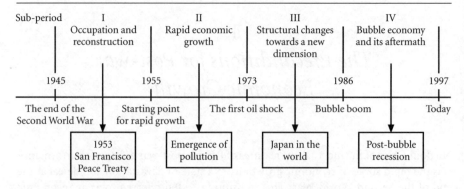

FIGURE 1.1. *A sketch of post-war economic performance*

capita GNP within less than five decades. Despite lower growth in the 1990s, Japan could perhaps be set to become one of the world's largest economies by the early twenty-first century. The term 'the rise of the Phoenix from the ashes' is most appropriate to describe the process of resurgence from the ashes of war and swift economic recovery with high-speed growth which Japan has successfully achieved (see Allen 1965, Patrick 1970, Tsuru 1993).

Since the fall of the Berlin Wall, many have begun to focus their attention on the reconstruction of Eastern Europe and the transitional process of remodelling the failed centrally-planned economies into market economies. In so doing, it is expected that the Japanese experience of transforming its wartime-controlled economy might provide a model for the introduction of market-based economies in Eastern Europe (see Teranishi 1994). Thus, it is possible that the period of Japanese occupation might be relevant to the Eastern Europe situation and is therefore an interesting case study.

Before proceeding to a major discussion, we provide a rough sketch of the whole picture of Japan's post-war economic performance in Figure 1.1. Roughly speaking, we can divide the whole period into four sub-periods, I, II, III, and IV, depending upon the major economic changes experienced since the end of the Second World War. Sub-period I covers the decade of occupation and reconstruction starting from 1945 and is the main issue in this chapter. Around the end of this period, the post-war economy managed to regain its pre-war level in terms of average output and the standard of living. Meanwhile, the San Francisco Peace Treaty with the USA, through which Japan regained independence in the international community, was signed in 1953.

Sub-period II is devoted to a typical time period of Japan's rapid economic growth, starting from 1955 and ending in the early 1970s with the first oil shock. During these years, the Japanese economy continued to grow at a rate far greater than that of any other advanced country in the world. Interestingly enough, this growth was precipitated by the single-minded emphasis of the government, businesses, and the general public on economic growth. However, rapid economic growth tended to bring with it its negative externalities as well, causing a great deal of environmental damage, especially in the form of water and air pollution. This has thrown the whole process of rapid economic growth into doubt.

At the outbreak of the first oil shock in 1973, followed by the second in 1979, the Japanese economy was confronted with the need for tremendous changes, which led to sub-period III. Since Japan relies almost totally on overseas markets for basic materials and energy sources, it is evident that its economy was highly vulnerable to the price shocks and oil embargoes. The big structural changes encountered by the Japanese economy lowered real growth rates to a significant extent. However, in spite of the disruptions caused by the two oil shocks, Japan's economic performance was much better than that of other industrialized countries in terms of real growth, inflation and employment in the 1980s, pushing Japan to the forefront of the world economy.

Since the late 1980s, a new dimension, known as the 'bubble economy', appeared replacing sub-period III where Japan established its position in the international community. This bubble phenomenon, delineated here as sub-period IV, generated the sharp rise of land and stock prices (i.e. asset inflation) in the period 1986–1991. After the collapse of the bubble boom, Japan's fortune has undergone a complete reversal as prolonged recession and stagnation have loomed over the Japanese economy. Despite the official announcement of the EPA that economic recovery was underway as of October 1993 after reaching a trough, the Japanese economy has showed no sign of buoyancy or upward movement until the late 1990s.

The Basic Nature of Occupation Policies

As a result of defeat in the Second World War, Japan was placed under military occupation by the victorious Allies. The eleven-power Far Eastern Commission in Washington officially determined relevant policies to govern Japan under the occupation. As a matter of fact, General MacArthur, Supreme Commander of the Allied Powers (SCAP)[1], was responsible for all decision making of any consequence, as well as for the implementation of occupation policy.

Rather than punishment, the occupation was regarded as possibly the greatest social experiment attempted by the Americans. The immediate objectives of the occupation were twofold: democratization and demilitarization. It was widely believed that Japan would be able to become a peaceful member of the international community only if it were democratized. No doubt, SCAP believed that Japan would not try to invade other nations as a democracy, and tried to recreate Japan as a democratic society not only in an economic and political sense but even in terms of culture and ideology.

Furthermore, in-depth attempts were made to demilitarize Japan by stopping all military production and destroying all weapons. In addition, war-related leaders in

---

[1] SCAP usually referred both to MacArthur himself and to the administrative bureaucracy of the occupation in general.

military, political and business circles were purged by SCAP as war criminals. Great emphasis was placed on the removal of the economic and political bases of military powers and the curtailment of Japan's attitude to employ war as a means of foreign policy.

In conjunction with these two objectives, there were a number of epoch-making economic, social, and political reforms in concrete terms. Focusing on socio-political reforms alone for the moment, particular attention should be paid to the following cases. The state was segregated from the Shinto religion, and the Emperor renounced any claims to divinity and became a mere symbol of the state. Also, the system of nobility with aristocratic titles was abolished and the general vote was expanded to admit women. All restrictions on political, religious, and civil freedoms were removed, and fundamental rights were guaranteed to all. Moreover, of primary importance was the establishment of a parliamentary democracy as a principal feature of the occupation process in which the Emperor was replaced by the parliament as the core of the political system. Instead of rule by a divine Emperor as in the pre-war era, the nation was governed by the Prime Minister and his Cabinet, both of which were elected by the Diet. In turn, members of the Diet were elected by the general public in both the House of Representatives and the House of Councillors (see, for a more expanded discussion, Reischauer 1977).

It is also important to note that many of these reforms were incorporated into a new constitution enacted in 1947 under great American influence. Perhaps this is one of the most idealistic constitutions in the world in view of the political, economic, and social rights that it pledges to the citizens. As an example of its idealism, attention often focuses on the manifestation in Article 9 which renounces the use of military force. The Japanese people have widely accepted this constitution from the beginning, despite its American origins (see, for general discussion, Yamamura 1967).

Major Economic Reforms

Not only the socio-political reforms, but also the economic reforms of the occupation period were extremely significant in providing a basis for Japan's outstanding economic performance during the entire post-war era. Obviously, the efforts towards democratization involved major economic reforms. There were several economic reforms which are worth noting, but special attention should be paid to the following four cases (see, for more detailed discussion, Patrick and Rosovsky 1976, ch. 1; Teranishi and Kosai 1993, part II).

First of all, the most sweeping reform was attempted in the sphere of farmland ownership. No doubt, land reform was one of the most valuable reforms in the occupation reform package for promoting sustained economic growth. This should be contrasted with the experience of other Asian countries, such as the Philippines. As far as the ownership of farmland is concerned in pre-war Japan, tenantry was predominant and widespread. For example, around 1910 approximately 45 per cent of the land was cultivated by tenants. The remaining land was owned by landlords who were relatively wealthy, powerful, and paternalistic individuals. The landlord–tenant relationship

TABLE 1.1. *The effects of land reform—area farmed (1000m²)*

	Before reform on 11 November 1945	Purchases by the government until 1 August 1950	After reform on 1 August 1950
Independent farming land	27639	367	46471
Tenant A	23483	18803	5107
Farming land owned by			
Resident landlord	16075	11494	4750
Absentee landlord	7418	7309	357
Total B	51132	19170	51568
Tenancy ratio % A/B	45.9		9.9

Source: Ministry of Finance, *The Financial History of Japan: The Occupation Period 1945–52*, vol. 19 (Toyo Keizai Shimposha, 1978), p. 78.

was symbolic of social class discrimination in the pre-war era, and reform programmes had occasionally been under consideration. However, Japanese bureaucrats had never implemented such a major task.

Although it was not the progenitor of the idea, SCAP was able to carry out substantial land reform as a substitute agent for the paralysed bureaucratic groups. In order to end tenantry, land ownership was transferred from landlords to their farming tenants by the method of sale and purchase, not confiscation, under the control of the government. In principle, it was the intention that landlords be fairly compensated for the sale of their land, the value of which was set at the market prices predominant in 1945. However, as argued below, the real value of the transaction price was tremendously reduced by rampant inflation when, in practice, transaction took place a couple of years[2] after the sale.

Consequently, farm tenantry and landlordism, which still remained untouched in many other countries, were eliminated in Japan by the post-war land reform. Table 1.1 summarizes the effects of land reform in terms of statistics on the farm land owned by independent and tenant farmers. Prior to the implementation of land reform in 1945, 45.9 per cent of total farm land was still cultivated by tenants. Subsequently, however, the tenancy ration fell drastically to about 10 per cent as a result of government purchases from landlords. Thus, the structure of land ownership was greatly altered and absentee landlords nearly disappeared. In spite of such a big revolution in the historical structure of agricultural land ownership, there were few changes in the methods of production based on family farms. The goals of stout farming families were achieved independently of landlord control. Land reform did not have any immediate effects in terms of increases in productivity, but it is evident that the new owners

---

[2] Indeed, the transaction price of land at that time fell to only 1 per cent of pre-war land prices. See Patrick and Rosovsky 1976, p. 10.

invested more actively in land improvements, encouraging a higher demand for food products with higher prices. Thus, the agricultural sector was able to satisfy the pressing need for food, and at the same time it became the first sector to regain the pre-war standard of living.

Second, a major objective of occupation policy was to foster a strong, independent labour union movement. Basically, SCAP aimed to create a 'mass of power' (i.e. industrial workers) to contend with the existing establishment of business and bureaucratic groups. For this purpose, SCAP decided to place American union leaders in key positions to promote the unionization movement. In a relatively short period of time— and far beyond expectation—Japan's unionization advanced with great rapidity. By 1948, around 56 per cent of industrial workers participated in their own labour unions (see Ono 1994, p. 75).

One of the marked features of unionization in Japan was that from the very beginning most of the bargaining between managers and workers took place at the individual company level. As a result, company unions have developed well throughout the post-war period, and are considered to be the fundamental basis for the efficient employment of good labour. Many unions at individual company level came together in industry-wide organizations which in turn amalgamated at the national level. Unions at the national level were sometimes aggressive and militant, clashing with company management over demands for wage increases in annual 'spring offensives'. In this sense, the SCAP objective was accomplished.

Parallel to the unionism movement, flexible labour markets were established after a few years of post-war turmoil. Based upon the equal partnership of employers and employees, Japanese managers regained the authority to hire workers and to attract new workers from the surplus labour force in agriculture. It is generally acknowledged that Japan's post-war growth was fuelled by the influx of surplus labour from the agricultural sector.

As an assessment of the effects of these two occupation reforms, it can be said that both land reform and labour unionism triggered an opportunity for farmers and individual workers to participate fairly and share the subsequent economic growth. Moreover, the reforms led to an attenuation of the social conflicts among differing groups that had seriously damaged communities during the pre-war period. In other words, social stability was brought about by these reforms.

Third, the Zaibatsu (i.e., Japan's industrial conglomerates) were thoroughly dissolved as part of the package of occupation policies. The Zaibatsu, the four largest of which were Mitsubishi, Mitui, Sumitomo and Yasuda, were family-owned conglomerates and were usually controlled by a holding company. They occupied positions of economic and political power to a great extent in the pre-war period, amassing a great deal of wealth in the process. Naturally, they were deeply involved in the war-time economy.

Zaibatsu dissolution was carried out along the following two lines. First, the Zaibatsu families were removed from the positions of ownership and control of their own companies. The holding companies were terminated and all stocks owned by the Zaibatsu family members were confiscated and sold. In addition, they were not even allowed to work in the firms which they had once owned. These measures were so sweeping that the Zaibatsu families themselves lost power forever. The other factor in the dissolution of Zaibatsu companies was the relative 'leniency' with which it was carried out. For example, the Mitsubishi trading company was separated into a hundred smaller, competitive units, but the established linkages of mutual transactions remained unchanged.

Lastly, and related to the third point, the SCAP's concern was with the establishment of anti-monopoly legislation. The primary intention behind this legislation was to reduce the concentration of business power and to create a competitive business environment in the markets. Interestingly enough, this policy was undertaken in the context of building strong unionism and an egalitarian agricultural system, as well as disbanding military power. For this purpose, in addition to Zaibatsu dissolution, cartels and monopolies needed to be abolished and fair rules for business groups enacted. Essentially, this enactment contained anti-monopoly legislation and the establishment of Fair Trade Commission to monitor these rules.

As a result of implementing such institutional reforms as Zaibatsu dissolution and anti-monopoly legislation, the competitive market conditions were ideally arranged by SCAP in a relatively short period after the end of the War. It was, however, very difficult to obtain a general acceptance of the merits and social benefits of free competition from the Japanese businessmen and bureaucrats. This contrasts sharply with American thinking on competitive markets (see Patrick 1970). In the USA, great emphasis is placed on the importance of free competition, with the role of government ideally being restricted to a minimum level for maintaining brisk competition in the market economy. On the other hand, it appears that greater importance tends to be placed on the costs of free competition in Japan, such as possible over-investment, excess capacity, and excess competition.

'Excess competition' has frequently been criticized by the Japanese government and business leaders. This attitude implies that free competition has been only partially accepted, while direct guidance on business decisions by the government has relative approval in Japan. As a consequence, the basic idea behind anti-monopoly legislation as an occupational reform has been gradually eroded in the business sector (see Allen 1979).

DIRECT CONTROL OF THE GOVERNMENT

Inflationary Trends

At the conclusion of the Second World War, real GNP in 1946 had fallen to two-thirds of its pre-war level (1934–36 average) and, similarly, production had fallen to about one-third.[3] To make matters worse, the rate of inflation had risen more than 300 per cent in the same year.

---

[3] The agricultural product index (the 1933–35 average = 100) indicates 92.5 in 1949, 98.9 in 1950, 99.2 in 1951, 111.2 in 1952, and 97.6 in 1953. See MOF 1978, p. 81 and also Kawagoe 1993.

TABLE 1.2. *Inflationary trends*

Year	Wholesale price		Retail price (Tokyo)		GNP deflator	
	Index 1934–36 = 1.00	Rate of inflation %	Index 1934–36 = 1.00	Rate of inflation %	Index 1934–36 = 1.00	Rate of inflation %
1934–36	1.0	—	1.0	—	1.0	—
1944	2.3	—	3.0	—	3.6	—
1945	3.5	51.1	3.8	26.7	n.a.	—
1946	16.3	364.5	18.9	397.4	40.9	—
1947	48.2	195.9	51.0	169.8	104.1	154.5
1948	127.9	165.6	149.6	193.3	187.6	80.2
1949	208.8	63.3	243.4	62.7	232.4	23.9
1950	246.8	18.2	239.1	−1.8	244.9	5.4
1951	342.5	38.8	309.5	29.4	298.9	22.0
1952	349.2	2.0	300.5	−2.9	302.3	1.1
1953	351.6	0.7	311.0	0.2	327.2	8.2
1954	349.2	−0.7	321.2	3.3	332.5	1.6
1955	343.0	−1.8	307.4	−4.3	329.9	−0.8

Source: The Bank of Japan, *Hundred-year Statistics of the Japanese Economy*, 1966, pp. 51, 77, 80.

Among the disastrous plight of the immediate post-war economy, inflation was the most crucial economic and social issue in Japan. Needless to say, inflation inflicted great damage on holders of financial assets (e.g. deposits, bonds, and so on), pensioners, rent recipients, and to some extent wage earners. Wages constantly lagged behind inflationary adjustment. In particular, ex-landlords and Zaibatsu families were hit most severely, while ex-tenants, corporate stock holders, and owners of other real assets did not suffer from inflation, and even benefited in some cases. It is interesting to note that these striking changes in income distribution and property ownership were incurred without any difficulty in social disorders. The reason is perhaps simple. Since Japan was thoroughly devastated and in a state of chaos, the need for tremendous sacrifices could be accepted by all. The forcible adjustment caused by inflation took the form of transfers from a small minority to a large majority of Japanese, who responded favourably. In the process, the previous possessors of wealth and power were not able to sustain their vested interests, because they were under attack economically, politically, and socially.

Table 1.2 depicts the inflationary situation in terms of the wholesale price index (WPI), the retail price index (RPI) in Tokyo and the GNP deflator during the immediate post-war period. The WPI, computed on the basis of pre-war level (i.e. 1934–36 prices), was 16 times higher in 1946, 48 times higher in 1947, 128 times higher in 1948, and rose up to over 200–300 times higher later on. Statistics for the RPI show a more or less similar pattern. On the other hand, a more drastic rise was seen in the GNP deflator for 1946–47. The phenomenon of inflationary trends can be more clearly observed from the rate of inflation. The WPI expanded at an annual rate of 364.5 per cent in 1946, 195.9 per cent in 1947 and 165.6 per cent in 1948. Likewise, the RPI delineates the same phenomenon while the GNP deflator shows a somewhat different pattern. The Japanese economy suffered from rampant inflation in the true sense of the term.

It is apparent that inflation was unavoidable to some extent, given the special circumstances after the end of the War. The government were held liable to a significant extent both to the general public and to firms in the form of latent compensation payments. A vast amount of compensation had to be paid both to the families of those who lost their lives, and to the firms that suffered damages due to the country's entry into the Second World War. Moreover, the urgency of post-war production shortages and the sharp bottlenecks of productive materials accelerated the rate of inflation. Obviously, strong inflationary pressures had been built in during the War.

By 1949, as seen in Table 1.2, inflation had finally calmed down, mainly reflecting the drastic measures of the Dodge Plan adapted by SCAP, as noted below. If the Japanese government had not at first been reluctant to take the initiative in adopting strong anti-inflationary policies, rampant inflation could have been mitigated by a combination of wage–price and budget controls. However, the government consistently displayed a non-cooperative attitude towards halting inflation during the period in question. By and large, the government placed greater emphasis on economic recovery even at the cost of inflation, which became a major policy stance during the high growth period of later years. The government feared that anti-inflationary measures would become unpopular, thereby losing widespread support among the people and firms. In particular, since the big businesses had to repay enormous amounts of wartime loans to banks, they wanted to raise the price of their products and to repay the loans with money sharply reduced in value.

Price Stabilization Programmes

Of course, the Japanese government did make a considerable effort to halt rampant inflation, but its efforts were completely futile. In accordance with the sharp rise in prices, the government attempted two sets of micro supply-side measures: price controls with the aid of subsidies and the allocation of invested funds for key industries. However, since these measures themselves were strongly inflationary, SCAP was finally forced to introduce macro adjustments for price stabilization: i.e. the Dodge Plan.

At the outset, the Japanese government launched a measure to freeze deposits as an element of its price stabilization programmes. The exchange from 'old' yen to 'new' yen was made compulsory by a decree in which new yen were frozen in depositors' accounts. Accordingly, depositors were only permitted to withdraw money from their bank accounts up to a certain ceiling that the government regarded as an amount appropriate to sustain a basic standard of living. This was intended to be a sort of 'shock therapy' to reduce money supply at a time of hyperinflation. Despite such a mandatory measure of deposit freezes to combat rampant inflation, the government failed to control budget deficits, which in turn continued to encourage inflationary trends.

In March 1946, the government established wage–price control as part of its stabilization programme. The wage rate was fixed by government officials and the prices of basic goods were also controlled in accordance with the wage restraint. For two basic goods, rice and coal, a dual price system was officially established, in which consumers' prices were constantly lower than producers' prices. The gap between the two prices was filled by price-stabilization subsidies in order to sustain consumers' prices at an artificially low level (Kuroda 1993).

In spite of the strong inflationary tendency of this programme, in July 1947 the government tried to expand the coverage of its dual price control system to choose five key products: including coal again, steel, non-iron metals, fertilizer and soda. The gap between the official dual prices requiring compensation by subsidies was further widened, producing a vast amount of fiscal deficits and more increases in the price levels. Obviously, the basic nature of this programme changed from one of price stabilization to one of price support, particularly in the key industries listed above. Since subsidies for stabilizing prices had to be financed from the budget, what would happen at the following stage would be as one might have anticipated from the outset. More money would be required to support this scheme via fiscal deficits. This point is substantiated by the data. For instance, the ratio of price-stabilization subsidies to the general account expenditure was 11.1 per cent in 1947, 13.2 per cent in 1948, and 28.7 per cent in 1949 (see MOF 1949 pp. 72–73, MOF 1962 pp. 126–7).

As seen in Table 1.2, the inflation rate remained at high three-digit levels for 1946–48. Clearly, successive programmes of price stabilization with wage controls could not halt the inflationary trend by itself and other anti-inflationary measures were needed to halt inflation. Inevitably, as a by-product of government control of the price system, black markets emerged; markets on which the people found they had to rely in order to survive during the earlier post-war period. Black market prices jumped to 40.1 times official prices in January 1946, based on fifty consumption goods in Tokyo. Such prices continued to rise, more or less, within a relative margin of two-digits until mid-1947, and thereafter they rose 4–7 times official prices in 1948. It was not until 1950 that black market prices were nearly extinguished (see MOF 1978, pp. 64–5).

Keisha Seisan Method

Let us move to the second micro supply-side measure, that is, the so-called Keisha Seisan method. The main causes of rampant inflation evidently relied upon both the monetary and real sectors, the former being the massive flow of money from fiscal deficits, and the latter the production bottlenecks. Given the enormous shortages of basic materials in the immediate post-war period, a priority-based system was needed to allocate restricted resources to specific sectors more effectively. The method employed was the 'Keisha Seisan' method, which was often called the *priority production system*, thereby implying a 'key-industry-concentrated' plan (see Tajika and Yui 1996). This was a kind of crude planning system intended to stimulate industrial recovery, and resume production in key industries, starting at the end of 1947.

The key industries targeted for this policy were coal, steel, fertilizer, plus a small number of others. In particular, the highest priority was given to coal production with the aim of becoming domestically self-supporting. The labour force was enticed into coal mining by the use of favourable measures that provided higher wages, housing, and other fringe benefits. Furthermore, the increased production of coal was channelled into steel manufacturing, which was given second priority, and in turn increased steel products were thrown into the coal industry as plant and equipment. After both coal and steel production reached a certain level by mutual supply, stocks were to be supplied afterwards to increase the production of other key industries. The main reason why targeting was feasible at all was that production bottlenecks could be identified and isolated in a few basic industries.

In addition to the regulation of production in selected sectors, corresponding financial resources were also allocated for the provision of concentrated funds to specific key industries. In order to accomplish the allocation of funds on a priority basis, the Reconstruction Finance Bank (RFB—the *Fukkin* for short) was established in October 1946, as a special government financial institution, being modelled after the US Reconstruction Finance Company. The *Fukkin* began its operation in November 1947, readily making loans to industries essential for reconstruction under the Keisha Seisan method. The *Fukkin* obtained funds by selling its bonds to the Bank of Japan (BOJ). Consequently, *Fukkin* financing resulted in increased issues of BOJ notes, and in turn stimulated inflation. However, this was a first priority objective attempted by the government to raise the level of production even at the sacrifice of price hikes. In fact, inflation had continued throughout 1947–48 at three digit levels and was often called the '*Fukkin* inflation'.

Under these circumstances, the production of coal was augmented to some extent. In total, however, it is difficult to properly assess the results of the Keisha Seisan method. The following comment may be of some assistance:

Because the Japanese economy faced at that time a serious shortage of raw materials, this policy was essentially an attempt to substitute domestic production of coal for interrupted imports, and made sense, at least in theory. How successful the policy actually was still remains a controversy today (Yoshikawa and Okazaki 1993, p. 97).

In spite of such a bold anti-inflationary policy, inflation was not abated and indeed became chronic, as if it were firmly built into the structure of Japan's economy. Thus, the next step required was to cure the chronic inflation by any means.

The Dodge Plan and Stringent Budgetary Policy
Facing prolonged inflation, the turning point of anti-inflationary measures came in the middle of 1948. Both the Japanese government and SCAP recognized the necessity of taking more powerful measures to combat inflation, but the relevant measures needed for stabilizing prices were not agreed upon between the two camps. While the former was fond of a gradual stabilization of the current inflation over a longer period

of time, the latter insisted upon prompt and thorough policy responses from a short-run point of view.

In pursuit of halting the rate of inflation, SCAP finally constructed, in December 1948, a comprehensive guideline called 'The Nine Principles for Economic Stabilization'. The basic framework of this guideline pointed out that fiscal deficits had to be reduced so as to stop inflation, requiring expenditure cuts, tax increases, more selective financing of investment, etc. Obviously, this was a package which consisted of belt-tightening measures for orthodox stabilization purposes. At the practical level, the measures were enforced by Joseph Dodge[4] who was sent as an economic adviser by Washington, DC in February, 1949.

The policy package adopted by Dodge was generally called the 'Dodge Plan', and was considered as typical of severe anti-inflationary policy. The following three programmes were of most importance in view of price stabilization:

1. top priority was given to balancing the budget on an overall basis, including all budgets in the government sector;
2. *Fukkin* financing was terminated;
3. subsidies to stabilize prices were eliminated.

In addition, the exchange rate was fixed at $1 = ¥360, and the US Aid Counterpart Fund (Mikaeri-account) was established to administer the aid from the USA.

No doubt, the most notable programme among them was the idea for a comprehensive balanced budget that was intended to cover not only the general account but also special accounts, government-affiliated institutions, and local government budgets in order to generate a budget surplus in total. This implied the need to compile a very stringent balanced budget in the fiscal year 1949. The true aim of the Dodge Plan was to diminish government debt from the BOJ through the curtailment of the *Fukkin* bonds. Particular attention would have to be paid to a drastic curtailment of price stabilization subsidies and, as noted above, a vast amount of subsidies in the general account began to disappear from September 1949.

Accordingly, the increasing rate of price index finally began to fall from the latter half of fiscal year 1948; both the WPI and the RPI of the BOJ were reduced from well over 100 per cent to two digits in terms of inflation rates. The rise in black market prices turned around to be negative in 1950.[5] As a result of the severe anti-inflationary policies in the Dodge Plan package, rampant inflation was finally terminated in 1949, producing acute deflation in the Japanese economy. Obviously, the remedy for rampant inflation in the Dodge Plan looked like shock-therapy and could not have been attempted at all had Japan not been occupied by foreign powers. In fact, direct government control was successful in stopping the inflation by intervening in the markets.

---

[4] Joseph Dodge was then a president at the Detroit Bank, and had participated in the US occupation policy of Germany in 1946.

[5] These figures are calculated from MOF 1978 pp. 547–9.

TABLE 1.3. *War damages of national wealth*

	Total of war damages (¥ million) (1)	Existed wealth at the end of WWII (¥ million) (2)	Percentages of war damages (1)/((1)+(2))
1 Buildings	22,220	68,215	24.6
2 Harbours and canals	132	1,632	7.5
3 Bridges	101	2,773	3.5
4 Machines and equipment	7,994	15,352	34.2
5 Railways	884	11,618	7.1
6 Vehicles	639	2,274	21.9
7 Ships	7,359	1,766	80.6
8 Electricity and gas	1,618	13,318	10.8
9 Telegraphs, telephones and broadcasting	203	1,683	14.8
10 Water supplies	366	1,814	16.8
11 Furniture and personal items	17,493	63,448	21.6
12 Miscellaneous unclassified	3,936	—	—
Total	64,278	118,852	25.4

Source: As Table 1.1, pp. 14–15.

ECONOMIC RECONSTRUCTION

The Process from Occupation to Recovery

Perhaps the initial occupation policies could have started by assuming that Japan brought devastation upon itself and therefore had to suffer the consequences. Following this reasoning, Japan would not have had any right to rely upon outside assistance for economic recovery. However, SCAP was not able to leave economic reconstruction issues untouched completely, because the difficulties in Japan were simply too great to ignore in the immediate post-war period.

As indicated in Table 1.3, Japan's national capital stock and infrastructure were entirely destroyed during the Second World War due to American bombing. For example, war damages of national assets as a whole shows total losses of one-quarter at the end of the War. The war damage ratios are 80.6 per cent of ships, 34.2 per cent of machines and equipment, 24.6 per cent of buildings and so on. A great number of human lives were also lost. Almost 3 million people died in the War, including military personnel and civilian casualties.

Moreover, Japan lost its colonial territories, including Taiwan, Korea, Manchuria and others. About 1.5 million people were expected to return from these old territories, and 7.6 million military soldiers came back from overseas. In addition to these people, 4 million employees working in military industries lost their jobs owing to the policy goal of demilitarization. Thus, the total number of job seekers in the labour markets amounted to more than 13 million (see Nishimura 1993, p. 3).

Indeed, by early 1946 Japan was on the brink of destruction and starvation, and desperately needed to obtain aid from outside sources. MacArthur persuaded Washington DC to provide large scale donations of food stuffs and medical supplies for the Japanese people to prevent disease and distress. As time went by, the form of US aid changed steadily from foodstuffs to petroleum, fertilizer, and industrial materials, reflecting the process of economic recovery.

During the period from the end of the War to the San Francisco Peace Treaty in 1953, occupation policy was, by and large, influenced by the changeable environment of international relations among major countries. The Cold War had divided the world by 1948, and China was not expected, from a Western standpoint, to be a stabilizing power in Asia. As a consequence, Japan's position was gradually highlighted to become a close partner of the West as a strong economy and a democratic nation. The USA began to regard Japan as the 'workshop of Asia' or 'a good friend of America', given the variation in the international community.[6] As a result of the shifting US attitude, increasing emphasis was placed on economic recovery while decreasing importance was put on economic reform.

The effect of this shift in US attitude implied that some parts of the occupation policies were to remain incomplete. Although both land and labour reforms had already been completed, the break-up of big industrial and financial firms was just about to be launched. The ambitious reform plan for industrial policy was forced to wither away at the implementation stage, and SCAP allowed most of the relevant firms to be split only partially.

Economic Recovery to the Pre-war Level

Rising up from the ashes, Japan regained economic power within a relatively short period. Table 1.4 summarizes the trends of GNP and production for 1945–55 compared to those of pre-war level. In 1946, Japan's mining and industrial production fell drastically to less than one-third of their pre-war level, and similarly GNP decreased to a great extent; about two-thirds. At that time, Japan suffered from large-scale war damages to basic industries, acute bottlenecks in scarce materials, and a shortage of production capacity caused by the military conversion of some civilian industries. The combined effect of these factors sharply curtailed the Japanese economic powers substantially below the pre-war level.

---

[6] Tsuru clearly pointed out the following: 'It can hardly be doubted that Japan's road to recovery was paved by coincidental developments on the international scene. With the heightening of the cold war psychology from about the time of the announcement of the Truman Doctrine (March 1947), reinforced by the demonstrably successful march of communists in China in 1948 onwards, the US government apparently became determined to make Japan 'a bulwark against communism' (see Tsuru 1993, p. 37).

TABLE 1.4. *Trends of real GNP and production*

| | Real GNP at 1934–36 Prices | | | |
	Amount (¥ million)	Growth rates (%)	Per head (¥)	Mining-industrial production index 1955 = 100
1934–36 Av.	16,672	—	244	61.9
1944	20,634	—	277	98.2
1945	n.a.	n.a.	—	43.2
1946	11,598	—	153	19.2
1947	12,573	8.4	161	23.9
1948	14,211	13.0	178	31.1
1949	14,524	2.2	178	40.0
1950	16,115	11.2	194	48.6
1951	18,207	13.0	215	66.2
1952	20,238	11.2	236	71.1
1953	21,657	7.0	249	85.8
1954	22,456	3.7	254	93.0
1955	24,967	11.2	280	100.0

Source: Economic Planning Agency, *White Paper on National Income*, 1965. Ministry of Finance, *The Financial History of Japan: The Occupation Period 1945–52*, vol. 19, p. 94.

However, as a result of strenuous efforts, attempted through successive reforms by SCAP and the Japanese government, economic recovery progressed steadily. As a matter of fact, in growth terms, economic recovery was swift; i.e. a real GNP growth rate of about 9 per cent had been achieved between 1947 and 1955. In 1949, the growth rate stagnated at only 2.2 per cent, reflecting the deflationary effects of the Dodge Plan, but the depressed state of the economy was soon stifled.

One chief reason for this was the outbreak of the Korean War in June 1950. In fact, an unexpected boom to Japan's economy was provided by the special procurement needs of the Korean War, which lasted for roughly three years. During these years, Japan became a giant supply base that could serve the US war efforts; that is to say, vehicles and armaments were manufactured and repaired, a great number of soldiers visited and stayed frequently, and massive amounts of money came into Japan. For three years, between 1946 and 1948, this special procurement expanded at an average rate of 2.3 per cent relative to nominal GNP.

As shown in Table 1.4, real growth rates have turned upward since 1950. Recovery started at a substantial pace, but it had begun from such a low initial level in 1945–46 that even rapid rates of growth were not sufficient to reconstruct the Japanese economy promptly. Analysis of the other columns of Table 1.4 reveals that per capita real GNP and mining–industrial production also began to rise steadily from around 1950.

Grossly speaking, Japan was unable to regain its pre-war level (1934–1936)[7] of per capita income and production until 1953 or 1954. Thus, Japan lost roughly 18 years of economic growth in the reckless adventure of the Second World War, as it would take that long to return to pre-war levels of economic performance.

What were the Preconditions to Rapid Economic Growth?

After reaching the pre-war economic level around the mid-1950s, the genuine economic reconstruction with rapid growth rates started from 1955. No doubt, the preceding occupation reforms and economic reconstruction outlined above provided an important economic base for the next stage of economic progress. However, what kind of fundamental base was constructed later on during the specific period of occupation? Stated differently, what were the preconditions for Japan's sustained rapid economic growth in the 1950s and 1960s?

It would not be adequate to compare Japan's occupation period with the transitional stage of an East European economy (see the Teranishi-Sachs argument in Teranishi and Kosai 1993), although great importance is often attached to this comparison. Like East European countries, Japan had experienced a huge number of difficulties in the transition from a wartime-controlled economy to a market-oriented economy in the chaotic state of the immediate post-war era. However, the specific period covered by a controlled economy continued for only nine years, from 1937 to 1945, and the Japanese maintained a working knowledge of the capitalistic economy even during wartime. Of course, the fundamental institutions of a market economy, such as the distribution channels, the tax system, financial transactions, etc., remained untouched and in a well-developed state. Consequently, Japan's transitional case was no doubt much easier and simpler. In this sense, Japan was equipped, to a considerable extent, with the necessary preconditions for the next step of economic recovery.

What is of most importance is how well the pre-war heritage could be replaced by post-war economic reforms during the occupation period. An overall assessment of occupation policies and the degree of their success are very difficult to quantify satisfactorily, but they must have deeply affected all aspects of the Japanese economy and society throughout the post-war period. In what follows, two points are worth noting as good bases or preconditions for post-war economic performance.

First of all, a more egalitarian society was established as a result of major economic reforms. Land reform successfully redistributed ownership of land previously farmed by tenants, solving the severe landlord–tenant problems that had long endured. Equally important, the labour union movement freed working groups from the predominant control of enterprise managers to some extent, although the encouragement of unionism tended to induce extremely aggressive labour disputes. The system of aristocracy was fully abolished, which, virtually on its own, brought about an egalitarian atmosphere

---

[7] The average of 1934–36 is often selected as a reference point of the pre-war level, because this was the last prosperous and peaceful period before the outbreak of the Sino–Japanese War in 1937. Indeed, the real growth rate of GNP was 5.2 per cent and the inflation rate of the WPI was 2.9 per cent during this period.

among the general public. These changes evidently contributed greatly to the enhancement of social mobility and economic vitality, stimulating small farmers and
workers to participate in economic activities for growth performance. Greater equality
of opportunity was secured, and personal incentives to behave economically were
encouraged in society. It should be noted that such an egalitarian sense was seen as the
extension to the people of economic powers actually enjoyed only by the few in the
past. Thus, rapid economic growth was promoted, given socioeconomic reforms,
towards an increased degree of egalitarianism.

Second, more competitive markets were established by the Zaibatsu dissolution
with the break-up of a few extremely large firms, the elimination of cartels and
monopolies, and the creation of the Fair Trade Commission. Later on, especially in the
1950s and 1960s, new industrial groups emerged as the remnants of ex-Zaibatsu, but
they were more loosely tied to each other than the Zaibatsu and thus were amenable
to highly competitive markets. No doubt market mechanisms are the most effective
means for determining which of the old industries ought to dwindle, and which new
industries should get the best opportunity for future success. The typical, successful
examples in Japan could be seen in the 1950s in the arrival of new, growing firms, such
as Sony, Honda, Matsushita and so on. As was argued previously, the term *competition* tended to be accepted by the Japanese in a different way to the traditional Anglo-
American view which exhorts that competition alone could automatically create the
maximum output and the lowest prices for the benefit of consumers.

On the contrary, in Japan, direct intervention in the markets by government was
normally justified as an adjuster to regulate over-investment or excess capacity in
certain industries, given the existence of oligopolistic markets. It is widely believed
in Japan, especially in the government bureaucracy and among big business, that
deviation from the Western competitive model would be rather desirable. This may
be called the Japanese-style competitive model which seemed to perform well during most of the post-war period, and continued to do so at least until the 1990s.[8]
Obviously, this model was derived partly from the imperfect accomplishment of
industrial economic reforms by the occupation policies, and partly from the process
of rapid growth that greatly influenced the conditions of industrial organization.

---

[8] At present, close ties between the government and business have been greatly criticized by many,
both within and outside Japan, for keeping the markets regulated and under control. Obviously, regulated
markets are conducive to protecting the benefits of vested interests, and deregulation is one of the most
effective weapons to making the markets more competitive.

2
Rapid Economic Growth and Its Effects

Contrary to the gloomy prospects immediately following the end of the Second World War, the Japanese economy started its genuine economic growth from 1955, based upon a number of major socioeconomic reforms during the occupation period. In fact, it continued its rapid surge of economic growth until the early 1970s, with one of the highest rates compared to many of the advanced countries in the world. This growth pattern, which lasted for about two decades, attracted worldwide attention because it was practically unparalleled in history (see, for instance, Boltho 1975).

Interestingly enough, rapid growth was derived from the single-minded, nation-wide emphasis on economic growth by government and business. Occasionally, the general public were also involved in the heated adoption towards growth-oriented policy. However, the rapid growth process was attained only at the cost of great imbalance and strain. Since the late 1960s, the 'downside' of economic growth began to capture the attention of the Japanese people, as environmental damage, spiralling price rises, inadequate infrastructure and other adverse side-effects of growth became evident.

This chapter analyses the process of rapid economic growth initiated by the government from 1955 to 1973. The three main topics are as follows. First, we will look at a rough outline of the pattern and causes of rapid growth from both the supply and demand sides of the economy. Secondly, we will pay special attention to the features of the government's growth-oriented policy which lie behind the growth performance. Lastly, to conclude our discussion, we take account of both the positive and negative sides of rapid growth during the period in question.

THE PATTERN AND CAUSES OF RAPID ECONOMIC GROWTH

Unprecedented Growth Patterns: 1955–1973

Roughly speaking, the two decades starting from the mid-1950s are usually called the period of high economic growth (*Kohdo Seichoki*). This high growth pattern, lasting almost 20 years, has drawn the attention of people around the world, keen to discover the process and causes as this 'economic miracle'. Before we embark upon the main argument, we will compare the pattern of Japan's growth performance against those of the G7 countries, as set out in Table 2.1.

The Japanese economy continued its upsurge of growth until the early 1970s at a rate far greater than that of any other major country. Of particular importance was the accelerated tempo of real growth rates from the mid-1950s to the end of the 1960s.

TABLE 2.1. *Growth patterns of real GNP among G7 countries, 1956–73* (%)

Year	1956–60	1961–65	1966–70	1971–73	1956–73
Japan	9.8	10.1	12.1	8.6	10.2
USA	2.2	4.9	3.2	5.0	3.8
UK	2.6	3.3	2.4	4.4	3.2
West Germany	6.4	5.0	4.8	3.9	5.0
France	4.8	5.9	5.8	5.6	5.5
Italy	5.5	5.3	5.9	3.8	5.1
Canada	3.3	6.0	4.8	6.1	5.1

Source: The Bank of Japan, *Japan and the World: A Comparison by Economic and Financial Statistics*, 1967, 1969, 1973, 1975, 1981.

Note: Figures are averages of annual percentages.

Indeed, average growth rates of real GNP in Japan for 1956–73 achieved 10.2 per cent, followed by 5.5 per cent in France, while the USA and the UK grew only at the rates of 3.8 and 3.2 per cent respectively. Almost half of the 18 years recorded two-digit rates of real growth in Japan, and Japan's real GNP in 1972 was 5.1 times larger than it was in 1955. This growth pattern was totally unprecedented worldwide. In some sense, the realized rates of real growth for those years might be said to be too high, if we consider the influence of the adverse effects—such as industrial pollution—caused by rapid growth. Thus, it would be more appropriate to denote this growth performance as 'rapid' or 'super-fast', rather than simply 'high', to imply a growth rate that is beyond a moderate or optimal level.

Major Supply-side Factors

What are the main factors to explain the remarkable achievement of Japan's rapid economic growth? It is necessary to analyse these factors from both the supply and demand sides of the economy. Let us begin with a discussion of the supply-side factors. There are several factors worth considering, but it is very difficult to reach an all-inclusive explanation of Japan's post-war economic growth. In what follows, the focus is upon three interrelated factors: labour, capital and technology (see Patrick 1970; Denison and Chung 1976; Patrick and Rosovsky 1976; T. Nakamura 1981; Allen 1981).

First of all, one of the key factors behind rapid growth was no doubt an ample supply of good quality labour (see, for general discussion, Galenson and Odaka 1976). Generally speaking, an economy with an abundant labour supply has a head start in achieving a higher rate of economic growth than a country not in this position, for two main reasons. First, an ample supply of labour ensures there are no bottlenecks in the process of production. Secondly, a large labour force implies relatively low wage levels, which in turn lowers product prices and thereby increases the competitiveness of exports in world markets. On the other hand, an economy with a shortage of labour finds its growth being held back by costs becoming inflated and the balance of payments deteriorating.

In the post-war period, Japan had a relatively abundant labour supply, with a large number of repatriations from overseas territories and rapid population growth due to a 'baby boom'. As a result, an enormous stock of labour had piled up in agricultural and other low-productivity sectors (e.g. small enterprises, retailing and other services). It was very easy to shift such a labour force to large-scale manufacturing industries, like the heavy-chemical industries which played a major role in the ensuing rapid growth. This favourable condition continued into the 1960s. For instance, the average growth rate of the total labour force for 1960–70 in Japan exceeded that of major OECD countries except the USA: that is 1.3 per cent in Japan, 0.8 per cent in France, 0.3 per cent in West Germany, −0.7 per cent Italy, 0.2 per cent in the UK and 1.8 per cent in the USA. Furthermore, it should be stressed that the average rate of growth in the number of wage earners and salaried employees was the highest in Japan for the same period with a rate of 3.4 per cent, in comparison with 2.0 per cent in France, 0.9 per cent in both West Germany and Italy, 0.2 per cent in the UK and 2.5 per cent in the USA (OECD 1972*a*).

In addition to being in ample supply, Japan's labour force was practically well-trained, industrious and hard-working. Needless to say, education is one of the most important elements in enhancing the quality of labour. It is widely acknowledged in Japan that the acquisition of education is an essential element of upward social and economic mobility. Most Japanese parents have been, and still are, highly education-conscious, stimulating their children to be better trained than themselves. The rising costs of higher education are likely to be met by sacrificing other expenses. An education-conscious society contributed greatly to the improvement of labour quality in view of both general and specific vocational skills. Thus we can see that this ample supply of well-trained labour had been a supportive and essential factor for rapid growth.

Secondly, the high rate of capital formation and saving was certainly another key factor to promoting rapid growth. Without a very high rate of new investment in plant and equipment, innovation would not have been prevalent and the growth of labour productivity would not have been feasible, as it would have been impossible to absorb excess labour forces into higher productivity sectors.

Throughout the 1950s and 1960s, Japanese enterprises in the private sector were eager to invest so as to expand productive capacity and output. Although investment was usually required to pay off in a relatively short period, business and managerial optimism about the growth of the Japanese economy were widespread with a strong perception of profit opportunities in the future. The majority of Japanese businessmen looked ahead with a bullish sentiment which was very much in contrast to the prudent attitudes of their foreign counterparts. For instance, a number of large firms made very aggressive attempts in undertaking investment to increase market share in Japan.

As a matter of fact, capital stock accumulation at constant prices had increased at great speed: at an annual rate of 10.3 per cent for 1955–65 and 12.1 per cent for 1965–75 in all private industries. The capital stock in 1975 was 8.3 times larger than

TABLE 2.2. *Gross saving as a percentage of GNP, 1952–72*

Year	Total gross saving	Personal saving	Corporate saving	Government saving	Capital consumption allowance
1952–54	24.2 (100.0)	6.7 (27.7)	3.1 (12.8)	6.1 (25.2)	8.2 (33.9)
1955–59	29.0 (100.0)	10.7 (36.9)	3.6 (12.4)	5.5 (19.0)	9.6 (33.1)
1960–64	35.8 (100.0)	12.1 (33.8)	4.8 (13.4)	7.6 (21.2)	11.2 (31.3)
1965–69	36.9 (100.0)	12.4 (33.6)	4.9 (13.3)	6.2 (16.8)	12.9 (35.0)
1970–72	39.5 (100.0)	13.4 (33.9)	5.8 (14.7)	7.4 (18.7)	14.0 (35.4)

Source: Economic Planning Agency, *Research Report on National Income Statistics, 1951–67* (1968), pp. 61, 69; EPA *1972*, pp. 37, 45; 1974, pp. 32, 33, 40, 41.

Notes: Figures are averages of annual percentages. Since statistical discrepancy is omitted, total figures have been rounded.

that in 1955. The growth of capital stock in manufacturing industries increased much more rapidly; by 10.5 times. Since capital grew at a higher rate than the labour force, the capital stock per worker also rose sharply and further enhanced the level of labour productivity (see Patrick and Rosovsky, pp. 17–18).

Investment must be financed out of saving, either domestic or overseas. Fortunately, no reliance was placed upon the borrowed savings of foreigners in Japan. In other words, the extraordinarily high rate of investment was well-matched by that of domestic saving. As seen in Table 2.2, one-third of gross saving was in depreciation funds which were generated by brisk investment itself and by a favourable tax device for depreciation allowances. Corporate firms also retained a high proportion of their earnings for investment in business expansion. What was most impressive of all was that the personal saving rate was a tremendously high component of gross savings. Private individuals continued to provide a higher proportion of domestic savings even though their income levels were below those of the Western nations. All groups, including wage and salary earners as well as dividend and rent recipients, farmers and unincorporated firm owners, tried to save a higher proportion of their income than that saved in any other advanced country (Mizouchi 1970).

Thirdly, technology was equally important for achieving rapid economic growth. As a result of incorporating new and innovative technology, Japan's high investment rate and labour supply became more productive. It is widely recognized that the post-war economic growth in Japan was highly dependent on the importation of foreign technology; that is the 'borrowed technology'.

In the 1950s and 1960s, there was still a wide gap between Japan's level of technology and the best level of Western technology. Japan managed to obtain the best new ideas and inventions at a relatively low cost and used its own skills to embody them swiftly in attractive new products. This may be called the strategy of a No.2, in that Japan followed after the No.1 Western countries endowed with the most advanced technology.

Two points should be stressed regarding the success of such a strategy. Japan lagged far behind many other advanced countries in terms of technology, and making up such a gap was bound to be beneficial. Japan had not reached the frontiers of advanced technology in the pre-war era, and in addition had been increasingly isolated from Western nations since 1937 at the outbreak of the Manchurian Incident. Thus, the technological gap had expanded enormously. On the other hand, Japan was domestically endowed with favourable conditions for the rapid introduction of foreign technology. Indeed, it had the capability to utilize foreign technology on a large scale. Around the end of the 1950s, there were a sufficient number and variety of managers, engineers and skilled workers who were able to learn the foreign technology and to turn it into newer products without excessive difficulty. Consequently, Japan was very quick to adopt as well as to adapt foreign technology.

Under the strategy of a No.2, the process of catching up with the advanced technology greatly benefited Japan in its achievement of post-war economic growth. Japan was able to borrow new technologies, that other advanced countries had invented with great effort, and put them into something new without having to invest large amounts of time or money. The borrowing of technology became a primary goal of Japanese technological policy to a great extent. On the other hand, much less emphasis had been placed upon the domestic advancement of basic research for the creation of technology over a long-run stretch.

Many of the major exporting goods, for example automobiles, cameras, TV sets, etc., were produced with a No.2 strategy. Obviously, Japan derived a great advantage from the catching-up process, through its easier and less expensive access to the most advanced technology in the world compared to the No.1 Western countries.

The Strength of Aggregate Demand

In parallel with the expansion of productive capability from the supply side of the economy, the demand-side effects had played an equally important role in post-war economic performance by the early 1970s. As noted earlier, Japanese economic growth since the Second World War had been exceedingly rapid, interrupted only by a series of short-run recessions as argued later (see Table 2.3). An actual decline in GNP in a particular quarter was incurred on one or two occasions, but all other recessions merely involved sharp slowdowns in the growth rate of GNP. Strong aggregate demand constantly prevented the actual level of GNP from dropping to any considerable extent. No doubt, one of the most marked phenomena about Japan's rapid growth was the strength of aggregate demand. The following statement is worth noting:

Western economists who study the postwar Japanese economy (especially, perhaps, those from the United States or Britain) cannot fail to be struck by what they may describe as the great secular vigor or buoyancy of aggregate demand in Japan, seemingly very unlike the usual situation of their own economies (see Ackley and Ishi 1976, pp. 162–3).

With no special stimulus aggregate demand in Japan seemed to be adequate enough to maintain a reasonably full realization of potential output. Given the strength of

TABLE 2.3. *Dates and duration of the business cycles, 1951–75*

Reference dates			Number of months		
Initial trough	Peak	Terminal trough	Expansion	Contraction	Total
	June 1951	Oct. 1951		4	
Oct. 1951	Jan. 1954	Nov. 1954	27	10	37
Nov. 1954	June 1957	June 1958	31	12	43
June 1958	Dec. 1961	Oct. 1962	42	10	52
Oct. 1962	Oct. 1964	Oct. 1965	24	12	36
Oct. 1965	July 1970	Dec. 1971	57	17	74
Dec. 1971	Nov. 1973	Mar. 1975	23	9	31

Source: Economic Planning Agency, *Monthly Report on Basic Data for Economic Analysis*, March 1980.

aggregate demand, the government deliberately took restrictive action to prevent the economy from overheating, resulting in policy-induced recessions as will be explained later.

This situation was quite different from that in mature economies like the USA and the UK over the same period. In these two countries, aggregate demands were met with full realization of potential output only during an occasional period of boom, which could not usually be sustained. Recessions took place frequently, and in the absence of continuing expansionary policies, GDP repeatedly remained stagnant. Alternatively GDP expanded insufficiently fast to employ the growing potential output in the economy, even if its growth was relatively low. Thus, policy stimuli were always needed to sustain an adequate level of aggregate demand to promote economic growth.

Of course, there were times when aggregate demand was sometimes either excessive or deficient in Japan, as well as in the West. Unwanted gaps between actual and potential output in Japan were probably smaller and less persistent than in other major countries, reflecting the consistent buoyancy of aggregate demand. As a consequence, little or no active stimulus by the government was required during the period under consideration.

How, then, should we explain the secular vigour or strength of aggregate demand in Japan? In order to answer this question, Figure 2.1 has been prepared to facilitate the examination and comparison of two aggregate demand components in Japan and the Western nations.

It is easy to observe the particular source of variations in the buoyancy of aggregate demand in each case shown in Figure 2.1. Obviously, the source of the unusual strength of demand in post-war Japan basically relied on investment demand, particularly in the private sector, and to a lesser extent on exports. Since Western countries normally depend on personal consumer demand, Japan's unique source is thus revealed by this international comparison.

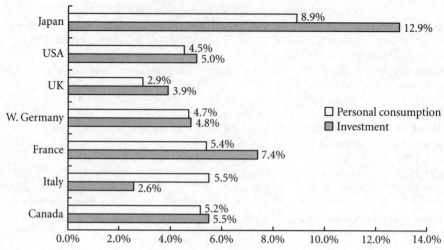

FIGURE 2.1. *Average growth rates of personal consumption and investment among G7 countries, 1963–72*

Source: As Table 2.1

Note: Investment is composed of plant and equipment in both private and government sectors

It is necessary to look for the specific reasons why investment demand was so high in Japan. Among a number of reasons suggested for the buoyancy of investment, one of the most important would be investor confidence in Japanese enterprises. This confidence, which had not existed in earlier periods, became increasingly important as time went by. Given strongly growing aggregate demand, the past experience which made yesterday's investment so successful proliferated the confidence of today's investment, and assured the persistent growth of markets for new products. By the mid-1960s, confidence had certainly been a crucial factor and it was not impaired by the frequent interruptions in business expansion due to the deliberate, restrictive actions of the government. Apparently, investors understood recessions to be temporary and easily reversible.

Furthermore, the situation was a 'virtuous circle': the strong and steady growth of investment demand was self-generating during this period in post-war Japan. Japan's capital facilities had grown swiftly as a result of the exceedingly high rate of investment previously noted, in order to restore the massive wartime destruction of plant and equipment. At the same time, the growth of total demand for the output of capital facilities was equally rapid and, to a significant extent, the result of the fast growth of investment itself. Therefore, new capital facilities could be profitably and fully utilized immediately upon completion, unlike the more mature Western economies, and there existed a number of unexploited opportunities which were able to increase output via massive investment.

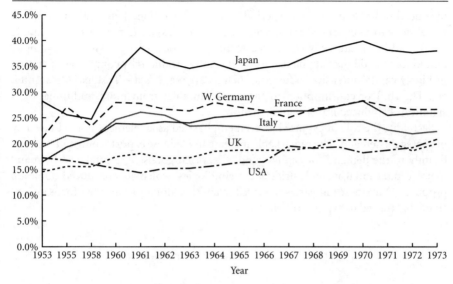

FIGURE 2.2. *Gross saving rates in major countries, 1953–73*
Source: As Table 2.1

Needless to say, it must be stressed, as argued earlier, that Japan's savings rate continued to be extremely high in the 1950s and 1960s. In Figure 2.2, gross saving rates in major countries are shown for 1953–73. Japan's position can be seen to have been not only higher, but significantly higher than the countries closest behind, West Germany or France.

Thus, the rapid growth of aggregate demand itself constitutes a general reason as to why investment demand was so vigorous in the 1950s and 1960s. Indeed, the rapid growth of investment encouraged the rapid growth of aggregate demand, and in turn sustained strong pressure on expanding productive facilities which relevant investment provided, thereby assuring that further rapid growth of investment would also be rewarding. This is a circular relationship, but it is not invalid.[1] Investment for growth in order to pursue more investment for even faster growth appeared to gain a value of its own.

In addition to this explanation for strong investment incentives, there exist a number of other reasons, for example government policies supporting investment or capital facilities such as the limit on output (see, for instance, Ackley and Ishi 1976, pp. 165–9). In relation to the argument on the strength of aggregate demand via buoyant investment, two further points are added for consideration.

First, although personal consumption was not a primary source of demand buoyancy, the growth of consumer demand for durable goods cannot be forgotten in the expansion of production. Since modern consumer durable goods were by and large

---

[1] Any way of describing mutual interrelations cannot avoid being impressionistic rather than rigorously scientific. It would be almost impossible to obtain quantitative evidence by using empirical data.

produced at the beginning of the period under consideration, there was a great deal of initial stock to be produced as the years went by.[2] The expansion of consumer durable goods had been indirectly connected to post-war industrial growth. For example, automobiles and home appliances were efficiently produced by companies operating in highly capital-intensive industries, such as Toyota, Nissan, Toshiba, Matsushita, etc. The shift of consumption to these new durables from more traditional ones significantly induced investment demand.

Secondly, the role of exports has been emphasized as an element in the buoyancy of aggregate demand. The remarkable increase in Japanese exports contributed significantly to the demand for capital goods. Exported goods were produced by many major capital-intensive industries and technologies, which also produced domestic products. Once these industries were well established domestically, their focus understandably turned to export growth.

MACROECONOMIC GOALS AND POLICIES

Growth-oriented policy and the role of Government

Several factors previously mentioned were important to Japan's unique growth performance. One of the most crucial factors, however, is the policy behind the rapid growth of the Japanese economy and the factors which contributed to this surge of growth.

Since the economy shifted into full recovery in the early 1950s, the Japanese government had placed domestic economic growth at the top of its macroeconomic policy priorities. In Japan, the direction of the nation's macroeconomic policies are not always stated on a formal basis, but economic planning usually tends to convey a verbalization of policy goals to the nation along with their quantification. While the plan was merely indicative and had no compulsory element, it was very effective in providing information and obtaining a national consensus (see Komiya 1975, Komine 1993). In fact, economic planning for multi-year periods (e.g. five or seven years) involved fully articulated goals that provided a good outline of the government's position for the purpose of private economic performance.

The first multi-year plan drawn up by the government appeared in 1955, entitled 'The Five-Year Plan for Economic Independence' (*Keizai Jiritsu Gokanen Keikaku*). The goals of Japan's post-war economic policy were vividly pronounced in that plan by the use of three key words: growth, investment and exports. The main idea—the total interlinkage of these policy goals—was summarized as follows. Rapid growth of output and employment in the modern industrial sectors of the economy was regarded as absolutely neccessary to absorb the large numbers of under-employed

---

[2] The importance of durable goods to the Japanese consumer is attached to popular slogans. One of the slogans prevalent between 1955 and 1962 was 'the three sacred treasures': refrigerator, electric washing machine and vacuum cleaner. From 1963 to 1970 the slogan turned into 'the three C's'; car, colour TV and cooler (air conditioner).

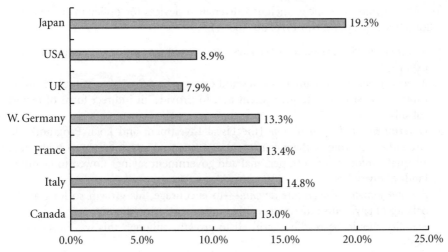

FIGURE 2.3. *Average growth rates of exports among G7 countries, 1963–72*
Source: As Table 2.1

workers in traditional low-productivity sectors like agriculture and small enterprises. Obviously the rapid expansion of modern capital-intensive sectors required massive investment and in turn a high rate of national saving. Also, the increased production of these sectors needed rapidly expanded markets, a substantial part of which had to be found overseas. Thus, a rapid growth in exports was an equally important goal, partly because the expanding output of modern industries could not be fully absorbed in the domestic markets and partly because the huge amount of raw materials being imported required exports in order that they might be paid for.

The very title of the 1955 plan, 'Economic Independence', had a significant implication. After massive economic aid or special procurement from the USA expired, Japan's need for expanded exports became an indispensable part of independent national survival. A rapid growth of exports seemed to be essential merely to pay for the imports required at the existing levels of output and income at that time. Thus, the government affirmed in the 1955 plan, as a basic policy goal, that Japan as a resource-poor nation would be required to export enough to pursue not only survival but growth—rapid growth. As can be observed in Figure 2.3, this policy goal was, more or less, attained with Japan, among the G7 countries, having the highest growth rate of exports in the period 1963–72. Japanese exports grew at a rate of 19.3 per cent while exports from the USA and the UK expanded at a relatively lower rate.

The goal of Japanese economic policy in 1955 provides us with a number of implications on a variety of other government policies (see Okita and Takahashi 1971). Many of the implications for microeconomic policies involved import protection, export subsidies, financial aid and guidance for selected areas of production and investment, extensive imports of technology, etc. Similarly, implications of the goals for macroeconomic policies included diversified devices for policy instruments as follows (see Ackley and Ishi 1976, pp. 160–1):

1. *Tax and public expenditure policies*—to encourage savings, investment, and exports.
2. *Monetary policy*—low interest rates and easy credit designed to stimulate highly capital-intensive private investment and to provide an indirect form of export subsidy.
3. *Government credit programme* (the Fiscal Investment and Loan Program)—to strengthen the role of the government as a financial intermediary to assure that adequate amounts of both personal and government savings flowed to favoured kinds of investment.
4. *A rapid growth of aggregate demand*—to encourage this growth so long as the balance of payments remained positive and export prices did not rise.
5. Stability should be readily sacrificed to growth, although this was never made explicit.

It is very important to stress that the growth–investment–export trial policy goals were well understood among various individuals and sectors in Japan. Indeed, such growth-oriented policies were advocated and popularized to the general public in Japan by politicians, businessmen, and the press.[3] The goals of government policies were widely accepted, partly because they were designed to utilize the incentives of private self-interest and partly because they were identified and observed by the public and viewed as important to the national interest.

No doubt, business was the front runner in promoting these policy goals among several groups. Japanese businesses were highly motivated to rationalize the process of production with an efficient combination of labour, capital, and technology. Major industries successfully improved their productivity, increasing the quality and diversity of their manufactured products while reducing costs. As a consequence, their competitiveness was greatly strengthened in both domestic and overseas markets. In particular, big business embraced an active management style, oriented towards growth performance, and closely tied with government policies. Given the strength of aggregate demand, technological innovations combined with buoyant investment activity and good labour supply, companies greatly improved their productivity and their competitiveness under an aggressive growth-oriented policy which was initiated by close cooperation between government and big business (see, for example, Abeglen 1970).

In order to clarify the process of growth-oriented policy and in particular industrial policy, special emphasis should be placed on the role of government from a micro-

---

[3] Popular slogans, such as 'prosperity through exports and stability through savings' were often employed to make the general public understand the government's position. Also, we can note an interesting argument of Huber by using the concept of 'strategic economy' (see Huber 1994).

economic standpoint. The Japanese government had primarily and consistently aided and encouraged big business by offering special tax concessions, favourable loans to important industries and special infrastructure facilities (e.g. harbours and roads) in order to maintain private production. More importantly, the government prevented big businesses from competing with each other in the markets to a great exent. As noted in Chapter 1, the Japanese seemed to have a unique view concerning the acceptable degree of competition in the market which was seen as unusual by foreigners. For example, in Japan more emphasis tends to be placed on the costs of a competitive system rather than the benefits of free competition.

Historically, most Japanese have not accepted the workings of the market's invisible hand, but have approved of the 'visible hand' of government guidance and business cooperation (i.e. cartels) in order to attain satisfactory economic results. Thus, the Japanese government and big business leaders were frequently concerned with 'excess competition', which they believe should be regulated to some extent by the government. By contrast, in Western countries, particularly in the USA, it is widely believed that the role of government should ideally be restricted to a minimum level, with government acting only as a referee or a rule-making body for the preservation of vigorous competition in the market economy. In this respect, there is a marked difference between the USA and Japan.

As previously discussed, the Zaibatsu were dissolved by SCAP reformers in order to establish competition among large firms after the Second World War. The Zaibatsu were dissected into a number of smaller companies and the monopolization of the market was further prohibited by law. The process of growth-oriented policy, however, gradually changed the economic and business structure from that intended by the Zaibatsu dissolution. In fact, based on the partial acceptance of direct administrative guidance in business, the government attempted to control 'excess competition' among big business.

In accordance with SCAP efforts for deconcentration, Japanese industry was certainly deconcentrated in the mid-1950s more so than before the War. With the passage of time, however, a gradual trend towards concentration of production began to emerge once again in many industries. By the late 1950s, the decentralization trend had reversed, and the top three or four firms in major areas such as automobile, glass, steel, and home appliance production occupied an increasing share of total output in their relevant industries. In 1963, for example, the share of output concentration among the top three firms was 100 per cent in both the film and glass industries, 97.1 per cent in the beer industry, 62.2 per cent in the automobile industry, 48.1 per cent in the steel indutry, etc. (see Matsushiro 1970). After the mid-1960s, the tendency towards concentration accelerated due to the increasing number of mergers among large firms in major industries. For example, a giant merger emerged from the two top steel companies, Yawata and Fuji, creating Nippon Steel in 1969, and also between the two big commercial banks, Daiichi and Kangin in 1971, creating the new top ranked bank of Daiichi–Kangin.

The past trend towards the restriction of competition resulted from the process of growth-oriented policy, as noted above. What was important was the fact that the government had taken the initiative to combine large firms and restrict competition in the markets. There exists a predominant view that the removal of excess competition by administrative guidance contributed significantly to the success of the post-war growth process. However, no decisive judgement can be made to evaluate, based upon empirical evidence, the post-war policy performance and its ability to control competitive markets. If we take the reverse side of the coin, we can say that, to some extent, the restriction of competition destroyed the climate in which new, small and independent businesses are able to come into being, to grow, and to prosper, a climate which is essential to the system of a capitalistic economy.[4]

The Limit on Rapid Economic Growth

The growth of GDP in any nation is by and large restricted by a certain limit on expansion. Actual production (GDP) is usually contrasted with potential output, which embodies the maximum feasible production currently permitted by the existing quantity and quality of labour and capital.[5] If actual GDP exceeds potential output, at least to some degree, it brings about an overrated economy. By contrast, when it falls short of potential output—as it often does in most countries—the insufficiency of GDP below potential output represents an unnecessary loss of production and income. Generally speaking, adjustment for maintaining both potential output and actual GDP at the same level cannot automatically be made in a market economy. Thus, the role of macroeconomic policy is to sustain aggregate demand at a level that keeps actual production (= actual GDP) close to potential output.

Normally potential output imposes a clear limit on GDP, as seen in many countries, because it physically sets a certain limit on the expansion of total output. However, this limit, of course, does not remain unchanged over time, and in particular this was not the case in Japan. As stressed previously, Japanese potential output expanded rapidly as productive inputs of labour and capital increased, generating the increased average productivity or efficiency of these inputs. As a consequence, potential output had little significance as a limit on GDP by the late 1960s.

Instead of potential output, greater importance had been attached to export, import, and the relation between them as a clear limit on expansion of the economy in the 1950s and 1960s. In fact, even at levels of GDP short of potential output, fear of potential balance-of-payments deficits usually emerged from a too vigorous expansion of aggregate domestic demand, at least under a system of fixed exchange rates, when pushed too hard against potential output, resulting in inflation. Such pressure

---

[4] Perhaps the truth exists in between the two extremes. Even if the Japanese government continued to intervene in the markets, we must note that Sony, Honda, Matsushita and the like appeared one after another in the 1950s from a group of small enterprises.

[5] It is not accurate to represent potential output in an economy accurately by a specific number, since the concept is ambiguous. Thus, it is more realistic to regard potential output as a range or band, not a specific figure.

tended to increase the rapid growth of demand for imports at a faster rate than that for exports. To the extent that inflation was frantically induced, there was likely to be a more or less consistent reduction of exports and an increase in the demand of imports, aggravating the balance-of-payments and decreasing foreign reserves in Japan. Particular attention was paid to the very low level of foreign reserves—$738 million in 1955, $1,824 million in 1960, or $2,107 million in1965 in comparison with about ¥80–90 billion in the late 1980s (see BOJ 1991, p. 6). Thus a demand management policy was required to control the level and speed of aggregate demand.

Since Japan holds few mineral resources and little arable land relative to its population, rapid growth of aggregate demand, industrial production, and income necessarily require vast increases in imports of fuels, raw materials and foodstuffs, which stimulate imports of all kinds of finished and international products. Unless exports grow with equal speed or unless capital imports expand, the balance-of-payments problem generally becomes more serious. Accordingly, it is important to stress that the effective limit on GDP and its growth during certain periods in post-war Japan may not always have been set by potential output, but rather by balance-of-payments considerations, based upon Japan's economic structure on policies. On this point, particular attention ought to be paid to the following statement:

Given the initial absence of international reserve assets in post-war Japan, and the government's commitment (as a badge of international respectability) to the value of the yen established in 1949, plus the policy decision (for reasons historical, ideological, and reflective of powerful economic interests) not to admit significant direct investment and a Japanese (and foreign) prejudice against appreciable long-term Japanese borrowing abroad, Japan's economic expansion could well have been limited, even short of potential output, by the extent to which its exports could expand (or its imports could be restrained) (Ackley and Ishi 1976, p. 170).

Although Japan's exports expanded rapidly, there was an incessant tendency during boom periods for imports to increase more swiftly, as noted below, which was designed to slow the expansion of aggregate demand, GDP, and, in turn, imports by the restrictive policy of government. As a consequence, a recession usually followed the imposition of such a restrictive policy, causing periodic policy-induced recessions in the business cycle as well as in what will be described below.

Around the late 1960s, changes began to be noticed concerning the nature of the effective limit on the expansion of Japan's GDP. Most importantly, the balance-of-payments problems began to be solved by the rapid growth of exports with a substantial rise in the amount of foreign reserves. One reason was the great improvement in Japan's international competitiveness in world markets. Another reason was that the USA became militarily involved in the war of Vietnam, and provided procurement demand to Japan. These two factors contributed significantly to the improvements in both Japan's exports and the balance-of payments structure.[6]

---

[6] Instead of balance-of-payment considerations as the limit on a nation's growth, there was a view that labour shortages gradually became the principal limiting factor after the mid-1960s (see Shinohara 1970).

Policy-induced Business Cycles

We have so far emphasized the importance of Japan's economic growth exclusively with no special reference to cyclical fluctuations. Of course, however, the Japanese economy did grow irregularly after the Second World War, with business expansions and contractions appearing one after another in a rather regular fashion.

Table 2.3 shows the business cycles which occurred in the period 1951–75 with the dates of peaks and troughs given according to the EPA's business cycle indicators. Obviously, the duration of each expansion was much longer than that of contractions, and during these expansion periods the rate of expansion was mostly high and often accelerated. Needless to say, such strong expansion was a main element in sustaining the long-run trend of rapid economic growth. Each expansion was followed by a brief period of recession typically for a year or a year and a half, and apparently the slow-down was short-lived.

What is most remarkable about the patterns of these cycles in post-war Japan is that real GDP did not decline even during contractions and it was only the rate of expansion which decreased. This implies that true business cycles mainly occurred in the rate of expansion, rather than at an absolute amount. In Table 2.4, the movement of GDP and its main components at constant prices are summarized during each phase, demarcated by calendar quarters corresponding to the month of the reference dates in Table 2.3. During the four contractions, real GDP increased at average rates of 4.4, 2.4, 4.0 and 5.3 per cent, which would have been regarded as relatively sufficient for expansion periods in the West. By contrast, during the five expansions, real GDP grew at a faster rate of more than 10 per cent.

Table 2.4 is also of great help in investigating which factors contributed most to such cyclical fluctuations. As stressed earlier, post-war business cycles were basically cycles in private investment. That is to say, each expansion was induced by a boom in fixed investment and, to a lesser extent, in inventory investment. Conversely, each contraction typically reflected a major decline in fixed investment and a drop in inventory investment. On the other hand, personal consumption constantly expanded during every post-war cyclical phase, irrespective of the ups and downs of business variations. Government expenditure showed some counter-cyclical patterns, in the sense that their rate of expansion was substantially faster during each contraction than during the previous expansion.

Greater importance should be attached to the movement of net exports of goods and services in conjunction with the initiatives of macroeconomic policy. Exports played a significant role in cycles; that is, they declined to a substantial negative figure during the two expansions until 1963, while they remained positive but increased slightly during those of 1962–64 and 1965–70, when measured from trough to peak.

Naturally, aggregate demand in light of private investment would have continued to expand rapidly if the policy had not turned to one of restraint. During each business expansion, potential output expanded equally swiftly, but its expansion showed no sign of surpassing the growth of aggregate demand. At the same time, there was no clear tendency for demand to outrun the growth of potential output, because demand

TABLE 2.4. *Changes in GDP and its components during expansions and contractions, in constant 1965 prices, 1954–73*[a]

Expansion or contraction	Gross domestic product	Consumer expenditure	Business gross fixed investment	Change in private inventories	Government purchases[b]	Net exports of goods and services
Expansion of 1954:4–1957:2						
Amount (¥ billion)	3,246	1,575	949	894	1,575	−430
Percent[c]	10.3	7.9	19.2	—	7.9	—
Contraction of 1957:2–1958:2						
Amount (¥ billion)	661	733	−206	−753	733	475
Percent[c]	4.4	8.0	−10.2	—	8.0	—
Expansion of 1958:2–1961:4						
Amount (¥ billion)	8,266	3,290	2,601	1,649	3,290	−646
Percent[c]	12.9	8.6	29.0	—	8.6	—
Contraction of 1961:4–1962:4						
Amount (¥ billion)	576	1,255	−109	−1,871	1,255	474
Percent[c]	2.4	9.5	−2.5	—	9.5	—
Expansion of 1962:4–1964:4						
Amount (¥ billion)	6,723	3,213	1,291	736	3,213	106
Percent[c]	12.9	10.6	13.6	—	10.6	—
Contraction of 1964:4–1965:4						
Amount (¥ billion)	1,241	863	−721	108	863	118
Percent[c]	4.0	4.9	−12.9	—	4.9	—
Expansion of 1965:4–1970:3						
Amount (¥ billion)	24,929	9,956	8,169	2,562	9,956	57
Percent[c]	12.7	9.5	23.0	—	9.5	—
Contraction of 1970:3–1971:4						
Amount (¥ billion)	3,845	2,187	76	−1,514	2,187	1,302
Percent[c]	5.3	6.1	0.5	—	6.1	—
Expansion of 1971:4–1973:4						
Amount (¥ billion)	12,429	6,072	4,896	359	6,072	−1,624
Percent[c]	9.7	9.5	17.2	—	9.5	—

Sources: Economic Planning Agency, *Annual Report on National Income Statistics* (1970 and 1974), table 4; for 1973: 4, EPA, *Japanese Economic Indicators* (April 1974), p. 42.

Notes:
   [a] All data are seasonally adjusted; yen data are at annual rates.
   [b] Government purchases represent the sum of 'general government consumption expenditure', 'gross fixed capital formation by government', and 'increase in stocks, government enterprises'.
   [c] Percentage change at annual rate.

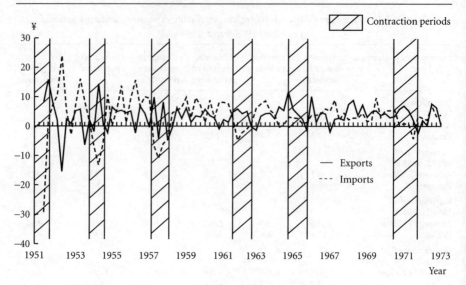

FIGURE 2.4. *Movements of exports and imports at 1965 prices, 1951–73*
(percentage changes from the previous quarter)

Source: Economic Planning Agency 1972, pp. 120–7

Note: Exports are those goods and services and factor incomes from abroad, while imports are those goods and services and factor incomes paid abroad. All data are seasonally adjusted on a quarterly basis.

grew creating its own supply. Therefore, the following question has to be raised. Why did the expansions in cycles have to be eliminated, slowing down the economy by restrictive policy? As is evident from previous arguments, the answer, until the late 1960s, lies mainly in the balance-of-payments problem.

Figure 2.4 depicts the movements of exports, imports and the relationship between them for 1951–73 by using quarterly data. Looking over the past trends of exports and imports in relation to post-war business cycles, we can clearly explain their unique features. Japan's exports expanded strongly, reflecting brisk world demand, effective export promotion efforts by business and government, and relatively low export prices. Exports increased rapidly throughout both boom and recession, but they tended to expand more quickly during recessions because of 'export drive'. Since domestic demand remained stagnant during recessions, firms were forced to find more demand abroad, accelerating exports.

Conversely, Japan's imports had a persistent bias towards increasing even more quickly during booms because the rapid growth of industrial production and income required more resources, raw materials, and imported consumer goods. During each contraction, however, the slowdown of consumer purchases prevented consumer goods imports from increasing and imports of capital goods were also reduced to a great extent, reflecting the decline of private investment. Thus, imports were highly sensitive to foregoing business cycles, causing systematic variations from one cycle to another. Accordingly, the Japanese economy encountered a sharp decline in net exports and went from a significant positive to a significant negative during expansions, which resulted in the appearance of the current account deficits seen in Figure 2.4.

The government had alternative countermeasures to cope with current account deficit problems: (i) yen devaluation, (ii) capital inflows, and (iii) the adoption of restrictive policies. The first and second policy instruments were historically adopted by the UK (sterling pound in this case) and the USA respectively. The Japanese government finally adopted the third type of policy measure, in particular the use of monetary policy. Since brisk investment played a vital role in cycles, monetary policy was no doubt most effective in slowing down the expansion of aggregate demand, GDP, and imports. Clearly monetary policy was the main instrument of short-run demand management in Japan in the 1950s and 1960s.

With regard to such causal factors, Ackley and Ishi emphasize the fact that Japanese post-war business cycles had essentially been policy-included by the late 1960s (see Ackley and Ishi 1976, pp. 184–95). They may also, therefore, be called 'government cycles' in the sense that turning points were determined by government intervention in order to achieve a specific goal (i.e. the reduction of current account deficits), rather than by the intrinsic forces built in the market economy. Therefore, the most distinctive profile of these cycles emerged as restrictive monetary policy which sharply diminished the expansion of demand, generated contraction or recession, and then subsequently eliminated monetary restraint and enabled expansion to resume promptly.[7]

In Figure 2.5, the relation of the phases in monetary policy and business cycles are delineated in the schematic presentation. Although it might be possible to reverse causal relations, we stress the critical role of policy restraints as follows: (i) every recession occurred after a period of policy restraint, (ii) most of the policy restraints were accompanied by recessions, and (iii) each period of expansion either started from the removal of policy restraints or took place at the same time as they were relaxed.

The observation in Figure 2.5 seems to indicate the 'on–off' character of monetary policy. Policy makers apparently needed only to switch monetary policy 'on' for special momentary restraint to curb an aggravated deficit in the current account through reduced demand, and to switch monetary policy 'off' for special restraint to rebound demand and output quickly. Little or no active stimulus was needed to buoy up aggregate demand. Thus, Japan's policy makers were allegedly given a considerably easier task to exercise control than their Western counterparts, and on the whole they seemed to succeed in achieving better results. This was particularly true of the fiscal authority which did not need to play any discretionary role in demand management, as will be discussed in more detail later.

This 'on–off' mechanism of restrictive monetary policies might have, by and large, slowed down the potential growth path of the Japanese economy. If the Japanese government had adopted other policy alternatives at that time, such as capital inflows or the floating of the exchange rate, the balance-of-payment problems might have been solved without sacrificing Japan's potential growth path.

---

[7] This is not to say that intrinsic cycles might not have occurred. Almost certainly these cycles would have occurred, but would not have been observed so vividly. In the present context less importance was placed on locating the nature of such hypothetical cycles.

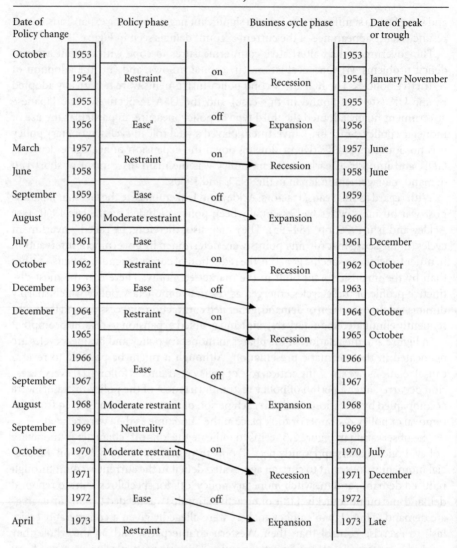

Date of Policy change		Policy phase		Business cycle phase		Date of peak or trough
October	1953				1953	
	1954	Restraint	on	Recession	1954	January November
	1955				1955	
	1956	Ease[a]	off	Expansion	1956	
March	1957				1957	June
		Restraint	on			
June	1958			Recession	1958	June
September	1959	Ease	off		1959	
August	1960	Moderate restraint		Expansion	1960	
July	1961	Ease			1961	December
October	1962	Restraint	on	Recession	1962	October
December	1963	Ease	off		1963	
December	1964	Restraint	on		1964	October
	1965			Recession	1965	October
	1966				1966	
		Ease	off			
September	1967				1967	
August	1968	Moderate restraint		Expansion	1968	
September	1969	Neutrality			1969	
October	1970	Moderate restraint	on		1970	July
	1971			Recession	1971	December
	1972	Ease	off		1972	
April	1973	Restraint		Expansion	1973	Late

FIGURE 2.5. *The relation of policy phases and business cycles, 1953–73*

Source: Policy data: OECD 1972c, pp. 87–91; Bank of Japan 1973, pp. 31–44; EPA, *Economic Survey of Japan* (various issues). Business cycle data: as Table 2.2

[a] The shift to ease in 1954–55 is impossible to date because it was not marked by any overt action

TABLE 2.5. *Social indicators, 1950, 1960 and 1970*

Indicator	1950	1960	1970
Subsistence			
1 Engel coefficient (%)	57.4	38.8	32.4
Safety			
2 Infant mortality rate per 1,000 births	60.1	30.7	13.1
3 Life expectancy			
male	58.0	65.32	69.31
female	61.5	70.19	74.66
Working conditions			
4 Annual working hours	2,306	2,432	2,252
Education and the level of life			
5 University and college students (percentage of age group)	n.a.	10.3	23.6
6 Senior high school pupils (percentage of age group)	42.5	57.7	82.1
7 Telephone per 100 persons	0.5	2.1	22.8
8 Sewerage (percentage of houses connected to public system)	n.a.	17.8	26.4
9 Water (percentage of houses connected to public system)	n.a.	53.4	80.8
Consumer durables			
10 Washing machines per 100 families	—	41.0	92.7
11 Refrigerator per 100 families	—	10.0	91.1
12 Vacuum cleaner per 100 families	—	8.0	70.1
13 Colour TV sets per 100 families	—	—	26.9
14 Passenger car per 100 families	—	2.8	22.1

Sources: Tabulated from EPA, *Summary of Economic Indicators* (Keizai Yoran, 1995), *White Paper of National Life*, 1985 and 1994, and Management and Coordination Agency, *Japan's Statistics*, 1995, etc.

WHAT WAS BROUGHT ABOUT BY RAPID GROWTH?

Improvements in Economic Levels and a Nation's life

Their outstanding post-war economic performance successfully led Japan to become the second largest industrial country by the late 1960s, surpassed only by the USA. Real GDP at 1985 prices in 1970 expanded to 4 times that of 1955, and per head real GDP equally increased with great speed from ¥4,929 in 1955 to ¥16,636 in 1970. The growth of economic levels as a whole naturally brought a major improvement in the nation's income and lifestyle. Virtually every Japanese was substantially better off as a result of the rapid growth, via higher wages and better employment. Likewise, turning our attention to the international sphere, Japan's resurgence to the top group of industrial nations provided the general public with a renewed self-confidence and national pride.

Table 2.5 summarizes the improvements of the nation's socioeconomic welfare between 1950, 1960, and 1970 by using the indicators of subsistence, safety, working conditions and consumer durables. It is rather difficult to evaluate a welfare indicator such as the quality of life in broader terms. From an historical perspective, however, it is incontrovertible that the objective economic conditions of almost all Japanese have improved immensely over the past 40 years as a result of rapid economic growth. Economic measures never capture the full range of changes in material welfare which are usually associated with economic growth. In addition to economic indicators, where we can observe remarkable improvements in economic levels, a much broader approach lies in the so-called social indicators that incorporate physical measures of safety, working conditions, education, culture, the consumption level of consumer durables and the like. While informative, this approach poses some problems in the selection of relevant indicators. No doubt, almost all the measures in Table 2.5 indicate absolute improvement. The Engel coefficient (i.e. the proportion of income spent on food) decreased to 32.4 per cent in 1990 from 57.4 in 1950.

Similarly, the infant mortality rate fell sharply, while the life expectancy for both sexes increased significantly. Working hours have constantly been reduced. The level of education has greatly improved over recent years. Also, the diffusion level of telephone, sewerage, and water have considerably enhanced the quality of life. Lastly, consumption of consumer durables has spread with great speed. For many households it has become possible to own physical goods such as domestically produced consumer durables. For instance, in 1970 91.1 per cent of Japanese families had a refrigerator, 92.7 per cent an electric washing machine, 70.1 per cent an electric vacuum cleaner, etc.

The Costs of Rapid Growth

No doubt, the very nature of rapid economic growth generated a number of problems which had been mainly derived from the growth-oriented policy performance of the government. Rapid growth was achieved in the 1950s and 1960s, based largely on heavy chemical industries while low-productivity sectors such as agriculture and small businesss lagged behind. In the process of rapid growth, it was not possible to synchronize completely the growth of every sector of the economy. The swift shift to heavy chemical industrial sectors caused various kinds of industrial pollution and the lagged sectors encouraged a rapid rise in consumer prices while achieving low productivity. Also, the rapidity of economic and social changes during the entire process of rapid growth resulted in overpopulation in major urban areas, which in turn led to a rising level of urban problems.

These are the imbalances or strains caused by a growing economy which may be called, so to speak, 'the costs of economic growth'. It was only in the late 1960s that the negative side of the growth process began to become clear to the Japanese people. Since that time, a large amount of doubt has been cast upon the past growth performance of the economy which was initiated by the government. Of course we should frankly assess the economic prosperity which was attained in the 1960s, but at the same time we must pay careful attention to the agonies of rapid growth and to the great effort made to rectify theses problems since then. In what follows, particular attention will be paid to both urban problems and industrial pollution.

In parallel with the rapid growth since the late 1950s, Japan's population began to concentrate in major cities, producing a variety of urban problems like traffic jams, packed commuter trains, land price increases, serious housing shortages, pollution and so on. The population concentration of Japan's three largest metropolitan areas (Tokyo, Osaka, and Nagoya) continued to grow throughout the post-war years. In 1970, about 44 per cent of Japan's total population resided in three areas and the Tokyo metropolitan area (including three neighboring prefectures: Chiba, Kanagawa, and Saitama) constituted 23 per cent of this percentage. Thus, one-quarter of Japan's population were massed together in this narrow area (which is only 3.6 per cent of total land area). Since major large cities provided a number of opportunities for higher education and better employment, they persistently attracted an influx of people.

Problems emerged from such a rapid urbanization of Japan in a variety of guises. Some of the major problems included housing, land, urban traffic, waste disposal, and disruption of the natural environment. These troubles impair the quality of life in Japan, and deprive the people of a healthy environment.

Most typical among these urban problems are the cases of housing and residential land.[8] The chief reason why the demand for housing and residential land remained so strong was that land costs were overwhelmingly high in metropolitan areas. The price of urban land (*Zenkoku Shigaichi land price*) rose by 1328 per cent between 1955 and 1970, in contrast to a 89.7 per cent rise in the consumer price index and a 16.6 per cent rise in the wholesale price index.[9] No doubt, the population concentration and precipitative urbanization in the post-war period caused this incredible rise in land prices.

Another unpleasant urban problem was the high level of congestion which adversely affected living conditions, and should be seen to include noise pollution, air pollution caused from auto exhaust gas, traffic jams, etc., and a lack of green areas in large cities. Motor vehicles were the principal source of pollution, because they were widely used in the confines of the city, which resulted in poisonous gas emissions, irritating noise, photochemical smog, and other related problems.

All the troubles including the kind of urban and environmental problems mentioned above were apparently promoted by the process of growth-oriented performance. In accordance with the basic policy goal, the Japanese government placed at the top of its priorities public investment activities for industrial use, such as the

---

[8] One of the highest ratios among applicants to the number of public apartments stood at about 1500 to 1 in 1967, when it was provided by the Tokyo Metropolitan Housing Corporation. Furthermore, in October 1973, the Japan Housing Public Corporation offered residential land lots in the city of Yokohama. Surprisingly enough, the number of applicants jumped to 5003 times the number of available land lots. This crazy competition was caused by the reasons that these lots of land were considered to be the last ones available within people's financial reach and within one hour's commuting time from the centre of Tokyo.

[9] The skyrocketing rise in land prices was partly induced by Prime Minister Kakuei Tanaka who proposed his grandiose scheme for the resolution of Japan's complicated urban problems. He suggested dispersing the metropolitan population by creating scores of new middle-sized cities throughout the country. But his proposal had the effect of encouraging land speculation by large firms, as he had failed to consider how far and how quickly the land problem would advance (see Kakuei Tanaka 1972).

construction of harbours, bridges, roads, etc. In retrospect, during the growth process more investment funds should have been reallocated towards housing, sewage, public parks, water supplies, etc. Greater importance should have been placed on enhancing the level of social infrastructures through the budgetary process.

Industrial Pollution

During the early period of post-war reconstruction in the 1950s and 1960s, great efforts were made to achieve rapid economic growth through business investment. Unfortunately, this growth-oriented policy performance was adopted by both private and public sectors without proper attention to the environment. As a consequence, it led not only to heavy pollution and irreversible damage to the natural environment, but it also resulted in serious health problems as noted below.

Industrial pollution, or environmental disruption, which had made its debut in the course of Japan's rapid growth, became one of the most serious economic and social problems around the year 1970. From the late 1950s, several new diseases like *Minamata* or *Itai-itai*, as will be described shortly, began to emerge in some specific local areas, but at that time nationwide attention was not being paid to these unique diseases caused by industrial pollution. Since then the production and range of industrial pollution has continued universally and has spread to cover virtually the entire nation.

It is necessary to explain briefly three examples typical of industrial pollution. First, what is probably the most famous case of all, *Minamata* disease. *Minamata* was once a charming fishing port on the west side of Kyushu and is now known all over the world through the media as the name of a painful, paralyzing, blinding illness. Industrial mercury from the Nihon Chemical Co., was deposited into the sea, contaminating its fish, and poisoning the inhabitants who ate the catch. As a result, hundreds of people were killed and thousands of them remained crippled. As the century closes, local victims are taking legal proceedings against the government seeking compensation for the physical damage caused.

The second example is of a cadmium disease which occurred in the Toyama prefecture in the north-central part of Honshu, making the bones of victims weak and brittle. A common nickname, *itai-itai*, or 'ouch-ouch' explains the intensity of its pain. Cadmium flowed into the Jintsu River from the Mitsui Metal Industry, poisoning the fish and the people who ate it.

Third, the city of Yokkaichi, which has famous oil refineries near Nagoya, produced an affliction caused by smoke-pollution called *Yokkaichi* asthma. The victims have to be hospitalized for frequently recurring asthma.

Why has such a miserable state of industrial pollution evolved? There are various explanations, but greater importance should be placed on the entire process of rapid growth in light of the development of heavy chemical industries. It is widely acknowledged that an excessive emphasis on single-minded growth performance provided a good basis for environmental damage, stimulating excess competition in the investment and production process. The overall strategy of rapid growth was to direct investment into the expansion of private production facilities in order to increase output. In general, most business investments were made without any effective anti-pollution equipment before industrial pollution posed serious problems.

Strong emphasis was placed on investment activity for industrial facilities that directly supported private production by growth-oriented policy. However, the government should have reallocated its investment towards relatively more social overhead capital in the growth process. Similarly, the government should have strongly guided business investment in order to halt the destruction of the natural environment by imposing special anti-pollution regulations on a compulsory basis. Obviously, these policy changes would have slowed down the realized growth rates in the 1960s, but it would probably have greatly contributed to the reduction of pollution related accidents. After the late 1960s, public concern prompted the adoption of pollution protection policies to avoid severe damage to the natural environment. In concrete terms, the Basic Law for Environmental Pollution Control was enacted in 1967, and furthermore the Environmental Agency was established in 1971 as a primary organization in charge of the environment, under the Prime Minister's office of the government. Both contributed a great deal to providing the main basis and impetus for major achievements in relation to pollution control efforts in environmental conservation.

Structural changes in the Japanese economy, as will be argued in Chapter 3, caused by two oil shocks in the 1970s, greatly affected the process of environmental conservation and control. As a result of the increased price of crude oil, energy-saving behaviour was adopted in industrial activities with a greater emphasis on the protection of the environment, which resulted in a significant reduction in pollution. Heavy polluting industries were socially criticized and obliged to introduce anti-pollution measures.

Both oil crises proved that the Japanese economy was founded upon a very vulnerable base of import dependency for basic raw materials. Thus, with the constraint of energy and raw materials, the rate of real economic growth essentially decreased from 10 per cent to 5 per cent. In turn, a slowdown of Japan's growth coupled with the promotion of pollution control measures and increased energy efficiency in the 1980s led to a reduction in environmental problems.

On this point, OECD has recently commended environmental policies in Japan as follows:

Over the past two decades Japan has had the largest economic growth of G7 countries, while substantially reducing emissions of a number of pollutants in the atmosphere and toxic substances in water, and further containing the growth of other pollutants and of waste production. For instance, while economic growth increased over the period by 122 per cent, SO_x emissions decreased by 82 per cent and NO_x emissions by 21 per cent, the best performance among OECD countries. This decoupling was achieved through economic structural changes, increased energy efficiency and effective environmental policies. These successes have proved that environmental policies and economic development can be mutually supportive; the competitiveness of Japanese industry has not suffered overall and has even benefited in some sectors (e.g., the automobile industry and the pollution control equipment sector) (OECD 1994, p. 182).

As noted above, pollution control policies in Japan have been quite efficient and have produced a number of success stories. As far as pollution control is concerned, Japan's performance has recently been highly evaluated by other industrial countries. However, these remarkable results of pollution control are limited to specific regions and sectors. In fact, great efforts have been made to abate the damages caused by air, water, or waste pollution in the natural resource sector.

3

Structural Changes Towards a New Dimension

The Japanese economy, with its high rates of growth and overall stability, has attracted worldwide attention in the post-war period. In fact, Japan successfully caught up with the West by 1970 due to a sustained surge of rapid economic growth. It is, however, widely acknowledged that a new era has emerged for Japan since the early 1970s, particularly in the context of international relations.

From the first oil shock of 1973 through the 1980s, Japan has undergone a sea of changes and has faced significant problems which have required solutions. These changes were induced by a drastic slowdown of economic growth, the occurrence of a large current account surplus, the sharp rise of the fiscal deficit and the far-reaching deregulation of financial markets. None the less, Japan has achieved more rapid economic growth than other major industrial countries, with a better performance in such areas as price stability, employment, and productivity. It seems that Japan has responded to its difficult problems with relative success when viewed from an international perspective.

The main purpose of this chapter is three-fold. First, we shall investigate the transitional stage after the first oil shock. Secondly, we shall trace the actual development of the Japanese economy in the 1980s with a consideration of the implications for the rest of the world. Third, we shall briefly appraise the results of Japan's economic performance in the 1980s. Of course, during each period, certain aspects of fiscal and monetary policies will be examined.

A TRANSITIONARY STAGE IN THE 1970S

The Slowdown of Economic Growth

As stressed earlier, the rapid growth of the Japanese economy during the 1960s was often called an 'economic miracle'. However, the era of high economic growth came to an end in the early 1970s, and has never returned. This change is depicted in Figure 3.1 in terms of real growth rates. From 1965 to 1970 the annual real growth of Japan's GNP averaged 10.3 per cent, but thereafter it began to slow down to much lower rates. The slowdown had actually started in 1970 with an average growth rate of 6.7 per cent between 1971–73.

We focus on the recession of 1971 to explain the slowdown of Japan's growth rates during the period in question. This recession had been caused by the revaluation of the yen under 'the Nixon Shock'.[1] Although the yen appreciation was marginal compared

This chapter partly depends on Ishi 1994*b*.

[1] The fixed exchange rate system was terminated in August 1971, when the USA abolished the convertibility of the dollar into gold. A ratio of 360 yen to the dollar was converted into a new ratio of 308 yen in December 1971, as a result of the Smithsonian Agreement.

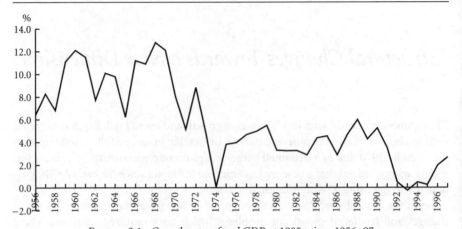

FIGURE 3.1. *Growth rates of real GDP at 1985 prices, 1956–97*

Source: EPA, *Annual Report on National Accounts*, 1982 and 1995; OECD, *Economic Outlook* p. A4

Notes: The years 1994–97 are estimations and projections by OECD.

to later exchange rate swings, this first experience was a great surprise to Japanese exporters. As a consequence, real GNP growth fell to 4.3 per cent in 1971, as illustrated in Figure 3.1.

In spite of a growth recession, inflation mounted due to policy's failure to make adjustments for a new era of yen appreciation (see, for a more expanded discussion, R. Angel 1991). Another policy mistake was induced by a grandiose idea of 'Remodelling the Japanese Archipelago' that Prime Minister Kakuei Tanaka had proposed, as noted earlier. The monetary authority also failed to control inflation as monetary expansion produced 'excess liquidity'.

Furthermore, dramatic change was incurred by the outbreak of the oil shock in 1973 which demarcated the end of Japan's high growth performance. The oil shock had laid bare the most vulnerable feature of Japan's domestic economy: its high dependency on imported crude oil, mainly from the Middle East. Consequently, Japan had to face drastic structural and institutional change in the economy. That first oil shock in 1973 brought an end to the post-war era of high economic growth, and began to create a Japan which was noticeably different structurally from the previous period.[2] In fact, Japan's growth from 1974 to 1989 had dropped to 3.9 per cent, including a year of zero growth. No doubt, the much slower rate had brought about substantial changes at both the macroeconomic and microeconomic level.

Stagflation after the First Oil Shock
Since the oil shock in the second half of 1973, Japan's economy encountered a new combination of prolonged recession and inflation. This recession began in the first

---

[2] Lincoln attaches great importance to 1973 as a convenient dividing line between major periods in post-war Japan. See Lincoln 1988, pp. 2–5.

quarter of 1974, moving quite differently from previous ones. Of significant importance was the zero growth of real GNP in fiscal 1974 for the first time in post-war
Japan. Although the economy hit the bottom in the first quarter of 1975, economic
recovery was still weak. In 1974 and 1975, fiscal and monetary policies were positively
employed, initially to restrict aggregate demand, and subsequently to move towards
stimulating it. Since the years of 1974–75 are really significant as they constitute the
immediate period following the oil shock, we ought to take special note of this period
in our further study.

During these two years, domestic business had continued to remain stagnant in a
protracted slump, showing no marked signs of recovery. This was chiefly attributable
to the continuing stagnation of private domestic demand. In a comparison of the
changes in private demand in the recession in question and those in past recessions,
there are several notable features.

Figure 3.2 illustrates the trends of four segments of domestic demand in four recessionary periods. The results may be summarized as follows:

1. Personal consumption expenditure, which in the past exerted a buoyant influence
   during cyclical depressions, showed little evidence of such movement in the 1974
   recession.
2. Private residential construction also continued to be sluggish, although it is usually
   expected to lead a business recovery. This prolonged slump was much more noticeable than that in personal consumption.
3. Plant and equipment investment fell sharply. What stands out here is that there was
   no upturn even after it was presumed that the economy had bottomed out (at the
   mark ▲).
4. Inventory adjustment was greatly delayed, reflecting the 'abnormal' inflation late
   in 1973. Its timing worsened the recession to an unprecedented extent.

Obviously, the pattern of business recovery was substantially different in the 1974
recession. Based on these observations, it was apparent that the 'on–off' character of
buoyant demand was not likely to work well this time. As will be noted later, a
special stimulus was needed to enable demand and output growth to resume the
pre-recession rate of expansion. This was a reflection of the seriousness of the most
prolonged slump in post-war Japan.

The trend of price levels was very important in explaining the basic nature of the
latest recession. The EPA emphasizes that:

The current recession has been brought by inflation and that, therefore, no recovery could be
hoped for without price stability (EPA 1975, p. i).

In fact, the 'abnormal' inflation due to the oil crisis touched off the sharp drop in
domestic final demand in the January–March quarter of 1974, as seen in Figure 3.2.
Moreover, inflationary expectations induced the increase in inventory investment which lasted until the April–June period of the same year, delaying inventory
adjustment.

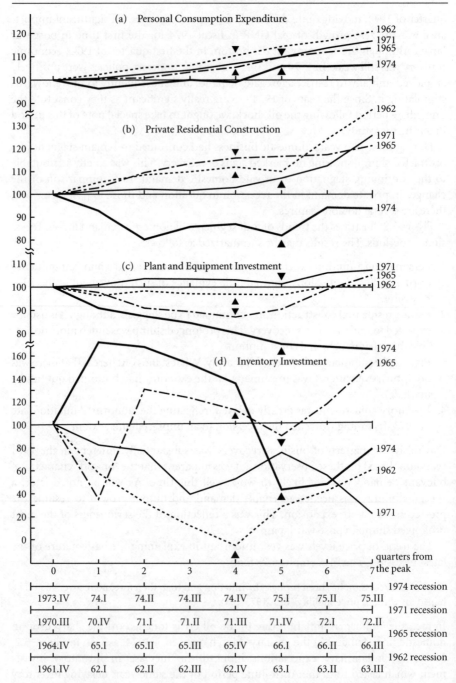

FIGURE 3.2. *Private domestic demand at constant prices during recessions*

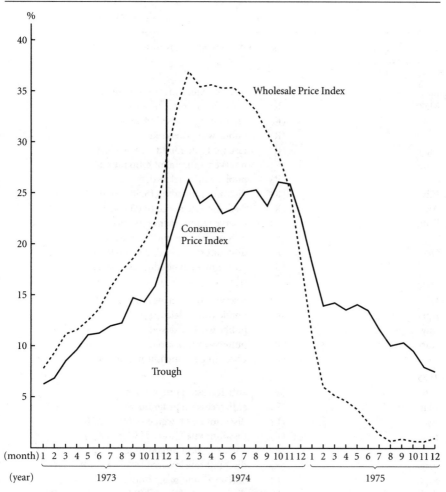

FIGURE 3.3. *Trends of price levels (rate of increase from the previous year), 1973–75*
Source: Bank of Japan, *Economic Statistics Annual*, 1976

The basic facts about price level changes during 1973–75 are shown in Figure 3.3.
Wholesale prices skyrocketed due to the oil crisis between October 1973 and February
1974, but thereafter their upward movement slowed down appreciably. However, the
rate of increase remained high until August 1974, maintaining the higher prices of
basic goods, such as oil, chemical goods, power and steel. The deepening of the recession greatly influenced the trend of wholesale prices. For instance, full-scale inventory
adjustment began to show stronger deflationary effects from about September 1974,
when wholesale prices started falling sharply.

The variation of wholesale prices in the 1974 recession showed a different pattern
from that in past recessions. While in the past wholesale prices had always peaked or

TABLE 3.1. *Demand management policies in 1973–75*

Year and Month		Fiscal and monetary measures
1973		
Jan.	(R)	reserve requirement ratio raised
Mar.	(R)	reserve requirement ratio raised
Apr.	(R)	discount rate raised (4.25 → 5.00)*
	(R)	public works delayed
May	(R)	discount rate raised (5.00 → 5.50)
June	(R)	reserve requirement ratio raised
	(R)	public works delayed
July	(R)	discount rate raised (5.50 → 6.00)*
Aug.	(R)	discount rate raised (6.00 → 7.00)
Sept.	(R)	reserve requirement ratio raised
	(R)	government expenditures delayed
Dec.	(R)	discount rate raised (7.00 → 9.00)
	(R)	government expenditures delayed
1974		
Jan.	(R)	reserve requirement ratio raised*
Apr.	(R)	public works delayed
July	(R)	public works delayed
Aug.	(R)	public works delayed
	(R)	government expenditures delayed
1975		
Feb.	(E)	anti-recession programme
Mar.	(E)	anti-recession programme
Apr.	(E)	discount rate lowered (9.00 → 8.50)
June	(E)	discount rate lowered (8.50 → 8.00)
	(E)	anti-recession programme
Aug.	(E)	discount rate lowered (8.00 → 7.50)
Sept.	(E)	anti-recession programme
Oct.	(E)	discount rate lowered (7.50 → 6.50)
Nov.	(E)	reserve requirement ratio lowered*

Note: (R) and (E) are designated for restrictive and expansive measures, respectively. The figures in parentheses are percentage levels of the official discount rate, and an asterisk * indicates that the policy change occurred at the same time as the changing of deposit and postal savings rates in the same direction.

begun to fall by the time business indicators peaked, this time they started falling only when full-scale inventory adjustment began in the second half of fiscal 1974. Unfortunately, it was just three quarters late.

Similarly, consumer prices rose sharply until February 1974, slowing down markedly only at the end of 1974. Throughout 1974, consumer prices remained at relatively high levels. Although the government faced both recession and inflation, more emphasis was put on price stabilization than on economic recovery. For example, the government was eager to stabilize the level of consumer prices, setting a policy target of holding down the rate of increase of consumer prices in March 1975 to 15 per cent relative to the same month of the preceding year. In reality, it was 14.2 per cent. The policy objective at that time was to reduce that same ratio of consumer prices to the one-digit level in March 1976.

In 1973 and 1974, the top-priority policy objective was slowing inflation, despite the continuation of the recession. Even before the increase in oil prices in October 1973, a virulent inflation was evident which simply accelerated the rate of inflation already prevalent in the economy. The government employed a series of demand-restricting measures to control inflation from the beginning of 1973.

Table 3.1 summarizes fiscal and monetary measures during the years of 1973–75. Demand-curbing measures began in April 1973, when the official discount rate was raised, and the public work contracts were carried forward. At the time of the oil crisis late in 1973, fiscal and monetary policies were shifted in a more restrictive direction to cope with 'abnormal' inflation. Broadly speaking, full-scale restrictive measures were enforced throughout 1973–74, while expansionary policies began to be put into effect only from the beginning of 1975. In these programmes, fiscal and monetary policies had operated as two different kinds of policy tools. Fiscal policy had been utilized through (i) a carry-over and carry-back of public work programmes and (ii) an adjustment of the schedule of the disbursement of government expenditures from the Treasury. The two monetary measures had been the raising or lowering of (i) the official discount rate and (ii) the reserve requirement ratio.

Of central importance was the manipulation of discount rate policy by the Bank of Japan (BOJ). During two years of tight money policy, the total hike of the discount rate amounted to 4.75 per cent. In addition to this, reserve requirement ratios were raised five times during 1973–74. Thus, this stringent monetary policy represented the most severe steps in the post-war era in terms of both duration and scale. Likewise, government fixed investment (excluding inventory) was substantially restricted by the postponement of both public works and government expenditures. The rate of change of government investment fell below that of GNP in the initial stages of the recession, as seen in Figure 3.4, although in past recessions the former had considerably exceeded the latter. As a consequence, it was often argued that the 1974 recession was basically a policy-induced one like all the others, due mainly to the reduced tempo of government investment in this instance, as well as stringent monetary restraint.

Why was the enforcement of such severe demand-management measures required over such a long period as an anti-inflationary policy? The chief reason for this was that inflation and/or inflationary expectation due to massive excess liquidity had been widespread for a long time. Thus, it took time to eliminate them, and without doubt inflation delayed the permeation of the effects of restrictive policies. With this view, the government often emphasized that it would be necessary to maintain strong measures to curb aggregate demand in order to achieve price stability.

Around the third quarter of 1974, demand-curbing measures gradually began to show more effect, including both a slowdown in price increases and a full-scale inventory

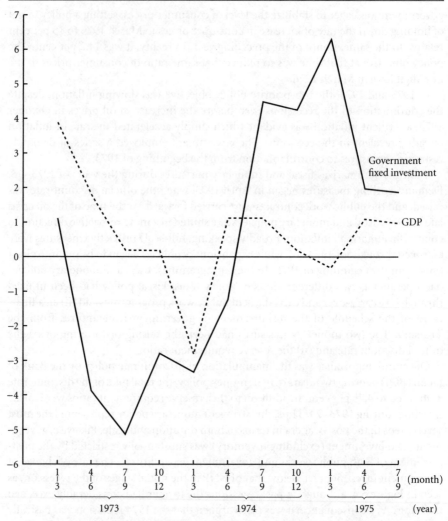

FIGURE 3.4. *Movements in GDP and government fixed investment (quarter to quarter rate of change, real, seasonally adjusted), 1973–75*
Source: EPA, *National Income Statistics*

adjustment. Expectations of an easing of the restrictions became increasingly higher, but the government was persistently reluctant to do so. Thus, the effects of the demand-curbing measures permeated at an accelerated rate, leading to a drop in wholesale prices. As the recession progressed, such social frictions as unemployment and bankruptcies began to appear in the economy. The recession, not inflation, became a more serious problem.

The government moved towards stimulative policies from the beginning of 1975, on the presumption that past demand management policies had achieved their primary goal of ending the abnormal inflation. Accordingly, anti-recession programmes were implemented four times by September 1975, as indicated in Table 3.1. The major aspects of these programmes were (i) the acceleration of public works programme, (ii) the increase of government loans for residential construction, and (iii) the expanded subscription of local bonds. Similarly, the BOJ lowered the official discount rate by 0.5 per cent in April, June, and August, and by 1.0 per cent in October, and began to relax the lending ceiling.

In spite of such a series of fully-fledged expansionary packages, the Japanese economy seems to have been too depressed to start vigorously recovering right away. Indeed, in its monthly economic report for February 1976, the EPA conceded that domestic business variation at that time might have been bottoming out, and amended its previous judgement that business hit the bottom in the first quarter of 1975.

In an appraisal of the demand management policies for those three years, it should be stressed that abnormal inflation nearly came to an end. By focusing on the price level, the demand-curbing measures from fiscal 1973 apparently were successful. It must be acknowledged, however, that such success had been achieved only with great sacrifice, that is a prolonged recession with social frictions. Economic recovery greatly lagged behind those following past recessions in which the economy promptly resumed the pre-recession level of output and demand within about one year or with a sharp V-shape upturn. At that time, the government expected that the anti-recession programmes would soon encourage a recovery in domestic business and a rally in economic growth. Nevertheless, such expansionary measures in 1975 did not prove to be as stimulative to business as the government had expected.

There were two reasons for this that are worth noting. First, although public works were believed to provide a key pump-priming boost to business recovery, fiscal stimulus remained discouragingly meagre because the financial crises of local governments acted as a brake. Second, the reduction of the official discount rate was limited to a great extent by the strong resistance to lowering postal savings rate. At the same time, we must note that the buoyancy of private investment came near to its end in the early 1970s, as will be discussed shortly.

The Hesitant Recovery in the Economy in the late 1970s

The Japanese economy after 1973 was transformed into the new era of 'stable growth', reflecting the reduced tempo of growth rates with the restraint of higher energy cost. The term 'stable' was generally taken to imply more steady, say in a range of about 4–5 per cent in terms of real growth. After Japan had experienced zero growth in 1974, the Japanese economy had recovered relatively sooner than that of any other major advanced country. However, the subsequent recovery was lacking in vigour and strength, unlike that of the 1960s.

The marked phenomena of weakening buoyant aggregate demand became notable since the outbreak of the first oil shock. In particular, great emphasis was placed on the sluggishness of private plant and equipment investment. The Japanese economy officially hit bottom in March 1975, but thereafter it never achieved a vigorous recovery. Although business expansions were considered to be prevalent during fiscal 1975–77 in the record of post-war cycles, economic recovery was still hesitant against widespread expectation of greater vigour and strength. In retrospect, such expectations were based on the belief that rapid growth in the 1960s could be substained into the next decade.

Obviously, the main factor for the retarded recovery was that private investment remained stagnant. As we have already seen in Figure 3.2, it began to diminish sharply around the turn of 1974, and continued to drop even in the expansion period after March 1975. There had been no conspicuous signs of investment increases for a while, which is to be contrasted with previous recovery phases. In the past, investment did turn upward immediately after business conditions reached a trough. In particular, the large-scale manufacturing industries, such as the steel and automobile industries, kept their investment decreasing for as long as five quarter periods. It was not until the fourth quarter of 1976 that it began to increase again.

Why did investment remain depressed so much for four years? What were the main factors behind the lack of vigour in investment? Two points should be stressed. First, excess capacity had been incurred by over-investment in the past. For instance, the productive capacity of crude steel and passenger car producers had sharply expanded over a period of 20 years.[3] Secondly, the tendency of over-investment was derived from an over-optimistic prediction of future demand in the 1972 boom immediately before the oil shock took place.[4] According to the published economic forecasts, a considerably higher level of private investment in plant and equipment had already been planned and even started to a significant extent.

It was in such a period that the Japanese government took initiatives on an expansionary fiscal policy in cooperation with the 'three locomotive countries' (the USA, West Germany and Japan) to stimulate the depressed world economy. Major financial sources for expanding public expenditures were sought by issuing national bonds, as will be discussed later. This experience could be thought of as the first adoption of Keynesian fiscal policies in Japan in the true sense of the term. Once again a second oil shock hit the Japanese economy in 1979, and its growth rate was widely believed to be lowered again by up to 3 per cent.

Particular attention should be paid to successful policy actions taken to confront the second oil shock of 1979. Table 3.2 shows what happened to price trends. Needless to say, the second large shock attacked the economy after the outbreak of the first oil shock, bringing with it double-digit inflation. Wholesale prices began to accelerate rapidly, and consumer prices followed. Import prices for energy were running high at

---

[3] Productive capacity in crude steel expanded 11.4 fold from 9.41 million tons in 1955 to 107.4 million tons in 1975 while domestic demand was estimated at about 60–70 million tons at that time. Likewise, demand for passenger cars increased enormously—238 fold—between 1955 and 1975.

[4] This boom was apparently intensified by Kakuei Tanaka's grandiose idea of the 'Remodeling of the Japanese Archipelago', as was argued earlier.

TABLE 3.2. *Trends of price changes, 1971–89*

Year	GDP deflator	Wholesale price index	Consumer price index	Import price index for energy	Wage index
1971	5.5	−0.8	5.8	15.3	13.7
1972	5.8	3.2	5.1	−3.5	16.5
1973	13.1	22.7	16.2	8.0	21.9
1974	20.1	23.5	21.8	193.3	29.1
1975	7.4	1.9	10.4	19.7	12.4
1976	7.8	5.5	9.4	7.3	11.8
1977	6.4	0.4	6.7	−3.9	8.1
1978	5.0	−2.3	3.4	−18.9	5.9
1979	2.7	13.0	4.8	32.3	6.1
1980	4.6	12.8	7.6	73.0	6.0
1981	3.7	1.3	4.0	9.7	5.1
1982	1.7	1.0	2.6	10.6	4.3
1983	1.4	−2.3	1.9	−11.8	2.4
1984	2.3	0.4	2.2	−4.9	3.5
1985	1.6	−3.3	1.9	0.4	3.1
1986	1.8	−9.4	0.0	−28.8	2.3
1987	0.0	−2.0	0.5	−12.5	2.0
1988	0.4	−0.7	0.8	−16.4	4.2
1989	1.9	3.5	2.9	9.2	4.8

Source: EPA, *Annual Report on National Accounts*, Bank of Japan, *Economic Statistical Annual*.

Note: Each index is computed for percentage changes from previous years.

193.3 per cent above the level of the previous year. Of most importance was the sharp rise in the wage level which in turn had induced cost-push inflation.

In 1974, the labour unions had successfully negotiated huge wage hikes to make up for high inflation, spurred by their strong desire to maintain current standards of living in terms of real income. Thus, wage increases reached 29.1 per cent. However, after the first real recession of the post-war period struck in 1973–74, a new realism emerged from a sober outlook conditioned by expectations of lower economic growth in the future. This was particularly noticeable in the behaviour of the labour unions. After 1974, the labour unions had diametrically altered their attitude into one of a more cooperative relation with management, adjusting quickly to the new realism. For example, wage demands were lowered, which in turn reduced strike activity.

The change in labour union strategy is evident from the fact that wage increases were restricted to 6 per cent in 1979–80 when the second oil crisis emerged. As a consequence, both the GNP deflator and consumer prices never increased rapidly, in spite of a sharp rise in import energy prices (Table 3.2). It is important to stress that the real wage never increased at a faster pace than labour productivity after the second oil shock. This means the relative share of labour was stable, and in turn corporate profits did not deteriorate as much, allowing businesses to invest in new plant and equipment.

It is noteworthy that the Japanese economy was able to pass successfully through the oil crisis of 1979 without a double-digit inflation or a recession, unlike in the previous experience. This success was clearly a result of the better performance of monetary policy with a much higher priority given to controlling inflation. Thus, the government regained confidence in guiding the economy through the 1979 experience. Although no one expected a return to high economic growth, a different kind of confidence was resurgent in Japan by the 1980s.

A NEW DIMENSION AS AN ECONOMIC SUPERPOWER IN THE 1980S

Macroeconomic Imbalance and Trade Friction

The move towards moderate growth[5] induced a basic macroeconomic imbalance in the form of a surplus of savings over investment in the private sector. When growth slowed down, the opportunity for investment was reduced as well. During the period of rapid growth, high levels of private savings, particularly as supplied by private households, had matched the high demand for private investment. However, while domestic investment demand fell, the economy continued to generate higher levels of savings which in turn created an imbalance in a way unfamiliar in the past. The excess of savings over investment in the private sector implied that this gap needed to be absorbed elsewhere in the economy; say, by any means within the government sector or by the rest of the world. If not, the economy could not have avoided recession or stagnation (see Yamamura 1982).

While fiscal policy played a vital role in absorbing most of the surplus savings in the late 1970s as argued above, the government was replaced as the major adjuster by the rest of the world in the 1980s. The chief reason for this change of policy was the government's resistance to a huge expansion of the fiscal deficit caused by expansionary policies. The fiscal deficit tended to fall steadily under the government's slogan of fiscal reconstruction as will be examined in Chapter 6, but the current account surplus rose sharply.

This is evident from Figure 3.5. The Japanese economy started to build surpluses in the first half of the 1980s. The ratio of the current account surplus to GDP moved upwards increasingly to a peak of 4.3 per cent in 1986. The increase in the current account surplus implied that the rest of the world would have to provide the demand instead of Japan, absorbing the goods and services not consumed in the domestic economy. Also, it implied that the surplus of savings had to flow out of Japan as a capital export.

---

[5] There are many factors to explain the slowdown of Japan's growth, but it seems that the most important was the closing of the technology gap.

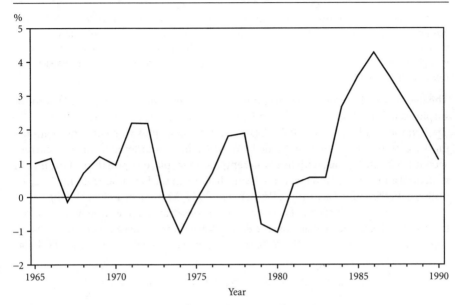

FIGURE 3.5. *Ratio of current account surplus to GDP, 1965–90*

Source: As Table 3.1

Note: Dollar values of current account surpluses are first converted into yen using the basic rate of foreign exchange, and then they are divided by GDP

No doubt, such a sharp rise in the external surplus in the balance of payments induced serious trade frictions, in particular with the USA (Schmiegelow 1986; El-Agrra 1988). Indeed, the expansion of Japan's exports was derived from rising demand in the US economy, caused by federal deficits. Thus, much of the international adjustment had to come from the USA.

In Figure 3.5, we can trace the long-run pattern of the relative weight of the current account surplus in GNP. Before reaching its highest peak in 1986, large current account surpluses had already occurred on more than one occasion. Prior to 1970, Japan was still a small economy and was far from provoking any interest in Europe and America. However, the rapid growth of Japan's exports was increasingly becoming a threat to producers in the importing countries, and frequent complaints of unfair competition and dumping began to surface. In large part, American steel and textile producers took the first initiative and were then followed by competitors in other countries. It was widely believed that the unfair advantages of Japanese firms could be ascribed to an undervalued yen and strong protection of the domestic market (see, for example, Komiya and Suda 1991).

As the economy entered the 1970s, rapid growth still continued and started to build surpluses in the balance of payments. To explain this situation, the following statement is worth noting:

All of a sudden, in the early 1970s, Japan was seen as a destabilizing factor in the world economy: a very large economy exporting vast quantities of manufactured products, importing primarily raw materials, and growing much more rapidly than the rest of the world. Concern was perhaps greatest in the United States, which was Japan's leading market (Patrick and Rosovsky 1976, p. 11).

The two oil shocks temporarily prevented Japan from running large current account surpluses in the 1970s, but as seen in Figure 3.5, Japan began to increase them vastly again in the first half of the 1980s. A large and rising surplus worsened international macroeconomic adjustment with the USA, which in turn suffered from large current account deficits. To cope with this issue, emphasis was placed upon the importance of structural adjustments and macroeconomic balance in the Japanese economy (see, for instance, Patrick and Tachi 1986; Pepper *et al.* 1985; Moriguchi 1989*a*, 1989*b*).

The sharp rise in the current account surplus was drawing to a close by 1986 when the yen greatly appreciated against the dollar. Variations in the yen exchange rates are depicted in Table 3.3 for 1971–89. Since 1971 the value of the yen to the US dollar

TABLE 3.3. *Variations of exchange rates of the yen against the dollar, 1971–89*

Year	Exchange rate[a] of yen	Percent change[b] from previous year
1971	349.66	3.0
1972	303.22	15.3
1973	271.80	11.6
1974	291.97	−6.9
1975	296.77	−1.6
1976	296.59	0.1
1977	268.72	10.4
1978	210.61	27.6
1979	218.96	−3.8
1980	226.88	−3.5
1981	220.48	2.9
1982	249.01	−11.5
1983	237.53	4.8
1984	237.55	−0.0
1985	238.54	−0.4
1986	168.51	41.6
1987	144.62	16.5
1988	128.15	12.8
1989	137.96	−7.1

Source: Economic Planning Agency, *Annual Report on National Accounts*, 1991, p. 69.
Notes:
  [a] Monthly simple average calculated from the middle inter-bank rate in the Tokyo market.
  [b] According to the IMF calculation method.

tended to appreciate over the long-run with some disruptions; that is ¥349.66 in 1971 appreciated in value to ¥137.96 by 1989. In particular, the yen appreciated by 41.6 per cent in 1986 relative to the dollar and likewise by 16.5 per cent in 1987. These successive appreciations discouraged exports by making them more expensive and promoted imports by providing the opposite price effect. As a consequence, the current account surplus began to fall, reaching 1.1 per cent in 1990 in terms of relative share to GDP as seen in Figure 3.5.

In summary, by the late 1980s Japan had become a successful, mature industrial economy. The level of per capita GNP exceeded that of the USA with a huge amount of foreign credit, as will be argued later. It is generally pointed out that Japan had grown to be at the forefront of the world economy and as a nation was in a position to perform as an economic superpower by 1990.

Structural Adjustments: The Maekawa Report

After shifting to slower economic growth in the 1980s, the fundamental macro-economic imbalance stemmed from surplus savings in the private sector. There are theoretically two alternative ways to solve this imbalance: one is to incur large fiscal deficits and the other is to produce sizeable current account surpluses.

Figure 3.6 illustrates the past trends in domestic demand and net exports (i.e. external demand) to clarify which factors had the greatest influence on movements in the real GDP growth rate. Obviously, domestic demand was predominant in the 1970s, reflecting fiscal expansion, while in the first half of the 1980s net exports began to occupy a substantial share of GNP in growth terms. This development urged foreign criticism, warning that the rising dependence on external demand was threatening Japan's trade relations with the rest of the world.

In particular, there was a great deal of argument and friction between Japan and the USA. Macroeconomic policies became important in bilateral (and sometimes multilateral) talks as Japan accumulated huge current account surpluses. The USA repeatedly requested that Japan stimulate domestic demand so that the debate in favour of an expansionary domestic policy intensified, even within Japan.[6]

To respond to both domestic and external pressures, Prime Minister Yasuhiro Nakasone in 1985 organized an advisory group of 17 members to conduct a study on policy measures as to how Japan's economic structure should be adjusted for a changing world economy. Chaired by the former governor of the BOJ, Haruo Maekawa, and after intensive discussion for approximately half a year, the advisory group published a report in April 1986. It was called 'The Maekawa Report', after the chairman.

The Maekawa Report had a strong impact on the policy debate, and still continues to lead Japanese discussion on the basic direction of macroeconomic policies in relation to structural change. The main idea of the report stressed the importance of encouraging domestic demand, by placing less reliance on increasing exports.

---

[6] The pressure for stimulative demand policies usually derived from the MITI, supported by scholars of Keynesian groups.

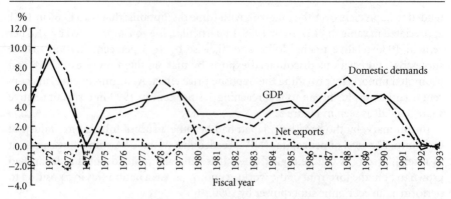

FIGURE 3.6. *Percentage points of real GDP growth rate due to domestic demand and net exports, 1971–93*

Source: EPA, *Annual Report on National Accounts*, 1955–89, pp. 26–9 and 1995, p. 47

Note: Net exports are exports minus imports. Percentages of domestic demand and net exports show the percentage points of growth rate due to expansion (or contraction) of the respective components. Thus the addition of both percentages is equal to GNP growth rate

Although criticized for being short and vague, the report at least raised the issue of finding measures to expand domestic demand as a response to foreign criticism. The USA strategically interpreted it as a very promising change of direction.

It would be worth summarizing the basic framework of the Maekawa Report, considering the significant influence it has on current policy issues.

At the outset, the Report sets a national goal for Japan as follows:

Setting as a medium-term national policy goal, the government should announce its determination, both domestically and internationally, to attain the goal of steadily reducing the nation's current account imbalance to one consistent with international harmony.

The large current account surplus is basically linked with Japan's economic structure such as being export oriented, and there is an urgent need for Japan to implement drastic policies for structural adjustment and to seek to transform the Japanese economic structure into one oriented toward international coordination (The Advisory Group, 1986).

Based upon the keynote statement mentioned above, six recommendations were made in relation to both domestic and international aspects of economic policy. First of all, domestic demand should be expanded in the form of housing and urban renewal, private consumption, and local public investment. Secondly, the industrial structure should be adjusted for the harmonious development of the world economy to encourage the international division of labour. For this purpose, direct overseas investment should be further increased, and the agricultural sector should adopt a more open-door policy.

Thirdly, great effort should be made to encourage imports of manufactured goods by improving market access and changing the exclusive behaviour of private companies. Fourthly, exchange rates should be kept in a more stable and sustained band of fluctuation. Also, financial and capital markets should become more liberalized in the process of facilitating the internationalization of the yen on a global scale.

Fifthly, Japan should contribute more to promoting international cooperation, for example by increasing imports from developing countries or by alleviation of the debt issue, and by implementing the new round of GATT agreements more actively. Lastly, some comments were added to manage fiscal and monetary policy. The dependency on deficit-financing bonds should be eliminated, but on a medium- and long-term basis a more flexible response should be taken in an effort to achieve economic balance. As for tax reform, it was recommended that the preferential tax treatment for savings be eliminated, along with the abolition of the tax exemption of interest on postal savings and small-amount bank deposits (Ishi 1993, ch. 8). Monetary policy should be managed more flexibly in order to create an economy led by domestic demand.

In addition to the major points noted above, attention should also be paid to the enhancement in the quality of the nation's standard of living, although this may not be directly related to the encouragement of domestic demand. In particular, an emphasis was placed on reducing working hours by the active use of paid leave for longer periods of time or complete five-day working weeks. The underlying assumption of the need for a reduction in working hours was that increased free time could be effective in expanding private consumption.

Overall, the Maekawa Report was positively welcomed by many, although the contents were not fully defined. While the report was being prepared, the appreciation of the yen began to put great pressure on Japan's export industries, making the need for policy change more evident. Thus, the debate over the desirability and feasibility of encouraging domestic demand played a crucial role in moving the economy away from the previous policy stance of export-led growth. In fact, it is widely acknowledged that the current account surplus has been reduced since 1986 largely as a result of policy measures proposed by the Report[7] (see Figure 3.5).

After the Maekawa Report was introduced, the term economic structural adjustment which was used in the title of the advisory group became popular as a strategy to guide the Japanese economy in the international context. The new way of thinking along the lines of economic structural adjustment seems to have developed concomitantly with the wave of neo-conservatism in the USA and the UK (see, for example, Moriguchi 1991). It seems that both 'Reaganomics' and 'Thatcherism' deeply affected the policy debate in Japan in the 1980s.

---

[7] The Japanese government took immediate action to implement the recommendations of the Maekawa Report. Its quick response was announced as the declaration of the Ministerial Conference for Economic Measures. In concrete terms, the government committed itself to the implementation of 'carefully thought out measures' in six major areas: (i) flexible monetary policy management; (ii) promoting the implementation of public works projects; (iii) passing along the benefits of yen appreciation and lower oil prices, and setting reasonable prices; (iv) promoting urban redevelopment by easing restrictions; (v) promoting housing construction and private-sector capital investment; and (vi) promoting small- to medium-sized firms.

Some Aspects of Economic Policies: Fiscal Consolidation,
Privatization and Financial Liberalization

The 1980s brought several new policy packages designed to cope with structural changes in the Japanese economy, both domestically and internationally. Worth noting among theses changes are three economic policies which characterize the movement of Japan's economic performance in the decade under consideration: (i) fiscal consolidation; (ii) privatization; and (iii) financial liberalization. These three aspects are closely tied to each other, as noted below. In the subsequent chapters, we shall argue them in detail, particularly the first topic, but a brief explanation will be made here to provide some important background information to understanding the development of Japanese economic policies.

The most marked feature of economic policy in the 1980s was the reluctance of the government to stimulate domestic demand through fiscal expansion. This reluctance constantly retarded efforts to stimulate the economy by reducing taxes or increasing expenditures. As a result, as noted earlier, the burden of encouraging domestic demand had shifted to expanding net exports in the first half of the 1980s, resulting in foreign criticism. The government had sustained its continued desire to reduce fiscal deficits under a slogan of fiscal consolidation. In particular, the MOF focused almost single-mindedly on deficit reduction, as will be discussed in Chapter 6. The prime objective of fiscal consolidation was to stop issuing deficit-financing bonds in the budgetary process until a specific year (see, for more detailed discussion, Ishi 1986*a*).

The policy debate for reducing fiscal deficits, based on fiscal austerity, had a close bearing on the promotion of privatization and deregulation. Initially, this was derived from a complete failure to introduce Japan's VAT in 1979, attempted by Prime Minister M. Ohira. The next step involved an administrative reform movement established to reduce the size of fiscal deficits and to make government expenditure more efficient (Ishi 1993, ch. 15; Lincoln 1988, pp. 116–22; Hollerman 1988, ch. 4).

Privatization was strongly promoted by implementing the process of administrative reform which was to be carried out without tax increases. According to the proposals of the Provisional Commission for Administrative Reform (*Rinji Gyosei Chosakai—Rincho* for short), three major government-owned corporations were to be privatized in succession from 1985–87: Nippon Telegraph and Telephone in April 1985, Japan Tobacco and Salt in April 1985 and the Japanese National Railroad in April 1987. Consequently, administrative reform pressure succeeded in separating major government-owned corporations from direct control of the government and urged new privatized enterprises to compete with private-sector companies.

Similar to privatization, deregulation became important in connection with *Minkatsu* (private-sector vitality), and was supported by the proponents of fiscal consolidation. It was widely believed that deregulation could give a strong boost to private investment, which in turn would provide the necessary stimulus to mitigate the imbalance between savings and investment.

The goal of achieving *Minkatsu* was based on the idea that private investment, for example investment in plant and equipment or in housing, could increase by easing government regulations. In fact, *Minkatsu* contributed to greater investment through the promotion of private-sector participation in projects normally undertaken by the government. Although *Minkatsu* did not provide a complete solution to the stimulation of domestic demand, it proved to be useful to a certain extent as a supplementary policy measure of fiscal expansion.

Behind the attempts of privatization and *Minkatsu*, there were no doubt some views in favour of 'small government' and 'government efficiency' that aimed at revitalizing the economy. Obviously, these ideas relied upon the ideology of 'neo-conservatism' in the USA and the UK. In any event, the first and second economic policies had remained predominant until fiscal consolidation was achieved in 1989 when deficit-financing bonds were finally left unutilized in raising government revenues in the general account of the national budget.

The third policy issue in question is how financial markets have been restructured in view of deregulation in the 1980s. Before the early 1970s, Japan had a highly regulated financial system which played an important role and served the economy very well. Virtually all interest rates were heavily controlled by the government, and the function of various financial institutions was segmented in narrow lines of business. Under such a regulated system, Japan's investors, individuals and firms, were forced to put most of their financial assets in deposit accounts at highly specialized banks with much lower interest rates than they would have earned under free market conditions. Bank loans, financed by these deposits, were channelled into corporations and fuelled plant and equipment investment for rapid economic growth. There are three aspects that explain the unique features of the financial sector before 1973: (i) the preference for indirect financing; (ii) direct control of monetary policy; and (iii) the role of the government budget (Patrick and Rosovsky 1976, ch. 4; Ishi 1982*b*; Viner 1987).

However, macroeconomic changes in the Japanese economy since the 1970s—the need for which arose due to excess savings, fiscal deficits and capital outflows—began to restructure financial markets to a great extent and to induce large-scale changes in the regulations and institutions governing them. Slower economic growth implied that firms became less dependent on bank lending. Under the controlled system of lower interest rates, the government found it difficult to float a massive scale of government bonds to finance expanding fiscal deficits. Moreover, after generating enormous current account surpluses, Japan was put under foreign pressure to liberalize extensively its international financial transactions.

These changes have inevitably pushed Japan towards a reorientation to liberalized financial markets, characterized by a greater use of market-determined interest rates. By the mid-1980s the pace of deregulation had greatly affected the economic activity of financial institutions, and continued to accelerate for more than ten years. However, change and deregulation have been gradual and have favoured marginal adjustments, thereby reflecting the level of importance placed on achieving consensus decisions, avoiding the possibility of failure, and reducing instability in the financial sector—all salient features of Japanese society (see, for example, Horne 1985; Feldman 1986).

TABLE 3.4. *Economic performance in Japan 1973, 1980 and 1989*

Indicator	1973	1980	1989
GNP			
Nominal (¥ trillions)	112.5	240.0	398.7
	(100)	(213)	(354)
Real (¥ trillions in 1985)	208.6	266.6	383.1
	(100)	(128)	(184)
Per capita (dollars)	3,814	9,137	24,463
	(100)	(240)	(615)
Per capita rank among OECD countries	16	17	3
Foreign trade			
Exports ($)	36.3	126.7	269.6
	(100)	(349)	(743)
Imports ($)	32.6	124.6	192.7
	(100)	(382)	(591)
Current-account balance ($ millions)	−136	−10,746	57,157
Overseas direct investment ($ billions)	1.9	2.4	44.1
	(100)	(126)	(2,321)

Source: As Table 3.1 and *OECD, National Accounts*, vol. 1, 1987.

Note: Figures in parentheses are an index computed for the 1973 base year.

ECONOMIC PERFORMANCE IN THE 1980S

What the Economy Has Brought in the 1980s

Japan's unprecedented high rate of economic growth had come to an end and, after 1973, along with the rest of the industrial countries, Japan experienced slower growth. As stressed earlier, Japan's economy had, nevertheless, relatively outperformed those of other major advanced industrial countries in the 1980s. However, the fact that economic growth had not risen to earlier levels clearly brought about changes in macroeconomic structures within the Japanese economy. These fundamental shifts created new problems, domestically and internationally, and required the government to take different policy actions (Balassa and Noland 1988; Inoguchi and Okimoto 1988).

Despite significant structural changes in the economy, Japan succeeded in joining the vanguard of the world's economies by the end of the 1980s. A new dimension as an economic superpower had been entered in the historical development of post-war Japan. Table 3.4 has been prepared to illustrate the changes in Japanese economic performance. Basic economic indicators, GNP and foreign trade, are shown for three selected years. Fundamental shifts become conspicuous between 1973 and 1989, that is in 1989 nominal GNP expanded by roughly four times and real GNP by 1.84 times. Although Japan had become the second largest economy in the developed world by

1973, its per capita GNP was ranked merely sixteenth among the 24 member countries of the OECD. Since 1973 its per capita GNP steadily increased, but its relative position remained almost unchanged by 1980. Finally, per capita income in dollars was pushed up by the large-scale yen appreciation in 1986 and 1987 to the level of that in the USA. In 1989, Japan's position in per capita GNP had risen to third, following two small wealthy countries; Switzerland and Luxembourg.

More attention should be paid to other indicators in relation to the trade sector. Japan encountered vast changes in its international balance of payments during the past two decades of the twentieth century. In 1973 when the first oil shock occurred under a new floating system of exchange rates, Japan ran a small current account deficit of $136 million, mainly reflecting both the sharp rise in crude oil prices and an appreciated yen. This deficit expanded to $10,746 million in 1980, as the result of the second oil shock. As time went by, by the late 1980s the current account surplus had drastically increased, as noted below, to $57,127 million, and was still rising. Needless to say, this sharp increase in the surplus resulted from the rapid expansion of exports over imports: exports increased by 7.43 times in 1989 as compared with 1973, while imports merely increased 5.91 fold during the same time span.

Furthermore, greater stress should be placed on the drastic jump of overseas direct investment in recent years. Obviously, this reflects the sharp rise of the current account surplus on a vast scale. In the process of increasing foreign investment, Japan was rapidly integrated into world capital markets, resulting in the liberalization of regulations in financial markets at home. Major shifts in the international balance of payments which resulted from macroeconomic developments in the Japanese economy posed an important problem for international trade, a problem which continues to plague Japan at the end of the 1990s.

Appraisal on Economic Performance

Comparing Japan's overall economic performance in the 1970s and the 1980s with that of Western Europe and the USA, we can conclude that Japan has successfully achieved better results. While the rate of inflation has been kept at the lowest level, no serious unemployment has been incurred. Thus, Japan has achieved the highest rates of real growth during the past two decades seen from an international perspective.

The Japanese economy continued to expand after November 1986 and had attained the longest duration of prosperity in the post-war period by September 1991. Upward movement of business activity had been sustained for over 58 months, a record-breaking length of time. Since this expansion began soon after the Maekawa Report was published, it became necessary to review the actual performance of the Japanese economy from the standpoint of the recommendations proposed by the Maekawa Report.

Before the London Summit was held in July 1991, the government published an appraisal detailing the results of the report. The main aim of the appraisal was to clarify to what extent the Maekawa Report's recommendations were realized in Japan's economic performance over the past five years, and to provide the then Prime

Minister, T. Kaifu, with important information prior to participating in the Summit in London.

According to this appraisal, the following four points were highlighted as fulfilling the recommendations.

1. The current account surplus was substantially reduced from $94.1 billion in 1986 to $33.8 billion in 1990: from 4.6 per cent to 1.1 per cent in terms of relative ratio to GNP.
2. Domestic demand led to substantial economic growth with increased investment. Indeed, the average growth rates for 1986–90 were 4.8 per cent in which the relative share of domestic demand occupied 5.4 per cent of the real growth rates as a whole (i.e. the counterpart of net exports was negative).
3. Imports had increased to a considerable extent. While imports of agricultural products were increased by about 1.5 fold from 1985 to 1990, the share of manufactured goods in total imports reached approximately 50 per cent in recent years, jumping swiftly from about 25 per cent in the early 1980s. In addition, tariffs on industrial products became much lower than those in other major countries.
4. Direct overseas investment and ODA (Official Development Assistance) increased promptly.

These four points summarize a successful story of structurally switching the Japanese economy's prime source of growth from net exports to domestic demand. As a consequence, it seems that foreign pressure and conflicts with trade partners have virtually disappeared, particularly with the USA. However, the appraisal report indicates that three points still remain unresolved.

1. The gap in the price level between the home and overseas markets still remained wide, although it had shrunk slightly. For example, assuming that the standard of living index is 100 in Tokyo, it is only 82 in New York and 79 in Hamburg (as of March 1991).
2. Attempts to shorten working hours have not yet been completely successful. Indeed, in Japan the average annual figure for working hours in 1989 was 2044, while in Europe and the USA the figure was approximately 1800 or less.
3. The high price of land prevented housing and social overhead investments from increasing at the necessary speed.

No doubt, these points pose problems which the government should continue to tackle in the future. While the Japanese economy was encountering a prosperous state of business expansion on the surface, another sea of changes has undermined its fundamental base since the late 1980s: the outbreak of the 'bubble' boom and its collapse. After the collapse of the unusual bubble boom with asset inflation, prolonged recession continued persistently in the early 1990s with almost zero rates of real growth.

4

The Emergence of the Bubble Economy
and Its Aftermath

Japan's economy achieved great success in its overall performance until the late 1980s. It had attained the highest rate of economic growth among major industrial countries with no serious problems of unemployment or inflation. Perhaps the first oil shock, caused by the oil embargo of the Arab countries, was an epoch-making incident in that Japan's weakness became evident, along with its vulnerability as a very resource-poor country. However, the damage of the first oil crisis was successfully limited by co-operation between private business and government policy. After overcoming the initial hardship of the 1970s, Japan emerged as an economic superpower in the 1980s. At the end of the twentieth century Japan is considered to be one of the more significant world economies, along with the USA and Germany, which should be responsible for the stable growth of the world economy.

However, from the late 1980s Japan induced a 'bubble economy', and after the collapse of the 'bubble', Japan's economy suffered through 'a stagnation of unprecedented length' for more than almost ten years after 1991 in spite of an expansion of business cycles. In one sense, prolonged stagnation as a result of the collapsing bubble might be seen as Japan's second hardship in the post-war period, next to the oil shock. There are a number of people, in- and outside Japan, who believe that Japan's era as a world leader is over and that its economy has been substantially weakened, deteriorating in its fundamental and potential capability. Is this true or not?—that is the main topic of this chapter.

There are three main points to be discussed in this chapter. First, the major aspects of the bubble economy as experienced by Japan in the late 1980s are clarified using statistical evidence and analysed in relation to policies taken by the government. Next, the basic features of post-bubble recession are studied with reference to both causes and effects. Lastly, Japan's economic performance and policy since the collapse of the bubble are explored in detail, covering recent developments, financial crises, and capital injections.

MAJOR ASPECTS OF THE BUBBLE ECONOMY

The Long Duration of Economic Expansion and the Bubble Phenomenon

The Japanese economy had been continually expanding since November 1986, attaining the second longest duration of economic expansion during the post-war period. When it ended in April 1991, as seen in Table 4.1, the upward movement of business

TABLE 4.1. *Dates and duration of business cycles, 1975–97*

Reference dates			Number of months		
Initial trough	Peak	Terminal trough	Expansion	Contraction	Total
Mar. 1975	Jan. 1977	Oct. 1977	22	9	31
Oct. 1977	Feb. 1980	Feb. 1983	28	36	64
Feb. 1983	June 1985	Nov. 1986	28	17	45
Nov. 1986	April 1991	Oct. 1993	53	30	83
Oct. 1993	March 1997	April 1999	54	25	79

Source: Economic Planning Agency, *Monthly Report on Basic Data for Economic Analysis*, March 1998.

activity had been sustained over a period of 53 months, second only in length to Japan's own record-breaking expansion of 1965–70, named the '*Izanami*' boom (see Table 2.3). Such a long upswing had not been seen in the previous three cycles whose expansion had lasted at most 22–28 months.

However, there exists a flip side to this coin, as it soon became apparent that this boom was induced by a 'bubble' economy from the second half of the 1980s. In fact, the bubble phenomenon had penetrated through the back door, without being noticed, into a range of economic activity. The bubble phenomenon essentially collapsed, as it historically turned out, and thereafter Japan's economy entered a prolonged recession for two and a half years. This period is often referred to as the 'post-bubble recession' or 'bubble-collapsed depression'. Since the end of this recession was officially announced by the EPA in October 1993, business expansion started again until March 1997 (as far as Table 4.1 is concerned). However, it has completely lost its vigour after hitting the bottom of the business contraction, trailing the depressed state of the economy in spite of such an official pronouncement.

In fact, the Japanese economy has merely shown weaker signs of recovery since that time, with economic activity remaining stagnant. People in Japan are acutely aware that they are in an economic crisis for the first time in their 50 years of post-war prosperity, as this is the first deflationary experience since the historic events following the end of the Second World War. Of course, Japan had already encountered some damage due to sharp inflation caused by the two oil shocks in the 1970s, but at that time it had successfully overcome such economic crises. However, what happened in the 1990s seems to be quite different from any previous crisis. It seems that the Japanese people have lost their self-confidence in their future and are wondering what has gone wrong (see, for general discussion, Bayoumi and Collyus 2000).

What is the 'bubble'?

It is necessary to begin with a definition of a bubble economy, even though the term has already appeared in this text. 'Bubble phenomena' are usually induced by asset price increases together with speculation. Asset prices, such as stock prices or land prices, rise suddenly and rapidly in a short period of time. Theoretically speaking, a 'bubble' is defined as a deviation from fundamental economic activities in the real sector. In terms of price, current prices rise sharply above fundamental prices over a large margin. This margin appears, we might say, as a kind of foam attached to real economic activities. As time goes by, the foam tends to disappear, characterizing a 'bubble phenomenon'.

Statistically, it is very difficult to estimate the magnitude of a 'bubble'. However, roughly speaking, a 'bubble' can be calculated as the difference between the current price and the fundamental price. The fundamental price of assets, such as stocks and land, can be derived from calculation of the discounted value of the future stream of expected returns[1] by using market interest rates as discount rates. Returns are normally dividends or rents. Since current asset prices generally include expected future capital gains, the gap between current and fundamental asset prices reflects the 'speculative bubble' caused by the acquisition of future capital gains.

Japan's 'bubble' actually evolved in the late 1980s. Historically, a 'bubble' is not an unusual economic phenomenon, although this one is the first Japan has experienced in recent years. We can note famous 'bubble' cases in history which many economists have already studied in detail. For instance, in the mid-sixteenth century the tulip bulb was the target of a great deal of speculation, inducing the crazy turmoil of a 'bubble' in the Netherlands. This is a famous historic incident called 'tulip-mania'. One hundred years later the Dutch experienced a similar speculative bubble, this time called 'hyacinth-mania'. Another famous example is the incident of the South-Sea Company of the UK in the seventeenth century. It was this incident which gave birth to the term 'bubble'. Also, in the late 1920s, the USA experienced a large scale land speculation in Florida, and later a stock market boom and bust in New York, triggering the great depression of the 1930s (see, for example, Kindleberger 1991, pp. 20–2; Chancellor 1999).

Similar scenarios actually occurred during the late 1980s in Japan mainly through stock and land speculation. One of the interesting facts about a 'bubble' is that few can conceive that they are in the midst of a 'bubble', thereby expanding its trend. Afterwards, by reflecting on the previous several years, it becomes clear that a 'specu-lative bubble' has been experienced. At the time of the bubble, however, everybody believes that stock and land prices will continue to rise upwards, without dropping. This is the lesson of the 'bubble' phenomenon that history can teach us.

---

[1] The fundamental price p is theoretically derived from the following formula:

$$p = \frac{R}{r + \tau + \sigma - n}$$

where R = expected returns; r = long-term interest rates, τ = tax rates, σ = risk premium, and n = expected growth of R. Of course, it is very difficult to obtain accurate values of the fundamental price, because these estimates have to rely on a variety of assumptions and are plagued by poor access to basic data. See The Institute of Fiscal and Monetary Policy 1993, pp. 100–6.

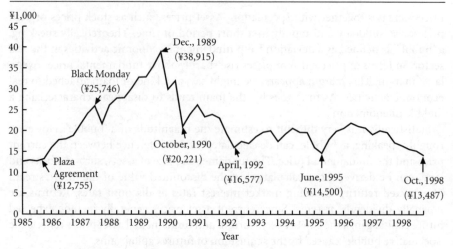

FIGURE 4.1. *Trends in stock prices (Nikkei 225 Stock Average), 1985–98*

Source: Tokyo Stock Exchange, *Monthly Statistics Report*

Note: Data are calculated on a quarterly basis

Major fact finding

Let us examine first the occurrence of the 'bubble' in the late 1980s in Japan by using basic data. Generally speaking, the economy is characterized by a state of asset inflation in terms of stock and land prices. As shown in Figure 4.1, stock prices continued to rise tremendously in the second half of the 1980s. The Nikkei 225 Stock Index began to increase from ¥12,755 during the Plaza Agreement in September 1985, with a minor drop after Black Monday, and reached its highest peak of ¥38,915 on the last trading day of 1989. Thus, it rose to virtually triple its level in about four years. The most marked feature was that the sharp rise in stock prices was maintained almost uninterrupted during that time. Parallel to such a swift rise of stock prices was the fact that the total market value of all outstanding stocks had also expanded from ¥196 trillion at the end of 1985 to ¥630 trillion at the end of 1989. In particular, it should be noted that their magnitude expanded to 1.6 times the size of the nation's GDP at its peak. From their highest level in December 1989, stock prices began to decline very swiftly to ¥20,221 in October 1990, and further to ¥16,577 in April 1992. Since then they have continued to fall: to ¥14,500 in June 1995 and further to ¥13,467 in October 1998 over the long term, although they have had occasional upturns.

Similarly, land prices showed a consistent upward movement from around 1983, as seen in Figure 4.2. The rise of land prices tended to differ from one place to another with time lags, unlike that of stock prices. Land prices for all building uses in the Tokyo Metropolitan area began to rise first, and their annual rates of growth were observed at 12.5 per cent in 1985, 48.2 per cent in 1986 and 61.1 per cent in 1987.[2] The upwards

---

[2] These figures are calculated in terms of percentage changes by employing the 'official land price' quoted by the National Land Agency each year.

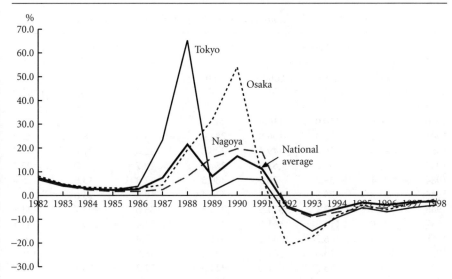

FIGURE 4.2. *Trends in land prices—percentage change from previous years, 1982–98*
Source: National Land Agency, Official Land Prices
Note: Tokyo, Osaka and Nagoya include their metropolitan areas

trend gradually levelled off, but the growth rates did not reach a peak until 1988. Thus the price level of land in the Tokyo Metropolitan area had increased 2.7 fold between 1985 and 1988. Afterwards the spiral spread of land prices was promoted in the Osaka Metropolitan area from 1987, generating a 3.3 fold increase at their peak in 1990 over land prices in 1985. In addition, the continuous effects of land price hikes were dispersed throughout the third largest area of Nagoya and other rural cities from 1988 to 1990. As a consequence, the market value of total land assets expanded to a total of ¥2,389 trillion in 1990, jumping up 2.4 fold from ¥1,004 trillion at the end of 1985. In fact, the 1990 value of total land assets in Japan was so enormous that it reached roughly four times that of the USA as a whole.

Thus, it is easily conjectured that vast capital gains were derived by such rises in stock and land prices in the late 1980s. In Table 4.2, the trend of unrealized capital gains is tabulated for 1980–93 relative to nominal GDP. This reflects the explosive emergence of the bubble phenomenon from 1986 to 1989. As a matter of fact, the total value of unrealized capital gains exceeded three times that of nominal GDP for the period under consideration.[3] As will be argued later, attention ought also to be paid to the process of the collapsing of the bubble after 1990. The sharp decline of asset prices generated a great number of capital losses, which have been a main cause of prolonged recession.

[3] Interestingly enough, stock and land prices indicated a sharp upsurge during the second half of the 1980s in many other countries, including the USA, the UK, Scandinavia, Korea, Taiwan, etc.

TABLE 4.2. *Trends of capital gains and losses, 1980–93 (¥ Trillion, %)*

Year	Capital gains			Nominal	Ratio to GDP		
	Stock (1)	Land (2)	Total (3)	GDP (4)	(1)/(4)	(2)/(4)	(3)/(4)
1980	0.6	110.0	110.6	240.2	0.2	45.8	46.0
1981	8.5	98.3	106.8	258.0	3.3	38.1	41.4
1982	−7.0	56.7	49.7	270.6	−2.6	21.0	18.4
1983	30.2	33.8	63.9	281.8	10.7	12.0	22.7
1984	37.1	39.2	76.3	300.5	12.3	13.0	25.4
1985	33.8	75.5	109.3	320.4	10.5	23.6	34.1
1986	121.4	253.2	374.5	334.6	36.3	75.7	111.9
1987	76.0	415.5	491.5	348.4	21.8	119.3	141.1
1988	177.5	166.7	344.2	371.4	47.8	44.9	92.7
1989	193.6	313.6	507.2	396.2	48.9	79.2	128.0
1990	−306.7	235.7	−71.0	424.5	−72.2	55.5	−16.7
1991	−4.8	−191.7	−196.6	451.3	−1.1	−42.5	−43.6
1992	−178.0	−228.9	−406.9	463.1	−38.4	−49.4	−87.9
1993	40.5	−133.2	−92.7	466.0	8.7	−28.6	−19.9

Note: EPA's estimates, based on EPA, *Annual Report on National Accounts*, NLA, *Official Land Evaluation* and Tokyo Stock Exchange, *Monthly Report of Tosho Statistics*.

Major Causes of the Bubble Economy

What were major causes of the 'bubble phenomenon' in Japan? This is still a contro-versial issue, which a number of economists have tried to solve. Analytical results are not decisive, but we can, in general, point to the following two causes (for a more comprehensive discussion see The Institute of Fiscal and Monetary Policy 1993):

1. mistakes in macroeconomic policies, in conjunction with a maladjustment to international policy coordination;
2. the speculative behaviour of financial institutions and non-financial firms.

It is widely believed that a large mistake had been made by maintaining a prolonged period of very low interest rates. During the period of 1986–89, the level of all inter-est rates initiated by the lowering of the official discount rate of the BOJ were kept at their lowest of the post-war period. This policy was initiated by the Plaza Agreement in 1985 which caused a rapid and drastic appreciation of the yen. In order to keep the value of the dollar from falling or preventing the value of the yen from appreciating further, Japan's monetary authority was obliged to adopt a policy of lowering the dis-count rate. Within about a year, starting from 1986, the discount rate of the BOJ fell to its lowest historic level of 2.5 per cent from 5.0 per cent. This continued for another two years until the BOJ turned to a policy of monetary restraint in 1989 (see Table 4.3).

TABLE 4.3. *Trend in the official discount rate of BOJ, 1983–95*

Dates	Percentage
22 October 1983	5.0
30 January 1986	4.5
10 March 1986	4.0
21 April 1986	3.5
1 November 1986	3.0
23 February 1987	2.5
31 May 1989	3.25
11 October 1989	3.75
25 December 1989	4.25
20 March 1990	5.25
30 August 1990	6.0
1 July 1991	5.5
14 November 1991	5.0
30 December 1991	4.5
1 April 1992	3.75
27 July 1992	3.25
4 February 1993	2.5
21 September 1993	1.75
14 April 1995	1.0
8 September 1995	0.5

Source: Bank of Japan, *Economic Statistics Monthly*.

During this period, the money supply grew at a high level of 7.5–11.5 per cent, while the real rate of economic growth was between 4–5 per cent.

In addition to easy monetary policy, fiscal expansion was also executed by the government's emergency spending package (¥6 trillion) in 1987, partly in response to foreign pressure. This spending package is considered to have spurred the onset of the 'bubble economy' in the late 1980s, because it was introduced when the economy was already out of the recession arising from the sharp appreciation of the yen. Expansionary policies through monetary and fiscal instruments obviously stimulated the expansion of security and real estate markets. Rapid increases of the money supply shifted a massive level of funds to these two markets.

As noted above, stock and land prices rose drastically during this period. As a matter of fact, the transaction of stocks in the Tokyo Stock Exchange sharply increased 5 fold from ¥264.7 billion in 1985 to ¥1,308.5 billion in 1989. Similarly, listed companies in the Tokyo Stock Exchange, consisting of mostly larger companies, increased by more than 10 times the total amount of their funds raised via equity finance from 1985 to 1989. At the end of 1989 when stock prices reached their highest peak, the Tokyo Stock Exchange became the largest in the world, surpassing the New York Stock Exchange in terms of equity capitalization value.; that is, ¥611 trillion in Tokyo and ¥438 trillion in New York. Likewise, land prices began to rise sharply from 1986 until the end of the 1990s. The real estate industry was booming, and increasing land prices raised borrower's creditworthiness as a collateral of loans from financial institutions.

Turning to the second point, great emphasis has been placed on the significance of speculative behaviour by financial and non-financial institutions in the creation of the bubble economy. Behind this speculative motivation, the deregulation of interest rates and financial activities in a broader sense played a vital role in accelerating the tempo of asset inflation. In 1986, a schedule for deregulation was announced by the monetary authority. Banks had to prepare for the expected rise in the cost of funds that the planned deregulation would prompt. Moreover, there were other factors that aggravated the business of financial institutions.

First of all, reflecting the slowdown of economic growth since the first oil shock in 1973, large companies tended to reduce their demand for bank loans due to the decline in investment opportunities. Secondly, in the 1980s industrial firms increased their financial resources directly raised from the capital markets, which were newly opened by deregulation. Corporate borrowing from banks was in relative decline. High and rising stock prices greatly encouraged industrial firms to raise long-term funds via equity financing, such as through the issuing of convertible bonds or bonds with warrants. Given such a worsening situation, banks had to compete with one another fiercely to seek new customers and to increase their loan opportunities in newly expanded businesses. In the circumstances described above, the lending behaviour of banks changed tremendously from traditional conservatism to aggressive expansionism.

The aggressive expansion of loans was a major source of the accelerating bubble economy in the late 1980s. All increased loans to these areas were basically made feasible by the increased value of collateral due to rising land and stock prices. The most important collateral was land. At that time, the 'land myth'—a belief that land prices would continue to rise forever—was prevalent among the Japanese people.

Until the early 1980s, prior to the advent of the 'bubble', it was common practice for banks to lend only 60–70 per cent of the market price of land serving as collateral. However, in the midst of the 'bubble', when the ever-rising trend of land prices was generally believed to be self-evident, it became common to make loans equal to 100 per cent, and sometimes even more than 100 per cent of the market price of the land. As it later became apparent, this was a very risky way of making loans.

While the bubble economy was widespread, the future outlook for the Japanese economy was very bright and bullish. It seemed that Japan acquired a high level of confidence and prestige in the international community on the basis of its good economic performance in the 1980s. No doubt, these factors affected the far-reaching optimism concerning the future trend for asset prices, and in turn the bullish sentiment on business expansion. There even appeared a grand illusion that the upsurge of asset prices could last forever and that the contraction phase of business cycles had ended. In fact, the economy had actually continued to grow at rates much higher than those of official projections attempted by the EPA each year.[4]

THE OCCURRENCE OF POST-BUBBLE RECESSION

Triggers to Curb the 'Bubble'

In 1989, the BOJ started to adopt a restrictive monetary policy, partly triggered by the growing social criticism of the sharp rise in land prices. Particular attention was paid to the complaints among the general public that rising land prices destroyed people's desire to purchase their own land and dwellings. The BOJ raised the discount rate five times from 2.5 per cent to 6 per cent within about a year, as indicated in Table 4.3, and in addition imposed regulations on loans related to real estate transactions. Land tax reform was enacted shifting a heavier tax burden into land holdings and capital gains on land sales. A new land-holding tax, named the land value tax, was created (for more detailed discussion, see Ishi 1993, ch. 17). Also, direct controls on the transaction price of land were introduced. All possible measures to lower stock and land prices had been triggered at once by the government.

As a result, the growth rate of the money supply dropped to 2.1 per cent by October 1991. Stock prices began to fall at the beginning of 1990. As has been quoted previously, the Nikkei Stock Average Index continued to drop with declining ratios turning into a 57 per cent drop from ¥38,915 in December 1989 to ¥16,572 in April 1992, and thereafter further followed by a decline to ¥14,500 in June 1995, a decrease of 62 per cent, as noted above. As seen in Figure 4.1, thereafter stock prices turned upwards for a while, but once again began to decline to a low level of ¥13,487 in October 1998, reflecting the recession in force at the end of the 1990s.

Land prices also ceased to increase and soon began to fall in 1990 (Figure 4.2). The number of real estate transactions fell drastically due to a lack of buyers, and in many cases real estate remain impossible to liquidate even at largely reduced prices. Consequently, the huge amount of loans made to the real estate industry and loans for collateral land stayed locked in for both borrowers and lenders. Given the stagnant situation in the land market, the declining trend of land prices has been measured in terms of a minus percentage change from previous years until 1998, showing no sign of an upwards movement.

Bank loans associated with real estate have caused serious damage due to reduced land prices, that is, the reduced value of collateral. There have been a number of large-scale bankruptcies of real estate companies, a situation that is continuing into the twenty-first century. In turn, every financial institution has suffered in some way from

---

[4] Realized real growth rates were 4.9 per cent (3.5 per cent) in fiscal 1987, 6.0 per cent (3.8 per cent) in fiscal 1988, 4.5 per cent (4.0 per cent) in fiscal 1989, and 5.0 per cent (4.0 per cent) in fiscal 1990. Figures in parentheses are the official projected real growth rates of the EPA.

the sharp drop in land prices. In particular, those banks which were most aggressive in expanding loans to the real estate sector have been the most seriously damaged. On the other hand, those banks at one time considered too timid and conservative have emerged suffering the least damage. The higher the reliance of banks on loans to real estate and non-banks, the higher the amount of bad debt and write-offs. As the 'bubble economy' collapsed, financial scandals began to emerge one after another. For instance, fake certificates of deposit were issued by the Tokyo Credit Association and many cases of compensation for losses to large customers by security companies came to light. The general public became increasingly concerned, placing less trust on the soundness of the financial transactions of banks and security companies (Shimizu 1992; Lincoln 1998).

The Dawn of Prolonged Recession

The 'bubble' boom finally hit its peak in April 1991, and thereafter the Japanese economy entered a very prolonged recession, which was widely recognized to have ended in October 1993. This was the second longest period of recession to hit Japan, lasting two and a half years, in line with the famous saying: 'the higher the peak, the deeper the trough' (see Table 4.1) which sums up the repetitive nature of business cycles in any country, and in Japan it turned out to be particularly true after the collapse of the bubble.

During the prolonged recession, the Japanese government tried to stimulate the economy by adopting expansionary policy packages six times during the fiscal years 1992–95. This could be seen in the increases of public investment and government loans, as will be argued in Chapter 6. However, such Keynesian-type fiscal expansionary policy was not effective in quickly propelling the economy into an upswing phase. It has been widely pointed out that fiscal actions can only restrain the further downward movement of an economy that is entering a 'double dip' recession. The monetary authority also attempted to make the economy more buoyant by lowering the official discount rate nine times from its top level of 6.0 per cent on 30 August 1990 to 0.5 per cent on 8 September 1995, a process which was still ongoing in 1999. In the same way as fiscal policy, however, monetary ease has not been very effective in promoting private investment.

Why have macroeconomic policies been so ineffective? The main factor behind weaker policy effects and a retarded recovery is no doubt the phenomenon of asset deflation caused by the collapse of the bubble, resulting in a tremendous level of non-performing assets remaining in the financial sector. So long as non-performing assets are accumulated and not liquidated, banks are unlikely to lend in a positive manner. Likewise, both firms and households are unlikely to increase their new business investment and investment in consumer durable goods, reflecting the massive amount of over-investment and over-consumption during the period of the bubble boom.

In the course of the sluggish recovery, an important economic co-issue emerged on the international dimension of the economy. Trade surpluses began to expand dramatically due to the sluggishness of domestic demand. As was observed in Figure 3.6, net exports increased to occupy a substantial share of GDP in growth terms from the early 1990s, while domestic demand was more dominant in the late 1980s. This development has generated foreign criticism, and in particular caused a great deal of argument and friction between the USA and Japan. The USA constantly requested that Japan enforce more expansionary policies and structural adjustments via a series of bilateral negotiations such as the SII (Structural Impediments Initiative) or the Japan–USA Framework for a New Economic Partnership. Of course, apart from external pressures, Japan needed to take more positive action to promote structural adjustments of its own resolve. For instance, further deregulation and liberalization and open-door policies were sought in several markets and particularly in the markets for telecommunications, finance and insurance, construction and agriculture (see Morris 1991; Mourdoukoutas 1993).

The Jusen (Housing Loan Company) Problem

One of the gravest problems relating to the collapse of the bubble was the so-called Jusen (Housing Loan Company) problem. In view of the crisis in Japan's financial system, this problem would in turn lead to economic turmoil in the Japanese economy. Even though stimulative economic packages continued to spend six times the levels spent in the past, the Japanese economy showed no active signs of a strong recovery. Many people believe that the main factors behind this hesitant recovery must have derived from the Jusen problem. Japan's leading banks encountered the so-called 'Japan premium' when they borrowed money overseas, forcing them to absorb the burden of an additional interest rate over average rates in the London market: 0.5 per cent in October 1995, 0.23 per cent in December 1995 and 0.02 per cent in February 1996, reflecting the unstable state of the Japanese financial system. It is in this context that we will now attempt to clarify the Jusen problem in the Japanese economy.

The government proposed the Jusen Resolution Plan in January 1996, and the Japan premium almost disappeared in the overseas lending market. However, there have been repeated arguments in the Diet concerning the pros and cons of the Jusen Resolution Plan in the fiscal 1996 Budget Bill, between the ruling coalition parties and the opposition parties. The situation was such that, if the Jusen Resolution Plan did not pass the Diet with the fiscal 1996 budget by the end of March, the 'Japan premium' may once again have been revived.

Then, what is the Jusen problem? The seven Jusen were founded by leading commercial banks, trust banks, and life insurance companies in the 1970s. Their purpose was to construct special channels of housing loans via specific non-banking institutions from the founding banks, separate from their main business of making loans. The Jusen borrowed money from both founding and non-founding banks, and lent it to individual home-owners as mortgage loans.

As time went by, and particularly during the bubble boom, the Jusen loans began to expand to the real estate industry, in addition to housing mortgage loans. As stressed earlier, the banks began to adopt a very risky attitude in making loans, reflecting the continuous rise of land prices. The risking of these practices has been revealed since the bubble burst in the early 1990s. Land value as first-class collateral began to fall sharply, and is still falling at the end of the 1990s (see Figure 4.2). Land prices have persistently continued to drop since the mid-1990s, never deviating from their declining trend, and this was particularly so in the case of commercial sites in Japan's largest cities such as Tokyo and Osaka. The real estate industry saw a rise in bankruptcies because of the poor business for rental and building activities caused by over-supply in the markets.

The land collateral of the Jusen turned into a massive amount of bad assets to be written off. In turn, founding and non-founding banks had to shoulder such non-performing assets accumulated by the Jusen, as the Jusen cannot liquidate them any more. This is the crux of the Jusen problem.

Around the mid-1990s, the institutions concerned began to consider a resolution plan for these non-performing assets, similar to that of the S & L Association of the USA in the 1980s. However, actually drawing up such a plan was continually postponed in anticipation of future land price increases. However, the time finally arrived when a decision to resolve the Jusen problem became imperative, because non-performing assets continued to lose their value as time went by. Finally, the MOF took the initiative to bail out the Jusen and proposed the resolution scheme in December 1995 as part of the fiscal 1996 Budget Bill.

This scheme calls for the founding banks to pardon all of their outstanding loans to the Jusen, that is, more than half of the Jusen's non-recoverable loans. The main reason behind this is that the founding banks have been accused of pushing their affiliated Jusen lenders into making these risky loans in the first place. Similarly, non-founding banks are required to pardon about 45 per cent of their outstanding loans to the Jusen. By contrast, agricultural cooperatives, the prime Jusen lenders, are to recover all of their outstanding loans and subsequently provide only a token 'good will gift' to the Jusen Resolution Corporation which is to be primarily in charge of resolving the Jusen problem.

It is widely believed that the share of the burden of agricultural cooperatives is too light in this scheme. Agricultural vested interest groups have performed well politically, posing a strong threat to politicians seeking re-election under a new single voting system. The light burden on agricultural cooperatives eventually required the use of taxpayers' money; ¥685 billion (about $6.85 billion) or around 10 per cent of the Jusen's non-recoverable assets of ¥6.4 trillion or $64 billion. After drafting the Jusen Bill in the plenary Diet of January 1996, Diet debates have become increasingly heated over the injection of ¥685 billion of taxpayer's money being used to liquidate seven mortgage lenders. According to a pubic opinion poll in March 1996, 90 per cent of those polled said 'no' to this use of public money. Despite such strong resistance, it is appreciated that the government decision to use taxpayers' money cannot be avoided if the crisis in Japan's financial system is to be resolved. However, it is widely asserted that to solve the struggles in the Diet regarding the Jusen, the share of the burden of agricultural cooperatives should be raised in relation to that of taxpayers.

Lastly, immediately before the plenary Diet ended in June 1996, the Jusen Bill did manage to be passed after a lot of conflicting political manoeuvres between the ruling and opposition parties. However, the original bill remained unchanged and is far from satisfactory.

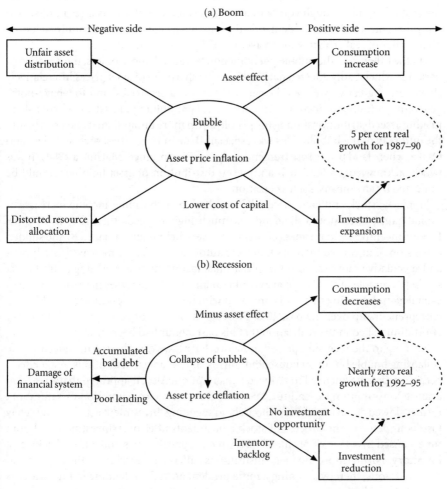

FIGURE 4.3. *The whole picture of the bubble process*

RECENT DEVELOPMENTS OF ECONOMIC PERFORMANCE AND POLICIES

Summary Review of the Bubble Phenomena

We will now summarize the total picture of the bubble process in both periods of boom and recession from the late 1980s. What phenomena have been incurred in the bubble process? Figure 4.3 illustrates both boom (a) and recession (b) periods. As seen in Figure 4.3(a), the bubble with asset price inflation generated both a positive (bright) side and a negative (dark) side of the Japanese economy and society during the boom period. The sharp rise of stock and land prices tended to increase household consumption as well as income levels and to stimulate investment activities by lowering the cost of capital through equity financing in capital markets. As a result of such a buoyant state of domestic demand, the Japanese economy successfully achieved higher rates of real growth with an average of 5 per cent for 1987–90.

On the other side, the bubble phenomenon produced, more or less, the negative or dark side which badly affected national life. The sharp rise of asset prices in a relatively short period greatly extended the gap between the asset 'haves' and the 'have-nots', generating a feeling of inequity. In particular, land holding played a decisive role in making asset distribution among the people much more unfair than it had been before the outbreak of the bubble. This was especially true in large cities, such as Tokyo and Osaka, where land prices rose tremendously (see, for instance, Matsuura 1994). It was widely acknowledged that such an uneven distribution of asset holdings should be mitigated by any means, such as taxation.

Similarly, stock and land price hikes resulted in such capital income increases as capital gains, interest and dividends, at much higher speeds than rises in income. Labour incentives and business efforts were overwhelmingly damaged by the sudden expansion of unearned incomes that were automatically led by increased asset prices and speculative motives. For example, a small factory manager owning a substantial site in the middle of the Tokyo area could obtain 10 fold increases in income through capital gains by selling this land compared with his total business income via his own entrepreneurship over the past 40 or 50 years. It would not be surprising if his work effort diminished in the realization that his past labour had been in vain.

Turning to the recession period in Figure 4.3(b), we can observe the effects of the collapsing bubble boom on households, firms, and financial institutions. Asset effects became negative which led to reduced consumption. Also, it appeared that a reaction against consumption expenditure, possibly due to over-consumption or saturation, further slowed down the tempo of household spending. Investment activity completely lost its impetus in the process of stock adjustments after over-investment in boom time, caused by a lack of profitable investment opportunities and a huge backlog of inventory. Furthermore, financial institutions suffered severely from their latent bad debt write-offs, thereby adopting a more prudent attitude to lending in the future, as will be argued later.

All of the above contributed a great deal to the slowdown in real growth rates during the period 1992–95 with successive growth rates of nearly zero ensuring a prolonged recession.

The Collapse of the Bubble Continues to Haunt the Economy

It was officially stated by the EPA in April 1991 that the bubble boom had ended, and that afterwards the Japanese economy entered a post-bubble recession until October 1993 (Table 4.1). In terms of real GDP growth rates, the economy had shown substantial growth in 1990, with a figure of 5.5 per cent, reducing slightly to 2.9 per cent in fiscal 1991, but since the bubble collapsed, real growth rates began to slow down at 0.4 per cent in fiscal 1992, 0.5 per cent in fiscal 1993, and 0.6 per cent in fiscal 1994, indicating that the nearly zero growth era lasted for three successive years. Even after the bubble recession ended in 1993, the Japanese economy has shown no sign of full recovery, and has remained sluggish. Meanwhile, the government has continued to take initiatives by introducing fiscal expansionary policy packages six times for fiscal 1992–95 to buoy up the depressed state of domestic demand (see Table 8.4). As a result, the economy managed to move upwards, achieving higher growth rates of 3.0 per cent in fiscal 1995 and 4.4 per cent in fiscal 1996, but it is widely believed that there has been no strong recovery at all simply a lot of weak and fragile movements in major components of aggregate demand.

Given such a stagnant state of the economy after the end of the bubble phenomenon, the Japanese people have clung to five long-cherished myths pertaining to the success story of Japan's economy:

1. the Japanese economy will constantly grow;
2. full employment is virtually guaranteed;
3. land prices are ever-rising;
4. the financial system is always maintained stable;
5. Japan has the safest society in the world.

However, these five myths are now being overturned. As stated earlier, real growth rates nearly reached zero, the unemployment problem has become crucial, and land prices have persistently fallen. The sharp decline in land prices inevitably damaged the stability of the financial system. In addition, both the Kobe earthquake and the violent acts of the AMU Shinrikyo religious group in 1995 have shocked the entire nation.

However, some bright signs of economic recovery did begin to emerge from the Japanese economy from around 1996, reflecting strong fiscal stimuli and an easing of monetary policy in the past five years. As we near the end of the 1990s, it appears that private investment is regaining some vitality and, assisted by increased housing investment, was stimulating a hesitant recovery. However, land prices continued to fall from 1990, continuing a sixth year of decline. For instance, commercial land prices in the three largest cities—Tokyo, Osaka, and Nagoya—fell 16 per cent compared with 14.8 per cent in 1994, while residential land prices in the same area fell by 4.6 per cent, against 2.8 per cent in the year before.

Once again, the Japanese economy entered into the sluggishness of downward movement in business conditions from fiscal 1997, triggered the raising of the VAT tax rate from 3 per cent to 5 per cent and the repeal of individual income tax reduction in ¥2 trillion in April 1997. Moreover, the co-payments of medical care insurance was lifted by as much as ¥2 trillion from September 1997, generating a greater fiscal burden on the nation. Thus, it is widely believed that such a fiscal burden being raised all at once must have retarded the recovery of the economy, producing a number of restraining effects on domestic demand, for example personal consumption, housing spending, and so on. What was worse, the Asian economic and financial crises which occurred in the fall of 1997 began to influence the Japanese economy through import reductions and the possibility of bad loans. At the same time, successive bankruptcies of major banks and security companies have accelerated the depressed tempo of the economy and plunged it into a gloomy and pessimistic state once again.[5] Reflecting the substantial slowdown of personal consumption and plant and equipment investment, the real growth rate of the Japanese economy in fiscal 1997 turned to −0.4 per cent, after a twenty-three year absence since 1974 and the first oil shock. In fiscal 1998 the economy has been worsened further and its real growth rate fell to as low as minus 2.2 per cent.

No doubt, these aggravated economic conditions have made other countries feel uneasy and Japan has lost some credibility overseas. In particular financial institutions have faced a great deal of difficulty in raising money in the Euro-market because of the increasing distrust there of the Japanese financial industry. For instance, the so-called 'Japan premium' began to emerge when the Japanese banks tried to purchase dollars in the markets. Table 4.4 depicts the trend of the Japan premium for October 1995–March 1999. It reached its peak at 1 per cent in December 1997 after the month when such big banks and security companies as Hakkaido-Takushoku or Yamaichi went into bankruptcy. Even in 1998, the premium level stayed high, reflecting the fragile structure of Japan's financial institutions with accumulated non-performing assets, but it finally dropped to zero in March 1999 due to a massive capital injection using public money, as discussed shortly.

What should we think of as the main factors which generate the continuous weakness of current economic conditions in Japan? Of course, we cannot neglect the increases of both tax and medical care insurance, and also the outbreak of the Asian financial crises. However, greater importance should be placed on the persistent unrest and instability in the financial sector with the huge amount of bad loans and non-performing debts, caused by the collapse of the bubble. Thus, the collapse of the bubble still remains to haunt the Japanese economy even if, officially, it is considered to be over. Suitable policy measures must be taken to cope with the current recession caused by the financial crisis, separate from Keynesian fiscal expansionary policies.

BIS Criterion and Capital Injections

One of the important factors behind the retarded recovery of Japan's economy is no doubt the occurrence of a financial crisis, as stated above. What is the nature of this financial crisis or unrest in the financial sector? We will consider it briefly here but, for a more expanded discussion, see Lincoln (1998). As a result of the collapse of the bubble phenomena, a large number of financial institutions were obliged to take on the burden of accumulated non-performing loans caused by the sharp decline of collateral values due to the tremendous fall in land prices. The drop in stock prices has also generated large capital losses among those holding assets in the financial sector. Thus, these increased capital losses have had a serious cumulus in financial institutions, which in turn has severely damaged their balance sheets.

---

[5] In November 1997, there were successive bankruptcy cases as follows: Sannyo Security Company failed on the 3rd, Hokkaido-Takushoku Bank on the 17th, Yamaichi Security Company on the 24th and Tokuyou-City Bank on 25th.

TABLE 4.4. *Emergence of the 'Japan Premium', 1995–99*

Dates	Premium (%)
25.10.1995	0.50
22.12.1995	0.23
12.2.1996	0.02
11.3.1996	0.18
29.7.1996	0.15
27.8.1996	0.03
16.12.1996	0.21
6.1.1997	0.06
24.3.1997	0.20
1.10.1997	0.01
14.11.1997	0.38
3.12.1997	1.00
9.12.1997	0.50
2.1.1998	0.69
9.7.1998	0.28
6.10.1998	0.53
5.11.1998	0.69
24.12.1998	0.22
8.1.1999	0.34
4.3.1999	0.0*

Note: The Japan premium is defined as the spread between the BBA-Labour and the offer-rate of three months' dollar purchase by Tokyo-Mitsubishi Bank.

In addition to such a damage by non-performing assets and capital losses, it has been decided that the Bank for International Settlements (BIS) criterion (i.e. international capital adequacy standards) should take effect for maintaining the soundness of the financial system from 1 April 1998 through the prompt correction measures of Japan's government. The BIS ratio α, which is defined as follows, mandates the capital adequacy requirements for the banks.

$$\alpha = \frac{\text{Self-owned capital}}{\text{Total asset}}$$
$$= \frac{\text{Tier 1} + \text{Tier 2} - \beta}{\text{Lendings} + \text{Security portfolio}}$$

(4.1)

Tier 1 = paid-in capital and capital reserves
Tier 2 = capital gains of holding assets, tax-free reserves for bad loans, subordinate
        bonds and loans, etc.
β = subtracted items, such as intended inter-bank stock holding

Depending upon the required capital ratio defined above, each bank had to meet the
following conditions in order to secure financial business, domestically or internationally.

$\alpha \geq 8$ per cent   for international business
4 per cent $\leq \alpha < 8$ per cent   for domestic business only
$\alpha < 4$ per cent   failed

Recent falls in the stock market threaten to reduce the value of equity portfolio that
banks count as capital, generating capital losses in Tier 2. As a consequence, each bank
has substantially suffered from the drop of α. How do banks meet the need of their
own capital ratio at the necessary level? Obviously, there are two ways to satisfy such a
ratio at the requested percentages; one is to increase the value of the numerator and
the other is to reduce that of the denominator in equation 4.1. In the light of the
depressed condition of the stock market, it was almost impossible for the banks to
increase their capital through the issuance of stocks. Thus, to achieve the target of
satisfying the necessary value of α, almost all banks were obliged to curtail lending
activities which has, in a number of cases, caused a credit squeeze. No doubt, such a
credit squeeze has slowed down the provision of investment funds for business
firms and hindered the growth of the economy. This is one of the main factors of the
sluggish economic recovery of these years.

    Thus, the government planned to stabilize Japan's vulnerable financial system in
December 1997, and constructed an emergency package called 'The Emergency
Measure to Stabilize the Financial System Law (EMSFS)'. Based on such an emergency
scheme, it decided to inject public funds into the banks to shore up their capital bases.
The bill was passed through the Diet on 16 February 1998, aiming to implement the
government scheme for capital injections, as seen in Figure 4.4. The total amount of
¥30 trillion was paid into the Deposit Insurance Corporation (DIC) from both the
MOF and the BOJ for two purposes: ¥17 trillion were designated to protect the depositors of failed banks by providing financial assistance from the special account in the
DIC, and ¥13 trillion were to be made available from public funds for an infusion of
new capital into banks from the account for financial crisis management. In both
cases, public money was paid into one place, the Resolution and Collection Bank (RCB),
from which relevant money could be channelled two necessary ways. One problem
was how to effectively screen the flow of public money into the relevant banks in times
of financial crises, although this would pose no problem in the case of take-over banks
of failed financial institutions.[6] To carry out this screening process, a neutral examining

---

[6] Hokuyou Bank, which has taken over Hokkaido-Takushiku Bank, is a good example of this case.

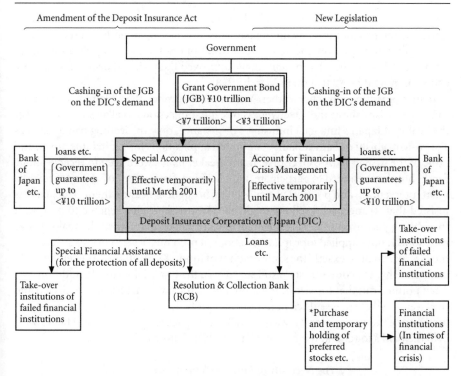

* Unanimous approval after a thorough review by a newly-established neutral 'Examining Board' is required.

FIGURE 4.4. *Framework of the emergency measures for stabilizing the financial system*

Notes: 1 The *special account* is intended to protect deposits that exceed ¥10 million. The new account for financial crisis management was established to purchase and temporarily hold preferred stocks, etc., issued by financial institutions, with the aim of stabilizing the financial system.

2. In addition to the accounts mentioned above, DIC has the *ordinary account* that serves to protect deposits up to ¥10 million.

board, called 'The Financial Crisis Management Committee', chaired by Professor Yoko Sazanami, was established as an in-house screening panel of the DIC to review the applications of capital injections for the banks in question. It was generally expected at that time that such a capital injection would encourage the banks to increase lending, thereby easing the credit squeeze that was hurting the Japanese economy.

In accordance with such a new government scheme, twenty-one commercial banks —nine major commercial banks known as city banks, three long-term credit banks, six trust banks and three regional banks—applied for capital injections of public funds in March 1998. These banks offered to issue either preferred stocks to increase Tier 1 or subordinated bonds (or loans) to raise Tier 2, to be purchased by public funds in order to strengthen their capital bases. As a result, the capital adequacy requirement in terms of the α ratio is expected to rise. When major banks decided to seek the injections of public funds to boost their capital, they were requested to submit streamlining restructuring programmes, including pay-cuts, downsizing of outlets, a reduction in the number of employees and so on. As a result of examining the applications from twenty-one banks, the government finally approved them all and decided to allocate a total of more than ¥2 trillion in March 1998.

In implementing this scheme, there were a small number of problems which caused some scepticism about the effectiveness of capital injections to allay suspicions over the health of Japan's financial industry. For instance, only the leading banks, such as Tokyo-Mitsubishi or Sanwa Banks, submitted applications for capital injections, and none of the weaker banks. Of course, many weaker banks were keen to receive public funds, but they hesitated to participate in the scheme, fearing the possibility of government intervention and political pressure being brought to bear on them. The LDP has insisted that stronger banks alone ought to take part in such a scheme to prevent it from being perceived as a 'bailing out' of weaker banks. Also, when the major banks mentioned above applied for capital injections, it presented a very curious spectacle— they seemed to need exactly the same amount of funds: ¥100 billion. Bizarrely enough, it appears that the convoy system still survives in the financial sector. In addition, it is often pointed out that the size of the capital injections was smaller than expected and they were unlikely to be sufficient to resolve rapidly the problems of the financial sector. Despite these misgivings, it was generally anticipated that such a new scheme must help the banks to rebuild their capital base and lend more to businesses.

The Necessity of Further Capital Injections

As 1998 passed, the anticipation with which the EMSFS had been greeted turned out to be falsely placed, as the scheme was seen to be a complete failure. Even though capital injection was attempted in March, the stock market reacted very badly to *de facto* failed banks. In particular, the stock price of the Long Term Credit Bank (LTCB), which had been under attack in the market, continued to fall even after the injection of capital by the government. Finally, the LTCB failed in September 1998. This was really a highly symbolic incident, signifying the end of the glorious history of Japan's financial institutions in the post-war period.

LTCB had been established in 1952 with the role of providing stable long-term loans to major industries, such as heavy chemicals. The LTCB had led the rapid economic growth of the Japanese economy. Like the other two long-term banks, the Industrial Bank of Japan (IBJ) and the Nippon Credit Bank (NCB), LTCB was allowed to issue bank debentures as primary financial sources and was not permitted to take individual deposits with the exception of deposits from corporate firms. LTCB had played an important role in fulfilling the financial needs of key industries in the 1950s and 1960s. As the liberalization of Japan's financial system progressed in the 1980s, the long-term credit banks began to be under attack from commercial banks, securities companies, and non-financial companies. In particular, LTCB, as well as NCB, faced great difficulties when large firms started to raise funds directly from the capital markets.

The capital injection to twenty-one banks in March 1998, based upon the EMSFS, was heavily criticized by the opposition parties for two main reasons. For one thing, the conditions for capital injections to LTCB and others, by purchasing their preferred stocks, was considered to be too lenient. The other criticism was that a capital injection should not be made before the failure of the bank. As a consequence, the opposition parties requested the establishment of more severe rules for capital injection and the construction of a new scheme for financial revitalization.

As a result of the political struggles, EMSFS was abolished as part of a political compromise, and was replaced by the Financial Revitalization Related Law (FRRL) in October 1998. The main points of FRRL can be summarized as follows.

1. The Financial Revitalization Committee (FRC) was established to be responsible for the supervision of financial institutions and for crisis management, such as the resolution of failed banks.
2. In order to develop a non-performing loan disposal system, the Resolution and Collection Organization (RCO) was established, as result of the merger of Resolution and Collection Bank and the Jusen Resolution Corporation, in which loan management and servicers (a collection business for bad loans) was introduced.
3. Early strengthening of financial functions ought to be achieved through promoting appropriate assessment of holding assets, preparing for appropriate reserves for loans, and enhancing the capital basis of financial institutions as necessary.
4. To carry out the resolution of failed financial institutions, management by a financial administrator and a bridge bank scheme should be instituted, and likewise special public management should be undertaken in relevant cases.

Based on such an idea of financial revitalization, a scheme of managing financial institution failures was established, as depicted in Figure 4.5. In addition to the DIC, that played a major role in stabilizing the financial system in Figure 4.4, the FRC is centrally responsible for managing the failures of financial institutions and judging the determination or the notification of failed cases (and forthcoming cases too). Figure 4.5 considers the example of the failure of Bank A; two channels are shown indicating how it should be managed by the FRC.

In the first case, where Bank A could suspend or has suspended deposit repayment, the FRC notifies its failure and determines its extent. Next, the FRC may request management by a financial administrator (the upper route from Bank A in Figure 4.5). The financial administrator investigates the sustainability of the bank up to that point, that is, its business and asset status, and its prospects in terms of transfer of business. The results and resolution plan must be reported to the FRC. Management by financial administrator is continued for one year (and a one-year extension is permissible). Meanwhile, if continuation of the bank's business could be made by any private successor institutions, the operations of Bank A are transferred to them. If not, a bridge bank will have to be established as a subsidiary of the DIC for the purpose of the temporary maintenance and continuation of the business of the failing bank. The

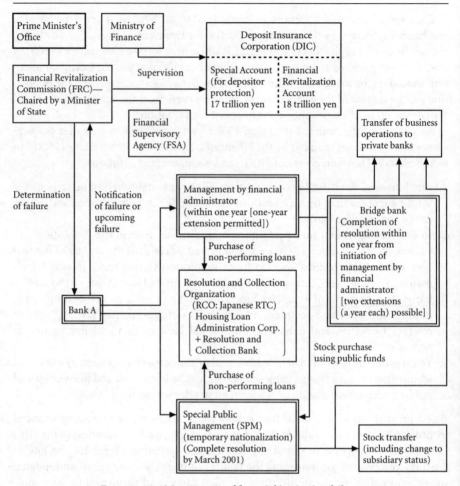

FIGURE 4.5. *Management of financial institution failures*

resolution by the bridge bank must be completed within one year, and if it is not successful, Bank A must be completely liquidated.

Another procedure may be taken when the failure of Bank A could have an extremely serious effect on financial markets, domestically or overseas, or on specific activities in certain regions or sectors. This is known as Special Temporary Management (STM), implying temporary nationalization (the lower route in Figure 4.5). In this case, the DIC acquires stock at prices set by the Stock Price Calculation committee, based on the net value of Bank A. On the other hand, Bank A under STM has to make reports on the past record of its business and asset status to the FRC, and to present the plans of management rationalization, business implementation, and rationalization. Since the second procedure is temporary, it has a termination date of

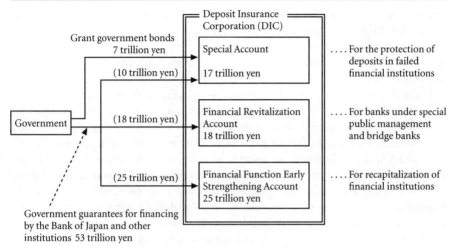

FIGURE 4.6. *Preparation of public funds*

April 2001 when the payoff scheme[7] will start with the guaranteed repayment of the principal amount of ¥10 million. For this purpose, such concrete actions as the transfer of business are needed to complete the failure resolution measures. In the two cases of these resolution procedures, the RCO takes initiatives in purchasing non-performing loans from Bank A as Japanese RTC. In addition, Bank A can expect to obtain such financial assistance from the DIC as protection of depositors, loans, and loss coverage.

In order to implement a resolution plan, public funds must be prepared for failed financial institutions by any means. Figure 4.6 depicts the scheme of public funds which total ¥60 trillion. In addition to the existing Special Account for the protection of depositors (Figure 4.5), two funds are established within the DIC. One is the 'Financial Revitalization Account' for the resolution of failed financial institutions with ¥18 trillion under the scheme of bridge banks and STM. The other is the 'Financial Function Early Strengthening Account' for recapitalization with ¥25 trillion. As financial sources, ¥7 trillion is prepared by grant government bond and the remaining ¥53 trillion is government guarantees for financing by the BOJ and other financial institutions.

Following the failure of the LTCB in September 1998, the NCB was also bankrupt by December 1998. Considering the widespread impact of their bankruptcies both nationally and globally, the government decided that both should be forced to be temporarily nationalized. By contrast, when Kokumin Bank, the Tokyo based second-tier regional bank, was declared insolvent by the FRC in March 1999, another resolution

---

[7] Until 31 March 2001, the Japanese government guarantees the repayment of all bank deposits without any upper limit, but it has been decided that the start of the payoff scheme will be postponed until 31 March 2002.

scheme was undertaken because the nationalization option was not appropriate for the smaller banks. In accordance with a new scheme of financial revitalization law, Kokumin Bank was first placed under the control of a financial administrator, and it will thereafter be turned into a bridge bank if a private buyer cannot be found within one year.

In April 1999, further capital injections were made to the nation's major banks using public funds. Fifteen of Japan's leading banks applied for a combined total of ¥7.45 trillion in public funds to clear the pile of bad loans which had been haunting the financial sector and the Japanese economy after the collapse of the bubble. As seen in Figure 4.5, ¥25 trillion were set aside to recapitalize banks whose funds had been depleted by writing off non-performing loans. The capital injection was made by buying preferred stocks and taking out subordinated loans from relevant banks, while the fifteen banks had to present restructuring and profitability improvement plans to the FRC when they filed their applications for public money.

The total amount of ¥60 trillion utilized for capital injections is approximately 12 per cent of GDP, and has been assessed as big enough and effective enough to resolve the long-standing credit squeeze and bad loan situation in the financial sector. In fact, the Japanese premium has been disappearing in the Euro market, and stock prices have continued to rise since the implementation of the capital injection policy in March 1999. This can be seen as the market indicating its acceptance of this policy decision adopted by the government.

How Should We Look Ahead?

Given the current state of the economy, how can we predict the future trend of the Japanese economy? After the collapse of the bubble, many bearish and pessimistic views have persistently hovered over the future outlook of Japan, depicting a scenario in which Japan will essentially wither in the years ahead. Such a view would be too pessimistic of the coming era in Japan, but it may continue to be prevalent for a while if the current prolonged depression continues. Of course, looking ahead, Japan can expect a number of difficulties in its economy and society, such as the rapid ageing of the population, a burgeoning debt accumulation in the public sector, expanded responsibility in the level of international cooperation, and so on. It should, however, be stressed that Japan still retains a great deal of potential economic resources for further development, given its current endowments of a high quality labour force, the high level of personal saving stock, a huge level of balance-of-payments surplus, and advanced technologies, as well as its strong competitiveness in the world market.

As we cited previously, 'the higher the peak, the deeper the trough'. This appears to be true of the current state of Japan's economy in the 'end of the bubble' recession. Consequently, it is going to prove difficult to make a swift and full-scale recovery from the damages inflicted by the collapse of the 'bubble'. Even after the signs of economic recovery begin to emerge, the tempo of recovery will be slower than that of previous phases of recovery. This time it may take longer for Japan's economy to turn upward again, solving the bubble problems.

In 1996, the EPA published a new social and economic plan[8] which still exists as an official economic planning tool today, but its use in the future is now in question as the ongoing movement of the economy evidently rejects it. However, it is helpful in clarifying the general recognition of the current situation facing Japan. Four points stressed in this economic plan are important in this context.

1. Globalization has thrust Japan into the world economy where it has to face stiff international competition.
2. Japan cannot achieve economic growth any longer by simply following the examples of other countries and must shoulder the burden and cost of the trial and error phase just as other front-runners do.
3. Japan is moving swiftly towards an aged society with families having fewer children, which will no doubt introduce a range of new difficulties.
4. Japan is making rapid progress in advanced communication technologies that will bring about important changes in various aspects of Japanese life.

Given the current state of the Japanese economy as described above, great stress is placed on the following structural problems which need to be solved as the country moves towards the twenty-first century.

First of all, Japan has not been successful in developing promising new industries to lead the economy, such as the automobile and home appliance industries during the period of rapid economic growth. On the contrary, the hollowing-out (de-industrialization) process of major industries has been accelerated in recent years, reflecting the sharp appreciation of the yen and the higher cost structure within Japan. Secondly, many employees feel uneasy about the prospects of change in the employment practices which have been characteristic of Japan, for example lifetime employment, the seniority system, and company unions. These practices were considered to be among the strengths of Japanese management and brought considerable competitive advantages. Thirdly, people have begun to worry about the unstable foundation of the welfare state, given the fact that a decreasing labour force will not be able to support an increasing number of elderly people. Fourthly, it is widely acknowledged that the rewards of post-war prosperity have not trickled down sufficiently to the life of the average citizen. In spite of possessing the second-largest economy in the world, the Japanese people do not tend to think that they have been rewarded with a fair share of the benefits. Lastly, Japan is expected to play a vital role in promoting the world economy and society by the rest of the world, despite its many unsettled domestic problems.

---

[8] This is a new economic plan for fiscal 1996–2000 published by the EPA, entitled the *Social and Economic Plan for Structural Reforms Toward a Vital Economy and Secure Life for the Japanese People*. According to this plan, the average growth rate for the coming five years is estimated to be 3 per cent in real terms and 3.5 per cent in nominal terms, on the assumption that structural reforms would make great progress. If these reforms cannot be effectively implemented, both growth rates would be reduced to a rate as low as 1.75 per cent. Inflation rates are estimated to be relatively lower, that is, less than 1 per cent as measured by the CPI and negative if the WPI is used, while the unemployment rate is expected to be higher than in the past. Obviously, this prediction is too optimistic and it is not feasible to believe it can be achieved during the period in consideration, given the recent real growth rates, say zero or below zero in fiscal 1997 and 1998.

The necessity of finding solutions to these structural problems in Japan has long been recognized by experts, but unfortunately these problems were concealed within Japan behind the bubble phenomenon. The collapse of the bubble revealed that these problems had been aggravated even more, and that the time had come to tackle them with renewed vigour. It is very difficult to find any decisive solutions to these structural problems, and the only way to respond, apparently, is through structural reform of Japan's economy and society. This is the reason why the new economic plan is entitled *Structural Reforms*.

To pursue these objectives, the plan emphasizes the importance of five categories: reactivating the economy; improving the quality of life; implementing responsibilities in the international community; promoting scientific and technological programmes; and accomplishing administrative and fiscal reforms. Without any doubt, reform of the economic structure is absolutely necessary for the Japanese economy to regain its vitality in the twenty-first century. If Japan could solve crucial economic problems caused by the collapse of the bubble in the future, it will be able to achieve a relatively higher growth rate of real GDP among major advanced countries in the coming century.

No doubt, the scenario developed by the EPA in the current economic plan has to be repealed, and the next plan is now being constructed in the Economic Council. Meanwhile, however, the main idea of future prediction is being replaced by the report of the Economic Strategic Council that was presented to Prime Minister Obuchi in February 1999. A more detailed discussion on this point will be developed in Chapter 6.

Part II
Fiscal Policy Responses

5

Budgets and the Budgetary Process

Government fiscal activity is reported to the nation through the budget. Governments perform a number of functions. Public expenditure and taxes are used to stabilize the economy, that is, when private demand is weak, expenditure may be increased or taxes adjusted downward or both. Even if stabilization goals are satisfied, the government would still have to fulfil other roles in the economy, such as resource allocation and income distribution. These roles are embodied in the provision of certain public goods and services to society at large or separately to a specific group of individuals. Given the multiple roles the public sector performs in the economy, how can we analyse the allocation or assignment of these roles within the framework of a multi-level government? Also, how can we understand the actual performance of government in the past and present? All of these can be conveyed to us via the budgets and the budgetary process. Each country has historically developed its own unique system of budgeting. It is difficult to find a great deal of resemblance between one country's budget and another. The budget system serves many functions which allow the government to execute its roles as mentioned above. The main tasks of budgets are to control government fiscal activities, to review previous actions and to identify future government programmes. In order to clarify the roles and functions assigned to government, we must first carefully explore the entire budgetary system and in turn the fiscal structure of the public sector.

This chapter starts with an outline of Japan's budgetary system with special reference to alternative concepts and uses under the present system. It then describes the budgetary process and procedures which are sometimes called 'budget cycles'.

ALTERNATIVE CONCEPTS AND USES OF BUDGETS

The Entire System of Japan's Budget
In Japan, there is no counterpart to the concept of the 'unified budget', or consolidated budget as in the USA (see A. F. Ott 1993, ch. 3). Each budget exists, independently of the other, to implement their individual function at different levels of government. At the same time, the budget system has traditionally been based on a narrower scope, and is not consolidated. In order to clarify the alternative concepts of fiscal deficits used for the analysis of the budgetary policy, we must begin with a discussion of the budget system. In Japan, the government sector is stratified into two levels: the national and the local governments, each one having some responsibility for a particular set of public functions. Each level of government has its own budget system, which is composed of more or less similar accounts.

This chapter draws primarily upon Ishi 1996*a*.

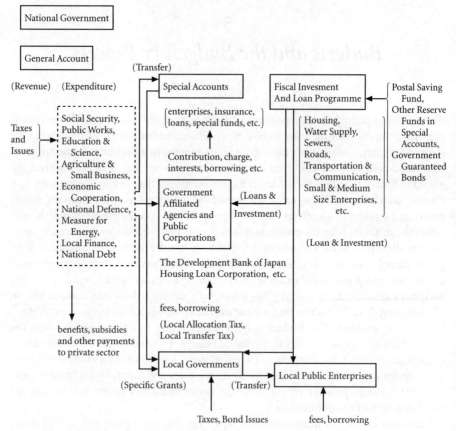

FIGURE 5.1. *A bird's-eye sketch of Japan's budgetary system*
Source: MOF, *The Budget in Brief*, 1985

Figure 5.1 illustrates the whole budget system, covering the entire scope of government. The national government's portion contains the *general account, special accounts,* and the *budgets of government-affiliated agencies and public corporations.* Among them, the *general account* is the most fundamental budget. In fact, almost all national tax revenues, except for earmarked taxes, belong to the *general account,* including revenues from national bond issues. These revenues are appropriated to such expenditure items as listed in Figure 5.1, but most of them become transfers and grants to various *special accounts* and to local governments. A small number of items are paid directly to the private sector from the general account, excluding wages and salaries of government employees.

The *general account* of the national government can greatly affect the entire system of the budget including that of local governments, although it reflects only a part of the whole budgetary system. When the word 'budget' is used in isolation, it often refers to the *general account budget*.

The *special accounts* are established when the national government needs to manage flows of specific funds to carry out specific government activities. For instance, such activities as government enterprises, insurance, loans, etc., are managed by one of the related *special accounts*. Each special account has its own specific revenue source, such as contributions, charges, interest and borrowing. In addition to these revenues, transfers from the *general account* are of great importance in the operation of the *special accounts*.

Government-affiliated agencies that are granted special legal status from the government also have their own budgets. The number of government-affiliated agencies stands at nine in 2000, including the Development Bank of Japan, the Housing Loan Corporation and so on. Since their activities are closely related to government policies, their budgets are included as a part of the national budget system. As a result, they must be submitted to the Diet for approval together with other budgets. Furthermore, there are also a number of public corporations, consisting mainly of the Urban Development and Housing Corporation, the Japan Highway Corporation, etc.

Similarly, special note should be paid to the function of the Fiscal Investment and Loan Program (FILP). This is not a budget item, but a programme of various investments and loans used by the national government. Mainly financed by postal savings and public pension funds, loans are made to support the funding of housing, water supply, roads, and so on. The budget system of each local government consists also of both ordinary accounts and public enterprise accounts. At the sub-national level, each is related to general administration and enterprise activities.

The National Budget Concept

Among the three different kinds of budgets, undoubtedly the most important is the *general account* which is the basic account of the government. The expenditure side of the *general account* contains such major government programmes as social security, public works, defence, education, etc., as listed in Figure 5.1. The *general account* (hereafter simply referred to as the budget) sets two basic principles for fiscal activities. First of all, every item of public expenditure or revenue must be represented in the budget for each fiscal year (from 1 April to 31 March). The expenditure of each fiscal year must basically be financed by revenue in that year, except for carried-over expenses, continued expenses, contract authorization, etc. This principle is usually called the 'single-year budget principle', the aim being to treat each fiscal year independently of another. This is to be contrasted with a multi-year budget system as used in the USA. Behind this single-year treatment, the revenue side of the budget is defined so as to include national bonds in addition to taxes. Thus, the total amount of revenues in the budget is constantly equivalent to expenditures in each fiscal year.

Secondly, certain limits are set in the budget when national bonds are issued as a supplemental revenue source to make up for shortfalls in taxes and non-tax revenues. In principle, the total amount of bond issuance must be restricted to the issuing of

TABLE 5.1. *The system of special accounts*

Type	Number	Explanation	Examples
The enterprise special accounts	5	To manage specific enterprises that the government administers.	• Mint Bureau • Printing Bureau • Postal Service

The insurance special accounts	11	Special insurance, reinsurance, and social insurance that are difficult for the private sector to provide (A) as well as insurance plans comparable to those provided by private insurance companies (B)	(A) • Welfare Insurance
			    • National Insurance
			    • Labour Insurance
			(B) • Postal Life Insurance
			    • Forest Insurance

The special accounts for public investment	5	To conduct specific public works.	• Port Improvement • Road Improvement • Flood Control
The special accounts for administrative business	9	To manage administrative business except for insurance, public works and loans.	• National schools • National hospitals • Foodstuff (especially rice) Control
The special accounts for loans	2	To administer the loan programme to the public corporations for specific purposes.	• Industrial Investment • Urban Development Loans
The special accounts for fund management	2	To manage public funds established for specific purposes.	• Trust Funds Bureau Fund • Foreign Exchange Fund (for sales and purchases of foreign exchange)
The consolidated funds special accounts	4	To consolidate the revenues and expenditures for specific purposes so as to make their accounting clear.	• National Debt Consolidation Fund • Local Allocation and Local Transfer Tax

construction bonds that are appropriated for capital expenditures in the current budget. This is the so-called principle of 'construction bonds', which will be described in Chapter 6. Of course, another form of bonds, 'debt-covering bonds', can be issued by a special authorization law when revenue shortages are too enormous to be covered only by construction bonds. Obviously, these two budgetary principles in Japan are different from those of many other advanced countries, presenting unique features to the budgetary system.

Let us now shift our attention to the other types of budgets. To begin with, let us explore in more detail what the special account budgets look like. When the government needs to achieve special projects, to control specific funds, and to perform specific functions separate from the general fiscal activity, the *special accounts* might be a more effective way of administering the related budget presentations. Thus, special account budgets are established by legislation for this purpose on the basis of a non-unified concept. Table 5.1 tabulates the current system of thirty-eight *special accounts* in 2000, classifying them into seven sub-groups. Each special account basically has its distinctive source of revenues such as social insurance contributions, interest receipts from loans, revenues from government enterprises and so on. For instance, the insurance *special accounts* which form the largest group have been established for handling the benefits and contributions to social insurance, reinsurance and pensions financially supported by tax revenues of the *general account*. The main tasks of the other *special accounts* are delineated in Table 5.1.

In general, the on-budget activities of the government are comprised of both the *general and special account budgets*. On the other hand, the government has found a need to extend its functions beyond the on-budget scope of the *general and specific accounts* mentioned above in order to perform these functions with greater flexibility and efficiency in view of management and accounting. As a result, government-affiliated agencies were established under special laws as so-called 'special corporations' with a corporate style of management. All of them are fully capitalized by the government, consisting of seven public finance corporations and two banks in 2000. Since they function in relation to government fiscal activity, their budgets must be approved by the Diet, just like other budgets. In addition, government-affiliated agencies play an integral role in the Fiscal Investment and Loan Program, as will be discussed in detail in Chapter 12.

When government behaviour is analysed or fiscal deficits are defined in Japan, the scope most commonly used is the *general account* (for a general discussion, see Ishi 1986a). For one thing, the *general account* can be thought of as representing the entire picture of Japan's fiscal activities, although it merely occupies the narrowest scope in the public sector. On the other hand, the fiscal data of the *general account* are more plentiful and available than those of any other budget. Ideally, as in the USA, a unified budget should be used for the budget presentation of the national government, combining the *general account* budget and the other two budgets.

Since such a unified budget is not prepared in Japan, our analysis must rely on the budget concept of the *general account*. Apparently, we must take careful note of the conceptual discrepancies between the Japanese budget and that of other countries. For example, social security contributions[1] (i.e. collected as a payroll tax in the USA) are not included in *general account* revenues. As seen in Figure 5.1, only transfers to the social insurance *special accounts* appear on the expenditure side of the *general account*. Consequently, the *general account* deficit is different from fiscal deficits in the US federal budget in which the total expenditures and revenues of social security programmes are included. To seek a US counterpart figure, we must include total outlays and revenues of the social insurance *special accounts*.

Local Public Finance Programme

Local governments in Japan also have their own budgetary system. On the sub-central level, Japan's local governments are composed of a so-called two-tier system: that is

---

[1] The social insurance system in Japan contains programmes related to health insurance, public pensions and unemployment compensation. See Chapter 11 for an expanded discussion.

prefectures and municipalities. They number 3,276 in total as of 2000, consisting of 47 prefectures and 3,229 municipalities (i.e. 671 cities and 2,558 towns-villages).

Each local government has its own budgeting account which compiles the revenues and expenditures necessary for its activities. There are two types of accounts. One is the *ordinary account* for general administrative services, such as education, fire, police, and so on. The other is the *public enterprise account* for such services as housing, sewage, and public transport. This budgeting system provides a common framework for comparing the financial situation of various local governments. These accounts must be reported to the Ministry of Home Affairs (MOHA) where they are statistically compiled each year and are utilized in the analysis of local public finance.

However, it usually takes a couple of years to compile and publish fiscal data on a national basis with a full coverage of the more than 3,000 local governments. Thus, a device is needed to provide an all-inclusive form of the total local budgets more promptly, because both the national and local budgets must be prepared to coincide for the same period.

Before the beginning of each fiscal year, the national government has to review the general situation of local governments in order to allocate revenue sources and to form basic fiscal policies among multiple levels of government. For this purpose, the MOHA is compelled by law to make official estimates of the total expected expenditures and revenues of all the local governments. Using this estimate as a basis, the MOHA is then expected to guarantee sufficient financial resources for each local government. The estimate and the revenue-sharing methods are consolidated into the Local Public Finance Programme (LPFP). This is an 'aggregated local public finance budget compiled of the annual budgets of more than 3,000 local governments'. It is considered to be comparable to the country's national budget (Ishi 1993, ch. 14).

The Position of the General Account *in the Whole System of Budgets*
Given the whole budget system described above, what is the relative importance of the *general account* in quantitative terms within the whole framework of budgets? Figure 5.2 illustrates the interactions between the *general account* and other budgets by using the 1996 initial budget figures. The total expenditure of the *general account* amounts to ¥70,987.1 billion, more than half of which is transferred into the *special accounts*, mainly into the local allocation tax (tax-share scheme) and the local transfer tax, national debt consolidation fund, welfare insurance, and other *special accounts*. The remainder is directly paid to the private sector. Removing the overlap between the *general and special accounts*, a net amount of ¥1,836,343 billion in the national budget is channelled in three directions into other budgetary accounts.

First of all, the national budget transfers ¥30,940.9 billion to local governments through intergovernmental transfers, such as the local allocation tax, the local transfer tax and national grant-in-aids. Conversely, local governments have to pay back ¥1,028.9 billion to the national government as the local governments' share in national direct projects. The second channel is concerned with the transfer to government-affiliated agencies and public corporations of subsidies (¥3,061.2 billion) and capital investment

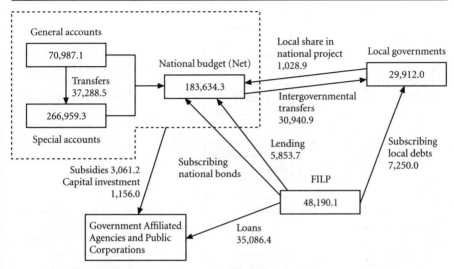

FIGURE 5.2. *Flows of financial funds from the general account to other budgets (¥ billion)*

Note: All figures are based on those of the 1996 initial budget and local finance programme in 1995

(¥1,156.0 billion) from the national budget. These agencies and corporations are provided loans in large amounts by the FILP (¥35,086.4 billion). Third, the national budget is closely related to the FILP, which is mainly financed by postal savings and public pensions. The FILP lends ¥5,853.7 billion to the national budget and subscribes a substantial part of national bonds.

The Government Sector in the System of National Accounts

Another concept of the budget can be considered to make up for the narrow scope of the *general account*. This concept covers the entire fiscal activity of the government in the economy and depends on the SNA (System of National Accounts) framework. The government sector in the SNA corresponds conceptually to the system of double-entry accounts used by the EPA to estimate current productive activity in Japan according to the international standard of calculation of the United Nations. When the SNA measures the market value of the currently-produced final output of goods and services, which are classified by type of expenditure, the government explicitly appears as the item of government purchases of goods and services, in addition to the other items, consumer expenditure, gross private domestic investment and net exports. The total amount of these items becomes the Gross Domestic Product (GDP), but government transfer payments do not appear conceptually in public expenditure.[2]

---

[2] In 1992, the GNP (Gross National Product) concept was replaced by GDP as a measure of national product and income in accordance with international treatment in Japan.

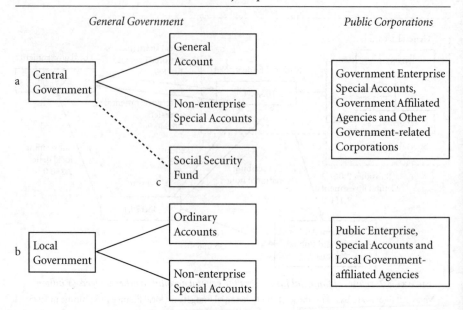

FIGURE 5.3. *The government sector in the SNA*

Source: EPA, *Annual Report on National Accounts*, 2000

In Figure 5.3, the government sector as defined in the SNA is illustrated in contrast to the *general account* of the national government. Generally speaking, the government sector in the SNA framework is further divided into two sectors, the general government and the public corporations within central and local governments. The scope of the general government which corresponds to the *general account* in concept has three major components: (i) central government, (ii) local government and (iii) social security fund. As is evident from Figure 5.3, the general government in the SNA framework not only includes the *general account* of the national budget, but also local ordinary accounts, non-enterprise special accounts and social insurance special accounts (i.e. the social security fund).

The government sector in the SNA is not a budget in the sense that it is not a fiscal plan for controlling, administering, or proposing the activities of the government. It is only a conceptual design of the government sector using the consistent framework of the SNA which is common to the international community. Of course, the SNA's treatment of government activity primarily differs from that of the budget in two ways, reflecting the difference between the concept of national income and fiscal operations. To begin with, transfers in the budget, including those to other accounts, interest payments or grants to local governments, are excluded from government expenditure in the SNA as a result of netting out when all sectors are consolidated into a summary account for the government and the nation as a whole. Only government purchases of goods and services are included in the SNA concept, because only that part of government ought to be included in final output.

Next, lending and financial activities are treated differently in the budget and the SNA. The budget includes such financial transactions of the government as the making of loans, loan repayments and land asset purchases, while the SNA excludes them because they produce no current output or income. For instance, the purchase of land for public works is counted as a payment in the budget, but is omitted from the SNA. Likewise, direct lending by government-affiliated agencies is excluded from the SNA since none of these transactions generate purchases of final output.

For economic analysis of fiscal policy, the SNA concept is preferred to the *general account* budget. By excluding items such as purely financial transactions (e.g. those involving the dealing of assets), the SNA concept provides a better measure of fiscal activities than does the *general account* budget. Moreover, perhaps the most important reason for the preference of the SNA concept is the need for consistency when relating relevant data to the economy as a whole. As noted earlier, it is important to stress that the SNA concept does correspond to the system of national accounts used to measure GDP while the *general account* budget does not. The framework of GDP is commonly employed as a yardstick of the level of economic activity in economic analysis. Thus, it is desirable to use a data series which is in concept consistent with the estimates of the SNA as an indicator of fiscal policy. This being the case, one can better observe how changes in fiscal decisions influence the level of economic activity.

Furthermore, the SNA concept has advantages in attempting international comparisons, because each country follows a common framework in measuring data. However, most of the SNA data have only become available since 1970 in the international context, and in addition they usually lack detailed information of fiscal data. Thus, it is difficult to use the SNA concept to analyse the behaviour of the fiscal authority in detail. By contrast, the *general account* budget is often much more useful for discussion of fiscal policy because of data availability. Thus, both should be treated as complementary sources and not as mutually exclusive ones.

Table 5.2 explores the relation of the *general account* to the SNA concept. In accordance with each item in Figure 5.3, it is possible to obtain relevant data on both final consumption expenditures and capital formation in the government sector in 1998 (EPA 2000). The relative share of the *general account* in the SNA framework is merely 17.0 per cent of final consumption expenditure and 1.7 per cent of capital formation. Obviously, nearly 75 per cent of both expenditures are occupied by local governments, given the current fiscal structure. Since transfer payments which occupy a substantial share of total government expenditure are included in the private sector, the *general account* only plays a minor quantitative role in government fiscal activities as a whole. However, as seen in Figure 5.1, the *general account* takes the initiative in controlling overall fiscal activities through transfers to other budgets, such as to the *special accounts* and local governments. Accordingly, it is likely to be considered as a representative of total budgetary activity.

TABLE 5.2. *Relation of the general account to the SNA concept, 1998*

Items in the SNA	Amount ¥ billion	Percentage distribution (%)
1. Final consumption expenditure of the general government	50,910.9	100.0
(1) Central	11,917.8	23.4
a. *General account*	*8,684.0*	*(17.0)*
b. Non-enterprise special accounts	2,145.9	(4.2)
c. Jigyodan	1,087.9	(2.1)
(2) Local	37,939.2	74.5
(3) Social security fund	1,053.9	2.0
2. Government Capital Formation	38,957.5	100.0
(1) Fixed investment	39,086.0	
a. Central	10,160.9	26.0
① General government	5,500.0	(14.1)
(i) *General account*	*649.7*	*(1.7)*
(ii) Non-enterprise special account	4,547.3	(11.7)
(iii) Jigyodan	303.0	(0.8)
② Public enterprises	4,660.9	(12.0)
b. Local	28,787.5	73.9
c. Social security fund	137.7	0.4
(2) Increases in inventory	−128.5	−0.3
Total	89,868.4	

Source: Economic Planning Agency, *Annual Report on National Accounts*, 2000, pp. 236–7.

THE BUDGETARY PROCESS

The Main Features of Japan's Budgeting

Fiscal policy can be executed in practice through budgeting,[3] in which the levels and composition of taxes and expenditures should be set to achieve certain policy goals. Therefore, it is crucial in any discussion of fiscal policy to understand the budgetary system, consisting of both the executive and the legislative process through which taxes and expenditures are actually determined every fiscal year.

Generally speaking, the making of a nation's budget is initially the purview of the executive branch of government. Then the legislative process approves the budget in the Diet where it is submitted by the executive. In a parliamentary system, the legislative power to alter the budget from the executive level is usually very limited. In fact, under the parliamentary system of Japan, as well as of the UK, Germany, and Canada, the government budget is commonly accepted without any serious amendments or

[3] In what follows, focus is placed largely on the national budget.

modifications. This implies that a single budget initially formulated by the executive plays a vital role in the budgetary process.

Budgeting is a continuous process, generating several steps referred to as the budgetary process. Among them, in Japan, the following three steps are important: (i) budget preparation and transmission, (ii) congressional action, and (iii) execution and settlement of the budget with audit. This process is by and large common to many other countries. Needless to say, the first step is of the greatest importance, because it is not customary to amend the budget at the Diet level, as noted above.

In Japan, the MOF has been given general jurisdiction over the whole process of making the budget. Within the MOF, the Budget Bureau is chiefly charged with the drafting of each budget. Although the MOF is practically responsible for the preparation of the budget at the initial stage, the Cabinet is solely responsible for its transmission to the Diet after having accepted the MOF's budget draft and adding minor modifications to it.

There are three points worth noting as marked features of Japan's budgeting. First, a revenue budget is compiled separately from the expenditure budget. Thus, unlike that of many other countries, Japan's budget to be submitted to the Diet is composed of both a revenue and an expenditure side. The revenue budget is formulated to clarify the resource needs of the budget programmes in the form of taxes, debt, and non-tax revenues in relation to the economic outlook and prospective revenues. For this purpose, at the end of every calendar year, the *Economic Outlook and Basic Policy Stance on Economic Management* is published by the government for the budgetary preparation of the forthcoming fiscal year. The growth rate of nominal GDP and other important data, which are indispensable to the estimation of tax revenues, are all included in this document in conjunction with current and projected economic conditions. As a consequence, a simultaneous consideration of both revenues and expenditures is made in general.[4]

Second, such provisions as continued expenses, approved carried-over expenses and contract authorization are submitted to the Diet in order to seek its approval. All of them are important as exceptional provisions of the single-year-budget principle, whose outlays can be extended over a stretch of multiple years. The maximum limit is five years. To begin with, continued expenses contain those on which the government has to make payments over a period of several years, for example, the construction of large-scale ships and submarines for defence purposes. Also, the Diet may allow some expenditure to be carried over to the subsequent fiscal year under a scheme of approved carried-over expenses. When an expenditure item is not anticipated to be spent within the current fiscal year, the carry-over treatment is permitted by Diet approval in advance. Moreover, the contract authorization scheme allows the government to contract certain projects on a multiple year basis. All or part of the necessary outlays are made within a given fiscal year or in the subsequent several years by prior approval of the Diet.

---

[4] Before publishing such official data, the Tax Bureau Staff at the MOF begin to estimate tax revenues on an informal basis using their own procedures.

Lastly, the budget cycle starts on 1 April and ends on 31 March every year; this is the fiscal year in Japan. With the exception of the three expenses noted above, outlays in the regular budget of each fiscal year must be made in that relevant time period. However, when the Cabinet expects that the regular budget cannot be approved by April 1, mostly for political reasons such as an upcoming general election, a provisional budget is specially compiled for a specific period from the beginning of the fiscal year and submitted to the Diet. Since the provisional budget is replaced by the regular budget once it is approved with a time-lag, expenditures in the provisional budgets must be limited to minimum requirement payments, such as the wages and salaries of government employees consistent with the upcoming regular budget. Furthermore, a supplementary budget is prepared for and submitted to the Diet when a shortage of revenue sources or special needs for expenditure occurs as the current fiscal year progresses. The supplementary budgets usually emerge a couple of times a year for a variety of reasons such as the necessity of recovering from natural disasters, wage hikes for government employees proposed in the recommendations of the National Personnel Authority[5] and so on.

Budget Preparation and Transmission

The making of a budget usually begins with the preparation of budgetary requests in the period of June–August at the level of ministries and agencies every year (eight to ten months before the next fiscal year begins on 1 April). The appropriate time sequence at each stage of the budget preparation is illustrated in Figure 5.4 in the case of the 1995 budget formulation process (for a general discussion, see MOF 1995). The figure shows the two-way flows of decisions from ministries and agencies on the left, and from the MOF on the right.

Budget preparation begins at the level of ministries and agencies. By August, or earlier in some cases, the individual units in every ministry and agency have to make plans for their expenditures and programmes. For this purpose, they review current operations and issues, programme objectives and future plans pertinent to the upcoming budget. Budget offices within each organization finally set up their own budget requests to be submitted to the MOF after making adjustments for intra-ministry review.

In parallel with these preparations, guidelines for the estimated budget requests are decided by the Cabinet about a month before the budget requests are made by the individual ministries and agencies. Under these guidelines certain 'ceilings' are fixed regarding the expenditure increments over the previous year's budget, depending upon each category of current and investment expenditures except for the two entitled expenditures (debt service charges and local allocation taxes, i.e. tax-sharing grants). Non-entitled expenditures are mainly targeted for the setting of such ceilings. As will be discussed in Chapter 6, the level and coverage of ceilings have become more

---

[5] Every year the National Personnel Authority rules to the government on recommended wage rises for government employees in order to make up for the gap between private and public sectors.

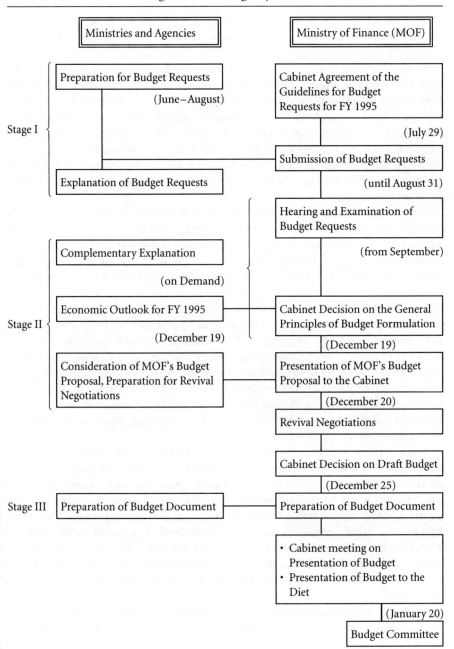

FIGURE 5.4. *Process of budget preparation for fiscal 1995*
Source: MOF, *The Japanese Budget in Brief*, 1995, p. 106

severe over the past decade or so.[6] Guidelines reflecting the basic attitude of the Cabinet for budgeting then flow back down through the MOF to ministries and agencies in the form of limiting targets to guide the preparation of the formal budget requests in August. They, in turn, must modify their budget requests to fit the guidelines and prioritize among various expenditure items themselves before submitting the requests to the MOF. As a result, these guidelines work effectively in controlling the latent excessive demand for expanding the budget at the level of each ministry and agency. It would perhaps be possible to assess that these guidelines have played a substantial role in curtailing expenditure levels in the past, although any critical view regarding the guideline strategy may be made and defended as will be described later. The first step of the budget process is over when budget requests are presented to the MOF on 31 August.

Subsequently, the second stage runs from September to December. This time is spent compiling detailed estimates and negotiating with relevant ministries and the MOF on budget allocations and figures. After budget requests are transmitted, budget examiners at the Budget Bureau of the MOF start a series of hearings and reviews with budget office staff in the ministries and agencies concerning the details of individual budget items. Additional supporting data and materials are requested in the hearing and review process. The budget examiners give considerable attention to the basis for each estimate of the budget items, review the past performance of relevant ministries and agencies, check the accuracy of the factual information presented and take account of the future implication of expenditure programmes. In addition, the examiners identify each item of expenditure, management issues and the like to be raised for discussion with the ministry and agency representatives during the MOF hearings. Conversely, all ministries and agencies have to defend their budget requests from one item to another in front of the examiners at these hearings, which are usually held from September to December.

Towards the end of December, the Cabinet issues the 'General Principles of Budget Formulation' and the MOF follows this guideline to complete the budget draft. For about a week after the MOF's draft is published, final negotiations are made to let some budget items be revived between the MOF and the relevant ministries and agencies, whose representatives attempt to justify higher amounts to the MOF staff. The process usually continues until the highest level of negotiations between the Minister of Finance and relevant Ministers or Director-Generals of Agencies are reached. After final reconciliation among the authorities concerned is reached, the MOF's budget draft is finalized and officially approved by the Cabinet at the end of December.

No doubt, budget making is always a political process, and the politics of making the budget is important in various ways. In particular, specific ministries and their

---

[6] For instance, prior to 1975 the guidelines were too generous, admitting increases of 25–50 per cent relative to previous fiscal years, but in the 1980s they have become very strict in restraining budget increase requests to a 'zero' or 'negative' ceiling.

'supporting politicians' frequently become advocates of increased expenditures for their own sake, backed politically by vested interest groups. It is commonly considered as natural and inevitable by the Diet and the MOF that they are very powerful in justifying their programme decisions and securing their budget requests. In Japan, this is quite true in such specific areas as agriculture and public works. It is widely acknowledged that politicians often intervene in the budgetary process for their own self-interests, and bias fund allocation efficiency in the budget.

Parliamentary Deliberation for Budgeting

After the Cabinet transmits the draft budget to the Diet, the third stage is launched in the budgetary process from the latter half of January. Of course, before its transmission, a series of budget documents have to be prepared by the MOF staff. In Japan's budgetary system, however, one can say that almost the whole process of budgeting has *de facto* ended by the second stage of budget preparation. Indeed, no serious amendments or modifications have been made so far in the past budgets during parliamentary deliberation, with minor exceptions in fiscal 1972, 1977, and 1991. This is to be sharply contrasted with congressional budgeting activity in the US.

The Japanese constitution stipulates that the House of Representatives (the Lower House) should be given first priority over deliberations concerning the draft budget presented by the Cabinet. In the plenary parliament, the Minister of Finance makes a budget speech in which he outlines the basic nature and structure of the forthcoming budget along with the government's stance on fiscal and monetary policies. On the same day, his budget speech is also repeated in the House of Councillors (the Upper House). In both Houses, the Budget Committee is organized to deliberate the draft budget intensively, but given the automatic approval of the budget, most of the items tend to become a formality without any meaningful discussions among the members of parliament. During the deliberations of the draft budget, public hearings are required by law, and a public attendant is selected by each political party.

After the approval of the Budget Committee in the House of Representatives, the draft budget is formally put to a vote at the plenary session of that House, and thereafter it is sent to the House of Councillors. There, the same procedure is taken by the Budget Committee to deliberate the budget and it is approved by voting. After its passage in that House, the budget becomes effective from 1 April. If the House of Councillors does not pass the draft budget within thirty days after it is transmitted, the budget is automatically approved in accordance with the decision of the House of Representatives. Moreover, if the decision differs from one House to another, a joint committee of several members from both houses is convened and enters into a reconciliation process. It is generally difficult to come to a common conclusion. This being the case, the decision of the House of Representatives can be given priority over that of the Upper House. As is evident from these facts, it is guaranteed by the constitution that the House of Representatives takes a superior position in the budget deliberation so as not to delay the budgetary action.

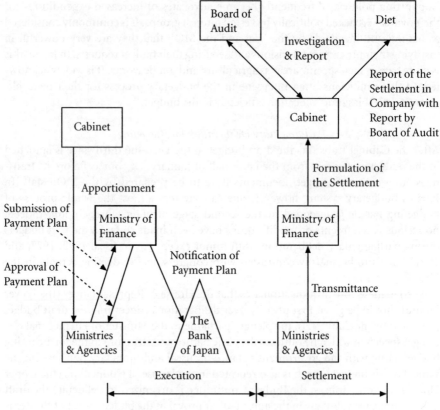

FIGURE 5.5. *Execution and settlement of the budget*
Source: As Figure 5.4, p. 113

Execution and Settlement of the Budget

Normally a new budget starts on 1 April, and thereafter the budgetary phase reaches the execution process. As shown in Figure 5.5, the Cabinet apportions the necessary funds of the expenditure budget to the relevant ministries and agencies for enforcement. Overall responsibility for executing the expenditure budget is given to the head of each ministry and agency, who cannot use them for any purposes other than those appropriated for in the respective budgetary items. Based upon the appropriated budget, they have to prepare payment plans on a quarterly basis in which the required disbursements must be clarified by each spending officer. After their submission, approval is needed by the MOF, which notifies the BOJ of the payment plans. Actual payments of the expenditure budget are made by issuing cheques drawn on the BOJ.

Every fiscal year ends on 31 March, after which there remain additional disbursement periods for a couple of weeks. After the close of the fiscal year, each ministry and agency have to transmit a statement of accounts for its expenditure to the MOF by the end of July which in turn carries out the settlement of accounts for total revenue and expenditure to cover all related budgets. Formulation of the settlement made by the MOF must be authorized by the Cabinet, and this is sent to the Board of Audit by the end of November. The Board of Audit is charged with inspecting the settlement of accounts, independently of the Cabinet as is stipulated by the Constitution.

The results of the inspection by the Board are returned to the Cabinet in the form of reports, together with which the settlement reports are presented to the Diet by the Cabinet around December. In both Houses, the Settlement of Accounts Committees are open to deliberate on these reports and to seek the possible responsibility of relevant ministries and agencies in cases of injustice or misuse of the disbursement of budgetary items.

As a consequence of the settlement, a fiscal surplus is usually generated to some extent which is called a 'carryover-surplus'. According to a rule of the Public Finance Law, not less than half of the carryover-surplus must be appropriated to redeem national bonds within two years under consideration. Such a surplus is transferred into the Settlement Adjustment Fund. Conversely, when revenue shortages are incurred in the settlement of the *general account* during recessions, the Fund is allowed to compensate these revenue shortages. When the Fund does not contain enough outstanding balances for this purpose, certain financial resources are transferred from the National Bonds Consolidation Fund to the Settlement Adjustment Fund to make up for the shortfall. However, they are required to be paid back from the *general account* by the end of the next fiscal year.

The Budget Process in Local Governments

In addition to the preparation of the national budget, let us investigate briefly the budgetary process in local governments. Since the total number of local governments is more than 3,000, it is impossible to explore the budgetary process of each prefectural and municipal government separately. Therefore, in what follows we shall focus on the case of Tokyo (the Tokyo Metropolitan Government), because Tokyo can be thought of as a representative example of the budgetary process applicable to other governments at the local level.

Figure 5.6 depicts a summary of the budget process in a typical year. Budget preparation begins with estimates of the individual units of each bureau of the Metropolitan Government, which are then submitted under the limiting ceiling by late August. From late September to late October, the budget request is presented to the Budget Bureau, divided between the first request and the second request, while the Budget Bureau staff examine them step by step, conducting hearings with the parties requesting the relevant budget items. Budget examination usually continues until early January within the Budget Bureau. Meanwhile, the Metropolitan Government makes any requests that it may have for preparing the coming budget to the national government, say the MOHA or other ministries, and a local debt issuance programme is published by the MOHA. Generally speaking, since local budgets are affected by the

FIGURE 5.6. *Budget process for the Tokyo Metropolitan Government*
Note: Tabulated by data from the Tokyo Metropolitan Government

national budget through the share of revenue sources and national grant-in-aids to a considerable extent, great importance is attached to reviewing the process of compiling the national budget around the close of the calendar year.

Before ending the process of budget preparation, municipal governments, including the 23 wards in the Tokyo Metropolitan area, also submit their requests for budgeting to the Metropolitan Government. At the final stage, the Governor's decision is made in early January to determine the existence of any significant budget items on which it may be very difficult to reach a decision at the level of budget examiners and whose importance is necessary to stress in view of specific policy issues. After including such decisions from the Governor, the draft budget is published around late January, and thereafter budget negotiations are begun to reach the final budget plan.

The local assembly is regularly held four times a year in March, June, October, and December. The budget plan is transmitted to the first meeting of the local assembly to be held every March and is deliberated mainly in the Special Budget Committee. After passing the budget plan at the local assembly by the end of March, it comes into enforcement. In sum, it seems that the budgetary process is more or less the same in national and local governments, although the time schedule differs slightly.

We have so far investigated institutionally the basic features of Japan's budgetary system and process. The scope of our discussion is not so ambitious, and more importance is placed simply on clarifying the fundamental framework of budgeting, in particular for the sake of foreign readers. One may criticize the present budget system in Japan on the following three points. The first is concerned with the 'single-year budget principle' which it might be better to replace with a multi-year one in view of allocative efficiency of budgetary funds. The second point is directed at the desirability of establishing both current and capital budgets, each in order to control relevant expenditure and revenue in separate accounts. Thirdly, a unified budget, as is utilized in the USA, might be constructed on a consolidated basis to make the narrow scope of the present budget system broader and clearer, avoiding overlapping transactions and double-counting. In spite of such criticism, it seems that Japan's budgeting system and process are working rather well at the present time, with no serious problems.

6
Budget Orthodoxy and Strategies for Deficit Reduction

Generally speaking, the government plays an important role in not only providing public goods and redistributing income, but stabilizing the economy in a non-inflationary environment. In order to execute the fiscal activities of the government sector, government expenditure, tax revenue and public debt are the main economic instruments. Apart from a balanced budget state, the budget frequently generates fiscal surpluses and deficits as a result of an expenditure–revenue gap, depending on the general level of economic expansion or contraction. Thus, fiscal deficits (or surpluses) provide us with a certain yardstick to express the basic nature of government fiscal activity.

It is worth noting that large fiscal deficits have long persisted in most advanced countries, and remain one of the most important problems to be solved in the years ahead. Many countries have begun to recognize the risks that continuing fiscal deficits entail in that they have the potential to explode into unsustainable debt accumulation, particularly in an environment of lower growth rates and high interest rates. In fact, a significant number of OECD countries have established fiscal targets in recent years to attain balanced or modest deficit positions in the general government account, as will be argued later.

Japan's fiscal position has worsened sharply since the early 1990s in terms of fiscal deficits and debt accumulation, reflecting the sluggishness of the economic recovery since the post-bubble recession. In Japan, officially great care has been taken by the fiscal authority, the MOF, to restrain fiscal deficits from expanding while Keynesian fiscal policies still remain predominant as an expansionary device. As a consequence, the central question addressed in this chapter is how fiscal policy issues have been handled among all the parties concerned in relation to the expansion of fiscal deficits in the past.

This chapter is divided into four parts. First, we briefly consider the recent development of Japan's fiscal deficits in comparison with those of other major countries. Secondly, we attempt to clarify the traditional budgetary rule adopted by the MOF in contrast to the Keynesian view. Thirdly, we note the strategies of deficit reduction in the annual process of budgeting. Lastly, we investigate the effects of the bubble boom and its collapse on the budgetary behaviour. These considerations would be of great help to understanding the underlying conditions of Japan's fiscal policy.

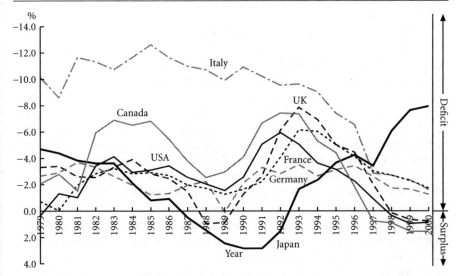

FIGURE 6.1. *Fiscal deficits (−) and surpluses (+) among G7 countries as a percentage of nominal GDP, 1979–2000*

Source: OECD, *Economic Outlook*, December 1999

Note: The scope of the general government in the national accounts is taken to include central and local governments and the social security fund

RECENT TRENDS OF FISCAL DEFICITS IN INTERNATIONAL PERSPECTIVES

Current State of Fiscal Positions in Major Countries

In Europe, the USA, and Japan, increasing importance has begun to be placed on the current level of fiscal deficits and accumulated debt in recent years. Policy makers tend not only to address policy management issues related to the immediate economic situation, but also to meet important medium-term policy goals to restore the annual balance of budgets. It is generally acknowledged that a stable fiscal environment would be essential to enhance the flexibility of the economy. For this purpose, well-designed macroeconomic and structural policies are required to reduce fiscal deficits in major countries.

Among many OECD countries, the deficit-reduction programmes have already assisted in lowering real interest rates and easing the pressures on currency markets through the enhancement of a nation's credibility. This effort is expected to continue to bring further beneficial effects in the future. However, in spite of fiscal consolidation efforts, large fiscal deficits, and the rising outstanding public debt still remain serious problems in each country.

Figure 6.1 indicates the past trends of fiscal deficits in the G7 countries for the period 1979–2000 with future projections. In order to obtain an adequate measurement common to each country, the relative ratio of fiscal deficits to GDP is employed in accordance with the SNA concept. There are a couple of points unique to Japan. First of all, Japan, in the 1980s, had successfully eliminated the large fiscal deficits which occurred in the late 1970s, and then turned them into a surplus after the mid-1980s. As will be argued shortly, this restoration of fiscal soundness was mainly caused by massive tax increases during the bubble boom.

Secondly, however, the fiscal deficit–GDP ratio had begun to rise again after the early 1990s. This recent trend in Japan ought to be sharply contrasted to those of other major countries, because all of them except for Japan have been able to decrease the relative size of their fiscal deficits to a considerable extent for several years. Thus, it is noted that in 1996 Japan's fiscal deficit surpassed those of the five other countries with the exception of Italy, reaching the worst situation among the G5 countries.

As described earlier, the general government is composed of three components: central government, the local government, and the social security fund. Inspecting each component in detail, it can be noted that the social security fund in Japan still accumulates a substantial surplus even now, unlike that of other major countries except for the USA. However, it is anticipated that such fund surpluses will start to disappear for some time to come as the population is ageing, given that the current scheme is partly on a pay-as-you-go basis. Thus it might be better to eliminate the ongoing accumulated surplus in the social security fund from the definition of fiscal deficits in the general government of both Japan and the USA.

If we use such a revised deficit–GDP ratio, Japan's fiscal position becomes much more aggravated: 6.0 per cent (3.4 per cent) in 1997, 8.5 per cent (6.0 per cent) in 1998, 9.9 per cent (7.6 per cent) in 1999 and 10.1 per cent (7.9 per cent) in 2000. The percentages in parentheses are those including the surplus of the social security fund. This being the case, Japan's fiscal deficits could exceed even the Italian level after 1996.

Turning to another measurement, we shall now consider the accumulated debt–GDP ratios depicted in Figure 6.2. Current fiscal deficits continue to increase the gross debt outstanding on a stock basis over time. Once fiscal deficits are generated in the budgetary process, public indebtedness must accumulate over a stretch of time.

The debt–GDP ratio had started increasing at a faster speed than that of other major countries, except for Italy, since the late 1970s. It slowed down once during the period 1987–91, reflecting the effects of deficit reduction on a flow basis for the same period, but thereafter it turned upward again until the present. That is to say, it has risen to be 105.4 per cent in 1999 and 114.1 per cent in 2000, exceeding 100 per cent, as Japan may catch up with Italy soon if the situation progresses as it is.

In retrospect, when have the fiscal deficit problems become evident in the major countries? Since the two oil crises in 1973 and 1979, the growth rate of the Japanese economy slowed down, and as a result, the nation's fiscal deficits expanded at a rapid pace. This story was, however, not at all unique to Japan, as many other countries of the world were plagued with similar problems.

Let us consider the outstanding debts of central government as a percentage of GDP since 1972 in 13 industrial countries. The ratio in Japan started to surge in 1974,

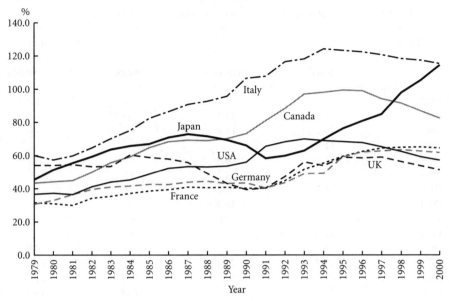

FIGURE 6.2. *Gross debt outstanding among G7 countries as a percentage of nominal GDP, 1979–2000*

Source and Note: As Figure 6.1

immediately after the first oil crisis in 1973. In 1974, the simple average of the rates among the G7 countries remained at 22 per cent while Japan's debts as a percentage of GDP in 1974 were merely 9.7 per cent, the second lowest next to 7 per cent for West Germany. However, the average ratio among the G7 countries had soared to 45 per cent by 1983, and the rate of increase in Japan was the fastest, increasing from 8.7 per cent to 44.7 per cent, reaching the second highest proportion after Italy's 78.6 per cent.

A similar phenomenon can be observed in the smaller industrial countries of Europe. The national debts have mushroomed during the decade of the 1970s in almost all Western free economies. This situation may be called a 'public debt explosion' (de Larosiere 1984).

Japan's Fiscal Position

The 'explosion' in Japan is particularly conspicuous. Naturally, the public debt issue has made it even more difficult for the government to compile the budget every year. Table 6.1 represents the bond dependency ratio (ratio of national bond issues to total government expenditures) in the general account of the national government in order to observe the past patterns of fiscal deficits in the narrowest scope since 1965. Japan has traditionally placed the highest priority on this ratio among relevant indicators in measuring the soundness of fiscal performance or fiscal discipline, although this is not

TABLE 6.1. *Trend of fiscal deficits in Japan: bond dependency ratio, 1965–2000 (%)*

Fiscal year	Total bonds		(Debt-covering bonds)	
	Initial	Settlement	Initial	Settlement
1965	—	5.4	—	(5.4)[1]
1966	16.9	14.9	—	—
1967	16.2	13.9	—	—
1968	11.0	7.8	—	—
1969	7.3	6.0	—	—
1970	5.4	4.2	—	—
1971	4.6	12.4	—	—
1972	17.0	16.3	—	—
1973	16.4	12.0	—	—
1974	12.6	11.3	—	—
1975	9.4	25.3	—	10.0
1976	29.9	29.4	19.3	14.2
1977	29.7	32.9	17.8	19.9
1978	32.0	31.3	18.4	16.5
1979	39.6	34.7	27.1	20.9
1980	33.5	32.6	22.0	20.9
1981	26.2	27.5	14.4	15.4
1982	21.0	29.7	9.5	18.3
1983	26.5	26.6	16.6	16.0
1984	25.0	24.8	15.2	14.8
1985	22.2	23.2	12.8	13.4
1986	20.2	21.0	11.3	11.0
1987	19.4	16.3	10.6	5.2
1988	15.6	11.6	6.5	1.8
1989	11.8	10.1	2.6	0.4
1990	8.4	10.6	—	1.6
1991	7.6	9.5	—	—
1992	10.1	13.5	—	—
1993	11.2	21.5	—	—
1994	18.7	22.4	5.2	7.1
1995	17.7	28.0	4.8	8.2
1996	28.0	27.6	18.8	17.1
1997	21.6	23.5	11.4	13.0
1998	20.0	40.3	9.2	21.9
1999	37.9	43.4	26.5	31.0
2000	38.4[2]	—	—	—

Source: Data from the MOF.

Note:
  [1] Provisional bond issuance to make up for revenue shortage
  [2] Provisional amount in the initial budget.

common to overseas countries. The bond dependency ratio originated in 1965 where the first debt-covering bonds were obliged to be floated to make up for the shortage of tax revenues in the supplementary budget of that year. Thus, the balanced budget position adopted by the MOF ended when the Japanese economy was faced with a depression and the MOF admitted to the necessity of stimulating the economy by generating fiscal deficits. However, after national bonds were issued on a substantial scale in 1966, the government made a strenuous effort to curtail them each year until the early 1970s, at least placing no reliance on debt-covering bonds.

The explosion of fiscal deficits in the general account of the national budget became serious after 1975. The harsh prolonged recession triggered by the oil shock produced an exorbitant deficit in the government sector, and the revenue shortage became evident during the implementation of the 1975 budget. Thus, a sharp increase in national bond flotation was necessary in the supplementary budget of 1975. The initial budget of 1975 planned to issue only ¥2,000 billion worth of bonds, but ¥3,400 billion more were added to the original plan as the large revenue shortage caused by the recession became more evident. Thus, debt-covering bonds had to be issued once again starting in fiscal 1975. In addition to the national government, local governments have also fallen into financial crises making it imperative for them to float local bonds in large amounts.

The bond dependency ratio reached 25.3 per cent after supplementation in 1975, and this ratio rose to 29.4 per cent in the 1976 budget. Furthermore, it continued to increase to reach a peak of 34.7 per cent in 1979. These dependency ratios are surprisingly high, compared with the 10.4 per cent average of 1965–74. After reaching a peak in 1979, the bond dependency ratio began a constant decline until 1986, mainly due to expenditure cuts. Thereafter, a further decreasing tempo in fiscal deficits can be observed during the period of 1986–90. In particular, during this period, the bubble boom was spread widely over the economy as a whole, and contributed to the generation of vast tax increases and in higher rates of nominal GDP. As will be argued below, such windfall type tax increases greatly assisted in reducing fiscal deficits, leading to a successful achievement of the target of fiscal consolidation and no issuance of deficit-covering bonds. However, once again, the bond dependency ratio began to rise sharply after 1991, mainly reflecting the stagnant state of the post-bubble recession.

Fiscal consolidation (in more fashionable terms in Japan, fiscal reconstruction) became increasingly important as a major policy target since the mid-1970s. The first objective of eliminating the issuance of debt-covering bonds as a slogan of fiscal consolidation was achieved in fiscal 1989 with a lot of budgetary manoeuvres, mainly due to a massive amount of unintended increases in revenues from the bubble boom. After the collapse of the bubble, however, the fiscal deficit problem has grown worse once again, as mentioned repeatedly. The bond dependency ratio began to rise up, reaching 43.4 per cent in fiscal 1999.

As is evident from the major fact findings described above, Japan's fiscal deficit poses a serious problem today. For example, a recent OECD report states the following:

Once an economic recovery is under way, Japan's fiscal position will have to be greatly strengthened in order to arrest and reverse the rise of public debt to GDP. This requirement is particularly urgent in view of the expenditure pressures that will soon appear due to the ageing of the population (OECD 1995, p. xii).

This statement is certainly true. Japan's policy makers should follow this policy recommendation, although it is very difficult for them to determine when deficit-reduction measures can be embarked upon, given the weaker signs of economic recovery. No doubt, concerns that fiscal retrenchment may have a negative impact on economic activity and employment frequently lead them to act prudently. In addition, apart from such a difficult judgement, they will have to make politically hard decisions to restore a sound fiscal position because of unpopular policy proposals such as expenditure cuts, tax increases, or both. In Japan, however, the policy of aiming for a balance in the fiscal position will be an absolute requirement once the signs of economic recovery convincingly appear.

One of the chief reasons behind the necessity for fiscal consolidation reflects the fact that the current situation of Japan's deficits has already deteriorated to a greater extent than that of other major countries, as stressed earlier. As a matter of fact, it would be almost impossible for Japan to satisfy the Maastricht criteria if it were a relevant target. In Europe, members of the European Union have made political decisions regarding two reference criteria, to keep fiscal deficits in line with a 3 per cent or less for deficit–GDP ratio and a 60 per cent or less debt outstanding–GDP ratio. Any European country that wished to join the European Monetary Union (EMU) in 1999 had to meet these Maastricht criteria. Thus, the Maastricht criteria are regarded as international standards of restricting fiscal deficits, but unfortunately the current situation of Japan's fiscal position is far from achieving such a standard.

Now each country in Europe is making assiduous efforts towards fiscal consolidation. The pace at which stronger fiscal positions could be established may vary from one country to another, and additional fiscal actions are clearly needed to implement concrete criteria. It is, however, generally believed that early, decisive fiscal actions have improved credibility, decreasing risk premia on interest rates and reducing the cost of debt servicing.

Japan has so far been the major exception in making progress to reduce fiscal deficits for two main reasons. For one thing, a hesitant recovery after the bottoming out of the post-bubble recession has repeatedly required additional expansionary packages. The other is that Keynesian fiscal policy still dominates the policy-making process. No doubt, these have contributed to a deterioration of Japan's fiscal balance as described above.

THE BALANCED BUDGET PRINCIPLE AND ITS AFTERMATH

Budget Orthodoxy and Fiscal Performance
It is very important to analyse how the fiscal authority has behaved to manage fiscal policy and control the level of fiscal deficits in view of government fiscal activity. On

this point, great emphasis has been consistently placed on the balanced budget rule by the MOF from a standpoint of budget orthodoxy.

In the following discussion, let us focus on the definition of fiscal deficits in the *general account* of the national government budget, because fiscal behaviour can be expressed very well within this aspect of the budget. Prior to 1965, as seen in Table 6.1, no fiscal deficits had been incurred in the operation of fiscal policies. The MOF had strictly maintained a balanced budget policy.

The MOF's budgetary orthodoxy prior to 1965 seems to have been based upon the following three empirical rules (Ishi 1973):

1. a balanced budget;
2. a tax policy with a constant ratio of tax burden relative to national income;
3. an intended underestimation of the 'natural increase in tax revenues' caused by a growing economy.

The first rule, the balanced budget, has been the dominant characteristic of fiscal policy in post-war Japan accompanied by the additional two rules. The basis for this lies in the traditional view of 'sound' finance, that is, all current expenditures must be financed by current revenues in the government sector. Following this axiom, the issuing of national bonds during the post-war period was rigidly restricted by a statutory limit to 'construction bonds' by the Finance Law to prevent the easy use of deficit-covering bonds. This concern for a balanced budget had been the result of the extravagant government spending and the inflationary pressures which had been experienced in pre-war Japan. At the outset of the Dodge Plan,[1] the balanced budget was actually implemented at all levels of the government, that is, not only in the general account of national government but also in its special accounts, in other accounts of government-affiliated agencies, and in local governments.

However, the balanced budget policy had to be altered with the passage of time. Indeed, government guaranteed bonds in the Fiscal Investment and Loan Programme (FILP) and local government bonds gradually began to be issued. It was not until 1965 that national bonds were issued and a deficit appeared in the *general account*. Not even 'construction bonds' were issued prior to this date. Thus, we should note that the meaning of the term 'balanced budget' has been slightly changed as the post-war period progressed. Nevertheless, it cannot be denied that the balanced budget should be emphasized as the most fundamental rule of government fiscal policy. Even after the budget became unbalanced after 1965, the MOF has constantly stuck to its desirable goal of restoring a balanced budget.

The second empirical rule has been to keep the ratio of tax yields to national income constant (i.e. 20 per cent). This rule for tax policy had been adopted, especially in the period 1955–65. In a growing economy like that of post-war Japan, this rule leads to a large amount of tax reductions. In particular, individual and corporate income taxes

---

[1] The Dodge Plan was a programme for economic policy drawn up by Joseph M. Dodge, then advisor to the Allied Forces in Japan. Its conservative and stringent recommendations, which emphasized a balanced budget as an important measure to counter inflation, were implemented for a few years after 1949.

must be significantly reduced every year. Had tax reductions not been implemented, income taxation would have considerably overburdened the taxpayers. Therefore, to avoid the overburdening of taxpayers, income taxes had to be reduced successively almost every year (Ishi 1993, ch. 3).

In addition to these two rules, the intended underestimation of the natural increase in tax revenues must be referred to as the third empirical rule. It bears close relation to the two rules discussed above. Some tax revenues, such as that from individual income tax, naturally registers increases as the tax base expands with the growth of the economy even if there are no changes in the tax rate and exemptions. The higher the rate of economic growth, the larger the amount of natural increase in tax revenue that can be expected. In actuality, a large volume of natural tax increases was realized each fiscal year up to 1965 which provided a substantial amount of new financial resources in the preparation of the annual budget. That is to say, a portion of the natural tax increases was appropriated to the financing of tax reductions, and another was devoted to the financing of new expenditure programmes. Thus a big, expansion-minded budget was actually created by means of such a large natural increase in tax revenue, without creating the problem of fiscal deficits.

A question can be raised about the estimation of the natural tax increases. It is largely based on the anticipated rate of economic growth which is usually computed five or six months earlier than the beginning of the fiscal year (see Chapter 5). For an illustration, let us suppose that the GDP will expand by 12 per cent in the next year. Based upon this anticipated rate, the MOF usually estimates what the natural tax increases will be; for instance, more than 500 billion yen. In doing so, some non-economic factors may be easily introduced into the calculation to bias the anticipated rate of economic growth. In most cases, an intentional underestimation of the GNP growth rate was proposed in order to decrease the expected amount of the natural tax increase used as a financial resource at this stage of budgetary preparations. Thus, since at the end of each fiscal year, the realized rate of growth was always much higher than the anticipated rate (Figure 6.3), an enormous natural increase in tax revenues materialized during the intermediate term after the implementation of a new budget.

To sum up, the MOF's balanced budget policy played a dominant role in fiscal activities prior to 1965. The most important reason for this was that a rapid growth in GDP had constantly continued to provide enough increasing tax revenue to keep the general account of the national budget balanced. As a consequence, the MOF did not need to issue national bonds and was successfully able to sustain budgetary orthodoxy (for more detailed argument, see Chapter 7).

The exploding phenomenon of Japan's fiscal deficits accelerated since the late 1970s, as is evident from Table 6.1. When the government was compiling the national budget plan for fiscal 1977, there appeared to be a general consensus urging the need to achieve an economic balance at the sacrifice of fiscal balance. At that time, in order to stimulate the depressed state of the world economy, the so-called 'three engine countries' scheme was adopted by the Japanese government as a result of its obligation to international policy coordination with the USA and West Germany. On the other

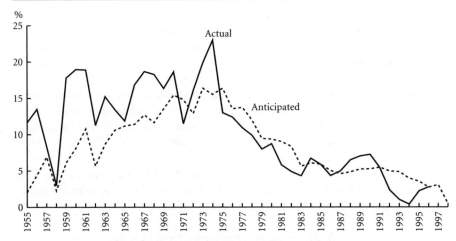

FIGURE 6.3. *Actual and anticipated rates of economic growth, 1955–98*
Source: MOF, National Budget; EPA, *Annual Report on National Accounts*
Note: In calculating the actual rate, SNA data are used after 1965

hand, the MOF was endeavouring to return to a balanced budget by stressing the importance of building the fiscal structure on the basis of sound fiscal operations. This policy is not a Japanese monopoly, and the fiscal authorities of the USA, the UK, Germany, and France have been adopting a similar stand. Why, then, are the fiscal authorities adhering to the principle of a balanced budget despite rising criticism?

The principle of a balanced budget is in opposition to Keynesian fiscal policy during the policy management phase. Under Keynesian policy, the government is called upon to manipulate the fiscal surplus or deficit in order to cope with a domestic business boom or slump. From this standpoint, a policy stance of the fiscal authority that attaches the highest importance to the balance of fiscal actions is considered excessively lukewarm. However, the theory that the policy prerequisite called fiscal policy could, in reality, function smoothly and efficiently could stand re-examination.

It is generally understood that the stabilizing effect of fiscal policy today is theoretically self-evident. Nevertheless, it seems that this has never been sufficiently utilized by fiscal authorities in any country. This is not because fiscal authorities have been ignorant of the theories, but because fiscal policy itself lacks adaptability to the real aspect of fiscal performance.

Japan's MOF has persistently entertained misgivings about the practical adaptability of fiscal policy in the following three phases. First, fiscal actions may be utilized as a measure for stimulating business. However, it may not be easily and effectively adopted in reverse to restrict business. The fiscal restriction of the business environment inevitably invites an increase in taxes and a decrease in government expenditure. Such an unpopular policy cannot be easily adopted, particularly when the political situation becomes unstable.

Secondly, under the circumstances, it is feared that an excessive fiscal deficit will ensue. Some argue that a fiscal deficit caused by a programme for stimulating business can be erased by the natural increase in tax revenue resulting from the improvement in business. However, the timing and the size of such a natural increase are not guaranteed.

Thirdly, the departure from a balanced budget is liable to obstruct resource allocation, the intrinsic function of fiscal operations. This principal function of fiscal operations to allocate limited resources efficiently without extravagance takes precedence over the economic stabilizing function, except under extraordinary circumstances, such as an acute recession.

The principle of a balanced budget should not be abandoned unconditionally when such adverse events take place, although it is stressed that the adjustment of business conditions through fiscal operations is extremely important.[2]

The Main Causes of Expanding Fiscal Deficits

Fiscal deficits began to expand rapidly after the first oil shock in 1973, and the situation worsened at the outbreak of the second oil crisis in 1979. The MOF made a great effort to restrict the bond dependency ratio to below 30 per cent in preparing the initial budget, but finally the effort failed. It is clear that the MOF has been reluctant to allow the pursuit of persistent deficit financing, as is evident from the past trend of fiscal deficits (Ishi 1986a). At the outset, national bonds were issued in accordance with the 'construction bond rule' which was strictly adhered to in each year before 1975. However, with the massive amount of bond flotation described above, the government was compelled to abandon this rule. Debt-covering bonds began to be issued on a large scale in both the 1975 supplementary budget and the 1976 budget, as noted above. In addition, the flotation of debt-covering bonds has continued to expand as if they were a regular financial source contrary to 'the construction bond rule'.

What, then, were the main causes of the sharp rise in fiscal deficits in the past? Particular attention should be paid to two periods: 1975–79 and 1991–96, when the bond dependency ratio expanded tremendously. A number of factors are considered to have been behind the rapid expansion of fiscal deficits in these periods, but the following two are most important.

First of all, emphasis should be given to the requirement to implement fiscal expansionary policies to stimulate the conspicuous slowdown of Japanese economic

---

[2] In this context, two compromise plans were advocated some time ago. The first plan calls for balancing fiscal operations on the basis of full employment. This is the important concept of full employment surplus (see, for instance, Okun 1971; Okun and Teeters 1970). The second plan aims at achieving a budget balance within a radius of one business cycle featured by a boom and a slump. The latter plan is considered to be a helpful suggestion for Japan. Generally called the 'Swedish Formula', this plan calls for erasing the deficit in the recession period with a surplus in the boom period. Whether this plan would function practically depends upon whether the fiscal operation may be applied for tightening business and whether the natural increase in income from tax in the boom period may be reserved as a fiscal surplus (Mydrdal 1939; Hart 1961).

growth, caused by the two oil shocks in the late 1970s and the collapse of the bubble in the early 1990s. Massive expansionary measures in light of public investment have been triggered during the periods under consideration, leaving vast fiscal deficits in its wake. Also, prolonged recessions accompanied by lower growth rates tended to produce large revenue shortages in the budget, which in turn accelerated the increasing tempo of fiscal deficits (Ishi 1982*a*).

As for the second factor explaining the large increases in fiscal deficits, we should take note of the expanded role that the Japanese government has played with respect to income maintenance, free health care, education, etc. This is particularly related to the first hump in the dependency ratio which occurred in the late 1970s. In the early 1970s, important institutional reforms were completed in the social security system as part of a programme to construct a welfare state in Japan. The target was to catch up with the Western level of social welfare programmes in public pensions, medical care, etc. It was generally pointed out that Japan had lagged behind Western countries in the development of social welfare policies. Ironically, it was in 1973 that new social welfare programmes were launched and they were expanded to match those in other countries. Therefore, 1973 is often called 'the first year of constructing the welfare state' (Noguchi 1983).

Although many new social programmes were built into the system at that time, it had been expected that the high rate of growth would continue in the future and would thus generate the additional resources needed to finance this higher public expenditure. Unfortunately, in the decade that followed 1973, the rate of growth fell considerably in Japan, as well as in most industrial countries.

Since 1973, in spite of reduced growth rates, the prevailing mood of the time created high expectations of the role that the government should play beyond its public sector activity. The boundaries of what was considered as justifiable public sector intervention were progressively pushed outward. The greater subsidization of public services, or even their free provision, made them cheap for the users, thus increasing the demand for them. People came to feel that they almost had a natural right to use cheap or free public services. In a democratic society where election campaigns are constantly needed for reelection, the political process generally favoured the expansion of public provision.

If the cost of the public provision had been totally covered by ordinary revenues, there would have been no problem in providing increased public services. However, while the electorate pushed for higher spending, it was far less supportive of the tax increases that would have been needed to finance that spending. To make matters worse, as noted below, tax revenues were substantially reduced, reflecting the slowdown in economic growth. The gap between government spending and revenue grew, contributing eventually to the higher level of fiscal deficits.

It seems that these two factors can explain why large increases in fiscal deficits tend to be common among major industrial countries, including the USA and Japan. The question is how this problem should be solved in each country.

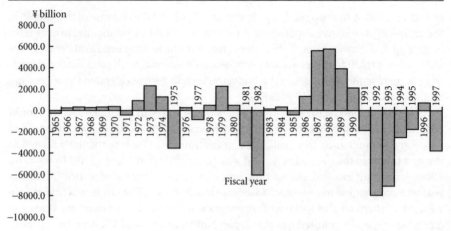

FIGURE 6.4. *Tax revenue shortages and surpluses, 1965–97*

Source: MOF, Tax Bureau, *Primary Statistics of Taxation*, each year

Note: Tax revenue shortages are defined as a negative gap between settlement revenues at the end of the fiscal year and the initial budgeted revenues in the scope of general account, while a positive gap indicates a surplus

Fiscal Deficits Caused by Tax Shortages

In addition to the above two policy measures as explanatory factors of expanded deficits, we must pay special attention to tax revenue shortages which automatically occurred during recessionary periods. Deficit financing is practically the only means available for dealing with revenue shortages. As a consequence, it is necessary to examine the nature and causes of the tax shortages in order to understand why deficits have been piling up since the debt explosion started in the 1970s.

By definition, a tax shortage is a shortfall in the tax revenue at the end of the year as compared with the amount of revenue forecast in the year's initial budget. Figure 6.4 shows the tax shortages and surpluses that have been recorded in Japan since fiscal 1965 in the national government. Fiscal deficits were virtually insignificant in the period of rapid growth, which lasted until the early 1970s, so consequently neither were tax revenue shortages. The only two exceptions were fiscal 1965 when a deficit of ¥238 billion was recorded, and fiscal 1971 when the shortfall amounted to ¥365 billion. These occurrences were closely tied with recessions.

During the mid-1970s, however, tax shortages began to take on serious proportions. The stagnation of the Japanese economy in fiscal 1975 following the first oil crisis resulted in a colossal shortfall of ¥3.6 trillion. Then the second oil crisis plunged Japan into economic recession again, bringing about the large revenue shortages of the early 1980s.

We can observe that huge tax surpluses have been incurred in the second half of the 1980s during the bubble boom, and that the situation turned to the reverse in the early 1990s as the bubble phenomenon burst. Evidently, tax revenue surpluses and shortages have been closely related to the variation in fiscal deficits, with a few exceptions.

Tax shortages have conventionally been attributed to a slowdown in the growth rate of the Japanese economy, but this interpretation is not entirely correct. The basic cause of shortages has been exaggerated predictions of the growth rate. Although separate estimates of revenue are compiled for each category of taxes, these estimates are based largely on the growth rate forecast in the economic outlook that the government releases at the end of every calendar year when it has almost finished compiling the next fiscal year's budget draft. Individual income and corporate taxes, which account for a major proportion of the revenue, are directly influenced by the growth rate. If the actual growth rate is lower than the forecast rate, the result is a tapering off of revenue during the year.

If we compare Figures 6.3 and 6.4, we can see that the unrealistically high growth expectations in 1971, 1975, 1977, 1981–82 and 1991–94 correspond to years of a tax shortfall. The important issue here is that the government has consistently over-estimated the growth rate since the mid-1970s except during the bubble period of 1987–90. We cannot gloss over this failure of the EPA's planners to estimate the growth rate accurately at the beginning each year. In view of the fact that exaggerated estimates of the growth rate are the prime cause of tax shortages, we must ask why this pattern has been repeated year after year.

Perhaps at times the forecasting problems have been purely technical in nature or due to unforeseen factors. However, if political motives are also involved, it would mean that, to some extent, past tax shortages were artificially created phenomena, not unavoidable and unpredictable deficits. For instance, we could conceive that this was the situation that arose during the process of compiling the budget for fiscal 1982. This view that exaggerated estimates of the growth rate by the government were politically motivated was beginning to gain a wide following. Unrealistic revenue estimates based on an excessively high growth rate made compilation of the fiscal 1982 budget easier, preserving a considerable amount of expenditure in areas of lower priority. Over-estimation of revenue made it possible to avert demands for drastic expenditure cuts. During the Diet debate on the 1982 budget, the opposition parties repeatedly pointed out that the revenue estimates were too high. Merely by recalling what happened in the Diet, we can see that revenue estimates for that year were considered excessive even while the budget was being compiled. Thus the fiscal 1982 revenue shortage was an anticipated result (Ishi 1982a, p. 10; Hollerman 1988, p. 95). The same phenomena have, more or less, occurred when anticipated rates of growth were higher than actual rates in the past years.

Obviously, the flotation of deficit-covering bonds is closely linked to tax shortages. Avoiding tax shortages is one way of reducing deficits. It will, however, be virtually impossible to eliminate shortfalls altogether because unforeseeable movements in economic conditions occur from time to time. Still, it should be possible to reduce shortfalls to a considerable extent by breaking the chain linking the overly high economic growth predictions with unrealistic estimates of tax revenue.

Lower revenue estimates necessitate greater strictness in the compilation of budgets. This strictness is, in fact, exactly what is needed for fiscal consolidation. It might even be advisable for forecasts of economic growth to be made to err on the low side and for tax revenue to be estimated conservatively. Even if the actual economic growth rate were to exceed the prediction—leading to a revenue surplus such as those seen during the 1960s, early 1970s, and the late 1980s—the extra funds could easily be used to reduce national bond issues.

Conflict between the Keynesian View and the MOF's View

Before 1973 when the first oil shock occurred, the government had almost never needed to employ expansionary fiscal policies in order to stimulate the Japanese economy. In fact, with a few exceptions, no Keynesian policies were required, reflecting the buoyancy of aggregate demand (Ackley and Ishi 1976).

However, the oil shock caused real income to fall to a great extent, not only in Japan but also in the rest of the world. Most countries fell into a depressed economic state with rampant inflation. The USA, West Germany and Japan were urged to take expansionary measures in accordance with the new idea of them being the 'three locomotive countries', as described earlier. In 1978, the Japanese government constructed a very stimulating budget in light of the large increases in public investment to expand the stagnant economy in the world. This experience is regarded as the first introduction of Keynesian fiscal policy to Japan.

With a background of prolonged recessions since the oil shock, fiscal activism in favour of stimulative measures began to emerge as a powerful device for attaining full employment. As a consequence, fiscal deficits became a means of achieving this objective. The same holds for the case of anti-recessionary policies after the collapse of the bubble in the early 1990s. In parallel with the expansion of the welfare programme as stated earlier, such fiscal activism clearly played a vital role in increasing the huge level of fiscal deficit. Faced with the continued rise of national bond issues, the economists views were divided into two groups, one being Keynesian, and the other anti-Keynesian.

The Keynesian group is generally composed of specialists majoring in macroeconomics, or the staff at MITI, the MOC, or the EPA. The Keynesians usually push the government to take on an expansionary budget, say, in the form of tax cuts and increases in public investment. Their target for achieving rates of real growth is always higher than the government's officially anticipated figure, mainly because they believe that the potential path of Japan's economic growth should be higher. As a consequence, the Keynesian groups too often ignore the accumulative effects of a chain of fiscal deficits. They feel optimistic about debt accumulation, which would naturally be reduced by the generation of tax revenues in a growing economy. According to the Keynesian view in Japan, it is more important to achieve a higher rate of growth than to eliminate fiscal deficits.

On the other hand, there is an opposing view, contrary to the Keynesian view, which is strongly supported by public finance specialists or the MOF staff. They compose the anti-Keynesian group. Generally speaking, a traditional embarrassment of fiscal deficits and growing public debts seems to be quite common to this group. They place more emphasis on the traditional principles of sound finance, that is, no deficit is justified if it is associated with unproductive investments, or current expenditures, or if permanent differences between expenditure and revenues result. In the view of the anti-Keynesian group, a fiscal deficit may be beneficial with respect to this year's economic performance especially when the economy is working at less than full capacity, but it may be harmful with reference to future economic performance if it leads to excessive increases in public debt. Thus, they are usually worried about debt accumulation, and emphasize the necessity of reducing it.

These two views, which are quite different with regards to debt accumulation, have conflicted with each over the past decades. Relatively speaking, the present author supports the anti-Keynesian position, although I admit the necessity of stimulating the economy by issuing national bonds in a severe depression. It seems to me that the present fiscal deficits are growing beyond acceptable cyclical deficits. If deficits were mostly cyclical, they would grow during recessions and swing into surpluses during the recovery period. This being the case, the public debt would not accumulate over time. The present situation seems to be different; today's deficits are not cyclical but structural. Structural deficits would remain 'high' even if full employment is achieved.

Also, the interest rate on national bonds has exceeded the nominal growth rate of GDP for the past several years. For example, the latter is estimated to be 3.5 per cent for 1996–2000 by the new economic plan of the EPA,[3] while the former has been fixed at about 5 per cent in recent years in order that the bonds sell well in the market. In accordance with the famous Domar model (Domar 1944), from a theoretical point of view, the ratio of interest payments to nominal GNP will not converge if the present rates of economic growth or interest rates continue. This being the case, it may be argued that a large debt at present would eventually bankrupt the government.

STRATEGIES FOR DEFICIT REDUCTION

Why is Deficit Reduction Necessary?

It is often argued that fiscal deficits need to be curtailed when accumulated, not only because of their harmful effect on the economic performance of a nation, but also because of the burden on the budget and future generations caused by interest payments on the public debt (see, for instance, Buchanan 1958).

Theoretically speaking, there are three negative effects on the macro-side of the economy derived from the expansion of fiscal deficits;

1. inflation;
2. a crowding-out effect in the fund markets;
3. currency depreciation.

[3] In 1995, the EPA published a new economic plan entitled the *Social and Economic Plan for Structural Reforms* to cover the period of five years from 1996 to 2000. Two kinds of average growth rates of real and nominal GDP (both are estimated to be the same) are presented as follows: 3.5 per cent with structural reforms, and 1.75 per cent without structural reforms.

These damages have in practice occurred during the past economic performance of major countries, such as the USA, the UK, France, Germany, etc. For instance, Germany has been constantly concerned with the potential inflation caused by accumulated debt in the past. France is suffering from a high rate of interest and crowding out in the fund markets after fiscal deficits have expanded rapidly. Moreover, all European countries are embarrassed about their currency depreciation due to a weakening of their credibility resulting from expanded debt. That is the reason why each country has been worried about the current debt accumulation and has embarked on its own deficit reduction, as argued earlier.[4]

By contrast, in contemporary Japan, fiscal deficits are not likely to induce possible harmful effects on the economy as a whole. In particular, it has generally been argued that Japan is still maintaining the highest rate of saving among major countries. This argument would perhaps have been supported in the 1970s and 1980s. For instance, in terms of the personal saving rate in 1983, Japan had 17.3 per cent while West Germany had 11.4 per cent, France 11.5 per cent, the USA 5 per cent, and the UK 7 per cent. The extent to which fiscal deficits crowd out private investment depend on the rate of personal saving of the country. A country like Japan with a high rate of personal saving that exceeds its domestic investment opportunities can easily finance its own investment as well as its fiscal deficit. This is to be contrasted with the US experience in which an increasing share of savings has been appropriated to fiscal deficits because of a very low saving rate.

However, Japan's advantage has begun to disappear in recent years. In fact, the personal saving rates in Japan, the UK, France, and Germany—excluding the USA—ranged between 13–15 per cent in 1992 (Tachi 1995, p. 304.) It is difficult to find evidence of Japan's superior position in terms of its personal saving rate in recent years. Furthermore, it is pointed out that Japan's saving rate will begin to diminish to a considerable extent from around 2005 when the baby-boomers begin to retire from their jobs (see, for example, Group of Ten 1995).[5]

In addition, the sharp rise in debt redemption and interest payments caused by an accumulating debt poses serious problems to the performance of government fiscal activity. As observed in Table 6.2, large increases in national bond flotations have made national debt service and interest payments by far the fastest growing component of public expenditure. This was true at least until the burst of the bubble. If we examine the movement of interest payments as a percentage of public expenditure in the *general account*, we note that it has increased rapidly since the balanced budget principle had to be abandoned. In 1971, for example, interest payments were 2.2 per cent of public expenditures, while by 1987 this payment increased over 7.5 times,

[4] See Ishi (ed.) 1996*b*. In this volume a number of overseas interviews, in which I myself participated during 1995–96, are included.
[5] Furthermore, C. Horioka's analyses should be noted. He is trying to explain that Japan's high savings rate among households has so far been dependent on the younger age group, but that it will decline as the population is ageing, in favour of the life-cycle model (Horioka 1996; Horioka *et al.* 1996.) See, for another interesting paper, Kawasaki 1986.

TABLE 6.2. *National debt charges and interest payments, 1971–2000*

Fiscal year	Debt services (¥ billion)	Interest payment (¥ billion)	As a percentage of general account expenditure	
			Debt Services (%)	Interest Payment (%)
1971	319.3	203.0	3.4	2.2
1972	455.4	313.9	4.0	2.7
1973	704.5	448.1	4.9	3.1
1974	862.2	574.7	5.0	3.4
1975	1,039.4	733.5	4.9	3.4
1976	1,664.7	1,328.9	6.9	5.5
1977	2,348.7	1,931.6	8.2	6.8
1978	3,222.7	2,628.0	9.4	7.7
1979	4,078.4	3,339.8	10.6	8.7
1980	5,310.4	4,417.3	12.5	10.4
1981	6,654.2	5,565.3	14.2	11.9
1982	7,829.9	6,465.0	15.8	13.0
1983	8,192.5	7,905.0	16.3	15.7
1984	9,155.1	8,865.7	18.1	17.5
1985	10,224.1	9,878.5	19.5	18.8
1986	11,319.5	10,604.8	20.9	19.6
1987	11,333.5	10,942.8	20.9	20.2
1988	11,512.0	11,082.7	20.3	19.5
1989	11,664.9	11,132.1	19.3	18.4
1990	14,288.6	11,069.4	21.6	16.7
1991	16,036.0	11,930.1	22.8	17.0
1992	16,447.3	12,125.7	22.8	16.8
1993	15,442.3	11,661.4	21.3	16.1
1994	14,360.2	11,587.5	19.6	15.9
1995	13,221.3	11,650.5	18.6	16.4
1996	16,375.2	11,830.2	21.8	15.8
1997	16,802.3	11,818.4	21.7	15.3
1998	18,150.0	11,399.7	23.4	14.7
1999	19,831.9	11,562.9	24.2	14.4
2000	11,050.9	10,743.2	25.8	12.6

Source: Data from Ministry of Finance.

Note: Figures are all from the initial budget of each year. National debt charges contain both debt redemption and interest payments.

reaching 20.2 per cent. Thereafter, this ratio has begun to slow down to 16.4 per cent in 1995 and 12.6 per cent in 2000, reflecting both the effects of deficit reduction during the bubble period and the lower rates of interest. However, it will turn upward again, and will grow swiftly, given the continued accumulation of fiscal deficits in the future. The same holds true for the long-run trend of national debt services, which has

TABLE 6.3. *The results of generational accounting in Japan (¥ thousand)*

Generational age in 1992	Present value of net burden	
	case 1	case 2
Over 60	−66,669	−52,526
50–59	−7,656	−15,221
40–49	9,625	9,976
30–39	20,734	26,490
20–29	26,266	37,322
Future generation	39,674	—
Difference from age 20–29	13,408	—

Source: Economic Planning Agency, *Economic Survey, Fiscal 1995*.

Note: The results in case 1 estimate merely the future net burden, excluding the past burden and benefit, while those in case 2 include them.

expanded sharply from 3.4 per cent in 1971 to 25.8 per cent in 2000. This growth will swell public expenditure, increasing the relative portion of entitlements in the total, which will essentially make budgeting more rigid every year. In Japan, such rigidity in the budget is considered to be a serious problem, related to expanded deficits. No doubt, fiscal deficits are feeding upon themselves through the interest component of public expenditure, making their curtailment more difficult.

Apart from such in-budget difficulties, the expanded deficits tend to generate another issue, that of intergenerational inequity, that is the future tax burden which will arise from redemption and interest payments. Although controversial arguments have been repeated regarding the shifting of the public debt burden to future generations, it would not be unreasonable to conjecture that future generations should certainly bear the burden of public debt through possible tax increases (see, for example, Buchanan 1958; Wiseman 1984).

In recent years, special attention has been paid to the generational accounting approach to calculate how much future generations will have to pay in net burdens (i.e. tax and social security contributions) as compared to today's generation (Kotlikoff 1992). The concept of generational accounting originally emerged as an alternative measure of the deficit. Alternatively, generational accounting would be of great use in calculating the intergenerational burdens implied by the current tax and spending policies. Thus, relevant calculations have begun to appear in relation to a number of countries, such as Sweden (see, for instance, Hhagemann and John 1995).

In Japan, the EPA calculates the result of generational accounts, as seen in Table 6.3, broadening the coverage of estimation to include not only future but also past burden–benefit relations. There are a couple of interesting points worth noting. First, the size of the net burden varies with age, with the generation over the ages of 50 and 60 enjoying a net benefit, rather than a net burden. On the other hand, the younger generation—under the age of 40—must pay more taxes and social security contributions than they will receive in public services over their lifetime, to a great extent.

Second, the net burden on future generations would be the largest among all age groups, with future generations paying an additional ¥13,408 thousand as compared with that of the youngest current generation in their 20s. This result is important in our context, because the accumulated debt is assumed to be borne by future generations. No doubt, it is conjectured that the public debt burden could be shifted to future generations in Japan, given the current budgetary system.

Given both the macro and micro effects, currently and in the future, of accumulated debt, it is very clear that the Japanese government should launch a programme to reduce fiscal deficits and to restrain the rise of the outstanding debt relative to the general economic activity in the nation.

A Strategy for Fiscal Consolidation

Since the public debt has begun to accumulate to some extent, greater importance has been placed every year on the establishment of specific targets for deficit reduction, or at least within certain periods in major countries. For instance in the USA, the federal government enacted the Omnibus Budget Reconciliation Act (OBRA) in 1990 and in 1993 expenditure cuts were made by imposing so-called 'caps' (upper ceilings) to restrain deliberate (non-entitlement) expenditures within a fixed limit (i.e. average growth rates of 0.1 per cent in real terms). Furthermore, an attempt to restore the budget balance by 2002 was established in fiscal 1995 by the Presidential Budget Statement and Budget Resolution, although strategies for expenditure cuts are different among the Democrats and the Republicans. As a consequence, government shutdowns were incurred twice in 1995. In addition to setting forth caps on deliberate expenditures, the pay-as-you-go rule[6] was permanently introduced to maintain a fixed level of entitlement expenditure to recover the balance of the federal budget.

Likewise, the UK government has attempted to restrain the real growth rate of general government expenditure to less than 1.5 per cent every year under the total control scheme which was executed in 1993. In Germany, the ratio of general government expenditure to GDP is targeted for reduction to 46 per cent (i.e. Germany's pre-unification level) by the year 2000 with a simultaneous reduction of 1 per cent in the deficit–GDP ratio. In addition, the tax burden relative to GDP ought to be lowered to 23.5 per cent by the year 2000. These targets are included in the *Mid-term Fiscal Strategy* of the Federal Ministry of Finance. The French government also constructed targets for reducing the deficit ratio by 1 per cent each year by fiscal 1997 in order to satisfy the 3 per cent target in the Maastricht criterion.

Similar to the strategies for deficit reduction in other major countries, the Japanese government established a target for fiscal consolidation: zero dependency on deficit-covering bonds by a specific year. The first target was set to eliminate deficit-covering

---

[6] Any increases in entitled expenditure should be ensured either by relevant tax increases or by across-the-board expenditure cuts. Hence the use of the term 'pay-as-you-go', which indicates that we are using here quite a different system from that implied by an unfounded pension fund.

TABLE 6.4. *The guideline of ceilings for budget requests, 1982–99*

Fiscal year	Ceiling		Ad hoc expenditure scheme (¥ billion)	NTT scheme (¥ billion)
	Current expenditure	Investment expenditure		
1982	0% increase			
1983	5% decrease	0% increase		
1984–87	10% decrease	5% decrease		
1988–90	10% decrease	0% increase		1,300
1991	10% decrease	0% increase	Enhancement of the quality of life 200	
1992	10% decrease	0% increase	1) Enhancement of the quality of life 200	1,300
			2) Promotion of public investment 200	
1993	10% decrease	0% increase	3) Enhancement of the quality of life 250	
			4) Promotion of public investment 200	
			5) Improvement of R&D 110	1,300
			6) Repayment to NTT scheme 80	
1994	10% decrease	5% decrease	Repayment to NTT scheme 290	1,300
1995	10% decrease	5% decrease	Promotion of public investment 300	1,300
1996	10% decrease	5% decrease	1) Fundamentals of economic development and R&D 140	1,300
			2) Promotion of public investment 300	
1997	15% decrease in non-entitlements 12% decrease in the rest	0% increase	Provisional measures for economic structural reform 300	1,300
1998	Cappings in the Fiscal Structural Reform Act (see Tables 6.5 & 6.6)			171.5
1999	Suspension in the FSRA, and removal in cappings		Special frame for economic recovery 400	159.5

Source: Data from the Ministry of Finance.

bonds as a source of financial revenue by the end of fiscal 1980, reflecting the rapid expansion of fiscal deficits in the late 1970s. However, the government failed to achieve its initial target for fiscal consolidation, given the state of over-expanded fiscal deficits. Thus, the government had to continue its efforts for expenditure cuts towards the second goal of fiscal 1984.

However, it also proved impossible to achieve the second target, that of avoiding the issuance of deficit-covering bonds within the period, mainly because a massive revenue shortage emerged from the world recession after the second oil shock. Once again the government was forced to set a third target to restore the budget balance by fiscal 1990. Fortunately the new goal was achieved in fiscal 1990 by employing a wind-fall increase of tax revenue due to the bubble boom, as will be argued in detail shortly.

In the process of fiscal consolidation, a guideline for budget requests was adopted from the second half of the 1970s. The guideline for expenditure cuts is the 'ceiling' strategy. In the course of preparing the budget, usually at the end of August of the previous year, the MOF sets a maximum ceiling for the budget requests of all ministries and agencies for the next fiscal year. Table 6.4 summarizes the guidelines in the 1980s when the ceiling strategy began to be applied strictly to government expenditures. A 'zero ceiling' means that budget requests are to be frozen at the level of budget appropriations for the previous fiscal year, and a 'negative' ceiling implies that the request must stay below the preceding year's budget allocations. During the period of rapid economic growth in the 1960s, even 30–50 per cent increases were sometimes allowed for budget requests as a whole, in sharp contrast to the situation in the 1980s.

With the fully-fledged introduction of the ceiling strategy, some categories of government expenditure have been held to the levels of the previous budget from fiscal 1978, and furthermore no increase has been allowed for any non-entitlement spending categories since the fiscal 1982 budget under the zero ceiling. Finally, a negative ceiling was adopted in the fiscal 1983 and 1984 budgets. The 1985–91 budgets were drawn up under the negative ceiling strategy with some exceptional cases for investment expenditure.

While the zero and negative ceilings were introduced into current and investment expenditure, an ad hoc allotment scheme has been applied to specific areas of expenditure on items which are generally considered to be of more importance, and this is kept separate from other expenditure. For example, certain lump-sum funds were allocated to the expenditure for enhancing the quality of life in 1991–93 and for the promotion of public investment in 1992–96. As noted below, similar financial resources under the NTT (Nippon Telegraph and Telephone) scheme have been given to certain public work projects on an ad hoc basis since 1988.

Since the ceiling strategy was introduced in the budgetary process, the government has succeeded in keeping the budget from growing, despite strong requests for budget increases from political interest groups, many ministries, and agencies.

As Figure 6.5 depicts, the rise in non-entitlement government expenditure, which exceeded 20 per cent per annum in some years during the rapid growth period, has slowed to less than 10 per cent per year since fiscal 1981. Of the various expenditure

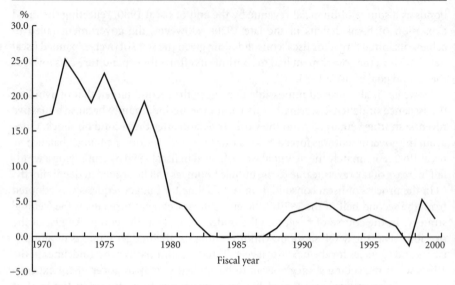

FIGURE 6.5. *Percentage changes in non-entitlement government expenditures*
over the preceding fiscal year, 1970–2000

Source: As Figure 6.4

Note: The figure for fiscal 2000 is based on the initial budget

categories, national debt services and tax-share grants to local governments are 'entitled' or not subject to expenditure cuts. Thus, the targets of the MOF's proposed expenditure cuts are other 'non-entitlement' government expenditure. Indeed, these expenditures have shown virtually zero growth in the mid-1980s, and thereafter their growth rates have been restrained to one-digit increases. However, a substantial rise in such expenditures have begun once again, reflecting the adoption of fiscal expansion in the early 1990s. The minus percentage in fiscal 1998 reflects the impact of fiscal structural reform, as will be argued shortly.

Figure 6.5 may be misleading. It is drawn using conventional non-entitlement government expenditures within the scope of the *general account,* but in the 1980s fiscal 'window-dressing' became prevalent on the expenditure side of the budget. To restrain the growth rate of non-entitlement expenditures to zero, fiscal 'window-dressing' on the expenditure side became more significant every year. It takes the form of excluding various categories of expenditure from the general account budget which should correctly be assigned there. For instance, a portion of the transfers to the social insurance accounts has been postponed, not appropriated. This represents borrowing which should be included in the expenditure side of the current fiscal year. In general, the MOF was successful in making the true expenditure position obscure and fostering the impression of adherence to 'fiscal consolidation with expenditure cuts' to the public.

The Rincho *and Administrative Reform*

Since the deficits in Japan are largely structural, they have to be reduced through basic changes in the level and pattern of public expenditure and in the tax system. In this case, it seems that a Keynesian type of policy cannot be of any help in reducing fiscal deficits. Keynesian policies are merely temporary, stop-gap measures. Of course, stop-gap measures help in reducing debt accumulation, but they do not bring a permanent solution to fiscal unbalance. Permanent solutions require permanent measures. Structural reforms become necessary when debt accumulation results from structural deficits.

Keynesian policies may be able to bring about a short-run reduction in the public debt through the natural increase of taxes generated by a higher rate of growth. However, they will not cure the disease of debt accumulation. Furthermore, we must note that economic reality since the oil shocks dictates that there will be no more continued high-speed expansion of business conditions. Given the future performance of the economy, tax revenue on a large enough scale to automatically reduce the accumulation of public debt could not be expected. The scenario drawn by the Keynesians is not likely to be realized.

Since the emergence of the public debt explosion in the late 1970s, the much needed reductions in Japan's huge fiscal deficits have progressed at only a snail's pace in the early 1980s because political considerations and other factors prevented the government from implementing either fully-fledged tax increases or expenditure cuts. The fiscal deficits afflicting Japan and many of the advanced countries were caused by structural and not cyclical factors.

Structural fiscal deficits can be eliminated only by sweeping reforms in both the expenditure and revenue structures. On this point, the new strategy of 'administrative reform' which the government adopted in 1981 can be highly recommended as the proper policy choice in Japan. At first, the government intended to contain the size of the fiscal deficits by tax increases, rather than expenditure cuts. In fact, the introduction of a new value-added tax (VAT), called the *general consumption tax*, was attempted by then Prime Minister Ohira in 1979, but it was a complete failure. As a result, it became politically very difficult to introduce enough tax increases to reduce the public debt, and the government had to change its policy stance from a reliance on tax increases to one on expenditure cuts (Lincoln 1988, ch. 3; Ishi 1993, ch. 15).

In particular, the Ad Hoc Committee for Administrative Reform (The Rinji Gyosei Kaikaku Chosakaior, or *Rincho* for short), established in 1981, had been playing an important role, backed by nation-wide support, in preventing the government from growing further. The *Rincho* recommended expenditure cuts and reviewed the activities and functions of government-affiliated institutions under the slogan of 'fiscal consolidation without tax increases'. As argued earlier, in accordance with the *Rincho* activities, the government set a maximum ceiling on the increase in public expenditures relative to the previous year for the compilation of the new budget every fiscal year. No doubt, this 'ceiling' method was supported and intensified by the *Rincho*.

The main aim of the *Rincho* was to promote administrative reform in order to solve Japan's fiscal crisis, which was at the core of the *Rincho*'s concerns. The *Rincho* embraced two other goals, that of reconstructing the fiscal structure and reducing the size of the government, as expounded in yet another slogan: 'small government'. When Prime Minister Zenko Suzuki established the *Rincho* in March 1981, he declared that he would stake his political life on the achievement of administrative reform, in particular pledging that he would restore a balanced budget by fiscal 1984. However, as previously mentioned, he decided to resign as prime minister in July 1982, mainly due to his failure to attain fiscal consolidation by the proposed deadline.

Administrative reform was widely approved by the general public, but inside the government it was true that both the bureaucrats and the politicians did not really want administrative reform and tried to avoid any significant changes. Strong resistance to such new reform was persistently shown to the members of the *Rincho*. Needless to say, the *Rincho* proposed various fundamental reforms which threatened to curtail certain ministerial privileges, and also to shift the relative distribution of ministerial power. In turn, politicians and vested-interest groups related to the relevant ministries and agencies were also threatened by the *Rincho* movement. They became allies when pressure had to be placed on the government to maintain their individual interests, although it was difficult to protest overtly against administrative reform. In other words, the typical tactic was 'to convey gestures of agreement in principle, but to disagree with the particulars' (*soron-sansei, kakuron-hantai*).

Despite such struggles among the individuals concerned, administrative reform, since its debut, has played a vital role in restricting the rise of government expenditure. In total, the level of non-entitlement government expenditure began to show a sharply decreasing tempo, as seen in Figure 6.5. In fact, the government's effort to restrict expenditure by imposing a strict ceiling strategy towards the ultimate goal of 'fiscal consolidation without tax increases' performed well in achieving its initial objective. All ministries and agencies slashed their budget requests to the minimum tolerable level. The government was compelled to revise laws and institutional systems to reduce expenditure. For example, two fiscal reforms were important. First, in fiscal 1984, the national health insurance system was revised to cut medical expenses to a certain extent. Secondly, in fiscal 1985, some of the national government grant-in-aids to local governments were scaled back. Both measures represented drastic fiscal reforms by traditional Japanese standards, and they seem to have been feasible only under the ceiling and the prevailing mood of administrative reform.

Although it sounds like an innocuous name, apart from the mere administrative formalities, administrative reform contained a broader scope for political and economic reforms as well. The most noteworthy accomplishments of the process of administrative reform were evidently in the move towards privatizing three public corporations on the basis of recommendations presented by the *Rincho* in 1982. In April 1985, both the Nippon Telegraph and Telephone Public Corporation, and the Japan Tobacco and Salt Public Corporation were simultaneously privatized to become the privately incorporated companies of NTT and JT (Japan Tobacco Inc).

Furthermore, in April 1987, the Japanese National Railroad (JNR) was also reorganized and split into seven regional companies for passenger transportation as the Japan Railway (JR).

In view of fiscal consolidation, great importance was attached to the JNR reform which was the *Rincho*'s chief priority. The JNR had continued to accumulate deficits since 1970, which had to be compensated by tax revenues from the national budget. The accumulated deficit was largely attributed to labour struggles, inefficient management, unprofitable local lines, and so on. Thus, the privatization of JNR into JR greatly contributed to restoring the budgetary balance (for an expanded discussion see Hollermman 1988, ch. 4).

NTT Scheme and Public Investment

When the Nippon Telegraph and Telephone Public Corporation was privatized into NTT in April 1985, two-thirds of its stock could be sold in the market, with revenues to be appropriated for the redemption of national bonds issued by the government in the past. At the outset they were reverted into the Special Account for the National Debt Consolidation Fund, and then a substantial amount of funds began to accumulate in this special account through the favourable sale of NTT stock in the market from fiscal 1986 to fiscal 1988.[7] Total revenues of about ¥10,000 billion were generated from the stock sales during these years.

Thus, a new scheme named the NTT programme was established by using the accumulated funds to promote the enhancement of social infrastructure in the fiscal 1988 budget. This was a device established to improve the level of social infrastructure in the midst of falling financial sources for public investment due to the ongoing process of fiscal consolidation. The revenues from the sale of NTT stock were appropriated for making interest-free loans, despite the fact that they were legally required to be employed for the redemption of national bonds. No doubt, the maturing loans should have been repaid to the Special Account described above, and the loans made restricted to safe opportunities.

The NTT scheme was composed of the following three types of loans, A, B, and C.

1. *Type A*—Interest-free loans for the construction of public facilities yielding profits for repayment within 20 years. A typical example is highway construction on the basis of self-liquidation by the Japan Highway Public Corporation. In a word, this is a type of profitable public works.
2. *Type B*—Loans were made to stimulate local governments to implement public works. However, these public works are not expected to produce any profits for repayment, and so the national government provided the subsidies necessary to repay the loans on maturity. This type of loan has to be repaid within 20 years. This is a kind of ordinary public works expenditure.

---

[7] The price of NTT stock was first bid up to ¥1.6 million in the stock market when it was sold in 1986, and it continued to rise sharply to top ¥2.55 million in 1987, reflecting the stock boom during the bubble.

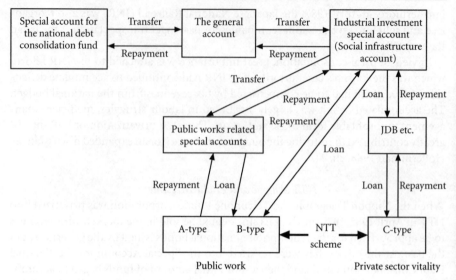

FIGURE 6.6. *The NTT scheme*

3. *Type C*—The loans made to the third sector had to be capitalized partly by local governments and/or other public corporations, such as the Development Bank of Japan. The basic aim was to apply the projects to revitalize the private sector. This type of loan must be repaid within 15 years.

An outline of the NTT scheme is roughly delineated in Figure 6.6. A portion of the revenues from the sale of NTT stock, which are deposited in the Special Account for the National Debt Fund, became interest-free loans that were picked up and transferred to the general account. Moreover, the funds for such a loan are transferred to the Industrial Investment Special Account (included inside the Social Infrastructure Account) in order to be administered on a consolidated basis. The NTT scheme provides interest-free loans of types A, B, and C either directly or indirectly (i.e. via public works related special accounts or the Development Bank of Japan, etc.) from the Industrial Investment Special Account.

FISCAL STRUCTURAL REFORM

The Original Reform Package for Fiscal Consolidation

In November 1997, the fiscal structural reform law was enacted at the Diet to eliminate fiscal deficits towards the target year of fiscal 2003 on a year-by year basis. This was proposed by the Hashimoto Cabinet as one of six major structural reforms,[8]

---

[8] Prime Minister Hashimoto proposed as his main political platform to achieve (i) administrative reform, (ii) economic reform, (iii) financial system reform, (iv) social security reform, (v) educational reform, as well as fiscal structural reform.

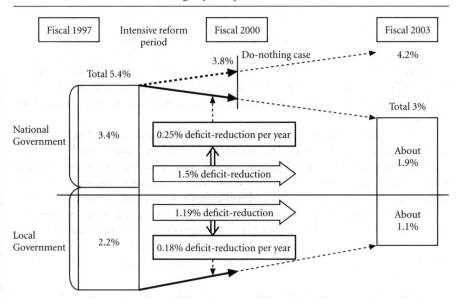

FIGURE 6.7. *Target of fiscal consolidation, fiscal deficits–GDP ratio*

Source: MOF

Note: In fiscal 1997, there is an overlapping component of 0.2 per cent of fiscal deficit between national and local governments. The effects of deficit reduction processes are estimated, based on an average nominal growth rate of 3.5 per cent in the future. If a lower growth rate such as 1.75 per cent is assumed, expenditure cuts should be accelerated to over 20 per cent

backed by the Primitive Measures for Fiscal Structural Reform under the Initiatives of Ruling Party Conference. Previously it had taken more than one year to prepare the draft of a basic plan for fiscal consolidation by the Fiscal System Commission, an advisory organ of the Finance Minister.

The outline of the reform package is summarized in the following three principles:

1. a fiscal consolidation target was fixed to reduce the fiscal deficit–GDP ratio within national and local governments to 3 per cent or less by fiscal 2003;
2. the issuance of deficit-covering national bonds should be eliminated by fiscal 2003;
3. in order to achieve this target, major government expenditure was capped to restrain its increasing tempo and promote its curtailment. In addition, the three remaining fiscal years of the twentieth century are designated as an 'intensive reform period' to further cut expenditure.

Figure 6.7 clarifies the basic framework of targeted fiscal consolidation. At the starting point of fiscal 1997, the national government has a fiscal deficit–GDP ratio of 3.4 per cent while local governments have 2.2 per cent, totalling up to 5.4 per cent in the scope of both governments, excluding any overlapping component. If a 'do-nothing' policy is taken by the national government at the beginning, this ratio essentially has to rise to 3.8 per cent in fiscal 2000 and 4.2 per cent in fiscal 2003. Thus, deficit-reduction should be planned annually relative to GDP as indicated in Figure 6.7; that is to say, 0.25 per cent in the national government and 0.18 per cent in local governments up to the targeted year of fiscal 2003. If such a periodic reduction could be implemented successfully, the 3 per cent target of fiscal deficit–GDP ratio can be achieved in fiscal 2003, dividing this ratio into approximately 1.9 per cent and 1.1 per cent for each level of governments.

In order to satisfy the second principle, the annual amount of cutting the deficit-covering national bonds was fixed in terms of ¥1.25 trillion as a maximum limit, which evidently indicates the political decision by the Hashimoto Cabinet to recoup fiscal soundness. Needless to say, this rule substantially restricts the budgeting practices which will be available afterwards and will give no room to admit tax reduction or increased government expenditure financed by deficit-covering bonds to stimulate the economy. As argued shortly, such a strict regulation under the fiscal structural reform law has deprived the government of taking a more flexible fiscal policy to combat current depressions and in the end the government was obliged to modify its plans to some extent.

The major instrument of debt reduction in relation to the third principle was to cut non-entitled deliberate government expenditure, rather than introduce tax increases during the targeted period. Table 6.5 shows the capping of major expenditure items after fiscal 1997. There are three points to be stressed here. First of all, social security expenditure is an important candidate for expenditure cuts, because its rise is expected to be inevitable given the ageing of the population. What is vital is to try and curb the amount automatically increasing due to the size of the aged population rising during the intensive reform period, that is restraining the growth rate in social security expenditure as a whole to a level lower than its inevitably increasing rate (approximately 2 per cent), given the aim of below-zero growth in non-entitlement government expenditure. In detail, the automatic increase of over ¥800 billion that will be projected under the current policy basis in fiscal 1998 will have to be limited to over ¥500 billion through the 1998 budget process. Of course, social security reform is absolutely necessary in the medical care insurance and pension system.

Secondly, public investment is a target for expenditure cuts. As mentioned previously, a large amount of public investment has been implemented to stimulate the weak recovery of the economy after the collapse of the bubble, but it has not been completely effective. On the contrary, a great deal of criticism has been made of the inefficient use of public work projects, for example the construction of unnecessary roads, harbours, airports, agricultural roads, etc. Thus, in implementing the expenditure cut, it has been decided to lower public investment to as little as minus 7 per cent in the fiscal 1998 budget. It is to be stressed that this was an epoch-making decision, given the current political environment in which the vested interests of the construction industry are strongly prevalent.

A third important measure is the minus 10 per cent cut of ODA (official development aid) in fiscal 1998. In the past one or two decades, the Japanese government has made

TABLE 6.5. *Capping of major non-entitled government expenditures*

Items	Fiscal 1998	Intensive reform period (fiscal 1998–2000)
Social security	Reducing above ¥500 billion	2% or below in terms of growth rate
Public investment	Minus 7% in terms of growth rate	Annual reduction
Education	Big cut	Zero or minus in terms of growth rate
Defence	Zero or minus in terms of growth rate	The same as above
ODA	Minus 10% in terms of growth rate	Annual reduction
Science and technology	5% or below in terms of growth rate	Big cut
Energy	Big cut	Zero or minus in terms of growth rate
Small and medium-sized enterprises	Big cut	The same as above growth
National grant-in-aid	Minus in terms of growth rate	Below nominal rate of GDP

Source: MOF, *Movement Towards Fiscal Structural Reform*, June 1997.

Note: The scope of government is the general account of national government.

a continuing effort to support the developing countries of the world by increasing or maintaining a high level of ODA. The cut in ODA proposed in the fiscal restructural reform implies that the basic principle of overseas aid policy will have to be changed to a considerable extent, which may have a significant impact on the rest of the world.

Other than the three major measures described above, the following expenditure items are under consideration for reduction: defence is to be pegged at a zero or minus growth rate; education, energy and small–medium-sized enterprises are all targeted for big cuts; and national grant-in-aid is restricted to a negative growth rate; while science and technology are to be allowed to increase by no more than 5 per cent.

The priority-based allotment system has been introduced into the initial budget of government expenditure at the initiative of the Hashimoto Cabinet under the fiscal structural reform law. However, looking at the results of the capping system as a whole, the measures have been far from satisfactory.[9]

[9] One of the defects in the Fiscal Structural Reform Law is to exclude the revenue and expenditure items of the supplementary budget. Thus, the government could use the supplementary items, if necessary, for any specific policy goal, and in fact PM Hashimoto tried to introduce temporary income tax reduction for the purpose of stimulating the depressed economy within fiscal 1997 before embarking on the Fiscal Structural Reform Law in April 1998.

Comprehensive Economic Policy Package

As discussed above, the Japanese economy continued to be sluggish in 1998, and it began to be widely proposed, both at home and abroad, that the ongoing austerity policy for fiscal consolidation should be changed into fiscal stimulus. In fact, the Japanese economy in fiscal 1997 showed a minus 0.7 per cent growth rate for the first time in 23 years after the oil shock, and both the USA and Europe have been urging Japan to implement fiscal expansionary measures to revive the flagging economy. In particular, they requested the stimulation of domestic demand to prevent Japan's external surpluses from rising to significant levels and to help absorb more imports from Japan's troubled Asian neighbours.

However, it was very difficult for PM Hashimoto to change his policy stance, since this was delicately linked to political responsibility. Thus, he had been holding back from specifically starting any fiscal stimulus until the fiscal 1998 budget—closely tied with the Fiscal Structural Reform Law –as enacted at the Diet in April 1998. Immediately after the passage of the initial budget for fiscal 1998, he finally decided to put fiscal consolidation on hold and to carry out a wide range of pump-priming measures as a comprehensive economic policy package to get the economy back on the track to recovery.[10]

In April 1998 the government proposed a comprehensive set of stimulus measures with the largest package ever competed. This accounted for ¥16.65 trillion, and the seventh economic policy package since the collapse of the bubble in 1991 in the hope of nursing the Japanese economy back to life. The fiscal stimulus package, as summarized in Table 6.6, contained about ¥12 trillion in actual fiscal spending as a portion of 'real water' in the total amount of ¥16 trillion that generates real aggregate demand.[11]

The key points of such a package can be broken down into the following three items.

1. One important pillar of the package was ¥4.6 trillion in tax reductions and other related measures. Major components were ¥2 trillion for the current calendar year and ¥2 trillion in 1999. Furthermore, other tax cuts and welfare handouts were added to these tax reductions.
2. The bulk of the package came in the form of an additional ¥7.7 trillion in public works spending by the national and local governments in light of a new type of public investment.
3. The package also indicated three types of other stimulative measures: that is, those in support of the land market; small and medium-sized businesses; and employment.

[10] Hashimoto said that 'The economy is in a very serious state, and while still upholding structural reforms, I have decided that we will take the steps seen as both necessary and sufficient to regain trust both at home and abroad' (The *Japan Times* 9 April 1998).

[11] Most of Japan's economic policy packages include both tax revenues (or national bonds) and other related financial sources (say, loans from government trust funds financed by postal savings or public pensions). Thus, the former financial scale of the total package is often said to be 'real water' as an indicator of a genuine injection into effective demand.

TABLE 6.6. *Fiscal stimulus package in fiscal 1998*

Items	Fiscal measures	Expenditures	
		¥ trillion ($ billion)	% of GDP
1 Tax reductions, etc.	a Temporary income and inhabitants' tax reductions	4.0 (31)	0.8
	b Other tax cuts	0.3 (2)	0.1
	c Welfare handouts	0.3 (2)	0.1
2 Public works by national and local government	a National public works	6.0* (47)	1.1
	b Anti-disaster works	0.2 (2)	0.0
	c Local public works	1.5* (12)	0.3
Sub-total 1 + 2		12 (93)	2.4
3 Others	a Land market measures	2.3 (18)	0.5
	b Measures for small and medium-sized business	2.0 (16)	0.4
	c Employment measures	0.05 (0.4)	0.0
Total		over 16 (124)	3.2

Source: EPA, *Summary of Comprehensive Economic Measures*, 24 April 1998.

Note: *Public works by both the national and local governments include land purchases (approximately 5 per cent of those expenditures).

The first tax cut package was planned to buoy up the economy through personal consumption and investment. The ¥2 trillion income tax reduction for the 1998 fiscal year was aimed at reinforcing the ¥2 trillion in similar cuts already implemented in February and March 1998. It is to be stressed that another tax cut of ¥2 trillion was also included in a similar package for the following year. Other tax cuts of roughly ¥300 billion were implemented by using the revision of special tax measures to raise tax deductibility for home purchasers and small enterprises in order to expand their investment. Another disbursement of ¥300 billion as welfare handouts was provided to pensioners and the bed-ridden elderly or low-income earners who cannot gain from income tax cuts.

The second package of public works is generally propagated by the government to change the form of public work programmes from the traditional type of construction industry to a new, broader social infrastructure investment. For instance, the works include ¥1.6 trillion for environment and energy-related projects, and ¥2.0 trillion for telecommunication networks, scientific research, and welfare and education-type projects.

Thirdly, the stimulus package also contained a comprehensive plan to boost land markets. An effort was made by the government to help firms, especially financial institutions, to dispose of their non-performing assets. Under the scheme, the government established a special body to assist and mediate between creditors and borrowers to hasten the transactions of land held as collateral. Within this third category, the necessary steps were taken to promote the creation of more venture-type small–medium-sized businesses, and to encourage rehiring of unemployed people, by offering subsidies.

The Resurgence of Keynesian Policy

PM Hashimoto has been in a severe political position when trying to combat the generally prevalent request for pump-priming policies to stimulate the stagnant economy. Thus, he finally had to shift from a fiscal stance of austerity to expansionary fiscal measures by introducing the comprehensive economic policy package described above.

No doubt, such a fiscal stimulus implies a plan to launch a pump-priming fiscal measure to expand domestic demands. In a word, the Keynesian policy re-emerged from a prolonged recession prevalent in 1997–98 against the ongoing wave of fiscal consolidation. In order to implement economy-buoying measures, it became necessary to modify the Fiscal Structural Reform Law because large scale income tax cuts must be financed through the issuance of deficit-covering bonds.

The opposition party strongly insisted that a whole package of comprehensive economic policy should be totally repealed as a symbol of policy mistake, but PM Hashimoto rejected this suggestion and only made a minimum revision on the original package. The three main policy revisions were as follows:

1. the target year for fiscal restructuring was postponed from fiscal 2003, as stated in the original Reform Law, to fiscal 2005;
2. a suspension clause was introduced to stop the annual reduction of deficit-covering bonds;
3. the capping system excluded social security expenditures for fiscal 1998.

As a result of expanding fiscal deficits to embark upon the fiscal stimulus shown in Table 6.6, the national government were forced to issue an additional ¥118 trillion of national bonds in the supplementary budget of fiscal 1998. Thus they led to a rise in the deficit–GDP ratio from the original 5.4 per cent to about 6.7 per cent in fiscal 1998,[12] and so both the national and local governments will have to reduce the annual ratio; that is 0.46 per cent towards fiscal 2005 rather than 0.43 per cent towards fiscal 2003. Since a sharply decreasing tempo of fiscal deficits may have a bad impact on the economy, the government decided to put off the target year to two years later.[13]

A more difficult problem was a revision in Article 4 of the Reform Law which stipulates the fixed amount of contracting deficit-covering bonds in each fiscal year.

---

[12] If we include ad hoc increases of fiscal deficits caused by liquidating the accumulated debts of national railroad and national forest special accounts, this deficit–GDP ratio will rise to 11.7 per cent.

[13] The original plan of fiscal consolidation itself had the target year of fiscal 2005 when it was established in January 1997. Consequently, the postponement of the target year was quietly accepted by many.

Evidently, this stipulation prevents the government from taking bold fiscal expansionary measures. To avoid such a rigid rule, it is necessary to suspend the stipulation temporarily, as happens under the USA OBRA (Omnibus Budget Reconciliation Act), to cope with economic emergencies. As a consequence, the following revisions were made as a suspension clause to stop annual cuts of deficit-covering bonds in the Reform Law. The suspension is triggered by three emergency situations:

1. real growth rates are totally less than 1 per cent on an annualized basis for two consecutive quarters;
2. the annualized growth rate is less than 1 per cent in a single quarter with conspicuously low figures in personal consumption, plant and equipment investment, and employment.
3. an unpredictable disaster occurs, causing an 'economic shock', like the oil shock or the Great Hanshin Earthquake, at home or overseas.

Furthermore, the Fiscal Structural Reform Law encountered the *de facto* collapse of capping. The fiscal stimulus package included a wide range of public works projects, neglecting practically a minus 7 per cent ceiling for fiscal 1998, as seen in Table 6.5. Also, as a result of political compromise, the limit of social security expenditure was excluded from the capping system as a special treatment for fiscal 1999.

Based upon these revisions of the Reform Law described above, the comprehensive package was launched into fiscal expansion. To what extent could the package be expected to stimulate the stagnant state of the economy? As is shown in Table 6.6, the ¥16 trillion package was 3.2 per cent of GDP in 1998. The EPA currently calculates that it would push up nominal growth rates by 2 per cent in the first year of implementation, even without any additional ¥2 trillion of income tax cuts in 1999.

However, there remains controversial debate about the stimulative effects of the package. For example, many economists have pointed out that its positive effects would only be temporary and would not be strong enough to put the economy on the road to recovery. In particular, spending on public works is thought to be of little avail towards generating any sustainable growth. Temporary income tax reductions are also expected to have only a limited effect on increasing personal consumption because a substantial amount of any tax cuts would be used for saving. Thus, it is widely maintained that such temporary income tax cuts should be changed into permanent tax cut measures to promote greater expansionary effects in the Japanese economy.

On the other hand, there are more optimistic views, which believe that the stimulative package will get the economy back from the brink of deflation. Some optimists believe that the fiscal stimulus will help the Japanese economy achieve a real growth rate of 1.9 per cent in fiscal 1998, as targeted by the government. It is also anticipated that consumer sentiment is no worse than it was due to the falling inflation rate and income tax cuts.

To summarize, what is of most importance from now on would be to facilitate further deregulation and structural reforms of the economy, mainly including the financial sector, to revitalize the Japanese economy towards full recovery, rather than implementing a simple fiscal expansionary programme as has been done so far.

The Debut of the Obuchi Cabinet and the Economic Strategy Council

The policy change of PM Hashimoto was too late to maintain his political leadership as the recession was worsened in 1998. In July 1998, he was completely defeated at the Upper House election, losing a number of LDP seats. As a consequence, he resigned from the position of Prime Minister and was succeeded by Keizo Obuti. This political change encouraged the government to switch from fiscal structural reform to fiscal stimulus, making business recovery in the Japanese economy rather than fiscal consolidation the policy priority. Indeed, a pessimistic view was prevalent concerning the prevailing business condition, and the forecast target of real growth rate was lowered to minus 2.2 per cent in fiscal 1998, rather than the previous target of 1.9 per cent.

Thus, Obuchi Cabinet began to take the initiative in constructing a fiscal expansion scheme in the light of the fiscal 1999 budget. Two points are worth noting. For one thing, the Fiscal Structural Reform Act was suspended in order to ensure that all measures possible can be taken to stimulate the depressed economy. The other was that the fiscal 1999 initial budget should be formulated together with the fiscal 1998 third supplementary budget, the idea being to draw up a combined 15-month budget to strengthen the continuity of fiscal expansion. Moreover, a 'special scheme for economic recovery' amounting to an additional ¥4 trillion was established, the major part being allocated to public works expenses once again.

In August 1998 when PM Obuchi took office, he instituted the Economic Strategy Council, chaired by Kotaro Higuchi, Chairman of Asahi Breweries Ltd., as a private advisory panel to collect the views of invited business leaders and academics. The main task of this Council was to design a scenario for the future process of economic recovery. After six-months of discussion and surveying economists and business leaders, the 10-member panel presented its final report to PM Obuchi in February 1999.

One of the most notable features of this report was the proposal of a three-step approach to attaining the full-scale recovery of the Japanese economy, as well as a potential path for fiscal consolidation in the future. The following are the key recommendations made by the Economic Strategy Council.

1. Japan still has the potential to realize 2 per cent real growth rate after fiscal 2001. Thus, fiscal 1999–2000 should be termed a rehabilitation period from the burst of the bubble economy, in which sufficient structural reforms of the economy should be taken. Meanwhile, priority should be put on economic stimulus and the stabilization of the financial system.
2. Fiscal 2001–2002 is the time for Japan to return to a sound path of economic growth. At the same time, drastic structural reforms should be launched in light of reducing public investment.
3. Fiscal consolidation should be initiated for 2003–2008 through austere budgetary policy, after which the full-scale recovery phase can be attained.

These are the three key recommendations. In addition more detailed items were proposed: switching from direct taxes to indirect taxes; a 25 per cent reduction in the number of public servants; the sale of government assets; the improvement of FILP; etc. The problem undoubtedly lies in the implementation process which is considered to be very difficult politically. However, after receiving the proposals from the Committee, PM Obuchi said:

I would like to direct and urge each Cabinet minister to start implementation of such proposals, beginning with the ones that can be realized (The *Japan Times* 27 February 1999).

It is widely acknowledged that PM Obuchi's political life will depend on the extent and speed of economic recovery, because he has officially committed himself to the achievement of 0.6 per cent growth rate in real terms in fiscal 1999. His target of 0.5 per cent of the real growth rate has finally been attained, but unfortunately he died suddenly in May 2000.

7

An Empirical Analysis of
Balanced Budget Policy, 1953–65

It is widely accepted that government expenditure and taxation can play an important role in the control of aggregate demand as a device for promoting economic stability. The purpose of this study is to evaluate the stabilizing effect of government fiscal activity in post-war Japan, and its scope is limited to two relatively simple considerations: (i) identifying empirically the cyclical behaviour of fiscal surplus and deficit, and thereby (ii) evaluating the planned and unplanned fiscal actions employed by the government during an earlier period of post-war Japan.

This chapter consists of three parts. In the first part, we attempt to clarify the state of business cycles and government fiscal activity in post-war Japan. This is followed by a statistical inquiry into the surpluses and deficits in the government accounts. Next, we examine the factors in the fiscal system to which the countercyclical effects of the government fiscal activity may be attributed.

POST-WAR BUSINESS CYCLES AND GOVERNMENT FISCAL ACTIVITY

A Specific Period for the Balanced Budget

Although extensive theoretical work has satisfactorily demonstrated the benefits of the countercyclical use of government fiscal instruments in the pursuit of economic stability, it seems that in practice the empirical aspects of the problem have not always been sufficiently investigated and thus significant conclusions concerning the actual working of fiscal policy have been difficult to reach. In the case of Japan, this description is particularly apt.

The present study primarily aims to provide a quantitative description of cyclical patterns of time series data related to government fiscal activity in the course of business cycles. Presumably, most changes in government receipts and expenditures are influenced by business cycles, and in turn have some feedback effect on the state of business conditions. In other words, there must be some reciprocal causative relation between those two elements. It would be desirable to estimate separately the influence of each of the causative factors, but our aim here is less ambitious. Indeed, an attempt is made only to ascertain the facts about the movements of fiscal data in the context of the swings of business conditions as actually experienced by the economy.[1] Thus, this

This chapter is heavily based on Ishi 1973.

[1] Furthermore, no effort has been made here to study the aspects of monetary, credit, and public debt actions that were closely related to the development of fiscal policy, although we must admit that it is impossible to ignore them completely. Therefore, it must be acknowledged that this will give only an incomplete picture of the total government activity affecting the economy.

is a straightforward factual account of how government revenues and expenditures have fluctuated.[2] It will provide, however, some new revelations and more exact knowledge to ascertain past sources of weakness and strength in fiscal policy.

As a first step towards clarifying the purpose of the analysis, let us specify the period covered by this study. For the following two reasons, we will concentrate on the period from 1953 to 1965 in this analysis from a standpoint of countercyclical policy in the national government. First of all, the year 1953 was chosen as the starting point because it is generally accepted as the completion date of the post-war recovery process (see Chapter 1), and the beginning of normal business conditions and cycles. On the other hand, since the years during which the so-called balanced budget policy was strictly adhered to is of central interest in this study, the year 1965 which marks the termination of this policy with the issuing of the first long-term national bonds in the post-war period is an appropriate closing date for the period to be studied. The peculiar characteristic of the government fiscal activity during the time period under consideration was that, unlike other nations, Japan incurred no public debt of any significant size. Therefore, the post-war Japanese experience seems to provide an interesting topic worth noting in the analysis of the operation and effectiveness of fiscal policy.

Fiscal Performance over Business Cycles

Let us first summarize the general properties of business cycles in post-war Japan. What caused the post-war business cycles and how likely they were to happen are beyond the field of inquiry. What is needed here is some business indicator of aggregate economic activity which can be contrasted with the cyclical behaviour of government surplus and deficit. For this purpose, we can consult the table prepared above from EPA data which gave the dates and duration of Japan's business cycle (see Table 2.3). Although the reference dates pretend to do no more than sketch the turning points of business conditions (i.e. the peaks and troughs), they are helpful to our analysis.

In so much as the EPA reference dates are accurate, there are a few marked features about the post-war business cycles in Japan. In the first place, the duration of each of these cycles has been from three to four years, as noted above. It has been suggested that these constitute minor cycles, not major ones, and should be designated as 'inventory cycles'. Furthermore, the historical records of business cycles clearly appear as a series of expansions followed by briefer periods of contraction. In fact, contractions have been short, normally less than a year each in length, while the periods of expansion have been longer, averaging two and a half years in length. Secondly, these results would indicate that Japan has experienced only mild recessions, not serious depressions, every three years. Accordingly, it was optimistically felt—up to 1965—that three years of upswing could be expected to be punctuated by a year of modest downswing.

---

[2] No attempt has been made to appraise the effectiveness of fiscal policy from a standpoint of policy target, such as 'full employment surplus' used in E. C. Brown's study or 'implicit federal surplus' used in W. Lewis' study. In Japan, it is almost impossible to set forth such a policy target as was developed in the USA in the 1960s since no emphasis has been placed on the target of full employment. (See E. C. Brown 1956; W. Lewis, Jr. 1962, chs I–III.)

Next, we shall briefly refer to the problem of government fiscal activity under such repetitive periods of business cycles. This topic was more fully discussed in Chapter 6. As argued earlier, it is possible to summarize the operation of the government fiscal activity until 1965 under the following three empirical rules: (i) a balanced budget; (ii) a tax policy with a constant ratio of tax burden relative to the national income; and (iii) an intended underestimation of the 'natural increase in tax revenues' caused by a growing economy. In what respect are these three empirical rules connected with the stabilizing effect of fiscal action? Judging from the fact that attitudes towards a balanced budget and fiscal responsibility remained strong, it may be suggested that the pursuit of countercyclical policy through the manipulation of fiscal surplus and deficit had never been employed at all, or at least had not been pursued intentionally. Also, it should be noted that the main target of the tax policy had been the enforcement of tax cuts (Ishi 1993, ch. 3). Hence, this tax reduction policy had been carried on continuously with no respect to the state of business cycles.

Similarly, the underestimation of the natural increases in tax yields did not work in favour of countercyclical policy. The government had always constructed a small number of supplementary budgets within the intermediate term of the fiscal year which are financed by the natural tax increases currently accrued. This indicates that the government surpluses from the natural tax increases were spent on an expanding economy which had attained a high rate of growth, although it should have been retained in the treasury for the sake of stabilization (for more detailed discussion see Chapter 8). Thus, it seems permissible to suggest that all the empirical rules had acted as an active constraint for countercyclical fiscal actions.

So far as such past experiences of fiscal operations are concerned, one might feel pessimistic about this study, the purpose of which is to seek some empirical evidence in favour of the countercyclical effects of fiscal policy in Japan. The reason for this is that the effectiveness of fiscal policy is restricted to a considerable extent by a number of factors, as we have already seen. The above discussion, however, is only part of the story. Despite the numerous constraints, there is good evidence, as shown below, to support the hypothesis that fiscal policy has had a countercyclical effect and has encouraged government surplus during prosperity and deficit in times of recession. Such evidence may be important in the clarification of the debate over the question of the effectiveness of fiscal policy in post-war Japan.

Before proceeding further with the problem of finding statistical facts, it would be useful to clarify here another assumption. In shaping government fiscal activity, the state of business fluctuations is never the only factor and seldom the most important factor. Indeed, its operation is under many constraints and is shaped by many considerations other than those of economic stability, for example resource allocation or income distribution. Stated differently, the government's action affecting revenues and expenditures is not confined to counteracting trends in aggregate demands. Therefore, the actual time series of government revenues and expenditures reflect the mixed results of the fiscal actions pursued in the past.

Ideally, it would be desirable to disentangle those actions from each other and to extract only the stabilizing effects of government behaviour from them. With the exception of a theoretical treatment, it is, in practice, impossible to decide definitely whether or not the motive for a particular action was primarily to counter recession or inflation. To deal with the problem, it must be assumed that the actual variations of government revenue and expenditure associated with actions other than economic stabilization are unchanged over time, and are ignored for the simplicity of the analysis. That is to say, the treatment of all the variations found in the statistical data as changes resulting solely from the stabilizing action of the government must be justified.

CYCLICAL PATTERNS OF FISCAL SURPLUS AND DEFICIT

The Data and the Scope of the Government

The principles of fiscal action in the interest of economic stability are simple according to the textbooks of fiscal policy. The government is theoretically supposed to use both sides of the budget as a stabilizing device to moderate business fluctuations, and so a cyclical pattern of government surplus in expansion and deficit in contraction is to be anticipated over a business cycle. Therefore, the first thing to be done as a simple but basic approach is to observe the movements of time series data relating to government revenues and expenditures from a stabilization standpoint.

In proceeding with the statistical operations, it should be noted that annual data are very crude and inadequate for testing the cyclical behaviour of government fiscal activity. However, many of the statistics which have so far been developed to investigate the countercyclical effects of fiscal actions are based on annual data. Such empirical estimates on an annual basis have generally left something to be desired, because they have obscured timing relations between the fiscal time series and the state of business conditions, making it impossible to trace cyclical patterns with confidence since business cycles cannot satisfactorily appear by annual unit. For this reason, in this study monthly data are used, even though their compilation and analysis are more difficult than annual data.

A definition of government revenue and expenditure is not as precise as it sounds, because they are measured in various different ways. Thus, it is necessary to clarify at this point the exact concept of fiscal surplus and deficit. This question has a close bearing on the problem of the definition of the aspect of government to be used. Of the alternative aspects of government for which there exist adequate statistical information, three are of central interest for our purpose. First, the *general account* of the national government can be referred to as representing the narrowest aspect. Secondly, a broader concept can be obtained from the addition of special accounts and government-related agencies. Thirdly, by adding the local government to the national government, the broadest aspect of government can be followed by the concept of national income accounts. To recapitulate, three concepts are presented as follows:

1. the *general account*;
2. the national government—concept (1) plus special accounts and government-related agencies;
3. the general government—concept (2) plus local government.

Each of them has its own advantages in the analysis. Let us first suppose the government is limited to concept (1). There are two advantages to concept (1) which need to be considered in reference to this study. For one thing, it provides a good framework for studying the government's behaviour while operating under a balanced budget, since much has been discussed concerning this within the aspect of the *general account*. The other advantages is that the stabilizing effect of tax revenues can be described more efficiently using concept (1). If the government were defined as a broader concept, the relative importance of tax revenue would be reduced because a number of revenue items other than taxes would be introduced into the picture. Also, the aspect of central government—that is concept (2)—may be regarded as an optimal concept in representing the policy performance of fiscal operation for economic stabilization, since it contains the FILP which is considered to have worked rather effectively as a countercyclical device. However, it cannot be utilized in practice because of the lack of detailed data. Finally, the aspect of general government is conceptually correspondent to national income analysis, although the social security fund is not included here. Therefore, the magnitude of government fiscal action in the overall level of economic activity can clearly be acquired by using concept (3).

Which concept is the proper one to employ primarily depends upon the availability of monthly data, so far as our analysis is concerned. In this respect the narrowest aspect of government is preferred, reflecting the fact that detailed monthly data can be compiled for concept (1) alone. In addition to this, however, concepts (2) and (3) will also be introduced below to check the possible bias which may be caused by choosing the narrowest concept.

The time series data of fiscal surplus and deficit are computed on a monthly basis by taking the algebraic difference between revenue and expenditure, after the necessary statistical calculations are done. Since government revenue and expenditure data are published by more than one statistical source, it is necessary to consider briefly the characteristics of the series analysed here. The basic data of government revenues and expenditures concerning the *general account* are compiled from a statistical source of MOF, entitled, 'Receipts and payments from or to the public in the Treasury', which is a single series on a monthly basis going as far back as 1949.[3] It represents the receipts and expenditures on a current cash basis for providing an accurate idea of the government's day-to-day business.

Throughout these monthly compilations, only those which are entered as current revenues are included. This implicitly eliminates national bonds from the government's revenue items, although national bonds had never been listed prior to 1965 in the sphere of the *general account*. Hence, the items of current revenues consist of (i) taxes, (ii) the profits of the Japan Monopoly Corporation (the Japan Tobacco Industry after

[3] More specifically, the Treasury's series are divided into two kinds of revenues and expenditures, depending upon the accounting method: (i) 'formal series'; and (ii) 'real series'. The 'real' series differs from the 'formal' one in that intra-governmental transactions have been eliminated from the 'formal' one. Since overlapping items should be omitted to get a true transaction from or to the public, the 'real' series are preferable. However, the 'real' series are not available before 1953. Therefore, for the years prior to 1953 a substantial amount of estimation was necessary to obtain the 'real' series from the 'formal' one which goes as far back as 1949.

privatization in 1985), and (iii) others.[4] They are to be contrasted with government expenditure including defence expenses, public works expenses, grant-in-aid to local governments, general shares in compulsory education expenses and others.[5] Let us now denote government current revenue and government expenditure as R_g and G, respectively. Fiscal surplus and deficit is defined, depending upon $R_g - G > 0$ (surplus) or $R_g - G < 0$ (deficit).

Statistical Procedures

The next issue to be dealt with is the statistical manipulation of the monthly data to be used in the formulae above. It is generally accepted that any monthly data consist of the following four components: (i) secular trend T; (ii) seasonal variation S; (iii) cyclical fluctuation C; and (iv) random movement I, where all components can be composed in terms of TSCI or $T + S + C + I$. Therefore, it is impossible to derive fiscal surplus and deficit series by computing directly the difference in the original data between revenue and expenditure. Some statistical adjustment must be made before subtracting one series from another. Indeed, all non-cyclical variations must somehow be eliminated in order to analyse the cyclical behaviour of fiscal surplus and deficit. Hence, we shall begin the statistical operation by attempting to isolate any cyclical fluctuation from the original monthly data.

The most important among the statistical procedures is to adjust for seasonal variations. The seasonal variation of some series is estimated by their compilers, but in most instances we have to carry out this operation ourselves. The individual series of government revenue or expenditure show an unmistakable seasonal swing—that is repetitive intra-annual variations are seen when the data are graphed. For example, the government revenue series have a few notable months every year which are periods of intensive tax collection because of the laws and practices of corporate and self-assessed individual income taxes. Likewise, a clear-cut seasonal variation is found in the government expenditure series by the same reasoning. Although techniques of seasonal adjustment have been greatly improved in recent years with the development of electronic computers, the problem of eliminating seasonal variation still remains troublesome in practice.[6] At the same time as the seasonal variation is eliminated, the random movement is also removed.

[4] This 'others' item is composed of (i) the government's business profits and receipts; (ii) receipts from liquidation of government property; (iii) surplus receipts during the preceding fiscal year; and (iv) miscellaneous.

[5] Comparing it with the terminology of national income analysis, the term 'government expenditure' used here includes not only government purchases of goods and services but also transfer payments and current subsidies. Thus, this makes a definition of fiscal surplus and deficit inconsistent with that used in the national income framework discussed later.

[6] In the present analysis, three techniques are utilized alternatively. (i) The 'centred' twelve-month-moving-average method. (This first entails a twelve-month-moving-average of the original figures, and then the placement of each average in the sixth month and half. Thereafter, these results are again moving-averaged. Systematic smoothing of a time series tends to eliminate short-run oscillations produced by random factors. In this respect the random movement of a series can be cancelled out by this operation). (ii) The US Bureau of the Census method (X-10). (iii) The EPA method. (This method was the one developed by the EPA. For further detailed information see, *Annual Report on National Income Statistics*, appendix, each year.)

After the laborious process of eliminating from the time series both the seasonal variation and random movement has been carried out, another problem remains to be solved. The data should be adjusted for the secular trend if we are to attempt a full analysis of cyclical behaviour. However, it is very difficult to separate cycle from trend. In fact, the isolation of cyclical fluctuation is a highly uncertain operation. Thus, the ideal procedure would undoubtedly be to make two sets of measurements for each series of government revenue and expenditure; that is one set based on the data unadjusted for trend but adjusted for seasonal and random factors, and the other based on the best attainable isolation of the cyclical component of the original data.

There remains one troublesome factor concerning the second set, because there is more than one method of computing the trend line: (1) the 40-month-moving-average method, and (2) a fit of least square trend line (both straight-line and quadratic education) method. Even if the trend were to be removed, it must be acknowledged that the analytic significance of the trend line is obscure. Since the most plausible results are obtained by using method (1), it is chosen for use in the succeeding analysis. By contrast, even if the revenue–expenditure data unadjusted for the secular trend are used in computing the government surplus and deficit, it may be suggested that the problem of eliminating the trend line can be settled itself by the nature of the method used here. That is to say, the trend line which would possibly be included in each of the revenues and expenditures might be cancelled out as a result of subtracting one series from another, provided that both series have the same trend.

Empirical Results

In the following Figures 7.1, 7.2, and 7.3, multiple series of government surplus and deficit are presented, reflecting the diverse statistical operations. Throughout the series, the statistical evidence seems to yield a fairly realistic picture of the 'cyclical components' and to provide clues to the actual behaviour of government surplus and deficit. Let us, first of all, take note of the basic series as defined by the narrowest aspect of government in Figure 7.1. It consists of the movements of two series (1) and (2), which could be considered to be the most reasonable of all the possible combinations of statistical adjustment. These two series, which show almost the same pattern over the period in question, promise to be more useful in explaining cyclical behaviour of fiscal surplus and deficit than results gained from highly fabricated series by the EPA or the Census (X-10) methods.[7] The monthly values of budgetary balances are depicted in Figure 7.1 for the years 1949–68 in series (1) and for the years 1951–66 in series (2), respectively, covering the four complete business cycles based on the reference dates as seen in Table 2.3.

There are two points that are especially worth noting. To begin with, although the actual fiscal operation in post-war Japan was broadly admitted as a balanced budget

---

[7] Of course, other series can also be employed in the present analysis. However, the series drawn in Figure 7.1 are preferable because of the more plausible and realistic result. In the results obtained from the application of the EPA or the Census (X-10) methods, there are more erratic and small oscillations which obscure the cyclical patterns which may be observed in Figure 7.1.

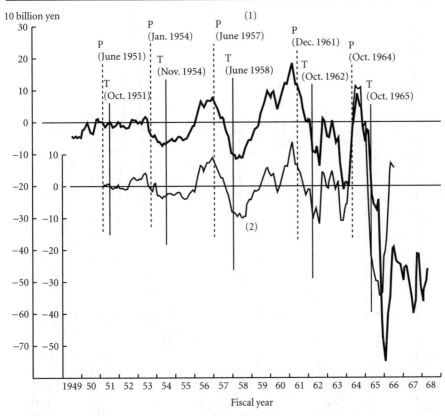

FIGURE 7.1. *Cyclical patterns of government surplus and deficit in the general account of the national government, 1949–68*

Source: MOF, *Monthly Report of Fiscal and Monetary Statistics* (in Japanese)

Notes: 1. Series (1) shows the monthly budgetary balances calculated using the data of trend-cycle components, while series (2) is obtained by using the data cycle component alone. See text for a more detailed explanation.

2. P, with broken vertical lines, and T, with solid vertical lines, here and in subsequent figures, represent the EPA reference dates, peaks, and troughs , respectively

principle, a fairly clear picture of cyclical patterns can be seen. Next, it might be emphasized that their cyclical patterns have been countercyclical over some periods. Let us now insert the troughs or peaks of the reference dates into Figure 7.1. The business cycles of 1954–58 and 1958–62 provide a good test of countercyclical movement. Indeed, in both cases the deficit with which the cycle began gradually became a net surplus as business expansion took place, while it dwindled again to a deficit during business contractions. In contrast to this, the experience of both the 1951–54 and 1962–65 cycles have not produced similar patterns. The 1951–54 period can be justifiably omitted from consideration since there is some obscurity concerning both the

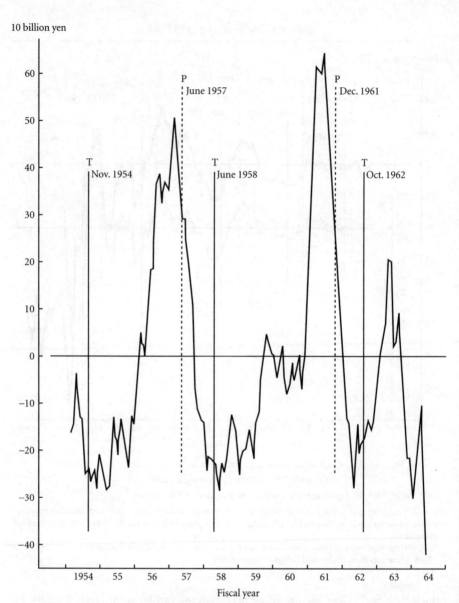

10 billion yen

FIGURE 7.2. Cyclical patterns of government surplus and deficit in the national
government, 1954–64

Source: Bank of Japan, *Basic Data for Economic Analysis* (Seasonal adjustments by the census method, in
Japanese), 1965, pp. 90–5

Notes: 1. The scope of government is enlarged to encompass the whole central government including the
special accounts and government-related agencies in addition to the *general account*

2. The budgetary balances are computed on a monthly basis in the form of 'treasury receipts from the
public' minus 'payments to the public', using the data adjusted by computer for seasonal variation and
random movement

occurrence of the business cycle and the estimation of our basic data. However, a reason concerning the 1962–65 period must be presented. In the post-1962 cycle, the countercyclical movements of the preceding two cycles are absent, as evidenced by the graph. This implies that some changes had already occurred in the fiscal system by 1962, although it was not until 1965 that national bonds were issued.

In order to verify these results obtained from using the narrowest aspect of government, we shall, alternatively, introduce two other concepts of government surplus and deficit into the analysis. Figure 7.2 illustrates the cyclical patterns of the national government's budgetary balances, using monthly data as reported by the Bank of Japan. It is clear that the patterns bear a close resemblance to those obtained from using the *general account* discussed above. That is, the surplus–deficit series reveal an obvious countercyclical pattern in the periods 1954–58 and 1958–62 while the pattern is disturbed in the 1962–65 cycle.

Similarly, Figure 7.3 is drawn for the total government,[8] although the data here are available only on a quarterly basis. Government surplus and deficit displayed a countercyclical effect in both the 1954–58 and 1958–62 cycles, corresponding to the evidence from the previous aspect of government. Thus, the original observations as obtained from the narrowest concept are vindicated by the cases of the two broader concepts. It should be stressed that the same patterns of government behaviour have been derived irrespective of the different aspects of government.

Such empirical evidence is very important when analysing the government's fiscal performance in promoting economic stability. Therefore, it is to these issues—why the surplus–deficit series displayed countercyclical movements in the periods 1954–62 and why it has failed to do so since 1962—that we now direct our analysis.

---

[8] Defining government surplus and deficit within the aspect of general government requires that it be done with reference to the concept of national income. In the exposition below, the notations used represent the following; G_c, government consumption; I_g, government gross capital formation (including gross fixed investment and inventories); S_u, current subsidies; T_r, transfer payment; F, net payment to the rest of the world; Y_g, government current revenues D_g, depreciation of government enterprises; and S_{gn}, government current surplus. By definition, S_{gn} is to be calculated as a residual item.

$$S_{gn} = Y_g - (G_c + S_u + T_r + F) \qquad (a)$$

Further, let S_g ($S_g = S_{gn} + D_g$) stand for government gross savings to be compared with I_g. By doing so, the government surplus and deficit used here are defined, following the fiscal terminology.

$$
\begin{aligned}
S_g - I_g > 0 \qquad &\text{surplus} \\
S_g - I_g = 0 \qquad &\text{balanced} \\
S_g - I_g < 0 \qquad &\text{deficit}
\end{aligned} \qquad (b)
$$

These relations are developed further, using (a).

$$
\begin{aligned}
S_g - I_g &= Y_g - (G_c + S_u + T_r + F) + D_g - I_g \\
&= Y_g - (S_u + T_r + F) + D_g - (G_c + I_g)
\end{aligned} \qquad (c)
$$

where the government surplus must be equal to the sum of government net revenues (i.e., $Y_g - S_u - T_r - F$) and D_g minus the government purchases of goods and services (i.e., $G_c + I_g$). The values of government surplus or deficit in the scope of total government were computed by the (c) formula.

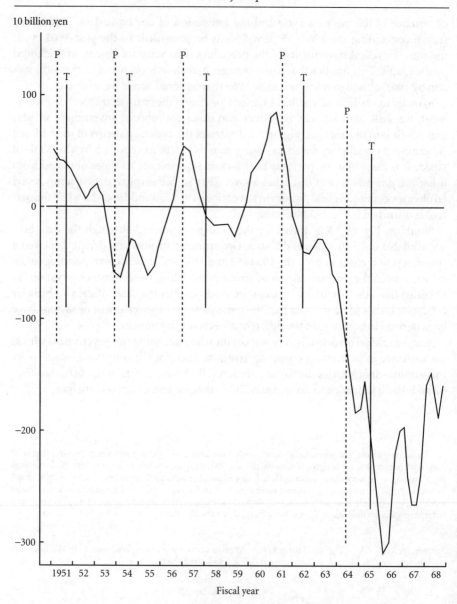

FIGURE 7.3. *Cyclical patterns of government surplus and deficit in the general government, 1951–68*

Source: EPA 1971

Note: The budgetary balances are computed on a quarterly basis using the data of trend-cycle components

SOME STABILIZING FACTORS IN THE FISCAL STRUCTURE

The Revenue Side of the Budget

The movement of government surplus and deficit can obviously be influenced by both sides of the budget, that is by the individual series of government revenue or expenditure. Therefore, it is necessary to consider revenue and expenditure separately in order to investigate which side of the budget has played a dominant role in directing the cyclical behaviour of government balances.

First of all, let us begin with a discussion of the government revenue side. Several important items are taken into account in the narrowest aspect of the government—the *general account*;

1. total government revenues;
2. total tax revenues—treasury bureau's data;
3. total tax revenues—tax bureau's data;
4. withheld income tax;
5. self-assessed income tax;
6. corporate tax;
7. liquor tax.

The items (1)–(3) and (4)–(7) are depicted in Figures 7.4 and 7.5, respectively. In drawing them, every series is composed of a cyclical component adjusted for seasonal variations, random movement, and finally for the secular trend.

Something further then is required to explain the statistical operations. When the secular trend rises rapidly, as in Japan in the post-war period, the strong trend tends to offset the influence of cyclical contractions in general business, or to make the detection of this influence difficult as noted earlier. In the case of computing the surplus–deficit series, it was not as important to eliminate the trend line from the trend-cycle composite since it could be cancelled out in the process of subtracting one series from another. However, when an individual series in the revenue or expenditure side of the budget is taken up, the importance of eliminating the trend should not be neglected. In the analysis that follows, the secular trend, which is computed by using the 40-month-moving-average method, is deducted from the trend-cycle composite obtained from the application of a 'centred twelve-month-moving-average method' to the original data.

Let us consider Figure 7.4. Three clear cyclical patterns are illustrated in the series of government revenue during the period 1950–62. If government revenue is to have a countercyclical effect for the promotion of economic stability, it would have to rise during expansion and fall during contraction. It is apparent that these movements, as observed here, satisfy the countercyclical condition. In fact, they correspond closely with the business cycles as outlined by the EPA's reference dates, although there were slight lags behind the trough dates in each cycle. In particular, the peaks of government revenues were perfectly synchronized with those of the reference dates. On the other hand, the experiences for 1962–65 reveal a partial exception. A sharp drop

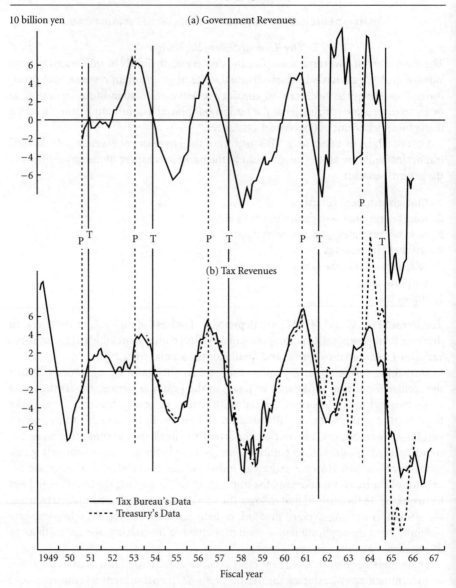

10 billion yen   (a) Government Revenues

FIGURE 7.4. *Cyclical patterns of both government and tax revenue, 1949–67*

Note: The scope of government, here and in the two subsequent figures, is limited to the *general account*

in government revenue took place at the peak of the reference date. This is quite similar to the government surplus–deficit series drawn in Figure 7.1. Thus, it may be suggested that the variations on the revenue side can have some significant effect on the fluctuations of government surplus and deficit.

10 billion yen

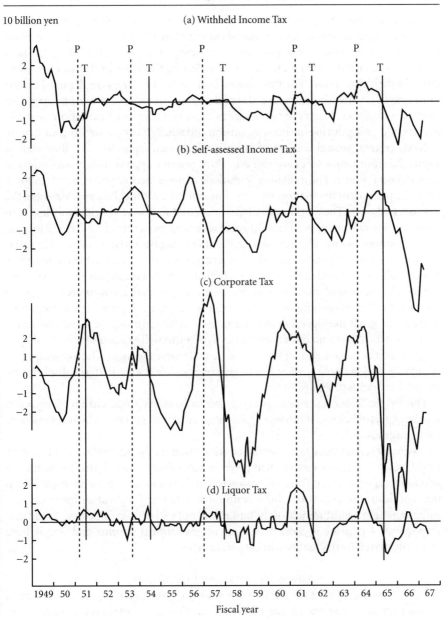

FIGURE 7.5. *Cyclical patterns of major taxes, 1949–67*

The major part of government revenue consists of tax revenue. As might be expected, the variations of tax revenue shown in Figure 7.4(b), bear a close resemblance to those obtained from government revenue in Figure 7.4(a). Two kinds of data are available in drawing the tax series, reflecting the fact that the tax collections differ in their time point. For this reason, both of the tax series are depicted on the same graph. On the whole, the two sets of data vary with almost the same pattern. In short, the resulting changes in the tax series show very sensitive fluctuations with the tax revenue, rising during business expansion and falling during business contraction.

Next, certain general sources of taxes are examined separately. As illustrated in Figure 7.5, four major taxes are chosen, which provide approximately two-thirds of national tax revenue. The individual variations of these taxes are explained as follows. First, the patterns of fluctuation are very similar for the withheld income taxes and the self-assessed ones. The amplitudes of their rises and falls were considerably less than those of corporate taxes because of the successive large reductions of individual income taxes, as argued below. This reveals that the stabilizing potential of income tax variations was substantially reduced. Indeed, it seems reasonable to assert that income taxes have not always behaved in the countercyclical manner that would have been expected.

Secondly, instead of individual income taxes, it appears that corporate taxes play a dominant role in promoting economic stability. As seen in Figure 7.5, the amplitude of their changes is the biggest of the four taxes, and furthermore the variations accurately counteract the trend of business cycles to perform well as a countercyclical device. Thus, it may be suggested that the corporate taxes were the most effective weapon of countercyclical tax policy, since it is largely responsible for the patterns displayed by the total tax yields in Figure 7.4(b).

Thirdly, the liquor taxes have, as a rule, shown no clear cyclical changes. This result is to be expected because it belongs to the category of indirect taxes which are insensitive to business cycles.

Having observed these facts, we can conclude that the cyclical patterns followed by total taxes, as well as by government revenue, can mostly be attributed to the fluctuations in corporate taxes. The chief reason is that corporate taxes have not experienced the significant tax-cuts which have continuously lowered individual income taxes. Although the expenditure side of the budget has not yet been examined, we found that in post-war Japan the cyclical behaviour of government surplus and deficit were primarily driven by fluctuations in corporate taxes.

Aspects of Government Expenditures

We shall now briefly shift the focus of our study to government expenditure. Using a method similar to the one employed in investigating government revenue, the three following items are examined:

1. total government expenditure;
2. public works expenses;
3. tax-share grants to local governments.

For the countercyclical purpose, government expenditure should decline during expansions and rise during contractions in order to mitigate the fluctuations of the general economic activity. If we consider Figure 7.6(a), we can see that the variations in government expenditure have not conformed systematically to the reference dates of business cycles. Indeed, they rose and fell irregularly throughout all the cycles of the post-war period, in a manner unlike that of the government revenue and tax revenue shown in Figures 7.4 and 7.5. However, this can easily be explained if we consider the basic nature of government expenditure. The volume of government expenditure should first of all vary in accordance with the variation of expenditure for social needs; that is a priori importance should be placed on the government's function of resource allocation. In other words, government expenditures can be justified, in part, on grounds other than pursuing a stabilization policy. Accordingly, when there are 'mixed motives' and fiscal actions are undertaken primarily for reasons other than the promotion of economic stability, there is often a negative effect on the countercyclical manipulations of government expenditure. Furthermore, it can be demonstrated, as will be verified below for the 1962–65 cycle, that expenditure has on some occasions shown a form of bias strong enough to overcome the countercyclical effect from the revenue side and to dominate the direction of budgetary balance.

Despite the fact that total government expenditure was wholly insensitive to business fluctuations, the public works expenses present one exception; that is, certain administrative procedures of accelerating and decelerating were carried out in spending on a list of public works in response to the recession and subsequent recovery. For instance, the public works expenses in the *general account* carried over to curb inflation on more than one occasion: in May 1957, September 1961, and September 1967. On the other hand, an administrative attempt was made to accelerate the outlays on public works to stimulate the economy in June 1965. Let us now consider Figure 7.6(b) with this fact in mind. The variations in public works expenses have not been as definite as those of tax revenue, but in some of the troughs which correspond to the reference dates (e.g. 1958, 1962, and 1965) it is possible to point out a correspondence between the peak of public works expenses and the contraction phases. Increase in public works expenses in these recession periods would probably be fortuitous since they cannot be regarded as discretionary counter-recession measures. However, they might have been helpful in stimulating the economy.

In addition, the variation in tax-share grants to local governments is illustrated in Figure 7.6(c), because it was expected that the series would reveal some sort of cyclical pattern. The reason for this is that the grants are financed by three kinds of taxes which themselves are sensitive to business fluctuations: individual income tax, corporate tax, and liquor tax. The result, however, did not show the meaningful pattern that had been expected.

Statistical Tests

The preceding exposition, as illustrated by Figures 7.1 to 7.6, and the findings, can be tested and ascertained in greater detail by computing the partial correlation

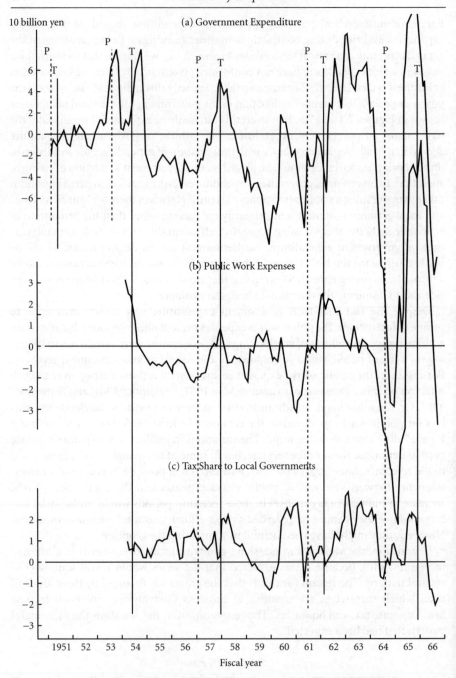

FIGURE 7.6. *Cyclical patterns of government expenditure, 1951–66*

TABLE 7.1. *Correlation coefficients among government budgetary balances (d),*
tax yields (t) *and government expenditure* (g)

I. The 2nd Cycle (Oct. 1951–Nov. 1954)				IV. The 5th Cycle (June 1962–Oct. 1965)			
	d	*t*	*g*		*d*	*t*	*g*
d	1.0000	−0.3256	−0.4373	*d*	1.0000	0.3956	−0.9164
t		1.0000	0.7712	*t*		1.0000	−0.3232
g			1.0000	*g*			1.0000
$\bar{R} = 0.3812$				$\bar{R} = 0.9176$			
$N = 38$				$N = 37$			

II. The 3rd Cycle (Nov. 1954–June 1958)				V. The 3rd and 4th Cycles (Nov. 1954–Oct. 1962)			
	d	*t*	*g*		*d*	*t*	*g*
d	1.0000	0.8973	−0.6200	*d*	1.0000	0.8079	−0.5802
t		1.0000	−0.2419	*t*		1.0000	−0.0517
g			1.0000	*g*			1.0000
$\bar{R} = 0.9884$				$\bar{R} = 0.9707$			
$N = 44$				$N = 96$			

III. The 4th Cycle (June 1958–Oct. 1962)				VI. The Whole Period (Oct. 1951–Oct. 1965)			
	d	*t*	*g*		*d*	*t*	*g*
d	1.0000	0.7752	−0.6141	*d*	1.0000	0.4761	−0.7923
t		1.0000	−0.0469	*t*		1.0000	−0.0226
g			1.0000	*g*			1.0000
$\bar{R} = 0.9658$				$\bar{R} = 0.9141$			
$N = 53$				$N = 169$			

Note:
[1] The figures in sub-tables are partial correlation coefficients. $\bar{R}$ and N stand for multiple correlation coefficients adjusted for a degree of freedom and sample sizes, respectively.
[2] The scope of government is limited to the general account.

coefficients between the fiscal variables. First, Table 7.1 indicates a matrix of partial correlation coefficients relating government budgetary balances (d) to tax revenues (t) and government expenditures (g), broken up into six time periods within the aspect of the *general account*. All the variables used here are composed of the cyclical components alone with d derived from series (2) in Figure 7.1, t from the Tax Bureau's data in Figure 7.4 and g from series (a) in Figure 7.6. The aim of the correlation analysis is to establish by a more precise statistical procedure which factors from either side of the budget have had a more dominant effect on the variation of government surplus and deficit. Table 7.1 is divided into six cases, consisting of alternative sets of the four reference cycles; that is, the four cases I–IV cover each of the four cycles, case V consists of the composite of the third and fourth cycles and the last case encompasses the whole period, taking in all the cycles.

Inspection of Table 7.1 suggests the following four facts concerning the six cases. First of all, in both case II and case III, in which a clear countercyclical effect has been noted, the correlation coefficients R_{dt} between the variables d and t are larger than the coefficient R_{dg} between the variables d and g. This reveals that the variable t can affect the variation of government surplus and deficit more than the variable g can.

Secondly, in the 1951–54 cycle (i.e. case 1) when the cyclical patterns of government surplus and deficit have not yet been found, the multiple correlation coefficients R_{dt}, and R_{dg} show all low values, and they are not statistically significant at the 5 per cent level. Accordingly, it seems appropriate to say that among the three variables, d, t, g, there was no meaningful relation.

Thirdly, the primary reason why the countercyclical effect of d tended to disappear in the 1962–65 cycle is clarified in case IV, reflecting a low value of R_{dt} and a high value of R_{dg}. That is to say, the variations of d can mostly be associated with those of g, not t. Indeed, the countercyclical variations of tax revenue, as was seen in Figure 7.4, have no relation to those of government surplus and deficit. This leads to the implication that g became a dominant factor in explaining the variations of d which showed irregular variations and as a result displayed a destabilizing effect.

Fourthly, the cases V and VI are presented to clarify the above discussion. The composite results of the 1954–58 and 1958–62 cycles (i.e. case V) carry a large value of R_{dt}, indicating the substantial stabilizing effect of taxation. Taking up all the cycles as seen in case VI, however, the value of R_{dg} is larger than that of R_{dt}. It appears that experience of the 1962–65 cycle has determined the direction of the whole period.

Next, let us turn our attention to Table 7.2, where we focus on several variables in particular. The variables selected for more detailed study are as follows: withheld income taxes (t_w), self-assessed income taxes (t_s), corporate taxes (t_c) and public works expenses (g_w). The statistical technique is similar to that employed above, although the variable g_w alone is dropped in the 1951–54 cycle because of a lack of data. It is obvious that the following results of the correlation analysis can support the observation made from Figures 7.1, 7.4, and 7.5.

First, the variable t_c is far and away the most important of all in cases II and III. In fact, the correlation coefficients R_{dtc} between d and t_c show the highest values during the periods under consideration. On the other hand, in both the 1951–54 and 1962–65 cycles (i.e. cases I and IV), the values of R_{dtc} are not significant at the 5 per cent level. Secondly, the coefficients R_{dtw} between d and t_w, and R_{dts} between d and t_s, do not necessarily carry high values. This suggests that income taxes do not play any important role in creating the cyclical movements of government surplus and deficit.

Thirdly, the coefficient R_{dgw} between d and g_w displays the highest negative value in the 1962–65 cycle. This implies that public works expenses have significantly contributed to the formation of the variations of government surplus and deficit, but they

TABLE 7.2. *Correlation coefficients among government budgetary balances (d), withheld income tax (t_w), self-assessed income tax (t_s), corporate tax (t_c), and public work expenses (g_w)*

I. The 2nd Cycle (Oct. 1951–Nov. 1954)

	d	t_w	t_s	t_c
d	1.0000	0.0389	0.5662	-0.4256
t_w		1.0000	0.0245	-0.2321
t_s			1.0000	-0.6891
t_c				1.0000

$\bar{R} = 0.5133$
$N = 38$

IV. The 5th Cycle (June 1962–Oct. 1962)

	d	t_w	t_s	t_c	g_w
d	1.0000	0.7161	0.5536	0.0684	-0.9156
t_w		1.0000	0.5286	-0.1783	-0.8206
t_s			1.0000	0.4855	-0.6580
t_c				1.0000	-0.1769
g_w					1.0000

$\bar{R} = 0.8466$
$N = 37$

II. The 3rd Cycle (Nov. 1954–June 1958)

	d	t_w	t_s	t_c	g_w
d	1.0000	0.3851	0.5290	0.6900	-0.6648
t_w		1.0000	0.3831	-0.3075	-0.5170
t_s			1.0000	0.3214	-0.2979
t_c				1.0000	-0.1376
g_w					1.0000

$\bar{R} = 0.9627$
$N = 44$

V. The 3th and 4th Cycles (Nov. 1954–Oct. 1962)

	d	t_w	t_s	t_c	g_w
d	1.0000	0.4397	0.1363	0.7066	-0.3914
t_w		1.0000	0.5405	0.2912	-0.2202
t_s			1.0000	0.4565	0.0000
t_c				1.0000	-0.1523
g_w					1.0000

$\bar{R} = 0.8466$
$N = 96$

III. The 4th Cycle (June 1958–Oct. 1962)

	d	t_w	t_s	t_c	g_w
d	1.0000	0.4951	-0.0379	0.7239	-0.3257
t_w		1.0000	0.6174	0.7989	-0.0814
t_s			1.0000	0.5032	0.1463
t_c				1.0000	-0.1483
g_w					1.0000

$\bar{R} = 0.8568$
$N = 53$

VI. The Whole Period (Oct. 1951–Oct. 1965)

	d	t_w	t_s	t_c	g_w
d	1.0000	0.4782	0.4155	0.3913	-0.7910
t_w		1.0000	0.4937	0.1984	-0.4203
t_s			1.0000	0.4560	-0.4369
t_c				1.0000	-0.1504
g_w					1.0000

$\bar{R} = 0.8466$
$N = 132$

Note: See the footnotes of Table 7.1.

did not play a stabilizing role in the economy because, during this period, government surplus and deficit showed no countercyclical pattern. Conversely, it seems that they became a factor which disturbed economic stability because they were strong enough to cancel out the countercyclical movements of tax revenue which were seen in Figures 7.4 and 7.5. By contrast, a substantial negative value of R_{dgw} can be seen in the 1954–58 cycle. In this respect, g_w may have played a considerable role in the countercyclical variations of d.

To sum up the above discussion, the countercyclical variations of government surplus and deficit during the periods 1954–62 (i.e. the third and fourth cycles) were chiefly due to those of tax revenue, particularly corporate taxes. In contrast to this, the experiences of the 1962–65 cycle or 1951–54 cycle can be explained by the fact that a stabilizing effect of corporate taxes was distorted by other forces (e.g. public works expenses) or was not fully felt. Thus, it must be acknowledged that corporate taxes had been the most influential factor for economic stability in the budgetary system.

THE COUNTERCYCLICAL EFFECT OF TAX POLICY

Discretionary vs. Built-in Effects

Hence, it is necessary to state briefly how corporate taxes have been able to vary countercyclically. This will be argued below in connection with changes in the tax laws. There are essentially two aspects to the problem. Special attention should be paid to two different devices in the operation of fiscal policy: discretionary actions and built-in stabilizers. For one thing, it is the intention of the government to use the fiscal weapons of government expenditure and taxation consciously or with discretion to compensate for business fluctuations. The other is that the government expects the forces built into the budgetary system to be working automatically as a countercyclical device.

Of course, it would be desirable to separate the two aspects of fiscal policy from each other in view of the stabilization policy, but it is practically impossible to disentangle them. The historical records of government revenue and expenditure are presented as a mixed compilation, influenced by both discretionary action and built-in stabilizers. For example, it is difficult to say to what extent the variations of tax revenues in historical records have been affected by any one factor and to what extent they have been associated with the other. If the tax system were to remain unchanged over a fairly long period of time, we might assume that the variations in tax revenue during this period could largely be attributed to the operation of built-in stabilizers. However, it is almost impossible in practice to find such a long period of an unchanged tax system in post-war Japan.

It is easily recognized that the main objective of the post-war tax policy has been the continuous reduction of individual income taxes in both the 1950s and the 1960s (see Ishi 1993, ch. 3). In fact, tax reductions have been implemented every year except 1960 without special reference to business trends. Tax reductions which have been legislated conform to some considerations other than achieving economic stability, for example an increased tax burden through creeping movements in tax brackets caused by inflation.

It is likely that the coincidence between tax reduction and business contractions may prove to be desirable, even if they have occurred unintentionally. Indeed, well-timed tax cuts might have somehow helped to cushion the decline, but were undertaken for a quite different reason, for example, to mitigate the tax burden of taxpayers from the viewpoint of tax equity. Thus it seems safe to conclude that in the post-war period in Japan, taxation was not subject to discretionary manipulations in the interests of economic stability. If the tax system had been operated with stabilization in mind, no legislative tax cuts should have been required at all during periods of business expansion.

Effects of Built-in Tax Stabilizers

Considering the basic aim of tax policy, it seems doubtful that discretionary actions can be assigned much importance in compensating for business fluctuations. Emphasis, however, must be placed on the fact that the variations in government revenue and tax revenue have actually contributed towards promoting economic stability during a specific period, despite the adverse or perverse effect that a large amount of tax reductions have had. In order to explain this interesting evidence, we need to shift our focus to another aspect of countercyclical devices: built-in tax stabilizers.

Since discretionary tax actions have proved to be ineffective in terms of stabilization policy, it must be stressed that the cyclical behaviour of government revenue, and in turn government budgetary balances, primarily depend on the strong operation of built-in flexibility in the tax system. If the tax laws had not been reformed so often, the cyclical pattern of tax revenue could have been depicted much more clearly. Therefore, it seems appropriate to conjecture that the role of built-in stabilizers in the tax system has worked greatly during the post-war period.

As opposed to individual income taxes, the effectiveness of the built-in stabilizers on corporate taxes is worth noting. The corporate tax reduction was relatively small compared to those for individual income taxes. It may be suggested that there was much more scope for the working of built-in stabilizers in the corporate tax system. Moreover, corporate taxes had occasionally even been increased countercyclically, although on a very small scale. These factors concerning the changes in the tax laws indicate why clear cyclical variations of the corporate tax are so clearly evident, compared with the individual income taxes in which no cyclical behaviour can be seen at all due to substantial distortions of tax cuts.

To recapitulate, the basic objective of this study was to investigate the actual performance of fiscal policy in post-war Japan and determine whether or not, in practice, it has been conducive to economic stability during the specific period of the balanced budget. In dealing with this question, the main feature of the study lies primarily in the examination of monthly data depicting the cyclical behaviour of the several elements of government fiscal activity—revenue, expenditure, and surplus and deficits in the budget.

When taking a general overview of the actual performance of government fiscal operations pursued under the balanced budget principle, the outlook for finding substantial evidence that government fiscal action contributed to economic stability appears unpromising, considering the constraints imposed on countercyclical movements by the empirical rules which have guided government fiscal activity. However, contrary to these initial expectations, the results of this study indicate the effective operation of some countercyclical devices.

In conclusion, the principal findings of the analysis can be summed up as follows:

First, the cyclical behaviour of government surplus and deficit indicates a much more clear-cut countercyclical pattern than was expected in advance. More specially, the surplus–deficit series depict a form of cyclical variation, and furthermore they correspond rather well with the peaks or troughs of the EPA reference dates. In particular, this is the case with the two cycles of the 1958–62 period. Conversely, no evidence was seen in both the pre-1958 and post-1962 cycles to support the cyclical pattern of government surplus and deficit. Some reasons for this should be defined. One reason is that, in the pre-1958 period, business cycles had not yet appeared in the economy as a whole due to the imperfect restoration of the post-war economy. The other main reason is that in the post-1962 cycle the Japanese economy as a whole reached a turning point in its economic structure. It must be emphasized that such evidence can be verified irrespective of the different aspect of government chosen for study—the *general account*, central government, and general government.

Secondly, greater emphasis has been given to the revenue side of the budget as the factor dominating the cyclical patterns of government surplus and deficit. The analysis was conducted by drawing each series of the revenue or expenditure side of the budget in the graph, followed by computing the correction coefficients between the relevant variables. As a result of the analysis, it was possible to conclude that the revenue side, composed of taxes, played a dominant role in forming the countercyclical movements of government budgetary balances, and that the expenditure side displayed some rather destabilizing effects.

Lastly, in examining the countercyclical effect of some important items in the budget by the same method, it must be acknowledged that corporate tax, which amounted to approximately 30 per cent of all tax revenues during the disputed period, are primarily responsible for the patterns displayed by total receipts and in turn by the surplus–deficit series. Furthermore, it appears valid to hypothesize that the built-in stabilizers of the tax system, especially within corporate tax, have generally been more helpful, when compared to deliberate action, in counteracting business fluctuations. Thus, in recounting the fiscal history of post-war Japan, special attention must be given to the working of built-in stabilizers in the corporate tax system in considering stabilization policy.

8

How Financial Resources were Generated in a Growing Economy

One of the most remarkable features about Japan, seen from the rest of the world, was the unstoppable phenomenon of its rapid economic growth. This was true at least until the beginning of the 1990s. Obviously, the fiscal performance or behaviour of the government must have been substantially affected by this post-war economic growth. In general, government fiscal activity interacts with the workings of the economy in many ways; that is to say, fiscal policy changes influence the growth performance of the economy while at the same time fiscal performance tends to be determined by a nation's economic growth.[1]

In this study, a greater emphasis is placed on the passive aspect of public finance in a growing economy: how the government has been influenced in its management of the budget every year through taxes and the public debt. What is of primary interest is how abundant tax revenues had been generated during the period of rapid economic growth before the outbreak of the first oil shock. As a consequence of these ample tax revenues, the government did not rely heavily on the issuance of national bonds during the period in question. The study in this chapter is divided into three parts. First of all, the main features of the Japanese experience are summarized in the context of the interaction between the government's fiscal activities and the economy, as compared with those of other countries. Secondly, empirical analyses are made to explore the mechanism by which ample tax revenues were generated during the era of rapid economic growth and of the subsequent phenomena occurring during the slowdown of growth rates. Thirdly, the focus is turned to the successful deficit reduction due to abundant tax increases during the bubble boom and the resurgence of expanded fiscal deficits after the collapse of the bubble economy.

THE MAIN FEATURES OF FISCAL PERFORMANCE

The Benefits of Growth to the Budget

We will concentrate on the effects of economic growth on the government's fiscal behaviour during the high growth era of the 1950s and 1960s. During this period, Japan achieved the highest sustained rate of growth that the world had ever seen, a phenomenon which must have been substantially related to fiscal performance. On this point, it is interesting to note the following statement:

[1] This chapter partially draws on Ishi 1990.

Japan's high rate of growth and moderate government expenditures (when compared with other developed countries) permit the Japanese to adopt tax policies that can well be envied elsewhere (Peckman and Kaizuka 1976, p. 323).

This argument suggests that rapid economic growth played an important role in sustaining a lower tax burden and keeping the size of the budget moderate. Also, it implies that a sort of 'virtuous cycle' was introduced into the budgeting process due to the massive amount of tax revenues generated by high speed growth. Thus, it is necessary to clarify the interaction between economic growth and the increased revenue sources which provided the main sources of tax reduction, and to a lesser extent, a reduction in government expenditures.

For the purposes of our analysis, the scope of the government budget is defined here as the *general account* of the national government. There are three reasons for this that are worth noting, as stressed previously. First of all, the *general account* is the most fundamental of all the budgets. It can have a great affect on the entire system of budgeting including that of the local governments, although it reflects only a part of the whole budgetary system in quantitative terms. Secondly, the *general account* concept, which is based on fiscal data, is much more useful for analysing the behaviour of the fiscal authority than other methods, such as the SNA concept. To put it another way, the *general account* budget is closely connected to the basis of government fiscal behaviour. Thirdly, almost all national taxes are directly linked with the financing of the *general account*.[2] Consequently, a study of the variation of such tax sources can play a major role in clarifying budgetary performance, although national bond issues are similarly important when taxes do not grow enough to cover total government expenditures.

Three aspects of fiscal behaviour are historically associated with the three specific sub-periods defined below, excluding the latest period of debt accumulation:

1. balanced budget—prior to 1965;
2. fiscal performance with national bond issues—from 1965 to the late 1970s;
3. fiscal consolidation—from the late 1970s up to 1990.

The first period of balanced budgets dominated fiscal behaviour in the post-war period. As noted above, the basis for this lies in the traditional view of 'sound finance' whereby all government expenditures must be financed by the current revenues of the government sector. The concern for a balanced budget was the result of extravagant government spending and inflationary pressures immediately after the end of the Second World War. Although some changes occurred in the broader scope of the public debt as time progressed, national bonds were not issued and a deficit did not appear in the *general account* until 1965. Indeed, not even construction bonds were floated prior to this year. It was at the time of the supplementary budget in fiscal 1965 that

---

[2] Other national taxes (e.g. the gasoline tax, the liquefied petroleum gas tax, the aviation fuel tax, the promotion of resources development tax, etc.) are earmarked to special accounts for the construction of roads, airports, energy resources, etc. They only occupy 2–3 per cent of total national taxes.

national bonds first appeared in the *general account*, reflecting the revenue shortages of the recession.

The second discernible sub-period of fiscal behaviour began with the annual issuance of national bonds. The basic aim of budgetary policy, however, was effectively to restrain the dependency on bond issues when compiling annual budgets. Following the axiom of the balanced budget principle, the issuing of national bonds was rigidly restricted by the Public Finance Law to 'construction bonds' to prevent the easy use of deficit-covering bonds. Fortunately, this target was achieved to some extent, as was the attempt to lower the bond dependency ratio (see Table 6.1) until the mid-1970s, chiefly because the Japanese economy still continued to grow and to produce a massive level of tax revenue. The fiscal authority had repeatedly made great efforts to reduce the issuance of national bonds to maintain the 'sound finance' principle. Thus, although fiscal deficits continued to appear, the government insisted on aiming to balance the budget. This was achieved to some extent, reflecting the massive amount of automatic tax increases which occur in a growing economy.

As large fiscal deficits began to emerge from the structural changes in the Japanese economy, the third period of budgetary policy was initiated after the late 1970s. Among the most important of these changes was the sharp reduction in economic growth rates, causing tax revenue shortages (Ishi 1982*a*). At the same time, a major expansion in spending on social welfare programmes was a crucial factor in the producion of structural deficits (see, for instance, Noguchi 1987*a*). With the emergence of expanding fiscal deficits, the MOF became concerned with the rising deficits and stressed the importance of their reduction as one of the most important objectives of fiscal policy in the 1980s. Eliminating fiscal deficits in light of deficit-covering bonds is officially called 'fiscal consolidation', a policy which was successfully achieved in fiscal 1990. This success can primarily be explained by the windfall increases in tax revenues caused by the bubble boom.

Japan's Fiscal Position—An International Comparison

The fiscal behaviour of a government depends mainly upon the growth of nominal income as opposed to real income in the economy. In the budgetary process, the amount of tax revenue which provides the major source of total revenue is increased or decreased by the speed of income growth in nominal terms. The higher the nominal growth rates in a nation's economy, the higher the tax revenue obtained for budgetary use.

In general, tax revenues, T, may be assumed to be a function of nominal income, Y, the level of exemptions and deductions, E, and the statutory tax schedule, t. The relationship between these variables is shown by the function: $T = (Y, E, t)$. Even if E and t are fixed by the institutional setting, T can increase rapidly so long as Y is growing at a high speed. What is important is the fact that revenue growth has been greater than income growth in Japan, reflecting the highly elastic structure of individual and corporate income taxes. In fact, the income elasticity of income taxes has been higher than unity, which has also helped to increase tax revenue in a growing economy (Ishi 1968).

TABLE 8.1. *Nominal GDP growth rates in G7 countries—five years averages (%)*

Year	Canada	USA	Japan	France	Germany	Italy	UK
1952–55	7.14	4.79	11.43[a]	5.69[a]	9.98[a]	9.13	6.93
1956–60	6.18	4.75	12.63	11.43	9.38	7.67	5.88
1961–65	8.12	6.46	15.74	10.29	8.70	11.04	6.82
1966–70	9.14	7.56	17.47	10.14	8.10	9.97	7.49
1971–75	14.03	9.44	15.22	13.17	8.78	14.94	15.72
1976–80	12.61	11.17	10.13	13.70	7.57	22.03	16.79
1981–85	9.15	8.09	5.66	10.84	4.37	15.62	8.80
1986–90	8.00	7.30	6.26	7.70	6.60	12.40	10.80

Source: Calculated from OECD, *National Accounts*, vol. 1, 1951–1980, and 1965–1985 (Paris, 1982 and 1988).
IMF, *International Financial Statistical Year Book*, 1995.
Note:
  [a] Three year averages in 1953–55.

One of the dominant factors in securing abundant revenue sources is how fast the economy has been expanding in terms of nominal growth rates. Table 8.1 shows the novel aspects of Japanese economic growth in comparison with the nominal GDP growth rates of other G7 countries. Obviously, Japan achieved a post-war growth rate far above that experienced by any other advanced country prior to the mid-1970s. Japanese growth rates reached the topmost rank of 11.43 per cent in 1952–55 to 17.47 per cent in 1966–70, and still maintained the second highest rank in 1971–75, after the UK. Thus, the era of high growth had been sustained for two decades, starting in the 1950s.

By contrast, after the mid-1970s, economic growth slowed down substantially. We should note in particular that the average annual growth for 1981–85 was 5.66 per cent, which was less than half the rate that prevailed during the previous thirty years, although it recovered to 6.26 per cent for 1986–90, mainly as a result of the bubble boom. As far as nominal growth is concerned, the era of Japan's high growth has ended,[3] and a new era of slower growth has been ushered in (Lincoln 1988, ch. 2).

It is important to clarify the kind of impact Japan's growth performance has had on the budget and on tax revenue. It seems clear that nominal income growth generated an affluent source of revenue which was appropriated for new expenditure programmes and large tax cuts, especially during the high growth period.

---

[3] Of course, in terms of real growth Japan still managed to outdistance all other advanced countries, albeit by a small margin. The gap between nominal and real growth rates is explained by the extremely low rate of inflation in Japan during the 1980s. In terms of average increases in the CPI during the period 1981–85, Japan saw a 2.52 per cent increase, while the USA saw a 5.52 per cent, the UK a 7.24 per cent, West Germany a 3.90 per cent, and France a 9.60 per cent increase.

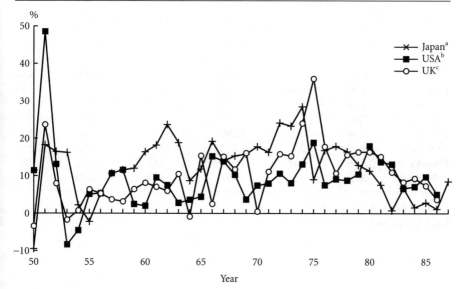

FIGURE 8.1. *Growth rates of budgetary expenditure of the central government*

Source: MOF, Tax Bureau, *Primary Statistics of Taxation* (in Japanese), each year

Note: Calculated from final settlement figures:
a. General account of the central government
b. Federal budget
c. Central government budget excluding national insurance payment

Our first task is to examine the impact of rapid economic growth on the size of the budget. Although there are some conceptual differences in the budgetary systems of each country, Figure 8.1 shows the trends of annual growth rates in the budgets of three countries in terms of central government expenditure. It should be noted that there is a close resemblance between the curves in Figure 8.1 and growth rates in Table 8.1. It appears that the growth of the budget in expenditure terms has changed in relation to the patterns of economic growth. It is striking to observe, in Japan in particular, the higher growth rates of budgetary expenditure compared to the two other countries during the pre-1975 period. Therefore, we can conjecture that the annual management of the budget is influenced by economic growth to a considerable extent.

Variations in the growth of budget expenditure are almost entirely reflections of the tax increases produced by the economic fluctuations in growth terms. In Table 8.2, the growth rates of national taxes in six countries are shown in terms of five-year averages, to simplify the comparison with the nominal GDP growth rates in Table 8.1. Japan and also France constantly maintained two-digit growth rates in tax revenue until the end of the period from 1976–80. Abundant financial resources for constructing annual budgets were provided by large levels of national tax increases. This growth in tax revenue, however, dropped sharply in the first half of the 1980s, and induced the necessity of fiscal consolidation. No doubt, this was caused by the slowdown in economic growth.

TABLE 8.2. *Growth rates of national taxes in selected countries—five years averages (%)*

Year	USA	Japan	France	Germany	Italy	UK
1951–55	6.39	10.89	12.84	14.84	14.66	4.66
1956–60	4.80	14.44	15.22	9.94	8.32	3.56
1961–65	4.74	12.94	10.76	9.52	12.29	7.70
1966–70	7.76	18.90	11.14	8.11	9.91	12.85
1971–75	6.46	14.21	12.89	9.11	15.03	13.92
1976–80	16.47	15.01	17.77	12.6	28.96	20.07
1981–85	5.56	6.66	11.25	3.68	20.31	10.02
1986–90	3.35	9.90	6.59	4.09	13.70	9.66

Source: Calculated from the MOF data.

Note: As Figure 8.1.

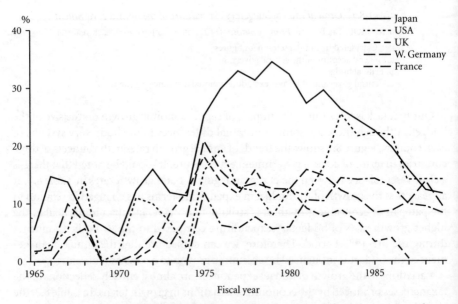

FIGURE 8.2. *Trends of fiscal deficits of central government: bond dependency ratio and expenditure–revenue gap ratios in selected countries*

Source: Japan—Fiscal Statistics (Zaisei Tokei); USA—the Budget of the US Government; UK—Financial Statistics; Germany—Finanzberricht; France—Loi de Finances, Loi Rectificatives, Loi de Reglement, Les Notes Bleus

Note: Japan uses the bond dependency ratio: the ratio of national bond issues to total expenditure in the *general account*. In other countries, the ratio of the government expenditure–revenue gap is used as an indicator of the fiscal deficit of the central government

A reduction in tax revenue augmented the reliance instead on public debt to obtain revenue sources for the budget. It is evident that debt issues tended to be stimulated by the reduction in tax revenue.

Figure 8.2 shows the trends of fiscal deficits in four major countries, starting from fiscal 1965 when the Japanese government issued national bonds for the first time in its post-war history. Until the late 1980s, the deficits in Japan grew, by and large, at a higher level than those in other countries. In particular, the gap between Japan and the three other countries began to increase tremendously after the mid-1970s.

A more detailed inspection reveals that the Japanese government started from relatively small deficits, measured as a ratio of bond issues to central government expenditures, from fiscal 1965 until fiscal 1975 (5 to 16 per cent). There was then a very rapid build-up of deficits, reaching a peak of 34.7 per cent in fiscal 1979. The level of the bond dependency ratio fell somewhat after that, but it remained in the range of 23–32 per cent in the early 1980s. It was not until the end of the 1990s that the dependency ratio fell to as low as 10 per cent. The resulting deficits turned out to be much larger than anything expected since the oil shocks, mainly because tax revenue failed to grow as originally predicted due to a slower growing economy. Thus, the importance of fiscal consolidation in the budget became a policy target of the MOF.

In short, even the trend of widening deficits can partly be explained by the variations in tax revenue generated in a growing economy. What is important in this context is to explore how tax revenues were generated in the process of economic growth.

HOW HAVE TAX REVENUES BEEN GENERATED BY ECONOMIC GROWTH?

The Conceptual Framework of Natural Tax Increases

Apparently, rapid economic growth has been closely tied to the natural increase in tax revenue from which the government derived the affluence it needed for constructing the budget. What exactly is meant by a natural increase in tax revenue? Even if the tax system remains fixed, tax revenue can increase naturally as it reflects the expansion of nominal income. The concept of natural tax increases plays a key role in explaining variations in the fiscal behaviour of the Japanese government.

The percentage increases in tax revenue given in Table 8.2 are derived from final settlement figures, which have already eliminated a certain proportion of the tax cuts from the new revenue sources used for formulating the budget each year. Thus, these tax figures are based on *ex post* data and only partly explain how economic growth can produce an increase in tax revenue. In order to analyse the impact of growth on tax revenue more comprehensively, we need to study in detail the natural increase of tax revenue before subtracting tax cuts. This is an *ex ante* concept based on the anticipated or expected figures for the coming fiscal year. This estimation is relevant to budget preparation, and is usually made several months before the beginning of the new fiscal year in April.

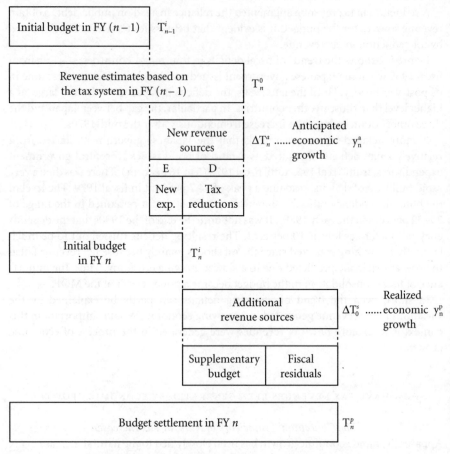

FIGURE 8.3. *The budgeting process and tax revenue sources*

Figure 8.3 delineates the budgetary process in an arbitrary fiscal year FYn, assuming that the budget is financed only by taxes. In constructing the initial budget, its revenue source, T_n^i, primarily depends upon the revenue estimates, T_n^0, with the tax system unchanged in (FY$n-1$), that would be produced by economic expansion. Thus, the gap between T_n^0 and T_{n-1}^i is defined as the natural increase of tax revenues, ΔT_n^a, appropriated for new revenue sources, which in turn are used for either new expenditure programmes or tax reductions. Only a part of the new government expenditures are added to the previous initial budget, resulting in the current initial budget in FYn.

In the high growth era, the Japanese government adopted an annual tax cut policy of a considerable size (Ishi 1993, ch. 3). These tax cuts were related to a specific tax policy, the purpose of which was to keep the ratio of tax revenue to national income

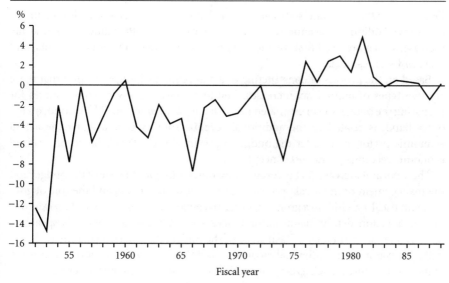

FIGURE 8.4. *Tax reductions as a percentage of new revenue estimates*
Source: As Figure 8.1
Note: The figure is the percentage change of D/T_n^0 in Figure 8.3

close to 20 per cent, as noted before. This policy was strictly enforced in the period 1955–65. In a growing economy like that of post-war Japan, such a policy leads to large tax reductions. In particular, individual income tax in Japan was significantly reduced every year to avoid overburdening the taxpayers through 'bracket creep'. If income tax reductions had not been implemented, the tax burden would have increased considerably.

Why were the large-scale tax reductions successful in the high growth period? Needless to say, the abundant revenue source, derived from the natural tax increases, enabled the government to reduce the tax burden to a great extent. In Figure 8.4, the trend of tax reductions is shown as a percentage of new revenue estimates for fiscal 1952–90. Almost every year prior to fiscal 1975, except for fiscal 1960, revenue sources for tax reductions were secured in the range of 2–15 per cent of total new revenue estimates for use in the initial budget. The trend reversed into tax increases after the mid-1970s, mainly reflecting the slowdown in economic growth.

Returning to Figure 8.3, let us consider the enforcement process of the initial budget until the end of the fiscal year is reached. Once the initial budget begins in April of each year, its process is generally affected by the actual performance of the economy, say by an unexpected recession, higher inflation, natural disasters, etc. Reflecting the changes occurring during the fiscal year in question, the initial amount of the budget does not normally coincide with the final settlement of the budget. In an era of high growth, additional revenue sources are expected to appear (this case is depicted in

Figure 8.3), while revenue shortages could also be induced by sharp slumps in the economy. Additional revenue sources are regarded as another kind of natural tax increase, which are used first for the supplementary budget, including tax cuts, and then for fiscal residuals.

Based on the process of constructing and enforcing the budget, we find that there are two types of natural tax increases. The first concerns new revenue sources for preparing the budget on an estimated basis, that is, an *ex ante* type. The second, on the other hand, is related to the additional revenue sources generated by the actual economic performance after the budget is put into force. This is based on realized economic relations, an *ex post* concept.

These natural increases in tax revenue obviously influence the size of the budget and the management of the fiscal performance each year. To understand the role of government fiscal activities in a growing economy, emphais should be placed on examining which factors determine the natural increases in tax revenue. Generally speaking, tax revenues are estimated at each stage of the budgeting process using micro-based data. For example, the individual income tax is divided into sub-categories, according to its income sources such as employment income, business income, interest income, etc. Each tax revenue is estimated from the trend of variations in these income sources and summed to obtain the estimated total tax revenue. The same procedures are applied in estimating other taxes: corporate tax, alcoholic beverages tax, the tax on gasoline, etc. Since such a micro-based approach is less useful for our analysis, we will employ nominal rates of growth as a general indicator to determine the natural tax increases, represented by the growth of each taxable base.

Empirical Results

Nominal rates of economic growth are classified into two distinctive categories: anticipated rates (y^a), an *ex ante* concept, and actual or realized rates (y^p), an *ex post* concept. In Japan, the EPA publishes the GDP series at three different stages, depending on the time of estimation: Y'' stands for preliminary GDP, Y' for interim GDP and Y for realized GDP.

Based on these data, we can calculate each n period growth rate as follows:

$$y_n^a = \frac{Y_n'' - Y_{n-1}'}{Y_{n-1}'} \tag{8.1}$$

$$y_n^p = \frac{Y_n - Y_{n-1}}{Y_{n-1}} \tag{8.2}$$

Figure 6.3 illustrates both the anticipated and the actual rates of economic growth since fiscal 1950. Actual growth rates noticeably exceeded anticipated rates until fiscal 1974 except for one year. After this date the relationship was reversed. In other words, the government tended to underestimate the trend of economic growth before the outbreak of the oil shock, but since the mid-1970s it has overestimated growth rates almost every year.

It seems that this phenomenon bears a close relation to the fiscal behaviour of the government. In particular, the natural increase of tax revenue seems to have been created intentionally until the mid-1970s, since the government consistently under-estimated the amount of tax appropriate for government expenditure at the first stage of constructing the budget. Natural tax increases, therefore, tended to emerge during the fiscal year as a result of the biased estimates of tax revenue. The higher the rate of economic growth, the larger the natural increase in tax revenue that can be expected. A question can be raised about the estimation of the natural tax increases. These increases are largely based on the anticipated rate of economic growth which is usually computed five or six months before the beginning of the fiscal year. As an illus-tration, let us suppose that GDP is expected to expand by 12 per cent in the next year. Based upon this anticipated rate, the MOF usually estimates the projected nat-ural tax increase. When doing so, some non-economic biasing factors can easily be introduced into the calculation of the anticipated rate of economic growth. Frequently, the GDP growth rate was intentionally underestimated in order to decrease the ex-pected amount of the natural tax increase used as a financial resource at this stage of budgetary preparations. Thus, since at the end of each fiscal year the realized rate of growth was always much higher (e.g. 18 per cent) than the anticipated rate, an enormous natural increase in tax revenue materialized after the implementation of the new budget.

As shown in Figure 8.3, there are close connections between the natural increase in tax revenue and the rate of economic growth in terms of both *ex ante* and *ex post* relations. Some estimates are made to clarify these relationships in crude terms. In order to ensure the functional relationship among the variables consistently exists, tax revenue is also reformulated in terms of growth rates:

$$t_n^a = \frac{\Delta T_n^a}{T_{n-1}^i} \tag{8.3}$$

$$t_n^p = \frac{\Delta T_n^s}{T_n^i} \tag{8.4}$$

where t_n^a is the rate of natural tax increase in the budget compilation of FYn, and t_n^p is the other rate relevant to the implementation of the budget in question. Using equa-tions (8.1) to (8.4), both *ex ante* and *ex post* relations are determined by the following simple formulae:

$$t^a = a_0 + a_1 y^a \tag{8.5}$$

$$t^p = b_0 + b_1 y^p \tag{8.6}$$

We estimate these regression equations in three sub-periods, roughly coinciding with the empirical rules of budgetary policy mentioned previously.

TABLE 8.3. *Empirical results: revenue increases in response to income growth*

Period	Ex-ante relations	Period	Ex-post relations
1952–64	$t^a = 5.295 + 2.583\, y^a$	1952–63	$t^p = -2.662 + 1.032\, y^p$
	(0.611) (2.170)		(−0.800) (4.069)
	$\bar{R}^2 = 0.320^*\ dw = 1.456$		$\bar{R}^2 = 0.648^{**}\ dw = 2.156$
1965–79	$t^a = -34.881 + 3.984\, y^a$	1964–78	$t^p = -16.967 + 1.335\, y^p$
	(−2.515) (3.864)		(−3.087) (3.888)
	$\bar{R}^2 = 0.576^{**}\ dw = 1.845$		$\bar{R}^2 = 0.579^{**}\ dw = 2.018$
1980–89	$t^a = -65.001 + 8.804\, y^a$	1979–86	$t^p = -10.896 + 1.737\, y^p$
	(−2.831) (4.179)		(−0.858) (0.855)
	$\bar{R}^2 = 0.716^{**}\ dw = 1.593$		$\bar{R}^2 = 0.128\ dw = 1.637$

Note: The maximum likelihood (ML) method was used to generate all these equations. $\bar{R}^2$ is the coefficient of determination adjusted for degrees of freedom, ** and * indicate significance at the 1 and 5 per cent levels, respectively, *dw* is the Durbin–Watson statistic, and the values in parentheses are *t*-statistics.

In Table 8.3, the empirical estimates are summarized, although one of the results is not statistically significant. We can find three points worth noting. First, roughly speaking there is a significant relationship between the rate of natural tax increases and economic growth in the two different stages of constructing and enforcing the budget. The higher the economic growth rates, the more tax revenue increases naturally.

Secondly, the equations generally show a downward movement as time passes. In particular, we can observe more clear-cut downward shifts in the *ex ante* relationships. This implies that in the earlier period of 1952–64 even a small value of y^a could generate a substantial amount of natural tax revenue for budgetary use. The same holds in large part for the *ex post* relationships in 1952–64. After the period of balanced budgets ended, however, major changes were made to the process of generating tax revenue. Since the intercepts of each equation rise negatively in 1965–79 and 1980–89, the economy would have to grow at a much higher rate to produce sufficient taxes to be seen as a new revenue source than it did in 1952–64.

Thirdly, we should note the relatively poor results of our estimates. The main reason for this is that economic growth rates play a limited role in determining the growth rate of natural tax increases.

A SUCCESSFUL DEFICIT REDUCTION AND EXPANDED FISCAL DEFICITS ONCE AGAIN

Enormous Expansion of Tax Increases

After the end of the rapid economic growth period in the mid-1970s, the government began to suffer from revenue shortages, reflecting the slowdown in growth rates. Since then, the primary goal of fiscal policy became fiscal consolidation. Fiscal consolidation which had been persistently targeted by the MOF was finally attained in fiscal 1990, mainly due to expanded tax revenues during the bubble boom. It is important to explore the background of this success story. However, the budget imbalance was aggravated once again soon after the collapse of the bubble economy. It is also important to investigate how rapidly fiscal deficits have expanded in a short period of time. In what follows, attention is paid the changing state of fiscal performance in more recent years in an attempt to explain fiscal deficits.

As can be conjectured from Figure 6.4, tax revenue tended to vary in response to economic expansion or contraction. Since the bubble boom became conspicuous, the growth rates of national tax revenue in the *general account* of the national government began to rise sharply at a much faster pace than in the pre-bubble period. Indeed, the figures were 9.6 per cent in 1986, 11.8 per cent in 1987, 8.6 per cent in 1988, 8.1 per cent in 1989 and 9.4 per cent in 1990, all of which exceeded the nominal growth rates of GDP by a large margin. As noted in Chapter 4, the phenomenon of the economic bubble induced brisk transactions with speculation in both security and land markets, and in turn expanded the taxable base to a great extent due to vigorous business activity.

As an example, we can consider the security transaction tax,[4] which continuously generated an enormous amount of tax revenue, reflecting the increased number of transactions which took place at a higher price level in the security markets. The revenue from security transaction tax grew at 103.9 per cent in 1986, 29.5 per cent in 1987, and 29.5 per cent in 1987. Similarly, corporate tax and self-assessed income tax expanded rapidly, partly because large corporate profits emerged from the business expansion brought on by asset inflation, and partly because the capital gains tax on land sales automatically swelled the income tax base for tax returns. Other taxes, such as the register licence tax, the property tax, the real estate acquisition tax, etc., also increased their revenue levels due to the expansion of related business activities.

We can attempt to estimate the tax revenue due to the bubble boom for the period 1975–96 in order to compare actual tax revenue with the assumed standard case shown in Figure 8.5. The standard tax revenue can be computed using the formula in equation (8.7). The relative change of tax revenue in a growing economy is represented as follows. Let η stand for the GDP elasticity of tax revenues, T for tax revenue and Y for GDP.

$$\eta = \frac{\dfrac{\Delta T}{T}}{\dfrac{\Delta Y}{Y}} = \frac{\dfrac{T_n - T_{n-1}}{T_{n-1}}}{\dfrac{\Delta Y}{Y}}$$

$$\therefore T_n = T_{n-1}(\eta \frac{\Delta Y}{Y} + 1)$$

(8.7)

Furthermore, tax revenues each year vary more or less due to deliberate changes in the tax code. Let us add $\pm \alpha$ for tax increases or decreases caused by such a deliberate

---

[4] The security transaction tax was created in 1953 when the capital gains tax on the sale of securities was repealed.

policy change, and T_n^* is defined as shown in equation (8.8) after adjusting for these institutional changes.

$$T_n^* = T_n \pm \alpha$$

$$= T_{n-1}\left(\eta\frac{\Delta Y}{Y} + 1\right) \pm \alpha \qquad (8.8)$$

Using the average η for 1975–85, it is assumed that η is equal to 1.1. By using the actual annual growth rates of nominal GDP $\Delta Y/Y$, we can obtain each year the value of T_n^* after 1986, starting from T_{n-1} in 1985. Regarding the pre-1985 values of the tax revenues, from (8.7) we get

$$T_{n-1} = \frac{T_n}{\eta\dfrac{\Delta Y}{Y} + 1} \qquad (8.9)$$

To make adjustments for deliberate tax changes, $\pm\alpha$ is added to the above formula from which the adjusted T_{n-1}^* is derived.

In Figure 8.5, the standard tax level is extrapolated after 1986 by the dotted line, assuming that a normal tax structure would appear in line with the period 1975–85 without the bubble phenomenon. The gap between the two lines can be explained as the additional expansion of tax revenue due to the occurrence of the bubble. Before 1985 the two lines move almost in parallel, while the gap between them begins to widen from 1986 to 1991. These expanded tax revenues may be regarded as windfall revenues in favour of the MOF. No doubt, they were of great help in reducing fiscal deficits, successfully leading to the attainment of the consolidation target for fully eliminating the issuance of deficit-covering bonds by the fiscal 1990 budget.

In order to investigate the background of fiscal consolidation, it would be worthwhile to discuss how the expanded tax revenues have been appropriated during the bubble period. For this purpose, Figure 8.6 is offered to clarify the fiscal performance regarding the allocation of additional revenues above the 1985 level to specific expenditure items during 1985–90. The accumulated tax increments for the six years were ¥63.5 trillion, as seen on the right hand axis, with the majority being appropriated for both debt reduction and entitlement expenditure (i.e. debt services and tax shared grants to local governments).

The dotted line in Figure 8.6 indicates the same level of standard tax revenue as that in Figure 8.5. Thus, the gap above this line shows the portion of tax increases due to the bubble which were fully appropriated for both debt reduction and entitlement expenditure. It can be argued that the bubble economy generated more tax revenue than a normal state of the economy would have done, and contributed greatly to the curtailment of the budget imbalance as well as to the necessary increases in entitlement expenditure. Fiscal consolidation was fortunately achieved as a result of these unintended windfall revenue gains due to the bubble.

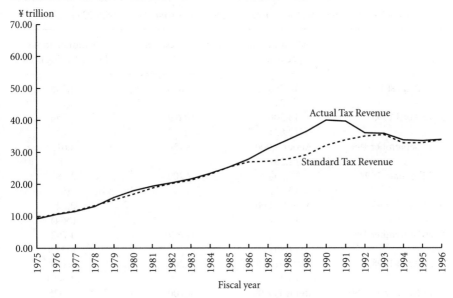

FIGURE 8.5. *Expanded tax revenues due to the 'bubble'*

Source: Data presented to the Tax Advisory Commission

Note: Actual tax revenue for 1975–96 is a final figure derived from the settlement budget. The 1995 figure is taken from preliminary data after the supplementary budget, while the 1996 figure is one estimated at the time of the initial budget. See text for the estimation of standard tax revenue

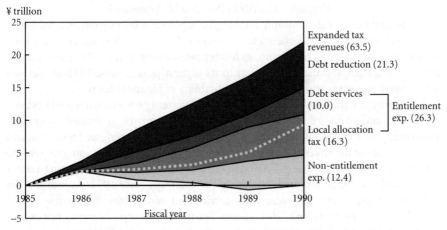

FIGURE 8.6. *How expanded tax revenues due to the 'bubble' have been appropriated, 1985–90*

Note: Figures in parentheses on the right-hand axis are the accumulated amounts of relevant revenue and expenditure for 1985–90. The dotted line indicates the case of standard tax in Figure 8.5

TABLE 8.4. *Economic packages and fiscal expansionary measures: 1992–99 (¥ billion)*

Dates	Total scale of the package	Public investment	National bonds (debt-covering bonds)
1 28 August 1992	10,700 (2.31)	8,600	2,256 (0)
2 13 April 1993	13,200 (2,83)	10,620	2,246 (0)
3 16 September 1993	About 6,000 (1.28)	5,150	3,616 (0)
4 8 February 1994	15,250 (3.21)	7,200	2,182 (0)
5 14 April 1995	About 7,000 (1.41)	n.a.	2,826 (564)
6 20 September 1995	14,220 (2.90)	12,810	4,702 (211)
7 24 April 1998	About 16,000 (3.22)	6,200	6,118 (2,000)
8 16 November 1998	About 17,000 (3.42)	8,100	12,325 (7,810)
9 11 November 1999	About 17,000 (3.40)	6,800	7,566 (3,740)

Source: Data from the MOF.

Note: Figures in parentheses under the heading of the total scale of the package are percentages relative to nominal GDP.

Expanded Deficits in Post-Bubble Recession

Since the collapse of the economic bubble, the Japanese economy has entered into a prolonged recession, and all the signs have pointed to a more hesitant recovery even though an upward trend has begun, as has repeatedly been argued. To make matters worse, a sharp appreciation of the yen to its highest peak in mid-1995 accelerated deflationary pressures and lowered the profitability of Japanese firms.

Accordingly, in the first half of the 1990s, the persistent policy requirement has been for a solid and sustained recovery, relying upon the growth of domestic demand. Economic growth rates have constantly been lower than projected (see Figure 6.3) and an urgent duty of the government has been the stimulation of the economy to pave the way for a faster recovery. The government has taken the initiative in triggering a series of economic packages designed to perk up the economy since 1992. As indicated in Table 8.4, these policy packages were carried out nine times during the period 1992–99, involving a total of ¥116.4 trillion. The policy measures originate not only in the *general account* of the national government, but also in the FILP and in the local government budgets. In addition, government loans with favourable interest rates are involved in these packages, as well as expenditure increases and tax reductions.

Each time, the total scale of the comprehensive packages amounted to 2–3 per cent of GDP in light of increased public investment. To implement such policy measures, the government was compelled to compile the supplementary budget within the fiscal year after the initial budget had started. Needless to say, both expenditure increases and tax cuts have essentially ensured the expansion of the fiscal deficits during the period in question.

Despite such a successive round of fiscal expansion in a relatively short period, the policy failed to generate a strong and early recovery. One notable factor behind this failure can be explained by the following statement:

Over one third of these packages was devoted to purchases of land and increases in lending by government financial institutions, much of which appears to have replaced private lending. Indeed, the additional demand impact of the packages amounted to only 20 percent of the total shortfall between actual and potential output in the current cycle (OECD 1995, p. 23).

Attention should also be paid to the reduced effects of fiscal stimuli through increases in public investment. In particular, the multiplier effect of public investment has shown a substantial decline during the 1980s and 1990s. If we employ the estimation results of the EPA models, the average multiplier values have continued to fall from 2.27 (1957–71), 1.47 (Q1 in 1976–Q1 in 1982) to 1.32 (Q1 in 1983–Q4 in 1992).[5]

Why have the expansionary effects of public investment been incrementally weakened? There are four factors worth noting. First of all, the Japanese industrial structure has changed from being based on the heavy-chemical and construction industries to being service and processed-based. As a result, production inducement coefficients have substantially decreased, curtailing the relevant multiplier effects. Secondly, international capital movements have begun to induce both increases in interest rates and yen appreciation via expanded public investment, and in turn have lowered the stimulative effect of fiscal expansion. Thirdly, the openness of the economy has promoted the overseas leakage of a portion of the multiplier effects through strong import growth. Lastly, as stressed earlier, the enormous rise in land prices in the 1980s has led to increased expenses on land purchases absorbing a substantial proportion of public investment in the budget. Given these structural changes, it may be argued that the contemporary economy is not flexible enough to respond smoothly to policy-induced shocks to continue to promote economic expansion.

Moreover, as pointed out in Chapter 4, the recent strains in the financial sector have apparently weakened the expansionary effects of fiscal and monetary policies. Even the most expansionary monetary policy has not been rapid and effective enough to provide adequate support to the depressed economy.

---

[5] These values are obtained from (1) Pilot Model SP-18 (December 1974), (2) The 2nd World Economic Model (March 1985), and (3) The 5th World Economic Model (December 1994). See, Economic Research Institute, EPA (1995).

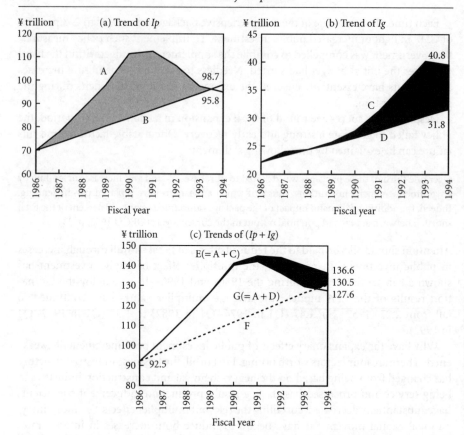

FIGURE 8.7. *Trends of private investment and government investment*

Note: *Ip* includes both private fixed and residential investment, and *Ig* is government capital formation. The lines A, C, and E are actual expenditure while the lines B, D, and F are trend lines extrapolated using nominal GDP growth rates

Whether the economic packages containing expanded public investment initiatives were completely ineffective or not remains an open question. Figure 8.7 analyses the relationship between private and public investment since the start of the bubble economy. The three parts of the figure depict the parts played by private investment, public investment, and both together, which actually expanded above their trend lines extrapolated from the growth rates of nominal GDP in the national account framework. Private investment in Figure 8.7(a) began to expand from 1986, mainly reflecting the brisk investment activity due to the bubble phenomenon. By contrast, public investment started its expanded role in 1991 to make up for the slowdown in private investment, as indicated in Figure 8.7(b) (take note of the different scales on the vertical axes in both figures). Public investment has increased markedly in line with the policy of pump-priming expenditures in the mid-1990s.

Figure 8.7(c) combines the trends in both private and public investment. No doubt, public investment has played a vital role in compensating for the decline in private investment by triggering, to a considerable extent, successive rounds of fiscal expansion. It appears that fiscal expansion was able to curtail the declining tendency in private investment and in turn restrain the further downward movement of the economy after the burst of the bubble, although it could not stimulate a full recovery of the Japanese economy.

A Further Public Debt Explosion?

Reflecting the weaker recovery and the large fiscal expansion after the collapse of the bubble economy, Japan's fiscal position deteriorated to a significant degree during 1992–96. This phenomenon entirely reversed the consolidation efforts undertaken by the government since the early 1980s. Although much of the rapid and spectacular widening of fiscal deficits was due to the influence of the past recession, there was no doubt a structural deterioration deeply rooted in the recent budgetary process.

In order to clarify the recent tendency towards budgetary imbalances, it is important to take into consideration the concept of structural deficits, to eliminate casual short-run fluctuations, thereby creating a better reflection of the real state of the budget. According to the IMF calculation (IMF 1996, p. 23), there was a clear turning point in 1993 with the structural balance moving from a surplus to a deficit of 1.0 per cent of GDP in the general government budget. In fact, there was still a structural surplus in1990 of 1.7 per cent of GDP, while a structural deficit began to emerge in both the central and local government budgets (excluding the social security fund from the general government) of 1.6 per cent of GDP. The structural deficit–GDP ratio is expected to rise from 1.2 per cent (4.5 per cent) in 1995 to 2.5 per cent (5.4 per cent) in 2001 (the percentages in parentheses are those excluding the social security fund.) Thus, quite apart from cyclical deficits which automatically disappear as business recovery progresses, reducing the current structural deficits will require the shifting of the government's efforts towards expenditure cuts and away from tax increases.

Anxieties about a public debt explosion abound once again, rivalling and perhaps even overshadowing the experience after the mid-1970s. How should we predict future fiscal positions? The MOF has estimated the future trend of fiscal deficits and debt accumulation in 1996, making several assumptions regarding the growth rates of non-entitlement expenditures. First of all, even if entitlement expenditures remain at the same level as in fiscal 1996 (i.e. a zero growth rate), it would not be until fiscal 2003 that deficit-covering bonds in the *general account* of the national government could be curtailed. This implies that a 20 per cent cut in expenditure is absolutely necessary by fiscal 2001, as compared with the baseline case of extrapolating non-entitlement expenditure growth at its current rate with no expenditure cuts.[6] No doubt, there would be a great deal of hardship if expenditures were cut every year.

---

[6] This is derived from the MOF's data on the 'Hypothetical calculations of the revenue–expenditure gap from a medium-term point of view, February 1996.

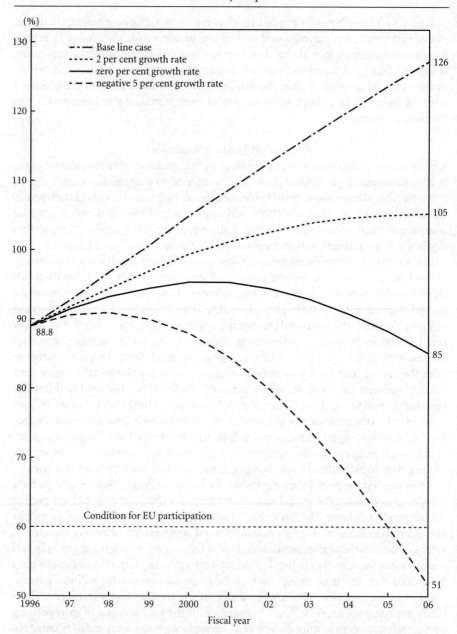

(%)

FIGURE 8.8. *Alternative predictions of the debt–GDP ratio in the general government*

Note: The four cases are dependent upon the assumed growth rates of non-entitlement expenditure. The base line case implies a growth rate in keeping with the past trend without any policy changes (i.e. 3.1 per cent after fiscal 1999)

Secondly, according to the MOF's calculations, we can predict how much out-standing debt will expand relative to GDP until 2006 in the general government,[7] as indicated in Figure 8.8. Given a growth rate of nominal GDP at 3.5 per cent as assumed in the economic plan of EPA in 1995, the debt–GDP ratio will increase to a level of 126 per cent in fiscal 2006, starting from nearly 90 per cent in fiscal 1996, if the trend of government expenditure continues to increase at its current rate and the government follow a non-intervention policy. If the same level of non-entitlement expenditures could be successfully maintained (i.e. at zero growth) from the mid-1990s until approximately 2005, the debt–GDP ratio would decline slightly below the 1996 level. However, it would still be impossible for Japan to attain the Maastrict criterion of 60 per cent. Therefore, the condition necessary for satisfying the 60 per cent rule would be to establish a 5 per cent reduction in non-entitlement expenditure.

As evident from the future predictions described above, fiscal consolidation is no doubt a high priority on the policy agenda. Greater efforts will have to be placed on the control of government expenditure, rather than running the risk of increasing taxation. Indeed, the current political and economic context is an invitation to make rapid progress in this field. It seems that the current level of debt accumulation is a powerful incentive not to postpone the adjustments to deficit reduction any longer.

---

[7] It is difficult to estimate directly the future forecast of the debt–GDP ratio in the general government. Consequently, the debt–GDP ratio in the *general account* of the national government, which is more easily calculated, is enlarged by the ratio 88.8/48.3, the relevant debt–GDP ratio between the two levels of government in 1996. It appears, however, that this estimate, made in 1996, is already out of date, given the successive rounds of fiscal expansion attempted by the Obuchi cabinet.

Part III
Specific Aspects of Budgetary Activities

9
Public Expenditure Trends in Light of Human Resource Development

Economic development in a country is by and large influenced by government policies, in particular through public expenditure in the budget. Thus, it is important to analyse trends in the allocation of public expenditures in order to clarify how efficiently they could affect the patterns of a nation's development. In recent years, the tendency has been to emphasize the role of public expenditure to develop human resources, via social services such as education and health, as well as real resources, in the public sector.[1]

The main objective in this chapter is to investigate overall trends of public expenditure in the light of human resource development. In what follows our concerns are with empirical findings about the changing patterns of public expenditure during the process of economic development in the last several decades of the twentieth century.

This chapter is divided into three parts. First of all, the overall patterns of public expenditure and GDP are summarized as an introduction to this study. Secondly, we will focus on the allocation of public expenditure by function in light of education and health. Thirdly, specific aspects of public expenditure allocation in the budgetary process are examined in view of an efficient and rigid public works programme.

TRENDS IN PUBLIC EXPENDITURE AND GDP

Available Data
Before conducting the necessary analyses, the availability of relevant data must be examined to achieve any meaningful results for this study. Broadly speaking, the necessary data can be derived from two statistical sources. One relies on national income (NI) statistics which can be obtained from the EPA's *Annual Report of National Accounts*. The other source consists of data from fiscal statistics at the national and local government level in which relevant public expenditure information is compiled by the MOF and the MOHA. For our purposes, NI statistics are more useful for public expenditure analyses, especially for international comparison.

Since fiscal statistics merely record transactions or outlays in budgetary terms (including fiscal transfers from one account to another), they would be of little use for economic analyses from an international perspective. On the other hand, NI statistics

---

[1] This chapter draws mainly on Ishi (1995a and 1995b).

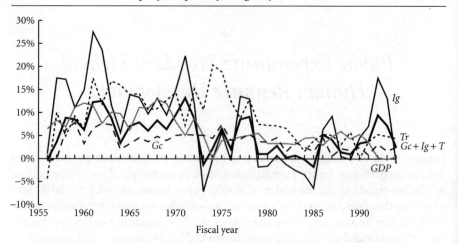

FIGURE 9.1. *Real growth rates of public expenditure in the general government and GDP, in constant 1985 prices 1956–94*

depend on the SNA (the System of National Account) concept which is based on a consistent framework of national income, which can easily be adopted to compare one country with another.

However, the data drawn from NI statistics have the disadvantage that they lack any detailed information of public sector expenditure by function. The data required for this study are only available to us from the following tables of the *Annual Report on National Accounts*, available for specific periods, as indicated:

1. gross national expenditure at nominal and constant prices: from 1955;
2. current and capital transactions by the sub-sectors of general government: from 1970;
3. selected outlays of general government by function1:[2] from 1970.

Data for public expenditure relating to periods dating to pre-1955 can be obtained from other statistical sources, but not all of them are consistent with those listed above. As a consequence, inasmuch as any systematic analysis within a consistent framework is concerned, our major attempt was necessarily restricted to relatively shorter periods than had been expected in the present study. It must be admitted that the coverage offered by the data is very limited (i.e. 1970–94) particularly in the case of classifying public expenditures by function which is of primary importance for this study.

---

[2] Nine functional classifications of public expenditure at the level of general government as a whole are available, but they are not divided between the central and local governments according to official data. Fortunately, however, the data were divided into the two levels of the government with the assistance of EPA staff, and figures have been calculated on an informal basis.

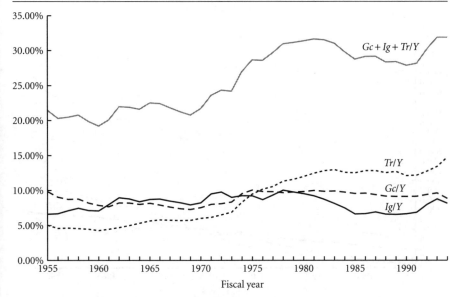

FIGURE 9.2. *Trends of Gc/Y, Ig/Y, Tr/Y and G/Y in the general government, 1955–94*

The Changing Patterns of Public Expenditures

The movement of growth rates of four of the general government's public expenditures (i.e. *Gc*—government consumption, *Ig*—government capital expenditure, T_r—transfers, and $Gc + Ig + T_r$—total public expenditure), as well as that of GDP, are depicted in real terms for 1956–94 in Figure 9.1. The trends of four public expenditures show the changing patterns in a larger band than that of GDP, and in particular, government capital expenditure varies in a wider fluctuation than government consumption. It is noted that government capital expenditure has moved in a counter-cyclical direction against GDP growth rates to some extent. Interestingly enough, these counter-cyclical movements can be observed during the recession periods of the 1970s or 1990–94. Attention should also be paid to the long-run variation of transfers which move in a volatile way, occasionally with greater speed than that of government capital expenditure. By contrast, government consumption shows a comparatively stable movement over a long period.

As a consequence of these growing patterns, it is interesting to explore whether the size of government has expanded in the economy as a whole or not. In Figure 9.2 the relative shares of public expenditures to GDP are computed in nominal terms for 1955–94. The upper line indicates the trends of economic activity through both the current and capital expenditures that the government has performed in a country. The relative size varies in the range of 20–30 per cent.[3] In Japan, this trend was moving up

---

[3] This level in recent years ought to be compared with that of the pre-war period. According to Ohkawa's estimates, the ratios of $Gc + Ig + T_r$ to GNP had already been higher: 22.4 per cent in 1900, 13.8 per cent in 1920 and 26.07 per cent in 1940 (i.e. wartime). See Ohkawa (1974).

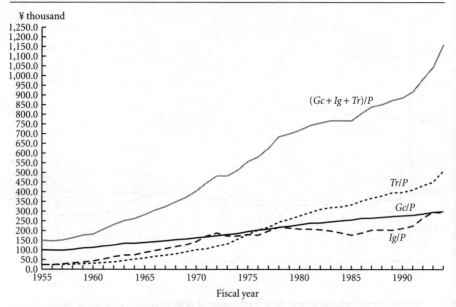

FIGURE 9.3. *Per head public expenditure in the general government*
at constant 1985 prices, 1955–94

Note: The money values in parentheses on the vertical axis are those of US$, calculated using an exchange rate of $1 = ¥85

towards the peak of 1979, but thereafter it obviously began to decline until 1990. This declining trend can be explained by the government policy of fiscal consolidation that was adopted in the 1980s, as discussed earlier. Thus, the relative share of public expenditure continued to drop to a considerable degree until 1990, when expansionary policies began to be adopted again to cure the deflationary effects caused by the collapse of 'bubble' boom.

While the long-run movement of government consumption to GDP was relatively stable, that of government capital expenditure has fluctuated more. Particular attention should be paid to both the declining trend during the period of fiscal consolidation in the 1980s and the upward trend to stimulate the economy caused by post-bubble depression in the 1990s. Government capital expenditure tended to be employed in a more flexible manner to allow for the achievement of specific policy goals. These policy changes must have affected the allocation of public expenditure to each function as will be argued below. On the other hand, the relative weight of transfers to GDP shows a steady upward trend from 1955, reflecting the expanded role of the welfare programme.

In Figure 9.3, the long-run variation of public expenditure per head, at constant prices relative to 1985, is shown to illustrate the benefit of public expenditure which has been allocated to the Japanese people. In the process of growing economic power in the nation, Japan's per head real GDP has greatly increased by 7.0 times from ¥490,000 in 1955, to ¥3,441,210 in 1994. In conjunction with this increased rate, per head real public expenditure had also expanded steadily over a period of forty years despite the variations between periods: that is, $(Gc + Ig + T_r)/P$ increased by 8.3 times from ¥138,700 in 1955 to ¥1,159,000 in 1994.

It is notable that Gc/P has increased for a long period with a straight upwards trend, reflecting that government consumption of the budget had to rise, mainly due to the constant increases of wages and salaries paid to government officials. By contrast, Ig/P has moved upwards across a wider range, occasionally surpassing the level of Gc/P. In Japan, government capital expenditure in the public sector has maintained a fairly high level, with a small gap relative to government consumption. This reflects the fact that the government has given priority in the past to capital formation in order to improve the poorer level of social infrastructure. It is important that the relative level of Ig/P against Gc/P would be much higher than that in any other countries. Moreover, particular attention should be paid to the sharp rise of T_r/P over this period. Obviously, it has greatly contributed to raising the level of public benefits.

How has Japan's outstanding economic performance brought about an improvement in socio-economic welfare of the people? It is rather difficult to evaluate welfare such as the quality of life in broader terms. From an historical perspective, however, it is incontrovertible that the objective economic conditions of almost all the Japanese people have improved immensely since the 1950s as a result of rapid economic growth. Economic measures never capture the full range of changes in material welfare which are usually associated with economic growth. A much broader approach lies in the so-called social indicators that incorporate physical measures of safety, work conditions, education, culture, the diffusion level of consumption durables, and so on. While informative, this approach poses some problems when selecting which indicators are relevant.

Table 9.1 presents time series data on a representative set of such indicators, although the scope of the data is limited. No doubt, almost all measures indicate an absolute improvement (see, for the 1950 and 1960 cases, Table 2.5). The Engel coefficient in line 1 (i.e. the ratio of income spent on food) decreased to 24.1 per cent in 1990 from 32.4 per cent in 1970. Similarly, the infant mortality rate in line 2 fell sharply while the life expectancy figure for both sexes, in line 3, has been increased to a great extent. Working hours, line 4, have constantly shortened. The level of education, as seen in lines 5 and 6, has greatly improved. Also, the diffusion level of telephone, sewerage, and water, in lines 7–9, have considerably enhanced the quality of life. Lastly, consumption of consumer durables has risen at a great rate, as indicated in lines 10–14. In particular, we ought to note the fact that each family unit has already utilized more than one washing machine, refrigerator, vacuum cleaner and colour TV since 1980.[4]

---

[4] In addition to major findings concerning the changing patterns of public expenditure mentioned above, the income elasticities of current and capital expenditures were calculated to examine the relationship between the growth of the nation's economy and that of public expenditures. These calculations, however, provided no significant results for our purpose, because the elasticities showed the variation to be in a very volatile manner from plus to minus. Thus, I stopped using this information. The average of such volatile values seems to give no meaningful results.

TABLE 9.1. *Social indicators, 1970, 1980, and 1990*

Indicator	1970	1980	1990
Subsistence			
1 Engel coefficient (%)	32.4	28.0	24.1
Safety			
2 Infant mortality rate per 1000 births	13.1	7.5	4.3
3 Life expectancy			
male	69.31	73.35	75.92
female	74.66	78.76	81.90
Working conditions			
4 Annual working hours	2,252	2,162	2,124
Education and the level of life			
5 University and College students	23.6	37.4	36.3
(percentage of age groups)			
6 Senior high school pupils	82.1	94.2	95.1
(percentage of age group)			
7 Telephone per 100 persons	22.8	72.1	
8 Sewerage (percentage of houses	26.4	46.8	43.8
connected to public system)			
9 Water (percentage of houses	80.8	91.5	94.7
connected to public system)			
Consumer durables			
10 Washing machines per 100 families	92.7	103.9	108.0
11 Refrigerator per 100 families	91.1	114.2	162.2
12 Vacuum cleaner per 100 families	70.1	109.5	130.8
13 Colour TV sets per 100 families	26.9	141.4	196.4
14 Passenger car per 100 families	22.1	57.2	77.3

Sources: Tabulated from EPA, *White Paper of National Life*, 1985 and 1994, and Management and Coordination Agency, *Japan's Statistics*, 1995, etc.

ALLOCATION OF PUBLIC EXPENDITURE BY FUNCTION

Trends of Human Resource Development

Total public expenditure is made up of three distinct categories: government consumption, government capital expenditure and transfers in accordance with the NI concept. The data needed to analyse the allocation of total public expenditure in the scope of general government, by function, are classified into the following nine categories:

1. general public services;
2. defence;

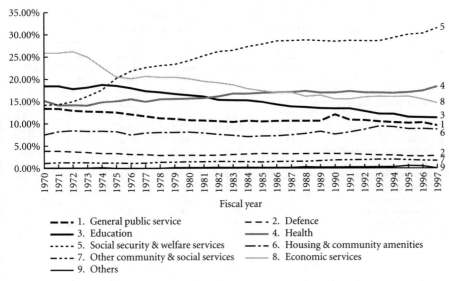

Fiscal year

‒‒•‒ 1. General public service   ‒ ‒ ‒ 2. Defence
——— 3. Education   ——— 4. Health
• • • • • 5. Social security & welfare services   ‒•‒• 6. Housing & community amenities
‒ ‒ • ‒ 7. Other community & social services   ——— 8. Economic services
——— 9. Others

FIGURE 9.4. *Patterns of relative shares of total public expenditure in the general government by function, 1970–97*

3. education;
4. health;
5. social security and welfare services;
6. housing and community amenities;
7. other community and social services;
8. economic services;
9. other purposes.

These is only one set of data available to us for this study, although the coverage of the time period for the relevant data is relatively limited.

Figure 9.4 depicts these nine categories of total public expenditures in the general government in terms of percentage distribution for 1970–97. If our primary concerns from the nine expenditures are with both education and health in view of human resource development, reference should be made to the statistical procedures of these two expenditures in Japan before observing the picture given in Figure 9.4.

According to the EPA's *Annual Report on National Accounts*, education is divided into three sub-categories. The first deals with general administration, regulation, and research all related to the provision of all school services in the form of current expenditure. The second deals with schools, universities, and other educational facilities, that is government capital expenditure appropriated for educational facilities of primary and secondary schools, universities and colleges, and other forms of education. The third covers subsidiary services, for example for school lunches, school buses, textbooks, etc.

TABLE 9.2. *Per cent distribution of total public expenditures in general government by function: annual averages of specific periods*

Items	Fiscal 1970–74 (%)	Fiscal 1975–80 (%)	Fiscal 1981–85 (%)	Fiscal 1985–94 (%)	Fiscal 1970–97 (%)	Fiscal 1980–97 (%)
1 General public services	13.1	11.6	10.6	10.9	10.5	10.3
2 Defence	3.7	3.1	3.1	3.3	3.0	2.9
3 Education	18.3	17.4	15.5	13.6	12.7	12.3
4 Health	14.5	15.4	16.6	17.2	17.4	17.6
5 Social security and welfare services	15.5	22.6	27.0	28.6	29.1	30.0
6 Housing and community	8.2	8.0	7.3	8.1	8.7	8.7
7 Other community and social services	1.3	1.3	1.6	1.7	1.7	1.8
8 Economic services	25.2	20.5	18.6	16.5	16.6	16.1
9 Other purposes	0.1	0.1	0.7	0.2	0.4	0.4
Total	100.0	100.0	100.0	100.0	100.0	100.0

Likewise, the health budget is composed of three sub-categories similar to education. One is general administration, regulation, and research whereby current expenditures are employed to provide all health-related services. The second concerns the construction of hospitals and clinics from capital expenditure. The last deals with individual health services, including the medical costs of doctors and dentists, their appliances and equipment, and the drugs prescribed by them.

There are three points worth noting in Figure 9.4. First of all, the most outstanding feature of all expenditures is the sharp rise in spending on social security and welfare services, starting in 1975, and, by the end of the 1990s, occupying nearly 30 per cent of the total. Thus, it predominantly affects the relative shares of other categories, most of which begin to fall from the mid-1970s. Secondly, health and education are ranked in the second and fourth positions among the nine items in recent years. Education shows a steadily declining trend, while health has followed an upward trend. As a consequence, the relative importance of education and health came to be reversed in 1981. Thirdly, among the other categories the large-scale fall in economic services is noteworthy in contrast to the big expansion of social security and welfare services. The reverse trend was induced around 1975 by ending the growth-oriented policies and encouraging the 'welfare state', that had been established in 1973.

More detailed information is given in Table 9.2, in which averages of percentage distributions in the allocation of total public expenditure are tabulated for specific periods. Inspecting successive five-year averages for each category, two different trends, accelerated or decelerated, can clearly be observed from the nine expenditure categories. Education and economic services show a decelerated movement, while health moves upwards at an accelerated rate, as do social security and welfare services. Other categories, such as general public services, defence, housing and community amenities, etc., continue their up-and-down fluctuations in the same time period.

TABLE 9.3. *Economic classification of total public expenditure by function in 1994 (%)*

	Government consumption	Government capital expenditure	Transfer expenditure	Total
1 General public services	83.4	10.5	6.0	100.0
2 Defence	97.0	0.0	2.9	100.0
3 Education	85.2	0.9	13.9	100.0
4 Health	10.3	0.4	89.3	100.0
5 Social security and welfare services	6.5	1.2	92.3	100.0
6 Housing and community	26.2	52.5	21.3	100.0
7 Other community and social services	54.7	34.2	11.1	100.0
8 Economic services	18.3	63.8	17.9	100.0
9 Other purposes	70.2	29.0	0.8	100.0
Total	30.8	17.9	51.3	100.0

The economic classification of total public expenditure might be equally important from an analytical point of view. Table 9.3 summarizes the relative shares of government consumption, government capital expenditure and transfers in the nine categories of expenditure in 1997.[5] The most important share of the total of public expenditure goes on transfers (51.3 per cent), and in particular on those for social security and welfare services which occupy more than 90 per cent in total, the remaining 6.5 per cent on government consumption and only 1.2 per cent on capital expenditure. Education and health contrast one another in terms of the combination of their respective contents: the largest share of education is taken up by government consumption (85.2 per cent), mainly because most of the educational services budget is made up of teachers' salary, as was pointed out; on the other hand, the figure for health services is mainly comprised of transfers (89.3 per cent), as is self-evident.

We should briefly explore the general background of the changes in the relative shares of education and health in view of public expenditure policies. In principle, the relative importance of each expenditure in total can be varied by the policy stance of government. It seems, however, that the two expenditures in question have had no bearing on the positive side of policy changes taken by the government in the post-war period. As argued previously, government policies have shifted from growth-oriented performance until the 1960s to the enhancement of welfare programmes since the early 1970s. In securing financial sources for annual budgets, large-scale tax increases in the 1950s and 1960s were replaced by both the depressed tempo of tax increases and the expansion of fiscal deficits since the 1970s.

[5] For the sake of convenience, I chose 1997 as a sample, but the situation in other years indicates almost the same pattern as the 1994 case discussed.

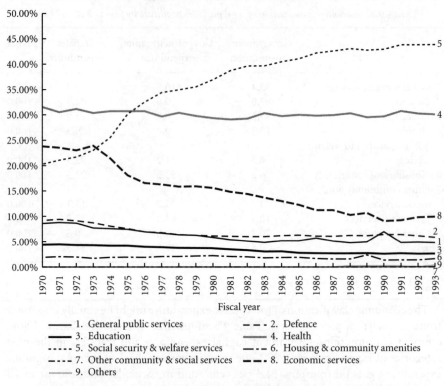

FIGURE 9.5. *Patterns of relative shares of total government expenditure in the national government by function, 1970–93*

Given these circumstances, the appropriation for education has gradually begun to slow down, reflecting the strategy of fiscal consolidation with the stringency of each budget. Education can be restrained relatively easily because it is not an entitled part of public expenditures, unlike pensions or medical services. Thus, it might be said that education has experienced a reduction in its relative size, due to changing fiscal policies, such as the reduction of fiscal deficits or the improvement of welfare services.

On the other hand, health has increased in line with social security and welfare services, as seen in Figure 9.4. Obviously, health has been partially or indirectly related to the process of promoting the 'welfare state.'

Intergovernmental Allocation of Public Expenditure
The main levels of the Japanese government are the national, the prefectural, and the municipal governments. The last two are called local governments, while the first is referred to as the national government. Thus, the general-term government which we have so far used within the framework of the NI concept is divided into the national and local governments to which social security fund is added.

Traditionally, the relationship between the national and local governments has been weighted predominantly in favour of the former in many respects. In fact, the extent of authority, the revenue share, and the degree of responsibility of the national government are all greater than those of local governments. Local bureaucrats must heed functional superiors at the central level: since functional lines of authority are dominant, local officials must be responsive to the central officials in each area (e.g. public works, health, agriculture, etc.). It is widely acknowledged that local administration has become vertically fragmented.[6]

In general, the national government performs its own functions, different from those of the local governments. Thus, the allocation of public expenditure by function essentially differs from one government to another, depending on the individual nature of public expenditure by each government. Typically, for instance, defence spending is exclusively made by the national government.

The allocation of public expenditure at the national and local government levels are delineated in Figures 9.5 and 9.6, showing the distinctive functions of total public expenditure in terms of percentage distribution. Patterns of their relative shares are drawn quite differently in the two figures. The most marked phenomenon in Figure 9.5 is the sharp rise of social security and welfare services as a proportion of total public expenditure in the national government, which have come to receive the dominant share since the mid-1970s. The second largest share is taken by health, which has remained relatively stable over a long period. On the other hand, education plays only a minor role at the central level.

On the other hand, the overall patterns of local government spending shown in Figure 9.6 are substantially different from those at the national level. Obviously, education is the most important spending function of local public services as a whole. It has maintained the highest share, keeping within the range of 25–30 per cent. That this is so should be apparent from the fact that it constitutes only a minor share of national government expenditure. By contrast, for local governments, providing a variety of local public services, health is not a main priority.

Based on empirical research, it is important to stress that developments in human resource management in Japan have created a 'division of labour' between the two tiers of the government. Local governments are mainly responsible for education, while the national government is charged with responsibility for health. Educational services for primary and secondary schools are compulsorily provided by the municipal governments, while provision for post-secondary education is charged to prefectural governments. By contrast, the national government plays an important role in fostering the activities of higher education in universities and colleges. However, a much larger share of educational expenditure is certainly taken up by primary, secondary, and post-secondary schools. Thus, spending on education is largely shared

---

[6] In Japanese, the term *tatewari gyosei* (vertical consolidation) is generally used. In order to get more grants from each ministry of the national government, local governments are constantly forced to accede to the priorities of national bureaucrats.

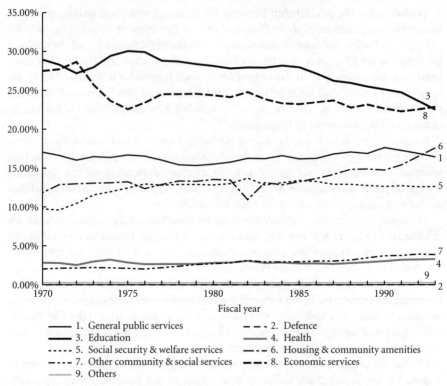

FIGURE 9.6. *Patterns of relative shares of total government expenditure in local governments by function, 1970–93*

at the local government level. Needless to say, in addition to public schools, there are a large number of private schools at every level of educational services, which are given a substantial amount of subsidies.

As is obvious from an examination of health service spending, health expenditure is mainly composed of transfers which have grown with the expansion of the welfare state and income redistribution. Since the provision of these public services is essentially centralized to maintain a uniform level of public benefit from relevant expenditure in the country as a whole, health has been primarily under the control of the national government.

Summary of Major Investigations

We have so far investigated the past trends of public expenditure in Japan's post-war growth in light of human resource development. What can we learn from the Japanese experience? It is difficult to choose one specific point as being the most distinctive feature of public expenditure policies. However, we will briefly summarize our argument as a conclusion to this study.

There are four points to note. First, the overall trends of public expenditure have been deeply affected by variations in the macroeconomic conditions, and in turn by the induced changes in fiscal policy. No doubt, both the yen revaluation and the oil shocks in the early 1970s could be listed as the most important economic incidents in post-war Japan, which together essentially led to the slowdown of growth rates and the structural changes made to the economy. These changes in the economy had also a major impact on the shift from one policy to another in the public sector. On this point, great emphasis should be placed on the effects fiscal consolidation had on the level and allocation of public expenditures.

Secondly, it seems that public expenditure on human resource development has not been given any special priority in terms of public expenditure policies throughout the post-war period. Generally speaking, greater importance has been given to education and health in parallel with other public services. It may be said that more importance was placed on human resource development as a contributing factor for economic development during an earlier period of pre-war Japan, for example the Meiji Era (1868–1911).

Thirdly, and related to the second point, both economic services and social security and welfare services have expanded more or have retained a larger share of public expenditure than social services for human resource development. Evidently, these two expenditures were closely tied with the growth-oriented policy and the enhancement of the welfare programme, respectively. Thus, given the limited source of financing, no special concerns have been made to deliberately increase the relative shares of education and health.

Fourthly, when we focus on the two-tier level of the government, the national government and the local governments have shown different approaches to the provision of public services and its financing. The so-called 'division of labour' has been introduced to ensure the roles are properly fulfilled at each level. Education has been shared by the local government levels which have therefore gained relatively abundant revenues. On the other hand, health has been provided at an increasing rate by the national government, funded by large-scale fiscal deficits, except during the period of 'bubble' boom.

Human resources have been accumulated over a period of about a century in Japan, which contributed significantly to the promotion of economic development. In more recent years, however, based on this past accumulation of human resources, no further stress has been laid on ongoing human resource development.

AN INEFFICIENT AND RIGID ALLOCATION OF THE
PUBLIC WORKS PROGRAMME

A Rigid Allocation of the Public Works Appropriation

Let us pay attention to the specific aspect of public expenditure allocation which is of great interest to our study. For a long time, the pattern of fixed appropriations in public works programmes at the national government level has been criticized from all sides as an example of inefficient resource allocation in the budgetary process. It is clear that this phenomenon was caused by the budget ceiling, along with the collusive ties between politicians, bureaucrats, and businesses (i.e. the 'iron triangle') that grew out of the LDP's long reign.[7]

As a result of the collapse of the LDP regime, circumstances surrounding the budget process have changed dramatically. It seems, however, that the perfect opportunity arose to correct long-standing abuses. Recognizing this, in October 1993 the MOF set up the Subcommittee on Public Works (hereafter called 'the Subcommittee') inside the Fiscal System Council and carried out a full-scale re-evaluation. Drawing on the findings of the subcommittee,[8] particular attention was paid to the status and problems of public works in Japan highlighted below and the steps which needed to be taken to correct those problems.

To sum up the problems briefly, it was found that the concept of public works was too broad. The appropriations examined here, which are called 'public works-related expenditures' in the *general account* of the national budget, reached ¥8 trillion in the 1993 budget. On top of that, there was ¥1 trillion for 'other facility expenses' for constructing school buildings, welfare facilities and so on. The image of 'public works' that most of us tend to have consists of projects undertaken under these two expenditure categories, but another important category of public works consists of projects carried out by local governments. The sum spent on these projects, ¥17 trillion, is actually larger than the amount allocated for public works in the national budget.

Across the board, public works appropriations—public fixed capital formation as defined within national income accounting—rose as high as ¥37 trillion in fiscal 1993. There is, in addition, a category that could be called 'comprehensive expenditures for general public works' (¥21 trillion), which includes projects carried out by public corporations (including those created for various specific projects). Among all of these, however, the most narrowly defined category is preferred in this study. One might ask why we must focus here on a category of public works that has such a limited scope. The answer becomes clear from the data in Table 9.4 where we can observe an interesting fact in the allocation of public work appropriations in the *general account*. More than 96 per cent of the total budget for public works carried out by the national government is controlled by three ministries: the Ministry of Construction (MOC), the Ministry of Agriculture, Forestry, and Fisheries (MAFF), and the Ministry of Transport (MOT). The remainder is passed out in small pieces to the Ministry of International Trade and Industry (MITT), the Ministry of Health and Welfare (MOHW), the National Land Agency (NLA), and other ministries and agencies.

For more than 30 years, the allocation of public works among the three principal ministries has remained virtually—and one might say skilfully—fixed. The pattern

---

[7] The dominant regime of LDP had continued for 38 years until August 1993, when a coalition party of non-LDP groups was established, headed by Prime Minister Hosokawa.

[8] I was the chair of that subcommittee.

TABLE 9.4. *The share of public works appropriations among the three major ministries (%)*

Fiscal year	Ministry of construction	Ministry of agriculture, forestry and fisheries	Ministry of transport
1965	69.36	20.14	7.46
1970	69.77	20.41	7.70
1975	68.47	20.38	7.23
1980	68.14	21.88	6.35
1985	68.20	22.01	6.25
1990	68.19	22.04	6.24
1991	68.37	21.85	6.24
1992	68.47	21.68	6.24
1993	68.61	21.49	6.24
1994	68.35	20.83	6.86
1965–93 magnitude of change	1.63	1.90	1.46
1980–93 magnitude of change	0.47	0.55	0.11
Difference between 1993 and 1994	−0.26	−0.66	−0.62
1995	68.50	20.54	6.87
1996	68.63	20.28	6.86
1997	68.51	20.05	6.94
1998	68.44	19.34	6.79
1999	67.00	18.58	6.77

Source: Ministry of Finance Publications.

Note: The proportion of public works expenditure is calculated using the data in the government proposal for the general budget of every year.

has been especially pronounced since the 1980s, when variations in the allocation fell to less than 1 per cent. This conclusion is supported by evidence that, during the annual budgeting process, interested groups (politicians and bureaucrats) make a great fuss over a variation as small as 0.1 per cent. One cannot observe this sort of phenomenon in any of the other previously mentioned categories of public works. Indeed, the crux of the public works allocation problem is clearly revealed in the rigidly fixed pattern of public works-related expenditure exhibited in Table 9.4. Until fiscal 1997, this distribution pattern has basically remained unchanged. It is no wonder that this category of expenditure, being the one that attracts the most attention, has come to be criticized as a symbol of the rigidity and inefficiency of budget allocations in the past.[9]

Over the past 30 years, the Japanese economy has undergone a significant structural transformation. Jolted by the twin oil crises of the 1970s, it left the path of rapid growth for the path of stable growth. The most notable structural change during this

[9] The same phenomena have still continued even now those data are available for fiscal 1995–99, see Table 9.4.

period was the relatively sharp decrease in the economic role of primary industry, measured in terms of both production output and number of workers employed. The primary industry's contribution to GDP dropped dramatically from 9.5 per cent in 1965 to 2.2 per cent in 1992, just as the number of agricultural households fell from 5.66 million to 2.94 million during the same period.

These are but a few examples of the social and economic realities surrounding public works. Although the social and economic mechanisms that such projects are supposed to address have undergone a huge transformation, the allocation of public works expenditure has hardly changed at all in 30 years. One could call this a classic case of inefficient resource allocation.

The fact that the entire Japanese socioeconomic 'vessel' has changed so much while the 'content' has stayed the same is a massive problem. The most deleterious effect of this mismatch lies in its violation of the basic rule of allocating scarce resources both effectively and efficiently. It is only proper that we alter the 'contents' in response to changes in the 'vessel'.

These rigid allocations perpetuate turf battles between the ministries and agencies that carry out public works, and lead them to undertake similar and often duplicative projects. Three ministries independently carry out these projects, subdividing them by function. For instance, both agricultural and coastal roads—initially designed to serve agricultural communities and fishing and shipping industries—have deviated from their original purpose, and have taken on the same characteristics as ordinary roads. Why, then, despite this fact, do three ministries continue, as they have for so long, to divide road projects that belong in the same category between themselves? This also applies to sewer and port projects, especially the latter. Coastlines are divided into four separate areas—A, B, C, and D—and the typical vertical administration is manifested as each relevant ministry independently carries out its own projects.

Under this sort of vertical system, ministries and agencies independently and arbitrarily evaluate their own projects.[10] As can be readily anticipated, investment efficiency is thereby seriously undermined, while appropriate selections and project coordination become exceedingly difficult. And when those public facilities are completed, the users—the beneficiaries of this work—find themselves inconvenienced in many different ways. Various problems—such as the lack of ordinary signposts on 'agricultural' roads and the extremely poor connections between those roads and common roads—are due to the fact that these projects have been undertaken because the ministry in charge builds 'agricultural roads' for the sake of building them, with little consideration for the convenience of users or efficiency of investment. In addition, it seems odd that cost-sharing formulas and user fees for sewers vary on adjoining lands according to the ministry or agency that has carried out such public works.

All such similar projects should be undertaken in a coordinated way with their specific purpose in mind. If this were done, it would help to reform the public works

---

[10] At that time, Prime Minister Hashimoto had taken initiatives to harmonize such duplicative projects in a more efficient manner.

appropriations process. At the same time, the efficiency of Japanese public investment and the effectiveness of the funding allocations should also improve significantly.

Collusion among Politicians, Bureaucrats and Businesses
Why did the allocation of public works projects become so inflexible? In the 1980s, fiscal consolidation became the highest budget priority. As a result of introducing ceilings to the level of increases for budgetary items, the growth in appropriations for necessary projects was restrained and it became difficult to make allocations based on need or other explicit criteria. More importantly, collusion between politicians, bureaucrats, and businesses under the LDP's long reign had borne the greatest respons-ibility, as a primary cause, for bringing about this situation. Every developed nation in the world formulates its policies in a distinct manner that has evolved over time, based on long-standing customs and traditions: Japan is no exception.

It is frequently pointed out that Japan's policy-making process has been influenced by collusion between politicians, bureaucrats, and businesses. According to public choice theory, every economic entity has its own specific, behavioural goals. That is to say, politicians strive to win re-election, bureaucrats try to increase their budgets or expand their own organizations, and businesses seek increased profits, following market principles. An important point is that these reciprocal power relationships have a general tendency to be biased in one direction. In other words, bureaucrats use their rule-making and licence-granting authority to control industries in the private sector. The business world exerts its influence over politicians through the supply of campaign funds. Politicians, in turn, wield power over bureaucrats because they determine whether bills are enacted in the Diet. The kind of politician referred in this case is the *zoku giin* (the tribe of politicians with vested interests) who represents the interests of specific industries.

Under the 38-year dictatorial rule of the LDP, there were a number of political scandals.[11] This series of corruption scandals, all of which have been criticized as manifestations of the collusion between politicians, bureaucrats, and business, no doubt grew out of the 'iron triangle' formed by those three entities. It is evident that the policy-making process has, until the closing decade of the twentieth century, been tied, to varying degrees, to this kind of structure. With its beginnings in 1993, how-ever, the political world changed dramatically. In Japan, the emergence of the ruling coalition under the Hosokawa Cabinet saw the old policy-making system collapse, at least temporarily. It is widely acknowledged that the *zoku giin* are experiencing a rebirth following the establishment of the second Hashimoto Cabinet in December 1996.

As the Kanemaru and *zenekon* (general construction industry) scandals clearly demonstrate, public works expenditure—of all the many items in the budget—are linked most closely to political interests, that is they are sources of political funds.

---

[11] The recruit, Sayama, and Knamaru Scandals occurred one after the other during the period from the late1980s to the early 1990s.

When *zoku giin*, wishing to secure their funding bases, conspire with bureaucrats who strive to enlarge or protect their own bureaucratic area, the task of cutting the budget for public works, which have become vested interests, is exceedingly difficult—even in the event that the need for such expenditures declines. Unless someone speaks out, this system of appropriations can continue indefinitely, just as it has in the past.

In searching for the cause of the inflexibility of public works allocations, we need to take a look inside the bureaucratic structure of ministries and agencies. Table 9.5 shows allocations for public works within the MAFF, by expenditure category, over the past 30 years. The relative share for each budget item, across the whole range of projects, is virtually unchanged from year to year. Since the 1980s, in particular, these shares have been remarkably fixed. Such a degree of rigidity is found in neither the MOC or the MOT, the principal bureaucracies engaged in similar projects.

So why does this phenomenon of fixed intra-ministry (not merely fixed inter-ministry) allocations arise? The key to unravelling this mystery lies in the fact that at MAFF there are an estimated 18,000 *gikan*—officers with engineering and other technical credentials—who specialize in public works. The number of such *gikan* at the MOC is 14,000 and at the MOT, 12,000. To maintain the bureaucratic system in which a certain number of *gikan* are employed in each segment of the system, MAFF must carry out a certain number of projects, guaranteeing a fixed budget level each year, despite the fact that the need for such projects may have declined. Thus, the ministry has built into its bureaucratic structure a mechanism to guarantee a fixed share of appropriations, even for public works projects for which there is no longer any noticeable priority. Under such circumstances, even MOF cannot use its budget assessment to trespass on this 'sacred' ground. Obviously, then, this represents a surrender of the assessment process.

Establishing Review Criteria

To bring about any substantial improvement in a public works appropriation process that has become so inflexible, a number of allocation criteria should be established. There are many different yardsticks which could be used as criteria for determining the appropriate allocation. The most important point is that these criteria must be able to function effectively in terms of the actual budgetary process. Perhaps the most general criteria would be (i) the extent to which each project contributes to overall infrastructure needs and (ii) how efficient it is as an investment. However, these are not necessarily objective, reliable criteria. For example, our idea of what constitutes adequate infrastructure—roads, bridges, sewers, etc.—tends to change frequently, based on the standards we desire or hope to achieve. In the case of investment efficiency, it is possible to use a cost–benefit analysis to compare similar projects to some extent. But if the projects are dissimilar, it becomes almost meaningless to compare the investment efficiency of one with the other. This means that, in response to changes in economic and social conditions, we need to develop some kind of subjective yardstick, even one that contains a certain amount of value judgement.

If one tried to outline the history of public works that supported the development of the post-war Japanese economy, one could perhaps divide it into three stages.

TABLE 9.5. *Public works allocation share within the Ministry of Agriculture, Forestry, and Fisheries (%)*

	Afforestation/ conservation	Coastal maintenance	Fishing harbour maintenance	Agricultural infrastructure	Reforestation	Forest road	Coastal fishing infrastructure	Hydro-electric dams, etc.	Total
1965	2.59	0.46	1.47	13.74	0.86	0.93	0.07	0.02	20.14
1970	2.28	0.40	1.71	14.20	0.68	1.06	0.07	0.01	20.41
1975	2.33	0.40	2.31	13.46	0.69	1.12	0.07	0.00	20.38
1980	2.55	0.37	2.58	14.12	0.64	1.30	0.32	0.00	21.88
1985	2.60	0.37	2.61	14.16	0.65	1.29	0.34	0.00	22.01
1990	2.69	0.37	2.61	14.13	0.64	1.26	0.35	0.00	22.04
1991	2.65	0.36	2.59	14.00	0.64	1.26	0.35	0.00	21.85
1992	2.62	0.36	2.57	13.88	0.63	1.26	0.35	0.00	21.68
1993	2.58	0.36	2.55	13.76	0.63	1.28	0.34	0.00	21.49

Source: The annual general budget of the year.

During the first stage—the period of post-war reconstruction before the mid-1950s —critical investments were made in projects to increase food production, as well as projects, such as tree-planting, flood control, and disaster relief, that served as national land conservation. During the second stage—the rapid growth period from the mid-1950s to the 1960s—roads, ports, and production bases to help promote industry were stressed. Finally, during the third stage—which began in the 1980s—emphasis was placed on projects that more directly improved the quality of life, such as housing, sewers, parks, and sanitation. This trend has continued to the end of the century.

The 'Report on Reforming Public Works Appropriations', which was released in December 1993 by the Subcommittee mentioned above, suggested a new scheme for allocating public works funding, based on these three types of projects. The basic ideas contained in that report are laid out in Table 9.6. Existing public works projects are classified into three groups—A (maintaining the living environment), B (national land conservation), and C (maintaining production infrastructure). Using this ABC order, an attempt is made to set priorities. It is widely believed that this system reflects economic and social changes in its own way, serving as a useful set of allocation criteria and priority rankings. Because it also identifies concrete cases, it should lend some rationality to public works appropriations when the time comes to review budget proposals.

To remedy the fixed allocation of public works, projects must be prioritized one by one, rather than allocations being made according to the share currently held by the ministries and agencies. It is crucial that a new way of thinking is adopted that emphasizes outcomes. Not all public works can be classified according to the three-tier structure mentioned earlier. As basic infrastructure for the future of Japan, freeways, regional airports, and so on should perhaps be treated as essential projects deserving special preference in the allocation of funds.

Obviously, the publication of these criteria for the allocation of funds caused a great stir among the interested groups. In particular, the ministries and agencies that found their projects being placed in the new category C fought desperately to repeal the criteria. As was often reported in the media, the proposals brought together all the interested groups, which then scrambled to preserve their vested interests. The sense of urgency was particularly strong for those tied to MAFF. However, they were undoubtedly saved by the partial opening of the rice market, which became a kind of 'divine wind'. As a result, regrettably, those projects ranked C were elevated to a higher position, because a subsidy from the 'Uruguay Round' (of WTO talks) was able to make some provision for maintaining Japan's agricultural infrastructure.[12]

Despite lobbying from the opposition, one might assume that MOF would have made effective use of this ABC prioritization scheme during the 1994 budget process as a means of doing away with fixed allocations. We thus face an interesting question: in the end, what kind of pattern characterized the allocation of public works?

---

[12] In order to mitigate the significant complaints of agricultural groups, a large-scale subsidy of about ¥6 trillion under the special scheme of the 'Uruguay Round' of talks was appropriated for five years from 1993.

TABLE 9.6. *Priority of public works*

Priority	Category	Reason for ranking	Projects
A	Maintaining life environment	Relative to other projects, efforts have been lacking up to now in these project areas and thus they are in need of increased allocation of funds to make serious efforts to reach the goals within a short period.	Housing, sewers, agricultural irrigation, water supply, waste disposal facilities, parks, roads in residential areas
B	Land preservation	Given the natural (geological, climatic, etc.) condition of Japan, the goals of these projects cannot be expected to be met within a specified period, and thus are to be continued steadily over a long period.	Afforestation and conservation to prevent erosion, maintain coasts, etc.
C	Industrial infrastructure	When the amounts of funds allocated to date and the relative weight of industries in the national economy are considered, these are projects to be funded selectively at reduced levels.	Industrial water supply, fishing ports, and other coastal fishing facilities, parks, agricultural roads, etc.

Note: Freeways and regional airports are not considered in marking this ranking.

In its draft budget for 1994, the MOF set aside about ¥100 billion in unappropriated funds, as was argued in Chapter 6, in order to reallocate these funds into more important items. When we compare the change in the allocation of public works among the three principal ministries in this budget with the previous year's budget, we find that the MOC's share dropped by 0.26 per cent, MAFF's declined by 0.66 per cent, and the MOT's increased by 0.62 per cent (see Table 10.4). Because one category of public works was reorganized (subway projects were, for the first time, added to the MOT), it is difficult to compare this year's allocation accurately with the previous year's. We can see, however, that some effort was made to change the allocation.

Table 9.7 presents the share of total public works appropriations by project category. What we should focus on is the difference between the 1991–93 share for each category and that for 1994. As an additional reference, the review criteria (A, B, and C) mentioned above are attached to the top row of the table. However, some projects are difficult to rank. For example, we cannot possibly rank road maintenance as a single entity. Furthermore, urban and arterial rail lines (with a 0.7 per cent share), such as subways, were included for the first time in the same category as forest roads and reservoirs for industrial water. Still, we can see at a glance that the share of appropriations going to the two groups of A-ranked projects increased, while the shares going to B and C decreased.

In MOF's draft of the budget in fiscal 1994, the biggest change was the 0.7 per cent increase in the allocation to housing. Although this was slightly better than the previous year's 0.1 per cent increase, it did not meet the initial expectation for a more significant change. It was also anticipated that the government would emphasize this category somewhat in its budget proposal, but this too was not the case. The whole picture changed slightly during the period of fiscal 1995–99, shifting the priority from conservation and agricultural infrastructure to housing and water supply and sewers.

As a whole, it seems clear that the final budget failed to make sufficient inroads. Although one must acknowledge that the MOF's budget bureau did make an effort, what has been accomplished to date falls far short of a real reform of the system for allocating funds for public works. However, the process of change has only just begun. It has continued in the formulation of the budgets in 1999 and beyond, when, one hopes, the government will make more decisive changes in the allocation process. For this to become reality, however, stronger leadership is absolutely required.

As the foregoing argument suggests, the subcommittee's review criteria were introduced and actually used in formulating the 1994 budget. This is perhaps not something that needs to be particularly emphasized here because, from the perspective of the average citizen, the priority ranking scheme (the three categories of A, B, and C) is nothing but common sense. It is significant, however, to note that these review criteria were developed with the participation of the Budget Bureau itself in the activities of the Fiscal System Council. Thus, what has been accomplished is tantamount to making a public declaration that the very agency in charge of budget assessment, not just some private group or research organization, is prepared to undertake a serious re-evaluation of the prevailing fixed appropriations for public works. Given this new

TABLE 9.7. *Distribution share by special public works category, 1970–99 (%)*

Priority Ranking	B	?	C	A	A	C	?	Other
(examples)	Conservation	Road Maintenance	Harbours, fishing, airports	Housing	Water supply and sewers	Agricultural infrastructure	Forest roads, industrial water supply	
Fiscal year								
1970	17.8	44.1	8.8	7.2	4.8	14.2	2.7	0.5
1975	16.9	35.8	9.0	11.0	10.7	13.5	2.8	0.4
1980	17.4	30.1	8.3	11.9	15.2	14.1	2.9	0.2
1985	17.4	29.4	8.3	12.2	15.6	14.2	2.7	0.2
1991	17.9	28.8	8.2	11.6	16.6	14.0	2.7	0.2
1992	17.9	28.8	8.1	11.7	16.8	13.9	2.7	0.2
1993	17.6	28.7	8.1	11.8	17.1	13.8	2.7	0.2
1994 MOF proposal	17.3	28.3	7.8	12.5	17.2	13.3	3.5	0.2
1994 Govt. proposal	17.3	28.3	7.8	12.0	17.6	13.3	3.5	0.2
1995	17.2	28.2	7.7	12.6	17.6	13.1	3.5	0.2
1996	16.6	28.1	7.6	12.7	17.9	12.9	3.6	0.2
1997	16.5	28.0	7.6	12.8	18.1	12.7	n.a.	0.2
1998	17.1	30.1	5.7	11.4	16.9	12.2	n.a.	0.4
1999	17.0	28.9	5.5	11.3	16.5	13.9	n.a.	2.5

Note: The 1994 MOF proposal included undistributed ¥100 billion. This amount is allocated in the government proposal. The 1999 figure is on an initial budget. Since classification has been changed in the 1990s, it may be difficult to compare the results each year in strict terms.

development, what then are the remaining issues that must be addressed in order to reform the public works appropriations process further?

The first issue has to do with this question: how far will the Budget Bureau be able to go in challenging the 'sanctuaries' or powerful vested interest groups? This is not to say that the Budget Bureau has, up to now, been totally powerless. However, the bureau has had to battle the vested interests of ministries and agencies that are backed by the LDP's *zoku giin*. In short, the resistance to change by those ministries and agencies has been strong enough to force the MOF, in effect, to surrender its budget assessment. Furthermore, we cannot overlook the fact that a series of unfavourable conditions due to fiscal consolidation with budget ceilings helped to foster the rigidity of public works appropriations. At the same time, however, it is simply unacceptable to neglect this problem indefinitely because the costs associated with the misallocation of resources are too high. Beyond the established criteria (priorities A, B, and C) that were newly delineated in 1993, the MOF ought to disregard the prevailing practices of individual ministries and agencies in the budgetary process.

Secondly, as previous experience clearly demonstrates, strong leadership from politicians is absolutely required to reform the politicized process of public works appropriations. Since the collusion between politicians, bureaucrats, and business has sustained the system of fixed allocations, breaking such collusive links is the first step towards resolving this type of problem. For such an effort to succeed, the Prime Minister must take a firm position and consistently support the MOF in the budgeting process. What actually happened was that ministries with many C-ranked projects quickly mounted increasing opposition to the Subcommittee's proposals. At the same time, *zoku giin* acted on behalf of the ministries and agencies that had suffered losses. As we enter the twenty-first century, such outdated political manoeuvring must cease.

Thirdly, in making recommendations that have to do with merging or abolishing various administrative units, the Subcommittee report was tentative and not as decisive as it should have been. As is often pointed out, behind the inflexibility of public works appropriations lies a bureaucratic personnel problem—that of the entrenched group of *gikan* in each of the ministries and agencies. This means that we simply will not be able to achieve a real solution to the problem unless and until we re-examine the goals of administrative reform and work towards changing both the structure and the operation of the related ministries and agencies. After witnessing what was attempted—and actually realized—in this reform effort of the Subcommittee, it must be concluded that a huge gap still remains between how much the government can or is willing to change and how much the average citizen hopes to see changed.

10
Ageing and the Social Security System

The ageing structure of Japan's population is moving sharply towards an aged society—one where the ratio of elderly people to non-elderly people is rising. No doubt, the process of societal ageing now under way will continue in the twenty-first century, and furthermore the speed of population ageing is considered to be faster in Japan than in any other developed country. Such a rapid ageing phenomenon must impose economic costs. In particular it will place a financial burden on all its members to support this aged-group through the expansion of the public pension system and medical and health care services. Generally speaking, the outcome looks profoundly pessimistic, because an aged society may lead to a proportionally reduced labour force, lower saving and growth rates, and higher levels of taxes or social security contributions. Obviously, the emergence of population ageing seems to generate a reduction in living standards and a social tension across all the generations.

Our aim in this chapter is to outline the basic framework of the social security system in Japan and to seek some desirable structural reforms in relation to the ongoing population ageing. First of all, we will begin with an overview of the movement towards an ageing society, discussing the demography of the population and the development of the social security system. Secondly, we will explore the current system of public pensions with respect to the national pension, employees' pensions and mutual aid associations. Thirdly, we will study various issues of the public medical and health care system in relation to the rapid expansion of medical costs. Lastly, we will discuss the necessity of structural reforms with special reference to the importance of nursing care services and future predictions of the financial burden to be borne by the entire nation.

OVERVIEW: THE MOVEMENT TOWARDS AN AGED SOCIETY

The Demography of Ageing

In Japan there is growing concern over the perceived increase in the dependency of large numbers of elderly persons upon a diminishing working population. Needless to say, the growth of the elderly group will impose increasing burdens on the non-elderly population in terms of pensions, health care, and other services. Before embarking on our main argument, it is instructive to look at the changing ageing structure of the population and the mechanics of that change from a demographic point of view.

The ageing phenomenon is derived from the expansion of the relative proportion of elderly people in comparison with other aged groups. The ageing structure of

TABLE 10.1. *Age structure of the population, 1920–2050*

	Population in '000			Percentage distribution			
	All ages	0–14 years old	15–64	65 years and over	All ages	0–14 years old	15–64	65 years and over
1920	55,963	20,416	32,605	2,941	100.0	36.5	58.3	5.3
1930	64,450	23,579	37,807	3,064	100.0	36.6	58.7	4.8
1940	71,933	26,383	42,096	3,454	100.0	36.7	58.5	4.8
1950	83,200	29,428	49,658	4,109	100.0	35.4	59.7	4.9
1960	93,419	28,067	60,002	5,350	100.0	30.0	64.2	5.7
1970	103,720	24,823	71,566	7,331	100.0	23.9	69.0	7.1
1980	117,060	27,507	78,835	10,647	100.0	23.5	67.3	9.1
1990	123,611	22,486	85,904	14,895	100.0	18.2	69.5	12.1
1995	125,570	20,033	87,260	18,277	100.0	16.0	69.5	14.5
2000	126,892	18,602	86,419	21,870	100.0	14.7	68.1	17.2
2005	127,684	18,235	84,443	25,006	100.0	14.3	66.1	19.6
2010	127,623	18,310	81,187	28,126	100.0	14.3	63.6	22.0
2015	126,444	17,939	76,622	31,883	100.0	14.2	60.6	25.2
2020	124,133	16,993	73,805	33,335	100.0	13.7	59.5	26.9
2025	120,913	15,821	71,976	33,116	100.0	13.1	59.5	27.4
2050	100,496	13,139	54,904	32,454	100.0	13.1	54.6	32.3

Sources: '1990 Population Census of Japan', Statistics Bureau, Management and Coordination Agency. 'Future Population Projection for Japan, estimated in September 1997 (Medium projection)', Institute of Social Security and Population Problems.

Note: Population Census 1920–1990
   Excluding Okinawa prefecture for 1947–1970
   Total figures for 1975, 1980, 1985 and 1990 include population of age unknown

a population is normally measured in three ways. First, in Japan, the group of elderly people is generally taken as the section of the population aged over 65. Thus, the elderly ratio is defined as the proportion of elderly people over 65 in the population. Secondly, the group aged 15–64 years is defined as the working population and it is this group which is considered to support the other age groups. Thirdly, the proportion of children in the population is the group under the age of 14.

In Table 10.1, this age structure is tabulated for the period of 1920–2050, obviously with the aid of future projections. The total population has steadily increased from the nineteenth century to the end of the twentieth century. In fact, the population of Japan has increased 2.2 fold, from 55,963,000 in 1920 to 125,570,000 in 1995, never ceasing its increasing tempo. However, the latest estimations suggest that it will reach a peak of 127,719,000 in 2009 and thereafter will begin to decline.[1] This has come as

---

[1] The projected population in Japan is classified into low, middle, and high estimates, depending on basic assumptions about fertility rates, average life-spans, and so on. Here we will normally be using the middle estimates.

something of a shock to the Japanese people who have always believed that there will continue to be an ever-rising growth in the population.

As is evident from Table 10.1, the proportion of the elderly population has been dramatically increasing since 1920. In 1930, the elderly ratio was merely 4.8 per cent, but by 1995 this ratio has risen to 14.5 per cent. According to the conventional classification of the United Nations, an 'aged population' or an 'aged nation' is defined as one in which more than 7 per cent of the population is over the age of 65 (United Nations 1985). Consequently, Japan entered the list of aged societies in 1970. Since then, the ageing of the Japanese population has continued to accelerate rapidly. It took only 25 years to double the elderly ratio from 7 to 14 per cent, which is generally accepted to be an extremely high speed development towards an ageing population.[2]

An even greater emphasis should perhaps be given to the future projections for the elderly population. The elderly ratio is expected to soar even further to the point where it will be almost doubled to 27.4 per cent by 2025. This growth pattern of population ageing will continue and will reach 32.3 per cent in 2050, implying that one citizen in three will be elderly by that time.

By contrast, if we look at the other end of the spectrum, the number of children aged 0–14 confirms this ageing trend. The proportion of children in the population has continued to fall from 36.5 per cent in 1920 to 13.1 per cent in 2025. As well as decreasing in size in relative terms, it is necessary to stress that the size of the under-14 population (19,400,000) was lower in absolute terms than that of the elderly population (19,743,000) in 1997. Likewise, the working population, aged 15–64 years, also turned to a decline in 1996 in both absolute and relative terms. Moreover, the proportion of the population aged over 75 will increase along with that of the population over 65. In fact, it will exceed that of the under-14 population by around 2020 in terms of relative size. The relative increase of over 75 year olds among the elderly population must pose further serious problems in an aged society as the burden in terms of pensions, medical and nursing care services must become even greater. It may in time be more appropriate to use the term 'ultra-aged society' rather than simply 'aged society'.

Japan is not the only developed nation to demonstrate such marked shifts in the age composition of its population. As is indicated in Figure 10.1, we can observe that the proportion of the population aged over 65 has increased dramatically for practically all major countries in the post-war period. Particular attention should be given to the projected surge in Japan's ageing population ageing at the beginning of the twenty-first century. As can be seen in Figure 10.1, population ageing in Japan has outstripped that in many other major countries, and is expected to continue to do so up to the 2020s. This ageing trend has been accelerated further by the statistics estimated in 1997 compared with the previous estimation in 1992. According to the former estimation, Japan will overtake Germany and continue to rise towards Italy around the year 2050. Thus, we can conjecture that Japan will become one of the most elderly

---

[2] The counterpart figures are 114 years in France, 82 years in Sweden, 69 years in the USA, 46 years in the UK, and 42 years in Germany (Tachi 1996, p. 147).

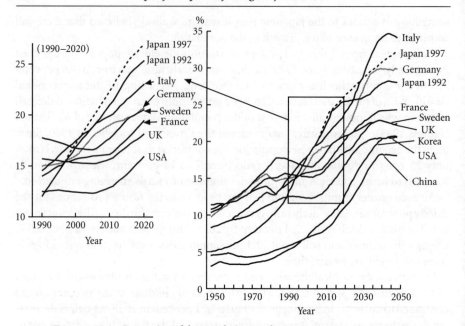

FIGURE 10.1. *Proportion of the population aged over 65 among major countries*

Source: East Asian Ministerial Meeting on Caring Societies, The Japanese Experience in Social Security, 5 December 1996, p. 21

Note: The line for Japan 1992 is based on the 1992 estimate of the Institute of Population Problems, while that for Japan 1997 is drawn on the 1997 estimate of the National Institute of Social Security and Population Problems

countries in the world in the twenty-first century. How did this change in the age structure of population come about?

In general, the age structure is the result of a complex interaction between mortality and fertility over time.[3] In the post-war era, public health has improved greatly and medical technology has made rapid progress. These two factors contributed significantly to the control of infectious diseases and other sicknesses, resulting in an acute drop in infant mortality as well as in the mortality rates for all other age groups. As a consequence, life expectancy at birth as a measure of mortality has lengthened from 59.57 years for males and 62.97 years for females in 1950 to 76.36 and 82.84 years respectively in 1995. At the end of the twentieth century average life expectancy in Japan is the longest in the world, followed by Sweden at 73.35 (males) and 80.79 (females), and Norway at 74.01 and 80.09.

Furthermore, if we consider the future trend of life expectancy in Japan, we will see that, according to the 1997 estimates, life expectancy will be 78.80 (males) and 85.83

---

[3] In addition to these two factors, there is one further factor of migration, but in Japan migration is negligible.

(females) by 2025 and it will continue to increase to as high as 79.43 and 86.47 years in 2050. We must conclude that the ageing of the population will continue with the ageing of the elderly population itself.

When a population is ageing, fertility is equally as important as mortality. The level of fertility determines the number of persons feeding into the population pyramid at its base, and the lower the number of new babies the greater the proportion of elderly people in the total population. The fertility rate (the average number of children that a woman gives birth to in her lifetime) has been in a constant decline from 3.65 in 1950, 2.13 in 1970, 1.42 in 1995 to 1.34 in 1999. This level is far below the rate of 2.1 necessary to keep the population at its present level. According to the population projections made in 1997, the fertility rate is expected to fall as low as 1.38 in 2000, but will take an upturn to 1.61 in 2025, after which it is expected to maintain that level. However, this was optimistic. The discrepancy in the elderly ratio in Figure 10.1 is due to the difference in the fertility rate between the 1992 and the 1997 estimates: that is, in 2025 the former is estimated at 1.80 and the latter 1.53.

Given the forecast of the population described above the ratio of the working population divided by the elderly population is falling rapidly from 3.8 in 1990, 4.0 in 2000, 2.9 in 2010, and 2.3 in 2020. According to OECD estimates (OECD 1997), the lowest such ratio in 2030 will be 2.0 in Germany, followed by 2.2 in Japan, while the ratio will be 2.5 in Sweden, 2.6 in France, 2.7 in the USA, and 3.0 in Canada. This implies that, in Japan in 2030, approximately every 2.2 people in the working population will have to support one elderly person.

Development of the Social Security System

Let us briefly outline the development of Japan's social security system during the post-war period.[4] Later more detailed analyses will be attempted. Amid the economic and social devastation after the Second World War, the basic principles of social security were established in terms of medical and health care services.[5] Given the poor state of nutrition and standards of living, the social security system first had to stress relief for the needy. This was one of the most urgent tasks for the government, which in turn played an important role in establishing Japan's public assistance policy later on.

As the economy was restored during the 1950s, people's living standards gradually improved. In addition to relief measures for the needy by public assistance, ordinary people were also in need of support by public means to prevent them from slipping into poverty due to sickness and ageing. Thus, medical insurance and pension systems to cover all members of the community were established in the 1960s, separate from public assistance. Although public assistance was financed by taxes, such social insurance

---

[4] Japan's social security system can be traced back to the Social Relief Regulations in 1874, but throughout the pre-war era under that system the relief offered was basically limited to the needy, and a spirit of mutual aid among relatives and neighbours was assumed to exist.

[5] The new Constitution of Japan enacted in 1947 explicitly states in Article 25 that 'All people shall have the right to maintain the minimum standards of wholesome and cultured living. In all spheres of life, the state shall use its endeavours to promotion and extension of social welfare and society, and public health.'

programmes were partly supported by social security contributions that the participants were responsible for paying in order to prepare themselves for the risks associated with poverty, sickness, and ageing.

It was in 1961 that both public medical care and public pension systems were created in the form of social insurance on a universal basis in Japan. After the Second World War, the medical insurance system that had been introduced in the pre-war period was on the verge of collapse due to the shortage of sufficient benefits. In particular, people such as self-employed farmers and professionals (about 30 million in 1956) did not participate in the Employees' Health Insurance (EHI), but they were all compulsorily enrolled in the National Health Insurance (NHI) by 1961. Therefore, the coverage of universal medical insurance was achieved for the entire nation. Similarly, the pension system was firmly established to include the entire population under the National Pension that was created in 1961. Japan's pension system was initially developed for employees, but the self-employed and farmers remained behind the development of employees' pension schemes. As the demand for aged income maintenance substantially increased, these workers also had to be covered by their own pension plans. Thus, the National Pension scheme began to include them, based on a universal pension for which everybody was eligible.

After establishing the universal basis of the public medical insurance and pension systems, both benefit levels were raised a number of times. Rapid economic growth before the first oil shock of 1973 enabled the government to expand the social security scheme, because it was then widely believed that greater efforts should be made to return some of the benefits of economic growth in the form of social welfare services. In fact, rapid economic growth resulted in steadily increased tax revenues, improved wages and a higher national standard of living as was argued in Chapter 2. Under such circumstances, the necessity of income maintenance, in particular for the elderly, was emphasized to a considerable extent.

In 1973, substantial improvements were made to the benefit levels throughout the social security system, which was considered to be comparable with that of Western nations. Thus, it is often pointed out that 1973 was the 'new year for the welfare nation'. For instance, free medical care for the elderly was introduced at that time which resulted in a sharp increase in the national health expenditure, as will be seen in Figure 10.6.

As the growth of the Japanese economy slowed down after the oil shock, the rebuilding of the social security system was begun by the government. Fiscal consolidation became one of the important policy targets in light of administrative reform, and structural reforms for the medical insurance and pension systems were also inevitably needed to avoid any worsening of their funding operations. Although the health service system for the elderly was newly created in 1982, the basic aim of social security policy in the 1980s began to be shifted from raising the level of benefits to ensuring the stability of the system from a long-term point of view.

This concern over structural reforms continued into the 1990s, and it was strengthened further in the midst of an ongoing trend towards population ageing with fewer

TABLE 10.2. *Trends of social security benefit expenditure by major categories (¥ billion, %)*

Fiscal year	Social security benefit expenditure							National income B	$\frac{A}{B}$
	Total A	Medical care	Ratio to total	Pension	Ratio to total	Public assistance	Ratio to total		
1971	4,022.5	2,249.8	55.9	1,015.2	25.2	757.5	18.8	65,910.5	6.1
1972	4,964.5	2,793.8	56.3	1,232.3	24.8	938.4	18.9	77,936.9	6.4
1973	6,253.8	3,422.7	54.7	1,670.2	26.7	1,160.9	18.6	95,839.6	6.5
1974	9,021.8	4,715.3	52.3	2,670.8	29.6	1,635.7	18.1	112,471.6	8.0
1975	11,771.5	5,706.4	48.5	3,886.5	33.6	2,178.6	18.5	123,990.7	9.5
1976	14,508.0	6,802.3	46.9	5,334.4	36.8	2,371.3	16.3	140,397.2	10.3
1977	16,877.7	7,597.7	45.0	6,599.3	39.1	2,680.7	15.9	155,703.2	10.8
1978	19,762.2	8,882.7	44.9	7,853.8	39.7	3,025.8	15.3	171,778.5	11.5
1979	21,973.2	9,734.6	44.3	8,998.7	41.0	3,239.9	14.7	182,206.6	12.1
1980	24,763.2	10,693.4	43.2	10,470.9	42.3	3,598.8	14.5	199,590.2	12.4
1981	27,552.6	11,481.5	41.7	12,061.6	43.8	4,009.6	14.6	209,748.9	13.1
1982	30,088.2	12,382.6	41.2	13,360.4	44.4	4,345.1	14.4	219,319.8	13.7
1983	31,964.5	13,068.4	40.9	14,431.9	45.1	4,464.2	14.0	230,805.7	13.8
1984	33,627.8	13,431.4	40.2	15,474.8	46.0	4,621.7	13.7	243,608.9	13.8
1985	35,668.2	14,248.3	39.9	16,915.4	47.4	4,504.5	12.6	260,278.4	13.7
1986	38,582.2	15,117.0	39.2	18,786.3	48.7	4,678.9	12.1	271,129.7	14.2
1987	40,659.2	15,904.2	39.1	20,011.2	49.2	4,743.8	11.7	283,895.5	14.3
1988	42,449.2	16,640.9	39.2	21,069.8	49.6	4,738.5	11.2	301,380.0	14.1
1989	44,871.1	17,496.7	39.0	22,564.5	50.3	4,810.0	10.7	322,143.6	13.9
1990	47,204.7	18,349.5	38.9	24,064.8	51.0	4,790.5	10.1	345,739.0	13.7
1991	50,120.3	19,476.4	38.9	25,636.7	51.2	5,007.2	10.0	363,054.1	13.8
1992	53,813.5	20,910.3	38.9	27,423.8	51.0	5,479.5	10.2	369,088.1	14.6
1993	56,791.1	21,777.9	38.3	29,059.4	51.2	5,953.9	10.5	372,750.0	15.2
1994	60,461.8	22,874.6	37.8	31,002.4	51.3	6,584.9	10.9	372,943.6	16.2
1995	64,726.3	24,059.3	37.2	33,498.6	51.8	7,168.3	11.1	380,214.5	17.0
1996	67,542.3	25,178.9	37.3	34,954.8	51.8	7,408.7	11.0	392,559.7	17.2

Sources: Policy Planning and Evaluation Division, Minister's Secretariat, MHW. National Income 'National Economic Calculations', Economic Planning Agency.

children. Now we need to explore in more detail the individual schemes of the social security system.

Social Security Benefits and Costs

Social welfare services are provided in the form of social security benefits, divided into three major categories: (i) medical care; (ii) pensions; and (iii) public assistance. No doubt, as the population has aged, expenditure on social security benefits has rapidly expanded in the 1980s and 1990s. Table 10.2 summarizes this increasing trend of social security benefit expenditure by category. The total amount of social security benefits was only ¥4,022.5 billion in 1971, but it had soared 17 times to ¥67,542.3 billion in 1996. The relative size of this expenditure to national income (*A/B*) increased constantly, from 6.1 per cent in 1971 to 17.2 per cent in 1996. As will be argued later, it is estimated that this trend will keep rising sharply to a level of approximately 30 per cent in 2025.

However, the relative share of social security benefit to national income is smaller in Japan, even at the end of the 1990s, when compared with other major developed countries. As can be seen in Table 10.2, Japan had a relative share of 13.8 per cent in 1991 while in the same year Sweden had 46.5 per cent, France 33.6 per cent, Germany 27.5 per cent, the UK 21.9 per cent, and the USA 16.6 per cent. Such a low percentage in Japan can be explained by two reasons: (i) population ageing had not at this stage progressed as rapidly in Japan as it had in the Western nations, and (ii) the pension system was still immature.

A breakdown under the major social security categories provides us with a number of points worth noting. First, medical care consumed more than half of total benefits in the early 1970s, but its relative share had continued to fall as low as 37.3 per cent by 1996. Secondly, and conversely, the proportion paid out on pensions was a mere quarter in 1971, but had rapidly risen to over 50 per cent of the total in 1996. Pension expenditure has expanded 34 times in absolute terms between 1971 and 1996 while the counterpart figure is only 11 times for medical care. As a result, in 1981 the former overtook the latter, reflecting the different growth rates in both. Thirdly, the relative share of public assistance expenditure has continually shrunk from 18.8 per cent of the total in 1971 to 17.2 per cent in 1996,[6] widening the gap between it and the other two categories.

The costs of social security should be financed by any available means. In Japan, the main financial source of social security expenditure is social security contributions, not taxes.[7] Needless to say, contribution revenues are earmarked for respective benefits through special accounts of the national budget. Table 10.3 summarizes the percentage distribution of financial sources for the social security system in six major countries. Although there are unique features pertinent to each country, Japan splits relatively evenly the costs of its social security scheme between three revenue sources: (i) employees' contributions, (ii) employers' contributions and (iii) state subsidies from tax revenue. This shared pattern adopted in Japan is, by and large, similar to those of the USA and Germany. By contrast, the UK, France and Sweden tend to rely heavily on any one of several sources.

Apart from the social security contribution the components of which will be studied in detail later, taxes related to social security benefits are compiled in the national budget. Tax revenue (and partly national bonds) from the *general account* of the national government have been appropriated not only to fund public assistance in the form of free provisions, but also to partly subsidize pension and medical funds which

---

[6] The most remarkable feature of Japan's social security system is such a small share of public assistance when compared internationally. Its relative share in Japan is only 10.0 per cent in 1991, while the international figures are 38.0 per cent in Sweden, 30.0 per cent in the UK, 26.8 per cent in France, 25.0 per cent in Germany, and 21.0 per cent in the USA (Tachi 1996, p. 152).

[7] Revenues from social security contributions are generally not included when studying tax policy issues in Japan. In fact, tax data do not include social security contributions, for two main reasons: (i) social security contributions are not treated as part of the *general account* of the national government, and (ii) they are administered mainly by the MoHW, not by the MOF. Thus, we are likely to neglect them when analysing tax issues because of the lack of combined data.

TABLE 10.3. *Percentage distribution of financial sources for the social security system*

Country	Contribution		Subsidy	State[a] operating revenues	Fund–others	(%) total
	Employees' share	Employers' share				
Japan 1991	28.3	31.8	24.0	12.6	3.3	100.0
USA 1989	23.8	31.6	33.1	11.0	0.5[b]	100.0
UK 1989	18.2	26.0	52.0	3.7	0.2	100.0
Germany 1989	36.9	34.3	26.1	0.6	2.1[b]	100.0
France 1989	23.4	50.6	20.9	1.7	3.4[b]	100.0
Sweden 1989	2.8	38.9	49.6	8.7	—	100.0

Source: Data from the MOF.
Note:
  [a] Including transfers from other public funds, as well as the NT (National Treasury).
  [b] Special social security tax is included.

are not sufficiently financed by their own contribution revenue. The total amount of social security expenditure that is financed by tax sources increased 8.9 fold from ¥1,642.2 billion in 1972 to ¥14,550.1 billion in 1997. The most remarkable feature of social security expenditure has been the continuous rise in non-entitled government expenditure from[8] 18.6 per cent in 1972 to 33.2 per cent in 1997. Among them, medical care expenditure has received the largest share of 40–50 per cent while the remaining share has been split fairly evenly between pensions and public assistance. Seen over the long term, the relative share going to pensions has tended to increase, while that of public assistance has shown a declining trend. We can, therefore, see the changing patterns in the relative importance of each category among tax-financed social security services.

THE PUBLIC PENSION SYSTEM

A Two-Tier Public Pension Structure

Pensions play a vital role in maintaining a certain level of income for daily needs in the case of old age, disability or the death of the main income-earner in a household. The public pension system was established during the pre-war era, when it was dependent on each occupational pension. As a result of restructuring and the integration of different types of pensions (see, for an expanded discussion, Horioka 1999; Tachibanaki 1996; Takayama 1992), the present structure of public pensions is rather simple, and consists of a two-tier scheme covering all residents in Japan, as shown in Figure 10.2.

---

[8] As the entitled government expenditures, there are two items of national debt services and tax shared grants to local government (*Chiho Kofuzei Kofukin*).

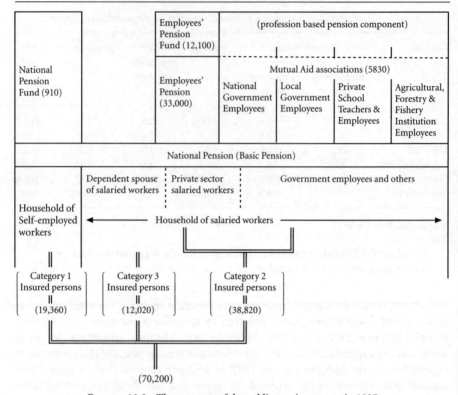

FIGURE 10.2. *The structure of the public pension system in 1997*

Source: Data taken from Social Security Agency

Note: Figures indicate the (rounded) number of insured persons in thousands

The first tier is composed of the National Pension (the so-called Basic Pension), under which all Japanese from 20 to 59 years old are included as contributors. The National Pension is sub-divided into three groups: (i) self-employed workers and others (19,390,000); (ii) waged and salaries workers (38,820,000); and (ii) dependent spouses of the second group (12,020,000) (figures in parentheses relate to 1997).

In addition to the first tier, there is another tier of the employees' pension scheme to supplement the National Pension in terms of pension benefits. Broadly speaking, employees' pensions are divided into two kinds: (i) Employees' Pension (EP) and (ii) Mutual Aid Associations (MAA). The Employee's Pension covers private sector salaried workers, amounting to 33,000,000 and the largest share of the employees' pension scheme (84.5 per cent). The MAA covers 5,830,000 public sector employees and other persons not covered by the above-mentioned categories (e.g. private school teachers and employees). Furthermore, the government stimulated each pension scheme to construct the third tier of pension in order to reinforce the insufficient benefits of National Pension, Employees' Pension and MAA. For this purpose, the

National Pension Fund (numbering 910,000 workers) and Employee's Pension Fund (12,100 thousand) have been established to supplement self-employed workers and employees, respectively.

It is necessary to clarify the background to the establishment of the unified system in place in Japan at the end of the twentieth century. As noted above, Japan's public pension had originally been developed by employees in various vocational groups. Thus, farmers and the self-employed tended not to be covered by the initial development of the public pension. In order to cover these persons, the old National Pension was established and all the Japanese citizens became fully covered by any type of public pension scheme on a universal basis. Under this system, they began to pay pension contributions into the old National Pension at the age of 20, and became eligible to receive a fixed old-age pension benefit at the age of 65. Moreover, fatherless families and disabled people were also eligible for pension benefit, and those who could not be eligible for receiving contributory pensions due to the elderly age at the start of the scheme were paid benefit in the form of welfare pension.

Since the old National Pension was so generous in terms of the pension benefits paid out from the beginning, it began to encounter difficulties in controlling its fund. For instance, it had introduced an indexation of pension benefits in 1973 due to which a sharp expansion of their payment was automatically ensured. Along with population ageing and further maturing of the system, the old National Pension had to shift its basic aim from raising the level of benefits to ensuring the long-term stability of the system as a whole. For this purpose, the public pension system had to be reviewed and restructured as a whole. In 1985, the old National Pension was drastically amended, and was transformed into the new National Pension (hereafter referred to simply as the National Pension) and it has since been this which has formed the basic pension.

The old National Pension covered only those who were not insured under the Employees' Pension, as noted above. However, the Basic Pension provided by the National Pension prescribes the basic necessities of life and pays a fixed amount commensurate with the insured period to all retired citizens, irrespective of their occupation, sex, employment status, or income level. Given its fundamental nature, the National Pension is the first-tier of the public pension system. Thus, employees are insured by both the National Pension and Employees' Pension systems, and receive an earnings-related pension as a second tier, in addition to the Basic Pension.

We should consider how pension systems secure the revenue necessary to cover the cost of the benefit. In general, the financing method of public pensions can be broadly categorized into the funding and pay-as-you go (i.e. unfunding) methods. In the funding method from which each pension scheme is initiated, financial reserves are funded in advance to meet the necessary cost of future pension benefits. Thus, future revenue is financed by both investment returns and contributions. Conversely, the pay-as-you-go method has no reserves in principle, and the cost of pension benefits must be covered by each year's contribution. Generally speaking, this has an advantages during a period of inflation, while it is vulnerable to demographic changes.

TABLE 10.4. *The framework of the National Pension in 1997*

Items	Contents
Legally initiated year	1959
Coverage	All the residents in Japan between the ages of 20 and 60
Insured persons (1000)	31,380[a]
Insurer	The national government
Pensionable age	65 years old
Pension benefits	
Old-age and retirement	Old-age basic pension (non-contributory old-age pension)
Disability	Disability pension (disability lump-sum benefits)
Death	Widow's pension (lump-sum, death benefits)
Pension contribution	
Insured pensions	¥13,300 per month[b] (additional contribution, ¥400 per month)
Subsidy from the national	$\frac{1}{3}$—Contributory benefits
government	All—Non-contributory benefits

Source: Social Insurance Agency, *Outline of Social Insurance in Japan*, 1996, p. 140.

Note:
  [a] Total of categories I and III insured persons, not including category II.
  [b] In fiscal 1998.

Historically, Japan's public pension systems started under the funded method in each scheme, but funded reserves have been reduced, reflecting population ageing in the past two decades. The present financing method partially adopts the use of revenue from each year's contribution, and it is termed a 'modified funded method'. It is estimated that funded reserves in the Employees' Pension will be phased out in the future, and thereafter this scheme will have to adopt a pay-as-you-go method.

The National Pension and its Fund

The National Pension is established, based on a social insurance formula as a means of ensuring financial security, although the payment of pension benefits is partly subsidized by the tax sources of the government. For instance, in the typical case of an old-age pension, benefits are paid on the condition that the insured person has paid contributions over a long period of time and has reached a certain retired age. Since the National Pension is intended to cover all citizens, an exemption has, from the beginning of the old system, been adopted for low-income earners who cannot afford to pay any contribution.

A pension as a form of insurance is a scheme covering insured conditions, such as old age, death, and disability, and which pays various sorts of pension benefits. Table 10.4 tabulates the basic framework of the National Pension as it stood towards the end of the 1990s, having been established in 1986. The most important scheme on the benefit side is obviously the old-age basic pension paid on the occasion of old age and retirement. Under this system, a person whose birth date is, for example,

2 April 1926 is entitled to the old-age basic pension when he or she has reached the age of 65, if at least 25 years of contributions have been completed as a qualifying period.[9] For such a qualifying period, the following are included:

1. periods for which contribution has been paid or exemption has been admitted under the old National Pension;
2. insured periods under the Employees' and MAA pension schemes;
3. periods of a dependent spouse of an insured under the Employees' and MAA pension schemes.

When the new system was initiated, the periods referred to in (2) described above are regarded as the 'contribution-paid period' in calculating the amount of basic pension under the National Pension.

The pensionable age is 65 years old, and the full amount of the old-age pension is ¥785,500 per year (as of April 1996),[10] which is payable to a person with a 40-year contribution-paid period. If the contribution-paid period is shorter than 40 years, the amount paid is reduced proportionally.[11] In addition to the old-age pension, several other pension schemes are included within the National Pension system to allow for cases of disability and death. The disability pension is paid when an insured person suffers a permanent inability to work due to injury or illness.[12] According to the degree of difficulty the person experiences in his or her daily activities, the disability pension is classified into first and second grade dependent on examination by qualified medical doctors. The benefits paid under this scheme are ¥981,900 for the first grade and ¥785,500 for the second grade annually.[13]

Survivors' pension is paid to the widow or to the bereaved children when an insured person dies, if he or she satisfies the same insured period as the disability pension requires. The amount of pension benefit is ¥785,500 annually to which additional benefits are paid for dependent children by the same amount as in the case of the disability pension. Also, the widow's pension was introduced to allow for a case where an insured person who has completed the minimum qualifying period of 25 years for the old-age pension dies before receiving it.[14]

---

[9] A person who was born before this date is provided with a pension under the old National Pension.

[10] In 1989, pension benefits were automatically indexed in conjunction with the rise of CPI even in the case of its increasing rate being less than 5 per cent.

[11] In the case of a person who is eligible to use the exemption for a certain period, one-third of the 'contribution-exempted period' is counted in computing the amount of pension benefit.

[12] Roughly speaking, the conditions for this benefit are as follows: (i) the claimant must be a member of National Pension or be aged 60–64; (ii) the total contribution-paid period should be at least two-thirds of the insured period; and (iii) a person is eligible in the case of permanent disability before reaching the age of 20.

[13] Moreover, additional lump-sum benefits are paid to the beneficiary with dependent children until they become 18 years old (20 years old if they are disabled). These additional pensions are annually ¥226,000 each for the first and second child, and ¥75,300 for each subsequent child.

[14] His widow is entitled to be paid as much as 75 per cent of the old-age pension which her deceased husband would otherwise have obtained, on the condition that they were married for at least 10 years prior to his death. In addition, a lump-sum death benefit is provided to the survivors when an insured person with a contribution-paid period of at least three years dies without receiving any old-age pension, leaving his dependants who are not entitled to the survivors' pension.

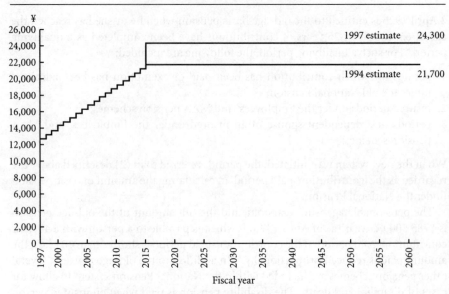

FIGURE 10.3. *Financing projections of the National Pension contribution*
Source: MOF
Note: Figures are monthly payments at constant 1994 prices

On the revenue side of the National Pension, there is the problem of maintaining a sound financial basis for pension fund, particularly in the long term. The National Pension is financed by both pension contributions paid by the insured persons and a subsidy from the national government. The way of paying pension contributions differs from one type of insured person to another. An insured person in category 1 must pay the fixed amount of contribution at the designated government or financial institution. The contribution of an insured person in category 2 is collected directly from the Employees' Pension and MAAs, and furthermore the obligatory contributions from persons in category 3 are covered by the payment of insured persons in category 3 through their respective pension schemes. That means that both the Employees' Pension and MAAs are responsible for the contributions to the National Pension fund on behalf of those in categories 2 and 3.

The amount of pension contribution must be reviewed every five years under the rule of financial recalculation, and must reflect the current state of inflation, interest, and income levels. The contribution applicable from April 1997 was ¥13,200 per month, but it is estimated that this level will increase rapidly through the 1990s and into the twenty-first century. Figure 10.3 depicts the long-run projection of National Pension contribution levels at constant 1994 prices, assuming that the present scheme is maintained in the future. Starting from ¥12,200 in 1996, the contribution increases annually by ¥500 until 2015 and thereafter reaches a certain stable level of ¥21,700 or ¥24,300 based on the 1994 and 1997 estimates respectively. Since the 1997 estimate uses a new series of population projections, it implies a more severe situation in terms of monthly payments by insured persons, reflecting further population ageing.[15]

Under the present system of paying contributions to the National Pension, there is one major problem. Since the whole population in Japan has to be insured at the basic pension level, certain groups of income classes, including lower income earners, all disabled pensioners and beneficiaries of livelihood protection benefits, must be exempted from paying contributions. Also, some insured groups, such as students over the age of 20 tend not to pay their obligatory contribution, although this is illegal. The ratio of exempted and unpaid contributions to the total amount paid is approximately 16.7 per cent. No doubt, these exemptions and the non-payment causes serious financial problems for the management of the National Pension.

At present, the national government subsidizes one-third of total benefits paid by the Basic Pension in the form of national grant-in-aid. As a consequence, Japan's Basic Pension does not constitute a complete social insurance scheme. The labour union leaders have requested an increase in the relative share of national grant-in-aid from one-third to half of pension benefits, because they are worried about the rapid increase in the payment contribution burden falling heavily on the workforce of the future.

Lastly, let us briefly look at the National Pension Fund as an additional tier of the National Pension. In order to supplement the insufficient category 1 benefits under the National Pension, the government promoted, on behalf of the self-employed, the construction of a supplemental pension to the National Pension Fund in 1991. There are two types of the fund: (i) a community-type fund which is established in each prefecture with a requirement that each has more than 1,000 participants, and (ii) an occupation-type fund which is organized across the entire nation by groups of more than 1,000 participants working in the same kind of industry and job. The number of participants gradually increased from 460,000 in 1991 to 660,000 in 1993 (MOHW 1996, p. 366).

The self-employed who belong to category 1 may choose to participate in one of these funds. The pension benefits provided by the National Pension Fund are varied, and are based on the level of contribution and the type of benefit selected by individual participants. For instance, if a person aged 40 pays into a lifetime pension with a 15-year plan, guaranteeing a monthly benefit of ¥30,000, the contribution is ¥11,700 per month. The ceiling for monthly contributions stood at ¥68,000 in 1997.

The Employees' Pension and its Fund

The Employees' Pension (old version) was established in 1941, and covered private sector employees in general. Since then, the original system has been modified a number of times to adjust pension benefits in line with improved standards of living caused by a variety of economic and social circumstances. In 1973, this pension scheme was substantially amended to secure the benefit levels in terms of real value. For example,

---

[15] Except for the population estimate, the same assumptions regarding future economic conditions are taken: 2.0 per cent for the inflation rate, 4.4 per cent for the income growth rate, and 5.5 per cent for the investment yield.

the actuarial revaluation method of pensions, using the standard remuneration of the insured persons was introduced, as will be explained below, and has continued to be applied every five years. At the same time, an indexed benefit system was adopted to link payments to the increasing rate of the CPI over 5 per cent, and later in 1989 it was altered to an automatic adjustment for inflation, even of less than 5 per cent.

In 1986, as stressed previously, the Employees' Pension was merged with the old National Pension and became the second tier as a remuneration-based pension under the new system, reflecting the thorough reorganization of the pension system as a whole. Furthermore, in anticipation of a rapidly ageing society, it has been decided that the pensionable age will be postponed from 60 to 65 years old from 2001, partly as a result of reforming the pension fund to allow for a sound financial basis in the future. Accordingly, a transitional pension plan had to be devised on behalf of the beneficiaries who will be aged 60–64 from 2001 to 2013.

Under the present Employees' Pension system, both benefit and contribution are proportional to the earnings of insured persons. In order to facilitate the calculation of them, the so-called 'standard remuneration' method is adopted, because remuneration in general is paid in a number of forms at different times, varying from time to time. Thus, the simplified standard amount of remuneration is absolutely required as a key measure to calculate both pension benefit and contribution. For this purpose, the average monthly standard remuneration is tabulated by grades, based on wages and salaries (excluding any bonus), with a certain level of upper limit.[16]

Table 10.5 summarizes the basic framework of the Employees' Pension scheme. There are a number of pension benefit schemes, the most important of which is the Old-age Employees' Pension. As a supplementary scheme, Disability Employees' and Survivors' Pensions are added, as in the National Pension System described above. Under the current Old-age Employees' system, the annual pension benefit is calculated as follows:

Pension benefit = Average standard monthly remuneration × 7.5/1000 × Number of insured months × Index rate

In addition to this amount, additional pension is paid if a beneficiary has a dependent spouse younger than 65 years old or children until the age 18 (or 20 in the case of a disabled child). Given the requirement of an insured period of at least 20 years, the annual additional pension payable for a dependent spouse is ¥226,000, and the same amount is paid to the first and second children. For each subsequent child it is reduced to ¥75,000.

Similarly, supplementary benefits are paid to disabled persons as a result of sickness or injury, and to the survivors at the time of the insured person's death. For instance, the benefit due from the Disability Employees' Pension is calculated in accordance with the formula of the Old-age Employees' Pension, and is increased by 25 per cent

---

[16] According to the table of monthly standard remuneration in 1994, the 30 grades provide us with each approximate amount of remuneration in relation to the range between ¥0–95,000 and above ¥575,000. The amount above ¥575,000 is all included in an upper limit of ¥590,000 even if it would further increase above this limit.

TABLE 10.5. *The framework of the Employees' Pension in 1997*

Items	Contents
Legally initiated year	1941
Coverage	Employees in the private sector
Insured persons (1,000)	33,000
Insurer	The national government
Pensionable age in 1997	60 for male and 59 for female
Pension benefits	
Old-age and retirement	Old-age Employees' Pension
Disability	Disability Employees' Pension
Death	Survivor's Employees' Pension
Pension contribution	
Employers	8.675%[a] (6.775–7.075%)
Insured persons	8.675%[a] (6.775–7.075%)
Subsidy from the national government	1/3 for pension benefits

Source: As Table 10.4.

Note:
  [a] Split contribution rates of 17.35 per cent and adopted to seamen and underground miners.

in the case of a first grade disability.[17] On the other hand, the survivors' Employees' Pension pays 75 per cent of the amount of the Old-age Employees' Pension to which the decreased person was entitled.

We will now briefly consider the revenue side of the Employees' Pension scheme. The contribution rate is fixed at 17.35 per cent for the standard remuneration as of October 1996 to secure the necessary amount to pay out pension benefits, given that one-third of the payment figure is subsidized by the national government.

Unlike the National Pension, pension contributions are split equally between the insured persons (employees) and their company (employers). In the case of insured persons who are members of the Employees' Pension, reduced contribution rates are adopted in the range of 6.775–7.075 per cent.

Thus, it is important to note that both pension benefits and contributions are calculated on the basis of the standard remuneration. Any pension is established as a long-term scheme in which it takes several decades from contributing to receiving benefits, and moreover pension benefits continue to be paid for a long period of time. Generally speaking, the whole amount of pension benefits starts from a comparatively small payment at the outset, and increases rapidly as the scheme matures. Two factors are significant to explaining the rising trend of pension benefits: one is population ageing and the other is the prolongation of an average contribution in which in turn the expansion of benefits has to be led.

---

[17] There are three grades of disability under the Employees' Pension, and no disability pension is granted in the case of entitlement to the third grade.

Obviously, to prepare for a rapid increase in pension benefits, it is necessary to draw up a financial plan to keep the pension fund well-managed. In doing so, great emphasis has been placed in Japan on maintaining the real value of the necessary benefit payments, reflecting the improvement of living standards. The financial plan initiated in 1973 was a method of actuarial revaluation, which depended on such assumptions as demographic factors (e.g. mortality and fertility rates), economic factors (e.g. wage increases and inflation rate), and employment factors (e.g. the size of the working population). Of course, periodic reviews are needed to adjust the basic framework of the plan to accommodate social and economic change as time passes. Thus, it is now stipulated in the legislation that the actuarial revaluation of both the employees' and national pension schemes ought to be made at least every five years. The latest revaluation was carried out in 1999, and the next will be performed in 2004.

Based on the actuarial revaluation for securing the necessary revenues systematically over the decades, future contribution rates are generally calculated as depicted in Figure 10.4. According to the latest financial plan by the MOHW, its contribution rate will be raised by 2.5 per cent every five years from 14.5 per cent in 1994, 19.5 per cent in 2000, 24.5 per cent in 2010 and 29.5 per cent in 2020 under the modified pay-as-you-go scheme.

If the assumption of a fund-balancing rate could be introduced to keep the balance at the same level so as to abate the cost burden for future generations, the uniform contribution rate is fixed at about 22 per cent. The current contribution rate should have so far been raised to reach the fund-balancing rate in every actuarial revaluation, but this could not be done. As a matter of fact, the fund-balancing rate itself has been raised in the past, reflecting an ad hoc improvement of pension benefits and population ageing.

If the system were to be changed into a fully pay-as-you-go method, what would happen to the level of contribution rate? As is indicated in Figure 10.4, the pay-as-you-go rate rises sharply from its lowest level in 1970 to a peak of 35.0 per cent in 2045. By that time Japanese workers will be paying 5.2 per cent more in contribution rates than under the modified pay-as-you-go scheme.

In 1998, the MOHA proposed four alternative plans to balance pension benefits against costs in the Employees' Pension scheme to delineate the nation's choice in the future.

1. Plan A—retaining the same level of pension benefit with the contribution rate of 34.3 per cent per monthly remuneration;   (6.5 %).
2. Plan B—a cut of 10 per cent in benefits with a 30 per cent rate of contribution per monthly remuneration;   (30.8%).
3. Plan C—a cut of 20 per cent in benefits with a 20 per cent rate of contribution per monthly remuneration;   (40.5%).
4. Plan D—a cut of 40% in benefits with the same rate of contributing as in Plan C;
                    (7.2%).[18]

---

[18] The percentages in parentheses are the results of a poll. This poll was carried out by the MOHW in March 1998, based on enquiries to 2175 persons who were working in various areas, for example enterprise managers, labour union leaders, academics, journalists, etc. (MOHW 1999, p. 119).

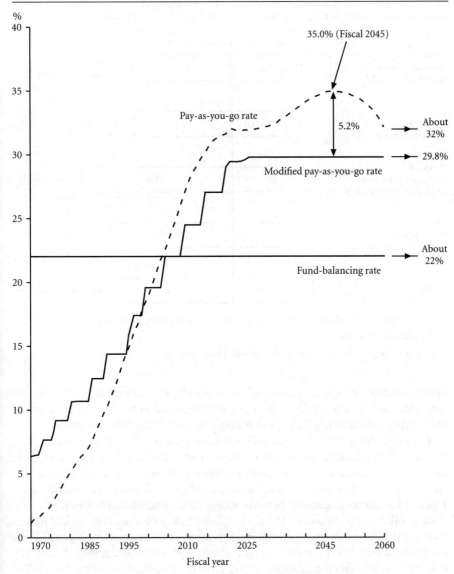

FIGURE 10.4. *Contribution rates of the Employees' Pension*

Source: MOF

Note: The fund-balancing rate is calculated based on the conditions under which the pension fund should be managed, given the uniform rate from the beginning, to keep its balance at the same level

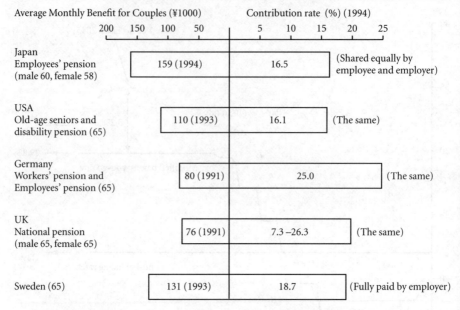

FIGURE 10.5. *Pension benefits and contribution rates among five major countries*
Source: Tachi 1996, p. 170
Note: Figures below country names indicate pensionable age

Plan A combines a high benefit and a high cost while Plan D combines a low benefit with a low cost. As a result of a poll among well-informed persons, it was evident that the intermediate cases of Plans C and B would be more likely to be acceptable.

No doubt, the contribution rate will rise sharply, up to 30 per cent or more, given the current structure of Employees' Pension scheme. It would be almost impossible for the younger generation to continue to shoulder the burden at such a high rate, considering all the other burdens, such as taxes and medical insurance contributions. Figure 10.5 compares pension benefits and the contribution burden in Japan with those in other major countries. Japan's Employees' Pension shows the highest benefit level of ¥159,000 while its contribution rate is merely 16.5 per cent, the second lowest level behind the USA. Given the current benefit–cost relationship, these figures can only forecast a worsening financial situation for the pension fund in the future. The need to restructure the present Employees' Pension system is crucial.

In view of the actuarial re-evaluation due in 1999, the MOHW began to deliberate possible future reforms. For example, the following points have been proposed as indispensable reforms for the Employees' Pension:

1. the benefit level should generally be lowered further;
2. the pensionable age should be further postponed to 67 from 65, based on the current revised plan;

3. the standard remuneration should not include wage increases and improved standard of living, but simply an inflationary factor.
4. wealthy pensioners above a certain level of income should have their benefits restricted to some extent.

At the third tier of public pension system, there is the Employees' Pension Fund. This fund was introduced in 1966 as a corporate pension to meet the various needs of elderly people and to allow pensioners to enjoy a more affluent life in their aged period. Of course, it implies an additional payment to supplement insufficient benefits at the first and second tiers of pension schemes. To set up the Employees' Pension Fund, a company has to set up a special legal entity with the consent of both more than half of the employees[19] and the labour union, under the approval of MOHW. The fund will then provide additional pension benefits suitable for its own financial conditions. There are two types of pension benefits provided by the fund: one is part of the Employees' Pension benefit (i.e. a remuneration-based portion, excluding the part related to indexation and re-evaluation), and the other is a supplementary lifetime benefit. The revenue necessary to pay such additional benefits is collected through contributions from participants and their employers. Contribution rates range from 3.2 to 3.8 per cent and are applied to the monthly standard remuneration by each fund as of fiscal 1996. These contributions are tax exempt.

Since its debut, the Employees' Pension Fund has so far developed smoothly, including one-third of those insured by the Employees' Pension. That is to say, there were 1,886 funds and 12,280,000 participants by 1996. In order to handle individual funds at the company level, the Employees' Pension Fund Association has been established at the national level. The reserves increased year by year, reflecting the development of the system, until by the mid-1990s assets exceeded over ¥40,000 billion. These reserves are utilized for portfolio investment in financial and security markets through trust banks, life insurance, and investment advisory companies.

However, after the collapse of the 'bubble' economy in the 1990s, the Employees' Pension Fund system has faced a new dimension, because its financial situation worsened rapidly, reflecting the lower rate of income growth and reduced yields for portfolio investment. A number of the Employees' Pension Funds have begun to dissolve, or have found themselves slipping into a situation where their reserves are insufficient to meet their future payments of pension benefits. Although some of the relevant companies in this situation are making an effort to reconstruct their funds by subsidizing them, the number of dissolution cases seems set to rise in the future. An overall restructuring of the system is requested in view of fund management.

Mutual Aid Associations

The third category of public pension system, the Mutual Aid Associations (MAAs), have developed with four distinctive pension schemes, each based on one of the employment groups: (i) national government employees; (ii) local government

---

[19] The number of employees in a company must be more than 500 to be entitled to this fund.

employees (iii) private teachers; and (iv) agricultural, forestry, and fishery cooperative employees. In addition, the employees of JR, NTT and JT were merged into the MAAs at the national government from March 1996 with certain lump-sum shares, because their pension funds had become aggravated to a great extent. Similar to the Employees' Pension, the objective of the MAAs is mutual aid through the provision of appropriate benefits to their members and their dependents when they suffer from sickness, injury, death, retirement, disaster, and so on.

Benefits under the MAAs are both short-term and long-term.[20] The former is nearly the same as medical care benefit, while the latter is a pension benefit itself. Thus, the MAAs cover both medical care and pension benefits at the same time in a unified system.

Short-term benefits contain not only medical care, but also various types of expenses and allowances related to members' daily life (e.g. removals, funeral, condolence, leave, etc.). Obviously, all these benefits indicate the nature of mutual aid among the members and their dependents. The scope and types of medical care benefit under the MAAs are similar to those of the Employees' Health Insurance system, as will be argued later.

By contrast, the long-term benefits of the MAAs are designed for old-age and retirement pensions, disability pensions, and survivor's pensions, similar to the Employees' Pension system. Indeed, mutual aid old-age and retirement pension benefit is calculated on the basis of standard remuneration. The same procedures are applied to two other pensions. Financial sources are collected by the contribution paid by members, and its rate is determined by the rules of each MAA: 5.40–10.26 per cent for the short-term benefits, and 18.39 per cent for the long-term benefits as of October 1996. Both contribution rates are split evenly by the members and the employers (i.e. the government). Moreover, one-third of the contribution for long-term benefits is subsidized by the national government, but no subsidy is paid towards short-term benefits.

The old-age and retirement pensions of MAAs are tabulated in Table 10.6 to allow comparison to be made. Depending on the financial situation, each MAA is slightly different to the next one in terms of pension benefits, contribution rates, reserves, maturity, etc. The most wealthy MAA is the Private School Teachers' MAA for which the contribution rate is the lowest, the monthly benefit relatively is higher and the reserve rate exceeds the lowest degree of maturity by 11 fold. In Table 10.6, both JR and JT have the worst performance record, as they offer pension plans whose maturity levels are extremely high. In particular, in the case of JR, the number of beneficiaries is larger than the number of contributors. JR has very low reserves and a low reserve rate, implying that its pension fund is in *de facto* bankruptcy. This is the reason why it had to be absorbed by the National Government Employees' MAA, as noted above. At the moment, other MAAs' pensions seem to be operated relatively well.

---

[20] The case of agricultural, forestry, and fishery cooperative employees is exceptional, because it owns only long-term pension benefit. Short-term benefits equivalent to medical care benefit is included in the National Health Insurance.

TABLE 10.6. *Old-age and retirement pensions of the Mutual Aid Associations in 1997*

	Members (1000) (1)	Beneficiaries of old-age and retirement pensions (2) (1000)	Maturity[a] (%) (2)/(1)	Average monthly benefits (¥1000)	Reserves (¥trillion)	Reserve rate[b] (fold)	Contribution rate[c] (%)
National Government[d] Employees' MAA	1,120	570	50.9	216	7.0	4.3	18.39
(JR)	190	290	152.6	197	0.3	0.5	20.09
(NTT)	250	140	56.0	202	1.8	5.1	17.21
(JT)	24	25	104.2	200	0.1	1.4	19.92
Local government employees' MAA	3,340	1,290	38.6	232	27.2	6.7	16.56
Private school teachers' MAA	400	50	12.5	218	2.3	11.5	13.30
Agriculture, forest and fishery cooperative employees' MAA	51	14	28.0	176	1.8	5.0	19.49

Source: Data from the MOF.

Note:

[a] round figures

[b] the ratio of reserve balance in the previous year to current pension benefit

[c] including both employers and insured persons as of October 1996

[d] excluding the cases of JR, NTT and JT

THE PUBLIC MEDICAL CARE INSURANCE SYSTEM

Rapid Expansion of Medical Care Costs

As the population is ageing, the demand for medical and health care services is increasing at a great rate, leading to a nationwide expansion of health care expenditure. According to the MOHW estimation, more than 62 per cent of all the necessary medical and health care costs for an individual's lifetime tend to be spent after they have reached the age of 60 years (see MOHW 1996, p. 109). No doubt, this increase in medical and health care expenditure will pose the most serious problem, in addition to pensions, in an aged Japanese society in the twenty-first century.

In Japan, all medical and health care costs are represented in terms of the national expenditure on health, which consists not only of necessary expenses from medical care insurance benefits and government subsidies but also the contribution paid by the patients themselves. Trends in national health expenditure are depicted in Figure 10.6 for 1970–98. Obviously, the long-run tendency is rising from ¥2.5 trillion in 1970 to ¥28.8 trillion in 1998, with a sudden large jump in the early 1970s due to the large-scale reforms of medical and health care services as a debut of the 'welfare state' in 1973. On average, such expenditure has increased by 5–6 per cent annually and has continued to add an amount of approximately ¥1 trillion each year since 1980. The relative share of national health expenditure to national income remained at about 6 per cent in the 1980s, but thereafter rose sharply to over 7 per cent. In the late 1990s, the growth rate of nominal income stood at a mere 1 per cent while national health expenditure is increasing at the rate of around 6 per cent each year. Obviously, this expansion must be caused by factors built into the structure of the medical and health care system.

It should be noted that there has been a sharp rise in the national health expenditure for the elderly over and above the ordinary type of public health insurance schemes, as will be explained later. This expenditure constituted less than a 20 per cent share of total health expenditure in the early 1980s, but thereafter it continued to increase by as much as a third. Evidently, with an increasingly ageing population the health expenses for the elderly will rise enormously in the twenty-first century.

To what extent is national health expenditure expected to expand in the future? The MOHW estimates that it will reach ¥38 trillion in 2000, ¥68 trillion in 2010, and ¥141 trillion in 2025, at an average growth rate of 5–6 per cent. Indeed, it will increase 5 fold between 1995 and 2025. As is expected, the increasing tempo health expenditure on the elderly will be much faster—in the range of 6–9 per cent—and its ratio relative to the total will be 35 per cent in 2000, 42 per cent in 2010, and 50 per cent in 2025. It is perhaps surprising to learn that half of the nation's health expenditure will be spent on those over 65 years of age. The problem is how we can restrain such a sharp rise of health expenditure in the twenty-first century.

In spite of the recent increase in national health expenditure, Japan's health expenditure relative to GDP is still at a lower level than in any of the other major countries (OECD 1997) The top three ratios in 1991 are 13.40 per cent in the USA, followed by

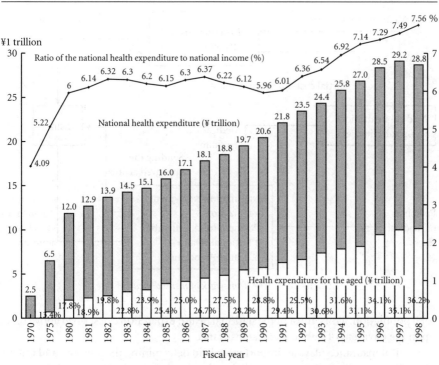

FIGURE 10.6. *Trends in national health expenditure, 1990–98*

Source: MOF

Note: 1. Health expenditure for the aged for January 1983 and thereafter is for those people who came under the now obsolete medical care expenditure provision system for the elderly. Thus, it is not possible to simpy compare the data just before and after 1983

2. The percentages for health expenditure for the elderly shown in the lower area are the ratios of health expenditure for the aged to national health expenditures

10.01 per cent in Canada and 9.05 per cent in France, while Japan's ratio is only 6.59 per cent. This reflects the fact that Japan's population was less aged when those statistics were drawn up, but such a fortunate condition will disappear early in the twenty-first century.

Outline of the Public Medical Insurance System

In Japan, medical and health care services are provided to patients by medical institutions (e.g. hospital, clinics, or practitioners) mainly in the private sector. For this reason, the public medical insurance system has developed as a social insurance that insures against illness and injury. All citizens participate fully in this system, through which they can purchase medical and health care services. That is to say, medical service expenses are paid for all citizens under such a publicly-established insurance system. This is in sharp contrast with the situation in the USA, where both Medicare and Medicaid services—the public medical insurance—cover only one-quarter of the

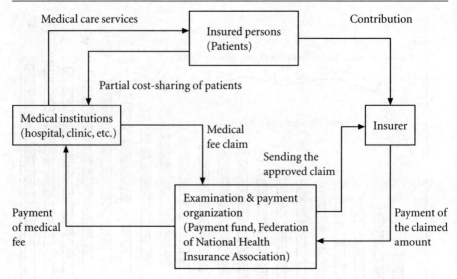

FIGURE 10.7. *The framework of insured medical care*

total population. Thus, most of the national health expenditure described above relies upon the payment of public medical insurance.

Medical insurance plays an important role in determining the quantity and quality of medical care services to be provided and managing the financial sources, such as insurance contributions or patient contributions. Figure 10.7 illustrates the basic idea of the present system. On one side, medical institutions provide medical and health care services to patients. Nearly all of the necessary medical fees for these services are reimbursed from the medical insurance system, although a proportion remains to be shared with the patients. On the other side, insurers, such as the government and health insurance associations, collect insurance contributions from patients and pay the amount claimed for medical and health care services through specific organizations in which medical fee claims are reviewed and examined.

Broadly speaking, Japan's public medical insurance system consists of (i) the Employees' Health Insurance (EHI) and (ii) the National Health Insurance (NHI), as tabulated in Table 10.7. Nearly the whole population is obliged to participate in either the EHI or the NHI, and each insured person has to pay an insurance contribution to insurers of the government and relevant associations. Basically, these health insurance schemes mainly operate on the basis of the contributions, but some are substantially subsidized by the national government.

The EHI, which was established in 1922, consists of two large health insurance systems, as well as seamen's[21] and MAAs' cases; one is the government-managed

---

[21] The seamen's insurance was established in 1939 to cover exclusively a 'seaman', as defined in the Mariners' Act. The insured persons numbered approximately 120,000 in 1996.

TABLE 10.7. *Outline of the health insurance system in 1997*

The kind of health insurance		The type of insured persons	Insurer	Medical care benefits	Financial Sources	
					Contribution rate	Government subsidy
Employees' Health Insurance (EHI)	Health insurance — Government-managed	Employees at small, medium companies	National government	90% for insured persons / 80% for dependents	About 8.5% of remuneration, split equally between employees and employers	13% of insurance benefits (16.4% as health service for the elderly)
	Health insurance — Association-managed	Employees at large companies	Health insurance associations 1814			Lump-sum subsidy ¥3 trillion
	Seamen's insurance	Seamen	National government		8.8%	Lump-sum subsidy ¥3 trillion
	Mutual aid associations	National and local government employees and private teachers	82 associations		7.6–8.6%	None
National Health Insurance (NHI)		Farmers, self-employed, etc.	Municipal government 3,249 NHI association 166	70%	Annual average amount per household ¥158,329	50% of insurance benefits 32–52% of insurance benefits
Medical Care System for the Retired		Retirees formerly under EHI	Municipal government 3,249	80%		None

Source: Tabulated from data from the MOHW.

health insurance for employees of small- and medium-sized companies, and the other association-managed one is for employees of large companies. The health insurance associations in the latter case can be established upon authorization of MOHW by an employer who employs 700 employees or more, or by employers working jointly in the community with a combined workforce of 3,000 or more. Instead of the government, they can manage their own independent health insurance schemes.

Conversely, the NHI was established in 1939 to cover all citizens not insured by the EHI, such as the self-employed, farmers, and the elderly. In contrast to the EHI, which is based on the workplace, the NHI is a community-type insurance mainly operated by municipal governments. After being restructured in 1958, the NHI has played a fundamental role in providing universal medical insurance in Japan. Since the NHI covers relatively low-income earners and has no employer fund, one-half of its insurance benefits must be subsidized by the national government, which should be contrasted with such wealthy insurance schemes as association-managed EHI or MAAs.

In 1984, the Medical Care System for the Retired was created with the NHI mainly with a view to securing an equitable balance of contributions against benefits over each generation. Those who retired and left the EHI used to participate in NHI, and tended to spend much more on medical costs than they had contributed. This was one of the major problems for the NHI fund and it had to be solved cooperating with the EHI. A new medical insurance was introduced exclusively to cover retired people who had previously been insured under the EHI. This was an important reform which began to prepare for an increasingly aged population and was intended to stabilize the medical insurance fund.

In addition to the EHI and the NHI, another health scheme had to be established to deal with health services for the elderly, in the way that Medicare does in the USA. Generally speaking, elderly people have a high rate of chronic sickness and disease. The ratio of elderly participants in the NHI was also essentially higher than in the EHI, which in turn tended to induce much higher health expenditure. In other words, the significant difference in the ratio of the elderly in each medical care insurance produced an imbalance of the burden among the insurers. Thus, it was becoming much more of a problem for the NHI, than it was for the EHI.

In 1983, a new scheme for the health and medical services system for the elderly was introduced to cope with these problems—a comprehensive health programme ranging from disease prevention and treatment to rehabilitation.[22] In order to correct disparities in the health expenditure for the elderly, it was to be borne equitably by the entire nation. Accordingly, medical costs began to be shared jointly by both national and local governments and by each insurer.

---

[22] Before introducing such a new scheme, the previous system enacted in 1972 brought about the sharp increase of medical care costs for the elderly, because co-payments of the elderly were paid out of public expenditure. As a result of easier access to treatment, hospitals and clinics were full of the elderly because of free medical services, disregarding the costs.

The health care and medical service system in place for the elderly at the end of the 1990s covers those who are insured by each health insurance and are aged over 70, or 65–70 if bedridden. Total costs are divided into 70 per cent from each health insurer and 30 per cent from the national and local governments (i.e. two-thirds by the national and one-third by the local government).

As shown in Figure 10.6, medical costs for the elderly have increased their relative share of national health expenditure from 13.4 per cent in 1975 to 36.2 per cent in 1998. Obviously, such a growth in expenditure on the elderly, which in turn has to increase the share of the burden for the contribution to the health service system, has led to financial crises for many health insurers.

Financial Crises in the Insurance Funds

Although the public medical insurance system was established to completely cover all citizens on a universal basis, each insurance fund has suffered financially in recent years. While health expenditure has steadily increased, reflecting population ageing and rising medical costs, revenue has constantly slowed down, due to sluggish wage and salary increments after the collapse of the bubble. Thus, major insurance funds have begun to build some form of insurance against financial deficits into the structure of their revenue and expenditure.

Table 10.8 summarizes the state of insurance finance for three major insurers in the mid-1990s. The government-managed health insurance turned into surplus in 1981 and continued to generate sound finance for 12 years, but from 1993 it began to show a deficit which expanded steadily, resulting in the largest deficit in 1996 of approximately ¥419.3 billion. In 1997, however, as a result of increasing the contribution rate and co-payment by patients, insurance finance was largely restored once again to a sound basis. However, the results of these efforts were beginning to disappear within a year or so, and deficits are estimated to increase again in 1999. According to estimates produced by the MOHW, the deficit having to be built into government-managed health insurance will expand in the range of ¥1,360–¥1,780 billion in 2001.

Similarly, the situation for association-managed health insurance schemes has continued to worsen since 1994 when the insurance funds first began to generate deficits, inducing more than half of insured associations into deficit-covering management. In fact, the amount of the deficits in 1995 increased sharply to ¥122.2 billion and ¥197.5 billion in 1996. In 1997, however, a sound financial footing was regained by utilizing the same procedures as the government-managed health insurance schemes, thus generating a very small amount of deficit. This better situation has not been sustained, however, and the balance began to swing the wrong way again from 1998. In fact, 84.6 per cent of total insurance associations were in the red in 1999. As indicated in Table 10.8, the NHI is financially in an even worse state having shown a deficit from as early as 1990.

This is the first time since 1961 that each health insurance fund has been in such a deep financial crisis. No doubt, the most influential reason for this is the sharp increase in the demand on the health service system for the elderly. The ratio of spending on

TABLE 10.8. *Financial crises in major health insurance schemes, 1983–99 (¥ billion)*

1 Government-managed health insurance

Items	Fiscal 1983	1990	1993	1994	1995	1996	1997*	1998**	1999**
Revenue	3,521.2	5,336.9	6,181.8	6,333.9	6,608.2	6,750.9	6,925.7	7,081.9	7,107.3
Expenditure	3,460.7	4,993.7	6,275.3	6,614.8	6,886.5	7,170.2	7,020.7	7,131.7	7,413.0
(Contribution to the elderly)	(540.0)	(1,139.8)	(1,492.7)	(1,611.8)	(1,705.7)	(1,856.6)	(1,889.7)	(2,127.5)	(2,354.4)
Balance	60.5	343.2	−93.5	−280.9	−278.3	−419.3	−95.0	−49.8	−305.7

2 Association-managed health insurance

Items	Fiscal 1983	1990	1993	1994	1995	1996	1997*	1998**	1999**
Revenue	2,877.8	4,561.6	5,335.8	5,386.8	5,506.4	5,625.7	5,922.4	6,020.7	5,944.1
Expenditure	2,667.0	4,330.3	5,218.4	5,464.2	5,628.6	5,823.2	5,924.1	6,154.4	6,341.0
(Contribution to the elderly)	(363.8)	(1,024.7)	(1,237.5)	(1,330.9)	(1,400.0)	(1,506.5)	(1,567.6)	(1,723.7)	(1,891.9)
Balance	210.8	231.3	117.4	−77.4	−122.2	−197.5	−1.7	−133.7	−396.9

3 National health insurance

Items	Fiscal 1983	1990	1993	1994	1995	1996	1997*		
Revenue	4,091.4	5,155.0	5,311.3	5,527.6	5,770.8	6,048.6	6,217.3		
Expenditure	3,897.9	4,966.3	5,399.4	5,664.6	5,879.8	6,164.0	6,246.5		
(Contribution to the elderly)	(1,068.3)	(1,433.0)	(1,503.8)	(1,674.8)	(1,774.3)	(1,926.0)	(1,995.9)		
Balance[a]	492	−66.8	−88.1	−137.0	−109.0	−115.4	−29.2		

Source: Data from the MOF.

Note:

[a] Balance is calculated to add both transfers to the fund and carry-over.

*Provisional figures, **Initial budget figures

the elderly relative to total expenditure by government-managed health insurance has jumped from 15.6 per cent in 1983 to 31.8 per cent in 1999, and the same holds true for the association-managed health insurance funds, which show an increase from 13.6 per cent in 1983 to 29.8 per cent in 1999. As a result of a cost-sharing scheme under the health and medical service for the elderly introduced in 1983, only the NHI has held the relative burden in terms of contribution to the elderly stable (at 27.9 per cent in 1983 and 32.0 per cent in 1997). Of course, in addition to the expanded spending on health services for the elderly, structural factors such as lower growth rates and population ageing became equally as damaging financially to the health insurance funds. It is widely acknowledged that the universal scheme of medical insurance in Japan is close to ruin, given the even more severe conditions facing the management of insurance funds in the future.

THE NECESSITY FOR STRUCTURAL REFORMS

Nursing Care Services for the Elderly

Since 1973, when the so-called 'welfare state' was launched, Japan's social security system has developed, following the framework of Western welfare states, with occasional patch-work amendments to adjust for the changing environment of socioeconomic conditions. However, until approximately 1990, the basic conditions surrounding the development of the social security system were still favourable due to the growing economy. Indeed, social security revenue was virtually secured by the steady growth in income and could maintain the sound balance of various pension and medical insurance funds. The situation changed completely after the collapse of the 'bubble economy' under which a sluggish growth performance tended to influence the badly managed operations of many insurance funds.

Looking ahead to the start of the twenty-first century, given such changed circumstances, the most serious policy issues for the social security system will no doubt depend on how we deal with the growing demand for nursing care services for the elderly in an ageing population (see, for example, Takayama 1998).

The advent of an aged society generates not only an increase in the number of elderly people themselves but also in the number of those who are needed to provide nursing care services. How should we take care of the elderly with senile dementia and those who are frail and bedridden? There are two alternatives: one is public care facilities (hospitals, homes for the aged, etc.) and the other to provide care in private houses. In pre-war Japan, it was quite natural for more than one generation of a family to live together in a single household, and care of the elderly was commonly considered to be the work of that family. After the Second World War, however, these multi-generational families were greatly reduced while nuclear families, consisting of a couple and their children, increased. As a consequence, the way of supporting elderly parents changed from being an aspect of the role of the family. Since the number of

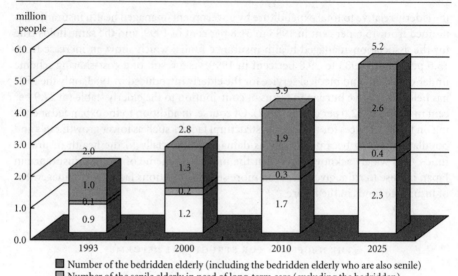

Number of the bedridden elderly (including the bedridden elderly who are also senile)
Number of the senile elderly in need of long-term care (excluding the bedridden)
Number of the frail elderly

FIGURE 10.8. *Future projections on the number of bedridden elderly people*
Source: MOHW, *The Welfare Vision for the 21st Century*, March 1994, p. 8

elderly people is expected to rise sharply, we have to solve this problem of the efficient provision of nursing care services.

Figure 10.8 shows future projections on the number of elderly people in need of long-term care. Starting with the most dependent, these elderly people can be classified thus: (i) the bedridden elderly; (ii) the senile elderly (excluding the bedridden); and (iii) the frail elderly. The total number of such elderly people amounted to 2 million in 1993, and thereafter it has been estimated that the figures will rise sharply to 2.8 million in 2000, 3.9 million in 2010, and 5.2 million in 2025. In particular, we must note that the most dependent group of the bedridden elderly will increase 2.5 times from 900,000 in 1993 to 2.3 million in 2025.

Given the increased demand for long-term care for the elderly, in 1989 the government formulated a Ten-Year Strategy to Promote Health Care and Welfare for the Elderly (known as the Gold Plan). This was a public assistance programme which was enforced in 1990. It has also been widely pointed out that the excessive burden on caregivers in families was turning into a social problem, and the capacity for in-home care was becoming difficult due to the ageing of the long-term caregivers themselves. The Gold Plan, which was to be implemented by municipal governments, prescribed various health and care services for the elderly as concrete targets to be reached by 1999 (e.g. 100,000 home helpers and special nursing homes for the elderly to accommodate 240,000 people). However, it became apparent quite soon that the targets under the Gold Plan were insufficient both in quality and quantity when compared to the actual demand for long-term nursing care. Thus, the government had to comprehensively review the Gold Plan and to reformulate it into the New Gold Plan in 1994.[23]

At the time of writing, long-term nursing care services are provided through both the public assistance programme for the elderly (i.e. free provision with co-payment) and the medical services financed by social security contributions and taxes. Furthermore, these services are divided into public facilities and home care. Facilities offering long-term nursing care services for the elderly can be divided into four main types: (i) nursing homes; (ii) care homes; (iii) medical service facilities; and (iv) general hospitals. As can be seen in Figure 10.9, there are distinct differences between the four facilities in terms of their cost-sharing structures and arrangements for co-payment (per person/month). While special nursing homes for the elderly are only available under the public assistance programme, the remaining three cases are all included in medical insurance schemes. General hospitals expenses are approximately twice as high in terms of care costs than the special nursing homes, but they request a lower burden of co-payment from patients per month.

The largest share of costs—except in the special nursing homes—is undertaken by insurers: 50–70 per cent in total. This is evidently one important reason why expenditure on the elderly in Table 10.8 and Figure 10.6 has risen tremendously as a proportion of each insurer's and national health expenditure. Despite the use of medical insurance schemes, we should stress that public money is largely utilized to support nursing care for the elderly under the current system. Also monthly contributions from patients has varied from ¥390,000 to ¥43,000 in each case.

In-home care services are provided through public assistance, such as the New Gold Plan, but the user contributions are sought in various cases, for example for home helps, day service/day care, short stay, etc.

What becomes evident from the discussion above, is that the biggest problem of the present nursing care system arises from the mixed nature of the medical treatment and nursing care required.

Generally speaking, given the current system of facilities for care services, even elderly people in need of simple nursing care tend to prefer long-term hospitalization in general hospitals to other forms of care, even if they do not need medical treatment. This is often known as 'social hospitalization'. Since the cost of looking after an elderly person in a general hospital is higher than it is in a special nursing home or other facility, this results in a waste of medical care resources.

Conversely, public assistance programmes for the elderly can also pose problems apart from there being a shortage of special nursing homes. For instance, users cannot always choose the service and are forced to follow the uniform services given the government allotment. Also, since the user contribution for long-term nursing care is charged according to income, middle-class income earners tend to bear the brunt of

---

[23] The New Gold Plan target for 1999 was enlarged from that of the Gold Plan: for example home helpers were increased from 100,000 people to 170,000 people, special nursing homes for the elderly from 240,000 people to 290,000 people, short stays from 50,000 beds to 60,000 beds, day service/day care from 10,000 locations to 17,000 locations and so on (MOHW 1996).

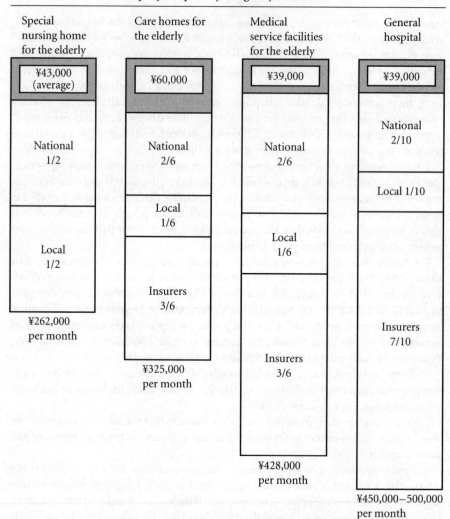

FIGURE 10.9. *Care costs by four service facilities (per person/month)*
and their cost-sharing: 1995

Source: Data from the MOF

Note: The shaded areas at the top of each column show the amount of co-payment per month by patients.
In the case of special nursing homes, it varies from zero to ¥240,000, depending upon patient's income level.
Thus, average amounts are used here. The figures at the bottom of the graph indicate total care costs per
month in each case

the burden. In addition, households entering a family member into a special nursing home for the elderly are compulsorily means tested. Needless to say, this generates a great deal of psychological stress for the family. Thus, it is quite common for a family to send an elderly person to a hospital where there is much more freedom to choose the appropriate nursing care, and lower co-payments.

In order to cope with the problems arising from the current schemes, there are demands for a new nursing care system to be established to strengthen the level of social support given to the elderly in need of care and to the relevant families. Accordingly, in 1996 the MOHW published a plan to introduce a new long-term nursing care insurance system. The main proposals are to build a basic framework which provides the necessary nursing care services through the social insurance system, based upon social solidarity. This is the same aim as medical and pension insurance. The relevant law has been passed through the congressional process with the new scheme coming into operation from April 2000,[24] producing a great deal of controversial argument among a variety of groups in Japan.

Expansion of Social Security Costs

The ongoing trend towards population ageing will obviously involve greater demands for public pensions, medical and nursing care, and will require an improved social security system. As noted earlier, the system in place for pensions and medical care at the end of the 1990s is suffering from a huge level of deficit in their funds. Demand for nursing care services also appears to be set to rise infinitely as population ages. Under these circumstances, it is necessary to resolve the public concern over the future of social security in Japan with special reference to the expansion of its cost. In particular, it is very important to learn to what extent social security costs will rise and how they should be shared by the government and relevant groups.

The MOHW has recently published future projections of social security costs towards 2025, assuming the existing system is untouched. Depending upon the assumptions of nominal growth rates (i.e. case A high, case B middle and case C low),[25] the ratio of social security costs to national income is estimated to be 28.5 per cent (case A), 33.5 per cent (case B), and 35.5 per cent (case C) respectively in 2025.[26] Of course, the faster nominal national income grows, the lower the relative share of social security costs will be. Not only such costs but also tax revenue will sharply increase the

---

[24] The main contents of the MOHW scheme are as follows. Insurers are municipal government. Insured persons are those aged 40 or older, dividing into category 1 (65 years or older) and category 2 (medical insurance subscriber for age 40–60). Insurance benefits are paid to insured persons in the form of various medical care and public assistance for both in-home and public facility services after confirming long-term care approval of the government. Total nursing care costs are shared by users' co-payment (10 per cent of insurance benefits), public funding (50 per cent) and insurance contribution (40 per cent).

[25] Case A assumes 3.5 per cent of nominal growth up to 2000, and thereafter 3.0 per cent. The counterpart percentages are assumed to be 1.75 per cent and 2.0 per cent in case B, and 1.75 per cent and 1.5 per cent in case C (MOF 1997).

[26] These results are estimated by using the projection of a less ageing population made in 1992, but the new projection of 1997 would apparently raise these social security costs by a couple of percentage points.

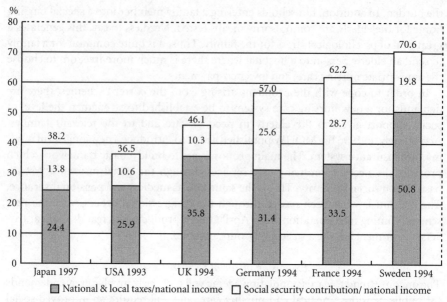

FIGURE 10.10. *Tax–social security contribution ratio*
Source: MOF

national burden as a whole. Thus, it is common to use the ratio of tax revenue and social security contribution to national income as a yardstick of the national burden ratio.

In Japan, we often employ the tax/social security contribution ratio in the general government within national income framework as an important policy goal. In Figure 10.10 these latest ratios are delineated for six countries to provide an international comparison. Japan's level is the second lowest at 38.2 per cent, following 36.5 per cent in the USA, while Sweden has the highest level at 70.6 per cent. The remaining three countries range from 46.1 per cent in the UK to 62.2 per cent in France. In 1983, the Ad-hoc Administrative Reform Commission stated that 'the tax/social security contribution ratio ought to be restrained below 50 per cent around 2020', and since then this statement has become the utmost objective of tax and social security policy. Obviously, however, it may merely be wishful thinking and very few in Japan believe it to be feasible.

Apparently, the tax/social security contribution ratio will exceed 50 per cent around 2025, if we consider the future projections of social security contributions according to the MOHW estimation. Even if tax ratio remains the same at 24.4 per cent, as in Figure 10.10, the estimates of 28–35 per cent in social security contributions would easily make the combined tax/social security contribution ratio outstrip the level of 50 per cent. Furthermore, we should not forget that this ratio does not contain the portion of current fiscal deficits that must be redeemed by tax increases on future generations. It may be better to include a fiscal deficit–national income ratio in the tax/social security contribution ratio as a potential burden on the nation. This being the case, the tax/social security contribution ratio in 2000 would rise to approximately 49.2 per cent. The EPA has recently estimated the future trends of tax/social security contribution ratio thus: 40.2 per cent (42.0 per cent) in 2000, 45.2 per cent (52.0 per cent) in 2010, and 51.5 per cent (73.4 per cent) in 2025 (percentages in parentheses are those including a fiscal deficit ratio) (EPA 1996).[27]

It is commonly acknowledged in Japan that the tax/social security contribution ratio should not lightly be allowed to rise above the limit of 50 per cent, as stressed above, although it may be very difficult to achieve this target. This is politically supported by many as a counter-example of an excessive welfare state model with high costs, as in a Scandinavian nation. Thus, it is most important to restrict the rapid expansion of social security expenditure through structural reforms of the social welfare programme itself.

In relation to the elimination of fiscal deficits, social security structural reform is being promoted by the Hashimoto Cabinet at the turn of the century in light of public pension and medical care schemes. To this end, greater importance should be put on achieving higher efficiency through reshuffling related programmes as a whole. User-oriented services ought to be emphasized to enhance the welfare level of beneficiaries in the social security system. Three points are worth noting for the future reform as we enter the twenty-first century.

First, public pensions should be reviewed in order to achieve the appropriate levels of benefits and contributions without causing any excessive burden in the future. For example, the pensionable age might be further deferred to 67. In addition, the periodic rises in pension benefits should be recalculated so as not to include any factor of wage increase rates, and taking into account the balance between the level of current benefits and the level of wages and salaries in the current working generations. Pension benefits themselves might be lowered; the arguments for this move come from an international comparison which shows that they are relatively higher than in other countries, as seen in Figure 10.5. It is noticeable that a proposal to switch the second-tier of public pensions into privatized management has gradually emerged among professional groups.

Secondly, greater importance should be directed towards reforming the entire structure of medical care services and the insurance system. It is widely believed that they encourage poor efficiency levels in the use of medical resources. Indeed, the increase in health expenditure has been substantially outpacing the growth in GDP, which might imply that the use of medical care delivery and drugs is wasteful. Both the demand and supply side of medical care services ought to be thoroughly reconsidered with a view to improving efficiency. The increase of co-payments from patients has recently been introduced into medical care treatment and drug sales to increase

---

[27] Other estimated results are more or less similar to those of the EPA. For instance, see MITI 1996; Daiwa Research Institute 1996.

awareness of the difficulties in maintaining the present level of health care service, and partly also to solve financial problems in the insurance funds. This has, however, been severely criticized by many because it completely neglects the supply factor of wasteful use of medical care and drugs. For instance, actually incurred medical costs are paid to the medical facilities (e.g. hospital, clinic, and practitioners) by the insurers, but a lump-sum payment method has been proposed to avoid excessive medical treatment. Also, since the pricing of drugs generates a price–benefit gap on the medical facilities,[28] such windfall revenue must be eliminated.

Thirdly, as argued in detail previously, a long-term nursing care insurance system for the elderly should be introduced into the current social security system to dissociate the mixed nature of medical and nursing care for the elderly. Its early establishment is desirable.

The Welfare State Withered?

The rate of population ageing and the decreasing number of children is occurring at an unprecedented speed in Japan, compared with any other advanced country. Accordingly, both the size and the form of the family is undergoing a huge change, with a sharp rise in the level of women's participation in society and a reduction in the number of family members. Given this transformation, the role played by the social security system is expected to grow in the areas of long-term care needs and child care.

On the other hand, the Japanese economy has slowed down substantially in terms of growth, as Japan faces the globalization of the economy with the 'hollowing out' of major industries. It is anticipated that the labour force will shrink, generating a labour shortage in the future. The government has already accumulated a large number of fiscal deficits and the proorest record of fiscal performance among the OECD countries. In such a handicapped state, greater attention should be paid to the future progress of the welfare state: that is, how should Japan maintain the present level of social security services and how will the welfare state have to be changed? Needless to say, this question is closely tied to how great a burden can be borne to maintain the social security system at a reasonable level. Evidently, this will be a crucial issue facing Japan in the first decade of the twenty-first century.

Given that the welfare state accounts for 59.1 per cent of all government expenditure (1995 figures),[29] its future is at the heart of most serious policy issues. It seems hardly credible that the provision of public services for social security will be able to continue at the 1990 level if the standards are to be maintained, let alone untouched. In particular, the medical insurance system may be extremely vulnerable as the population ages. Public pensions will also encounter major financial problems.

From the start of the so-called 'welfare state' in 1973, Japan has repeatedly made piecemeal amendments to accommodate occasional changes in the economy and

---

[28] In the medical insurance system, drug expenses are paid by the insurers following market prices, but in practice a lot of discounted prices are available, and this is where the medical facilities actually buy the drugs.
[29] This is the relative ratio of the total expenses of education, health, and social security/welfare services to general government expenditure according to national income statistics (EPA 1996, p. 221).

society with no long-term consideration of the overall design of the social security system. It is now time to reconsider the current framework, and reconstruct the basic idea of Japan's welfare state, although political parties which constantly claim undying commitment to its preservation are unwilling to provide the means.

There are two related issues in the financing of social security costs in the years ahead. One is public versus private financing, and the other is tax collection versus the social insurance method. With the current level of debt outstanding in the public sector, it is not possible to put increased public money into maintaining better public services. Even so, an aged society and the higher standards which greater affluence demands dictate that such a refusal to spend public money must mean more private spending. On this point, patients' co-payments for medical care have steadily increased during the 1990s to compensate for deficits in the insurance funds. In the longer term, private provision has to start with pensions and long-term nursing care. It might be necessary to privatize the second-tier pension (e.g. Employees' Pension) for the next generation with a return from the partial pay-as-you-go method to the fully-funded method. Since this reversion implies an undeniably radical plan to bring forward costs in the pension insurance rebates to be paid out over the period, it is not likely to be feasible. However, to cope with a potential deficit in the funds in the future generations and to retain the necessary public pension alone at a minimum level, privatization may be worth investigating, at least theoretically (see, for an expanded discussion, Takayama 1998).

Attention should also be paid to the alternative choices of tax collection or social insurance to secure the necessary financial sources for pensions and medical and nursing care. On the surface, Japan's social security programme takes the form of social insurance, but in practice a substantial amount of the necessary funding is dependent on tax subsidies. Should Japan move towards a genuine form of social insurance as seen in Germany, or towards being fully tax sourced as in the UK? It appears that Japan faces two such distinct alternatives. If we put more importance on redistributing income by class, a tax-financed method would be desirable. Conversely, if the relation between contribution and benefits is found to be more important, a social insurance method would be needed. At present no preference is being shown for either case, but funding from tax sources should not be increased any more. In other words, a social insurance form of social security might be accentuated further.

Looking ahead towards the twenty-first century, will the welfare state in Japan wither or not? This question relies upon the nation's choice concerning the future burden of the tax/social security contribution in relation to the expected level of public services. Which of two cases should we consider more desirable: a self-sustaining society, like the USA, with low benefits and low costs or a society with a high level of government intervention, as adopted by Scandinavian countries, with high benefits and high costs? As an increase in the tax/social security contribution is inevitable in the future, we Japanese will need to reach a public consensus about the concrete image of the welfare state that we should have.

11
Tax Incentives for Export Promotion, 1953–1964

Exports have played a vital role in Japan's economic performance throughout the post-war period. In terms of balance-of-payments, a sharp contrast can be observed between the growth of the Japanese economy during the years leading up to the early 1970s and the years since then. In the latter period, Japan's exports continued to increase rapidly, leading to huge current-account surpluses and a widening trade imbalance with much of the world. By contrast, for a decade and a half following the early 1950s, Japan suffered chronic trade deficits and a shortage of foreign exchange reserves. Particular attention is paid here to the earlier period, when the balance-of-payments situation was perceived as limiting economic expansion.[1]

The primary goal of this chapter is to explain the relationship between exports and specific export-promoting tax incentives during the period 1953–1964, particularly government policy to foster exports. The discussion that follows is divided into three parts. First, we shall briefly discuss export trends and the role of tax incentive measures. Secondly, we shall examine the institutional setting of export-promoting tax incentives and their possible effects. Thirdly, we shall explore certain aspects of such tax policy in a historical perspective with respect to conflicts in the international community.

EXPORTS AND THE ROLE OF TAX INCENTIVES

Export Trends

Japan possesses few mineral resources and little arable land relative to the size of its population. Rapid growth of its national income through expanded industrial production requires huge increases in imports of raw materials, fuels, and food. The following statement is worth noting:

> Given the initial absence of international reserve asset in post-war, given the government's commitment [...] to the value of the yen established in 1949, given the policy decision [...] not to admit significant direct investment and a Japanese (and foreign) prejudice against appreciable long-term Japanese borrowing abroad, Japan's economic expansion could well have been limited, even short of potential output, but the extent to which its exports could expand (or its imports could be restrained) (Ackley and Ishi 1976, p. 170).

---

[1] This chapter draws on Ishi 1994.

In fact, as was argued in Chapter 2, the government often used macroeconomic policy (particularly, monetary policy) to slow the expansion of GDP, domestic demand, and imports when expansion was generating a negative current-account balance, leading to untenable losses of foreign exchange reserves. As a consequence, promoting the rapid growth of exports was of the utmost importance and a variety of policies were employed by the government to stimulate export growth. Tax policy being the most noteworthy,[2] tax incentives were frequently used to achieve this policy goal.

It is instructive to examine export trends during the period in question before proceeding with the major focus of this chapter. As shown in Table 11.1, high rates of export growth were experienced during most of the 1950s and 1960s. These rates typically exceeded 20 per cent. During the early post-war period, leaders in government and business placed great emphasis on export-generated growth, often exhorting the population to recognize its importance with such popular slogans as 'prosperity through exports', as stressed before.

Japan's exports expanded rapidly. However, imports often grew even faster, particularly in boom periods. As a result, Japan continued to run a negative balance of trade through the late 1960s. Japan's rather low level of gold and foreign exchange reserves ($524 million in 1957) and its balance-of-payments deficit invariably threatened the government, which began imposing restrictive demand management policies. Policy-induced recessions through deliberate reductions in exports were followed by economic upturns (see Chapter 2). This pattern of export and import ended in the late 1970s and resulted in a shift to current-account surpluses. At the same time, Japan began to accumulate substantial international reserves.

Tax Measures to Promote Exports

Fearing balance-of-payments deficits in the 1950s and 1960s, the government targeted export promotion. To achieve the targets established for exports, the government formulated a number of special tax incentives[3] for individuals and corporations involved in export activities, including tax exemptions and deductions, tax-free reserves, and accelerated depreciation (see, for a more comprehensive discussion, Ishi 1993, ch. 3). It is difficult to quantify the effects of these policies; however, data on a series of revenue losses associated with the special tax measures, unofficially compiled by the MOF, are instructive.

Table 11.2 shows estimated revenue losses from the incentive tax measures for individuals and corporations during the period 1953–63. Total revenue losses from special tax measures for export promotion were between 5.42 and 16.42 per cent of

[2] In addition to tax incentives, government policies for the promotion of exports include import protection, export subsidies, financial aid, and guidance to favoured lines of production, and investment in export-related industries.

[3] In Japan, the term special tax measures generally refers to tax incentives. These can also be called tax preferences, tax benefits, and tax expenditures. Although the MOF constructs the list of special tax measures, their scope seems to be narrower than that of tax expenditures in the USA in terms of tax incentive policy. (See, Peckman and Kaizuka 1976, p. 352.)

TABLE 11.1. *Exports, imports and foreign exchange reserves, 1945–70 ($ million)*

year	Exports (1)		Imports (2)		Net exports (1)–(2) (3)	Gold and foreign exchange reserves (4)
1945	1		3		−2	
1946	6		11		−5	
1947	28		56		−28	
1948	144		168		−24	
1949	472		790		−318	
1950	828	(75.4)	967	(22.4)	−139	
1951	1,358	(64.0)	2,048	(117.8)	−690	
1952	1,273	(−6.3)	2,029	(−0.9)	−756	930
1953	1,274	(0.1)	2,410	(18.7)	−1,136	913
1954	1,629	(27.9)	2,399	(−0.5)	−770	637
1955	2,011	(23.4)	2,471	(3.0)	−460	738
1956	2,501	(24.4)	3,230	(30.7)	−790	941
1957	2,858	(14.3)	4,286	(32.7)	−1,428	524
1958	2,877	(0.7)	3,033	(−29.3)	−156	861
1959	3,456	(20.1)	3,599	(18.7)	−143	1,322
1960	4,055	(17.3)	4,491	(24.8)	−436	1,824
1961	4,236	(4.5)	5,810	(29.4)	−1,574	1,486
1962	4,916	(16.1)	5,637	(−3.0)	−721	1,841
1963	5,452	(10.9)	6,736	(19.5)	−1,284	1,878
1964	6,673	(22.4)	7,938	(17.8)	−1,265	1,999
1965	8,452	(26.7)	8,169	(2.9)	283	2,107
1966	9,776	(15.7)	9,523	(16.6)	253	2,074
1967	10,442	(6.8)	11,633	(22.2)	−1,191	2,005
1968	12,972	(24.2)	12,987	(11.6)	−15	2,891
1969	15,990	(23.3)	15,024	(15.7)	966	3,496
1970	19,318	(20.8)	18,881	(25.7)	437	4,399

Source: Bank of Japan, *Economic Statistics Annual*, 1970, pp. 227, 231, and 241.

Notes:
  [1] (1) and (2) are commodity exports and imports on a customs clearance basis.
  [2] Figures in parentheses are percentage changes on previous year.

total revenue losses.[4] The percentage of revenue losses from total special tax measures was 11–18 per cent of total income taxes. These two shares were much higher in the 1950s than in any other decade, indicating that tax incentives were employed most actively to promote economic growth and exports during this period.

  [4] These percentages fell drastically to between 1 and 2 per cent in the 1970s (see Ishi 1993, Table 3.2, p. 43). Other revenue losses are those for the promotion of individual savings and housing, the promotion of business saving and investment, and the promotion of environmental quality.

TABLE 11.2. *Revenue losses from special tax measures*

Fiscal year	Revenue losses from[a] special tax measures		Total individual and corporate taxes (¥ billion)	Relative share (%)	
	Total (¥ billion)	promotion[b] of export (¥ billion)		$\frac{(2)}{(1)}$	$\frac{(1)}{(3)}$
	(1)	(2)	(3)	(4)	(5)
1953	54.9	5.0	491.2	9.10	11.18
1954	65.8	4.5	485.9	6.84	13.54
1955	88.5	4.8	470.8	5.42	18.80
1956	88.5	4.9	564.8	5.54	15.67
1957	69.3	7.9	615.9	11.40	11.25
1958	80.4	13.2	567.6	16.42	14.16
1959	100.2	10.0	668.6	9.98	14.99
1960	140.7	11.5	964.0	8.17	14.60
1961	147.5	11.0	1,210.1	7.46	12.19
1962	169.5	21.5	1,359.9	12.68	12.46
1963	199.8	23.5	1,553.6	11.76	12.86

Source: Unpublished data estimated in May 1963 by the Tax Bureau, MOF.

Notes:
  [a] Based on an initial budget basis in full fiscal year.
  [b] Includes the special deduction for export income in 1953–63, the tax-free reserve for losses from export transactions in 1953–58, accelerated depreciation for the equipment of overseas branch offices in 1953–58, and accelerated depreciation for exporting firms' equipment in 1962–63.

The specific provisions of the special tax measures for the promotion of exports and the periods during which they applied are as follows.

Special deduction for export income	1953–64
Tax-free reserves for losses from export transactions	1953–58
Accelerated depreciation for the equipment of overseas branch offices	1953–58
Accelerated depreciation for the equipment of exporting firms	1961–67
Tax-free reserves for overseas market development	1964–67

The special deduction for export income, in effect during the entire period of 1953–64, accounted for by far the greatest share of special tax measure revenue losses—almost 90 per cent.[5] Thus, any discussion of the role of tax incentives in export promotion can, for all practical purposes, be limited to this deduction.

---

[5] Tax incentives for export promotion are often applied through indirect, not direct, taxes, particularly in developing countries. For a general discussion, see Sanchez-Ugarte, 1987, pp. 267–9.

THE INSTITUTIONAL SETTINGS OF EXPORT-PROMOTING TAX INCENTIVES

Special Deduction for Export Income

The special deduction for export income was established in August 1953 and was based on a similar system in effect in West Germany in 1951. According to the original provisions of this measure, traders and producers of exported goods making transactions between 1 August 1953 and 31 July 1956 were allowed to reduce certain portions of gross sales or net operating income derived from exports. The two criteria for calculating such a special deduction were: (i) gross sales criterion—3 per cent (1 per cent in the case of trading firms) of gross sales from exports, and (ii) net income criterion—50 per cent of net income from exports.

Using these two methods, export-related traders and producers were allowed to deduct the smaller of the two amounts from their taxable incomes. In March 1954, favoured treatment was extended only to export manufacturers with 5 per cent, rather than the usual 3 per cent, being applicable to them in the calculation of the special deduction based on gross sales. In fiscal 1955, the allowable deduction of exports derived from net income was raised from 50 per cent to 80 per cent in all cases.

Because expanding exports were considered a necessary condition for economic growth, the original export-promoting tax-incentive provision, due to terminate in 1956, was repeatedly renewed until 1964, when it was, as will be noted later, finally eliminated because it was in direct violation of the rules of GATT (the General Agreement on Tariffs and Trade). In the meantime, two supplementary deductions were added to the original export-oriented tax incentives. First, an additional deduction was attached to the original (i.e. standard) deduction in 1957 for those export-related firms raising their proportion of exports over the previous year's level.[6] Secondly, in 1959 a new deduction for technical services transactions was established to stimulate the export of Japanese technology. Accordingly, beginning in 1959, the special deduction for export income became increasingly sophisticated as three different deductions (i.e. standard, additional, and technical services) were made available to exporting firms.

Figure 11.1 depicts the hypothetical application of the standard deduction for export income. Let us assume that a firm achieved 1,500 of gross sales and 300 of net income in one business year. To calculate the standard deduction by the gross sales criterion, export sales (800) are multiplied by 3 per cent, producing a deduction of 24. In the case of calculation by the net income criterion, the assumed export income (160) is multiplied by 80 per cent, creating a deduction of 128. Because the smaller of the two figures is allowed as a deduction, taxable income on the hypothetical exports may be reduced by 24.

The case of a firm that increases its ratio of exports over the previous year's level is illustrated in Figure 11.2. Such an increase necessitates a combination of the standard and additional deductions. First, it is assumed that export sales doubled in one year

---

[6] The increased rate for deduction was 1.5 per cent for trading firms and 7.5 per cent for the exports of plants.

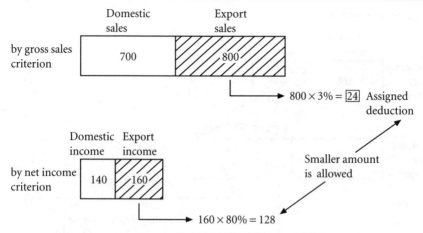

FIGURE 11.1. *Hypothetical application of the special deduction for export income, Case 1 standard deduction only*

Note: Initial figures of gross sales and net income are all assumed for the purpose of exposition

from 400 to 800. Current exports are divided into parts A and B. Part A, which is called the 'standard amount of export', is calculated by multiplying the previous year's exports by 50 per cent. This portion, in turn, is multiplied by the standard deduction rate of 3 per cent. Thus, the standard deduction amount is 6 (i.e. 200×3 per cent). Part B is defined as the current year's export (800) minus the just-described standard amount of export (in this case 200), creating a figure of 600. This portion is then multiplied by an increased rate of 4.5 per cent, resulting in the 'additional deduction' of 27. The combined deduction is calculated by adding the standard and additional deductions (i.e. 6 and 27) totalling 33, which is larger than 24, the deduction derived in Figure 11.1. The gap between the two figures represents the net effect of the additional deduction.

Secondly, calculation of the increased deduction through the use of the net income criterion is presented in the lower part of Figure 11.2. Export income is also divided into A and B by using the same 1:3 ratio as in the case of gross sales in the current year. A is multiplied by the standard deduction rate of 80 per cent, and B is multiplied by the additional deduction rate of 100 per cent. The combined deduction is achieved by adding the two figures. This figure (152) is larger than the deduction calculated in Figure 11.1 (128). Finally, the smaller deduction of 33 is the allowable deduction from taxable income.

Some Possible Effects of Tax Incentives

The question of just how effective such tax incentives were in promoting exports during the period 1953–64 is of central importance. From available empirical data, however, it is very difficult to determine the direct impact, in quantitative terms, of tax incentives on exports. In particular, it is almost impossible to distinguish between tax and non-tax factors on exports.

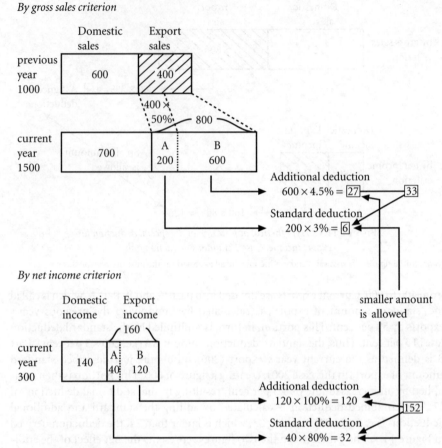

FIGURE 11.2. *Hypothetical application of the special deduction for export income,*
Case 2 standard and additional deductions combined

In spite of these difficulties, there are several areas worthy of analysis. Figure 11.3 shows the movement of exports in monthly increments from 1953 to 1967. At first glance, a strong upward movement can be observed during the entire period, with an acceleration occurring around 1964. Institutional changes in the special deduction for export income appear chronologically as points on the export graph. It would appear, however, that no meaningful relationship between the institution of the special tax measures and fluctuations in exports can be inferred. From a macroeconomic point of view, the effects of tax incentives on exports seem ambiguous.

Microeconomic data do, however, shed some light on the effects of the special deduction on exports. Evidently, export-related trading and manufacturing companies must have benefited from the special tax measures for the promotion of

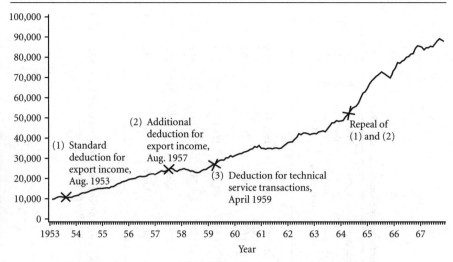

FIGURE 11.3. *Export trends and the time frame of the special deduction*

Source: EPA, *Annual Report of Observing Economic Fluctuations* (Keizai Hendo Kansoku Shiryo Nenpo) June 1968, pp. 22–3

Note: Monthly series of exports on a custom clearance basis are depicted from January 1953 to December 1967. Data are seasonally adjusted and given three-month moving averages

exports. Sample survey data of individual firms of different sizes in two sectors appear in Table 11.3. Individual firms were able to use alternative criteria in the calculation of the special deduction, but there was a clear-cut bias against the expectations of the tax authority in Japan. Trading firms were permitted to deduct some portion of their income only by the net income criterion; manufacturing firms were merely assigned another alternative. This was primarily due to structural factors peculiar to Japanese industry, factors quite different from those prevailing in West Germany.

Attention should be paid to the relative shares of total deductions to both export and net income. In terms of the ratio of total deductions to export income, the three trading firms presented in Table 11.3 succeeded in deducting more than 85 per cent of export income. Likewise, the four manufacturing firms surveyed were able to deduct more than half of their export income. There are a variety of relative percentages in their shares to net income, depending on the greater or smaller reliance on exporting activity of each firm. Obviously special attention is paid to the trading company with the highest value of 46.8 per cent. It is noteworthy that this small-scale corporation exempts almost half of its income from taxation.

The tax benefits of the special deduction for export income in Figure 11.4 can also be instructive. Tax benefits are defined as the ratio of special deduction to net income, and the variable to be considered here is the number of half-year accounting periods. Generally speaking, trading firms seem to enjoy more benefits in the range of 5–15 per cent. By contrast, manufacturing firms showed a greater percentage in smaller tax

TABLE 11.3. *The special deduction for export income in trading and manufacturing companies, 1959–60*

Company	Net income (A) (¥000)	Export income (B) (¥000)	Standard deduction (¥000)			Additional deduction (¥000)			Total deductions (¥000) (E)	B/A (%)	E/B (%)	E/A (%)
			by net income	by gross sales	assigned deductions (C)	by net income	by gross sales	assigned deduction (D)				
Trading												
A	1,156,591	194,621	61,113	158,658	61,113	108,230	337,178	108,230	169,434	16.8	87.0	14.6
B	45,410	755	402	1,337	402	253	1,010	253	655	1.6	86.7	1.4
a	8,373	4,188	1,072	1,436	1,072	2,848	4,636	2,848	3,920	50.0	93.6	46.8
Manufacturing												
X (Electrical machinery)	6,899,099	262,604	109,871	74,786	74,786	170,496	79,408	79,408	154,194	3.8	58.7	2.2
Y (Ship building)	1,625,548	441,944	48,656	29,124	29,124	380,026	257,282	257,282	286,406	27.1	64.8	17.6
x (Dyeing)	14,153	4,895	1,436	590	590	3,100	1,966	1,966	2,556	34.5	52.2	17.7
y (Cosmetics)	57,777	3,194	1,119	543	543	1,796	1,669	1,699	2,212	5.5	69.2	3.8

Source: Unpublished data collected by the Ministry of Finance.

Note: Companies A, B, X and Y are large-scale corporations with paid-in capital of over ¥200 million, while companies a, x and y are small and medium-sized corporations whose paid-in capitals are ¥3–12 millions. Data are collected during each accounting period from 1959 to 1960.

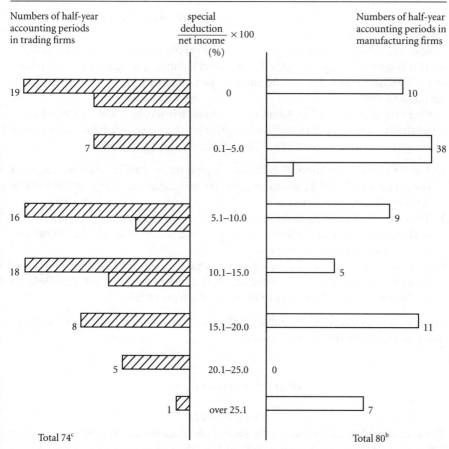

FIGURE 11.4. *Tax benefits of the special deduction for export income in trading and manufacturing firms, 1956–58*

Source: Sample data collected by the Tax Bureau, MOF in October 1958

Notes: a. Tax benefits are defined as a percentage of special deduction to net income

b. Includes total numbers of four half-year accounting periods in twenty manufacturing industry firms from the second half of 1956 to the first half of 1958

c. Three trading firms from twenty have the full-year, not semi-year, accounting period, and six half-year accounting periods are dropped

benefits. For instance, more manufacturing than trading firms experienced smaller benefits of 0–5 per cent.[7]

It is clear from these observations that there were a variety of differences in the level of benefits from using the special deduction based on the type of firm and sector. It would appear that excessive tax benefits were received by a number of exporting firms.

[7] A single manufacturing firm, however, showed 47.6, 51.0, 74.2, and 0 per cent in four successive half-year accounting periods.

Such large deviations in the benefits received by firms compelled the tax authorities to adjust the deduction system.

After extending the original measure for the special deduction for export promotion for two three-year periods, the Tax Advisory Commission began a detailed review of the effectiveness of this tax incentive system and whether another renewal was advisable in 1959.[8]

After careful study, the Tax Advisory Commission made the following three recommendations with respect to the continuation of the special deduction for export promotion provision beyond 1960 (Tax Advisory Commission 1960):

1. The standard and additional deduction should be merged. In addition, the gross sales criterion should be abolished, and the deduction percentage of the income criterion should be lowered.
2. The extent and coverage of the special deduction should gradually be reduced over the long term, with the possibility of temporary measures to avoid sharp, short-run fluctuations in specific industries.
3. A limit should be set to prevent some large firms from obtaining undue tax benefits. For instance, accumulated special deductions might be restrained below a certain percentage of paid-in capital in specific types of firms.

These proposals clearly had a substantial impact on the reformulation of such tax incentives for the promotion of exports.

CONFLICT WITH GATT RULES

Export Subsidy

The pace of review and reform of the special tax measures accelerated in November 1960, when the General Assembly of GATT reached an agreement to repeal export subsidies in order to eliminate undue disturbances to world trade.

Generally speaking, Japan's special deduction for export promotion should be regarded as an export subsidy because a certain amount of income from export transactions is exempt from taxation. This is a sort of 'disguised' export subsidy. Traditionally, however, the Japanese government took the position that these special tax measures were enforced mainly to strengthen capital accumulation in export-related industries, not to promote exports.

Even earlier, GATT had requested that all contracting parties submit a report if they were engaged in granting any export subsidies to firms in their country. Article 16 of the GATT reads as follows:

---

[8] The Tax Advisory Commission, which is one of the most important organizations in assisting the formulation of tax policy and reform in Japan, was established by the Prime Minister in 1953. (For a comprehensive discussion of the Tax Advisory Commission, see Ishi 1993, ch. 1). The main function of the commission was to assess Japan's entire system, to formulate annual tax changes, and to develop long-term tax policy.

If any contracting party grants or maintains any subsidy, including any forms of income or price support, which operates directly or indirectly to increase exports of any product form, . . . it shall notify the Contracting Parties in writing of the extent and nature of the subsidization (GATT 1958, p. 30).

Although Japan was a contracting party, it had not announced anything about its special deduction for export promotion, primarily for the reasons mentioned. Whenever the contracting countries debated export subsidies referred to in Article 16, the exemption of direct taxes for exporting firms, which certainly encompasses Japan's special deduction for export income, was the issue at hand. 'Additional Provisions on Export Subsidies' in Article 19, Section B, stressed that:

as from 1 January 1958 or the earliest practicable date thereafter, contracting parties shall cease to grant either directly or indirectly any form of subsidy on the export of any product (GATT 1958, p. 31).

In this international atmosphere, it was inevitable that Japan's tax incentives for the promotion of exports would have to be abolished, sooner or later. As noted earlier, the barring of export subsidies was proposed in November 1960 by the USA and by European countries at the Seventeenth General Assembly of GATT. It was, however, difficult to reach a unanimous agreement to immediately repeal export subsidies among the contracting parties. Therefore, two plans were presented for adoption by each country:

Plan A   Export subsidies as defined in Article 16 will be immediately and completely terminated.[9]

Plan B   Any country that cannot immediately accept such abolition is permitted to maintain temporarily its existing system (one year with the option to extend for two more years).

At the same time, a concrete list of export subsidies was drawn up in which the exemption of direct taxes was included. Thus, Japan's traditional position that its special deduction for export income was not an export subsidy was widely disallowed by the international community. Of course, Japan selected Plan B from the two aforementioned alternatives, indicating that it would make efforts to eliminate its special deduction system as promptly as possible.

Repeal of the Special Provision

During this period, there was much controversy among Japan's ministries about the future treatment of the special export-promoting tax measures. The Ministry of Foreign Affairs (MOFA) supported their immediate repeal; the Ministry of International

[9] Even among contracting parties that accepted Plan A in 1960, a number of countries continued to employ a variety of export-promoting tax measures. For example, there were the Western Hemisphere Trade Corporation, China Trade Corporation, Export Trade Corporation in the USA, the Overseas Trade Corporation or tax-sparing system in the UK, and special tax measures (i.e. accelerated depreciation, tax-free reserves) in West Germany, France, Canada, and Italy, all of which were equivalent to those in Japan.

Trade and Industry (MITI) wanted to maintain them as long as possible. MITI viewed Plan B as the better alternative because it would extend export-promoting tax incentives for three more years.

After much heated debate, the tax authority finally decided in 1961 to extend the special provision for the promotion of exports for one year, with the implication that, if necessary, it could be renewed for three additional years. Basically, it was agreed that the nature and extent of the export-promoting tax incentives would be reduced and the additional deduction removed, permitting only the use of the standard deduction.[10]

In March 1964, when the last allowable extension ended, the special deduction for export income was finally eliminated in accordance with the original proposals of the Tax Advisory Commission. Further renewal could not be permitted, given the increased tension among the members of the international community towards trade liberalization. Thus, in keeping with the wishes of the international trading community, the Japanese government was forced to discontinue its main policy instrument for export promotion. There were, however, three special tax measures that were added or extended in order to compensate for the repeal of the special deduction for export income:

1. The use of accelerated depreciation for the equipment of export industries was extended.
2. The deduction for technical services transactions was extended.
3. Tax-free reserves for overseas market development were established.

It was not until the early 1970s that export-promoting tax incentives were largely eliminated from the Japanese tax system.

It seems that tax incentives were relevant factors contributing to Japan's high level of exports during the 1950s and 1960s. Specifically, it was not possible to establish a significant relationship between export trends and the use of special tax measures to promote exports over time. It would appear that non-tax factors such as the competitiveness of export firms and industries, the role of the general trading companies, and the development of new products for overseas markets were responsible for Japan's superlative export performance. Even if no special tax incentives for exports had been enacted, export growth would probably still have remained at a high level.

Export-promoting tax incentives, however, clearly had a positive impact on the export activities of specific firms. From a microeconomic point of view, certain traders and producers of goods for exports benefited greatly from tax incentives, resulting in substantial revenue losses to the Japanese government and distortions of the tax system. It is uncertain whether such tax benefits to individual firms could have led to the increased trend of exports as shown in Figure 11.4. In sum, although the effects of tax incentives on exports are ambiguous, their negative impact on tax neutrality is quite clear. There seem to be few lessons to be derived from the Japanese experience with tax incentives for export promotion.

[10] The additional deduction was revived in 1962 with the minor amendment that only the net income criterion could be used to calculate it.

12

The Role of the Fiscal Investment and Loan Programme

In addition to its fiscal activities, such as tax collection, borrowing, and public spending, the government also collects a substantial amount of public funds through credit programmes such as the postal savings and public pensions. By using these funds, the government can make loans and investments in various public institutions to seek specific policy goals. One such credit programme is the Fiscal Investment and Loan Programme(FILP) separate from the on-budget activity in the *general account* of the national government. One of the marked features in the FILP is that the MOF centrally manages public funds to carry out a variety of national goals in line with fiscal and monetary polices. This is a very unique system that has attracted worldwide attention in relation to the promotion of economic growth in the past, but the FILP has recently posed a number of problems to be rectified in the wake of financial liberalization.

In this chapter, we will clarify the four main characteristics of Japan's FILP. First, we explore the basic framework of the FILP, both its sources and uses, as well as its purpose and scope. Secondly, we will discuss the historical background of the FILP, tracing back to the pre-war period with special reference to the postal savings system. Thirdly, we will pay special attention to government financial institutions, one of the biggest schemes in the FILP, whose functions and objectives are analysed in detail. Lastly, we will focus on recent developments of the FILP in the context of changed financial markets.

THE BASIC FRAMEWORK OF THE FILP: AN OVERVIEW

Purpose and Scope

The fundamental role of the government is to collect taxes, borrow money, and provide public goods and services. Apart from these activities, the government operates the financial functions of capital investments and loans, mainly at the national level. For example, postal savings, public pension funds, and insurance funds are all important financial sources besides tax revenue, and they can be used to make loans and to invest in public institutions for the promotion of specific policy objectives.

To foster investment and loan money, the government annually constructs a credit programme called the FILP. The FILP provides a comprehensive instrument for government investment and loans, financed by the special sources mentioned above.

This chapter is primarily based on Ishi 1982*b*, 1983 and 1986*b*.

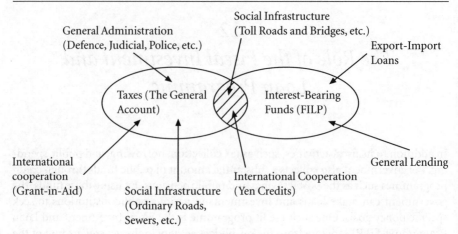

FIGURE 12.1. *The role of the FILP compared with the tax source activity*

This programme is not a budget as argued in Chapter 5, but the FILP is considered to be as important as the *general account* of the national government, and it is often called the 'second budget'. Therefore, each year the FILP is compiled and presented to the Diet for approval, excluding loans with maturity of less than five years, in the same period as the regular budgets.[1] The most marked trait of the FILP is that its financial sources have to depend on such interest-bearing funds as the postal savings. Thus, the FILP funds should not only be utilized to meet financial demands for public purposes, but should also be operated in a sound and profitable way, unlike the *general account* expenditure financed by taxes. Stated differently, FILP funds must be allocated to projects whose objectives can basically be achieved to generate profits for interest-bearing financing.

Obviously, the FILP funds ought to be used in a fashion supplementary to the *general account* from tax sources. In Figure 12.1, the role of the FILP is depicted in relation to fiscal activities financed by taxes in the *general account*. Three areas are demarcated, each with a shaded area of a joint nature. Tax revenues should be spent on general administration, defence, international cooperation (grant-in aid), and social infrastructures (ordinary roads, sewers, etc.), while the interest-bearing funds have to be used for general lending and export–import loans for the purpose of receiving both the principal and interest. The joint area is considered as a combined financing of taxes and loans to promote another type of social infrastructure (toll roads and bridges, public housing, etc.) or for international cooperation with yen credits. Generally speaking, the FILP provides financing for the investments of public institutions (including some local governments). It also makes loans to selected categories of private business that are regarded as having special importance for the purpose of development and social policy or to fund projects that cannot find adequate financing

[1] They contain the *general and special accounts*, and *government affiliated budgets*. See Chapter 5 for a more expanded discussion.

in the private sector. Most government loans to private enterprises are administered through a variety of special banks or finance corporations.[2]

Table 12.1 indicates the relative size of the FILP relative to the *general account* and the GDP for a period of 47 years. In 1953, the FILP was 31.7 per cent of the size of the *general account* and 4.3 per cent of the GNP. Its percentage relative to the *general account* rose to 47.2 per cent in 1972, immediately before the outbreak of the first oil crisis. Thereafter, this percentage began to diminish, mainly because funds from the Trust Fund Bureau were used to purchase substantial amounts of national bonds, not to make loans or investments through public corporations and government financial institutions. However, in the 1990s the relative share of the FILP began to expand, going beyond the 50 per cent level. The size of the FILP as a percentage of GDP continued to increase over a long period and reached a high of 8.3 per cent in 1995, but thereafter it tended to decline to some extent up to 1999.

Sources

Figure 12.2 is a graphic presentation of the FILP and its sources and uses in order to give an overall picture. The major sources raised from the public are postal savings, public pensions, and postal life insurance. These sources combined with the financing by bonds are placed in the following four funds.

1. Funds of the Trust Fund Bureau: postal savings, public pensions (e.g. National Pension, Employee's Pension), which are collected from the private sector and reserved in related special accounts, are deposited in this fund.
2. Postal Life Insurance Fund: postal life insurance and postal annuity also form a reserved fund, which is channelled through special accounts.
3. Industrial Investment Special Account: the investments, not the loans of the FILP, are made through this special account to which the *general account* of the national government transfers the funds.
4. Government Guaranteed Bonds and Borrowings: domestic bonds are issued by some government enterprises and public corporations to raise money from private financial institutions. The payment of both principal and interest is guaranteed by the government.

As shown in Figure 12.2, various kinds of public funds that are collected by government credit are brought together in the Trust Fund Bureau and controlled in a unified manner. Its main purpose is to utilize them most efficiently for national interests. The deposit interest rate of the FILP called the 'Yotaku Rate', which the Trust Fund Bureau usually pays on the postal savings and public pensions, is identical to the lending rate. Since there is no spread of interest rates between deposits and lendings, the FILP has no intention of earning profits as a financial intermediary.

Once the funds are collected from the private sector in various forms, the FILP dispenses them through four channels to the public, mainly in the form of loans. As

---

[2] The scope of government financial institutions was generally restricted to two banks and ten public finance corporations, as argued below in the text.

TABLE 12.1. *The relative size of the FILP, 1953–99*

Fiscal year	FILP ¥ billion (1)	General account ¥ billion (2)	Nominal GDP ¥ trillion (3)	per cent (1)/(2)	per cent (1)/(3)
1953	322.8	1,017.1	7.5	31.7	4.3
1954	282.0	1,040.8	7.8	27.1	3.6
1955	321.9	1,018.2	8.9	31.6	3.6
1956	349.7	1,069.2	9.6	32.7	3.6
1957	410.7	1,187.7	11.1	34.6	3.7
1958	417.4	1,331.6	11.8	31.3	3.5
1959	532.9	1,495.0	13.9	35.6	3.8
1960	606.9	1,743.1	16.7	34.8	3.6
1961	773.7	2,063.5	20.2	37.5	3.8
1962	905.2	2,556.6	22.3	35.4	4.1
1963	1,109.7	3,044.3	26.2	36.5	4.2
1964	1,340.2	3,311.0	30.4	40.5	4.4
1965	1,620.6	3,723.0	33.8	43.5	4.8
1966	2,027.3	4,459.2	39.7	45.5	5.1
1967	2,388.4	5,113.0	46.4	46.7	5.1
1968	2,699.0	5,937.1	54.9	45.5	4.9
1969	3,077.0	6,917.8	65.1	44.5	4.7
1970	3,579.9	8,187.7	75.3	43.7	4.8
1971	4,280.4	9,561.1	82.9	44.8	5.2
1972	5,635.0	11,932.2	96.5	47.2	5.8
1973	6,924.8	14,778.3	116.7	46.9	5.9
1974	7,923.4	19,099.8	138.5	41.5	5.7
1975	9,310.0	20,860.9	152.4	44.6	6.1
1976	10,619.0	24,467.6	171.3	43.4	6.2
1977	12,538.2	29,059.8	190.1	43.1	6.6
1978	14,887.6	34,096.0	208.6	43.7	7.1
1979	16,832.7	38,789.8	225.2	43.4	7.5
1980	18,179.9	43,405.0	245.5	41.9	7.4
1981	19,489.7	46,921.2	260.8	41.5	7.5
1982	20,288.8	47,245.1	273.3	42.9	7.4
1983	20,702.9	50,635.3	285.6	40.9	7.2
1984	21,106.6	51,480.6	305.1	41.0	6.9
1985	20,858.0	53,004.5	324.2	39.4	6.4
1986	22,155.1	53,640.4	338.4	41.3	6.5
1987	23,731.3	57,731.1	354.0	41.1	6.7
1988	25,344.0	61,471.1	376.9	41.2	6.7
1989	26,340.5	65,858.9	402.3	40.0	6.5
1990	27,622.4	69,268.7	432.6	39.9	6.4
1991	29,105.6	70,547.2	455.9	41.3	6.4
1992	32,262.2	70,497.4	464.2	45.8	7.0
1993	36,595.6	75,102.4	466.8	48.7	7.8
1994	39,408.2	73,430.5	475.5	53.7	8.3
1995	40,240.1	70,987.1	492.8	56.7	8.2
1996	40,533.7	75,104.9	491.2	52.1	8.3
1997	39,327.1	77,390.0	507.8	54.4	8.2
1998	36,659.2	77,669.2	495.8	47.2	7.4
1999	39,238.9	81,860.1	488.8	47.9	8.0

Source: Data from the MOF, the EPA and Japan Center for Economic Research.

Note: FILP figures are limited to the general type of FILP, excluding the amount of portfolio investment starting from fiscal 1987.

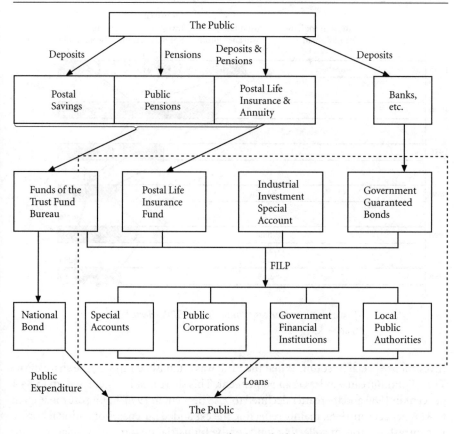

FIGURE 12.2. *Basic framework of the FILP*

Note: The area enclosed by the dotted line indicates the scope of the FILP

indicated in Figure 12.2 they are: (i) special accounts; (ii) public corporations; (iii) government financial institutions; and (iv) local governments.What is important in Figure 12.2 is the limited scope of the FILP in the areas surrounded by the dotted line. A portion of funds of the Trust Bureau Fund is devoted to the purchase of national bonds directly from the *general account*,[3] and the flow of this fund is out of the FILP. This allocation of funds has expanded recently, reflecting the difficulty of selling large amounts of national bonds in the financial markets.

Let us investigate the movement of each source in the FILP. Figure 12.3 presents figures for the different sources for selected years in terms of percentage distribution. There are two phenomena worth noting: one is the continuous increase in the size of the Trust Fund Bureau; the other is the sharp decline in the share of the Industrial

---

[3] The issue of national bonds mainly relies upon the subscription of syndicate groups which are organized by private financial institutions.

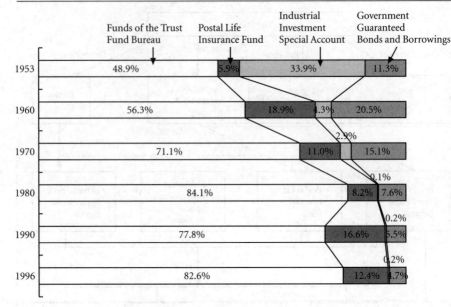

FIGURE 12.3. *Sources of funds in the FILP, selected years*
Source: MOF

Investment Special Account. When the FILP was established in 1953, the share of the Trust Fund Bureau was less than 50 per cent. This share steadily increased up to 84.1 per cent in 1980 and thereafter declined to 77.8 per cent in 1990, but it rose once again to 82.6 per cent in 1999, mainly reflecting the expanded purchases of national bonds. In contrast, the role of collecting funds of the Industrial Investment Special Account decreased in importance. Its relative size declined from 33.9 per cent in 1953 to nearly nil after 1980. The Postal Life Insurance Fund and the Government Guaranteed Bonds and Borrowings now share a substantial portion of the total fund, although the relative importance of the two funds has varied from year to year.

FILP funds must be allocated to revenue-producing projects through government financial institutions. Because FILP funds are financed from sources on which interest must be paid, say, in the case of postal saving accounts, the FILP is required by law to make loans on a profitable basis. This requirement is different from the principles of government expenditures that are financed by tax revenue. However, funds in the FILP can be employed in less profitable areas to accomplish special policy objectives (e.g. housing, urban renewal, regional development), supported by interest subsidies from tax sources, as will be argued later.

In addition, only long-term (i.e. over five years) financing and loans are annually included in the FILP. The shorter-term loans are not part of the FILP, although there are a number of short-term capital investments and loans in both the *general account* and several special accounts.

Uses

Funds collected from various sources are used for loans and investments to the private sector. This is the use side of the FILP, which is operated by special agencies relevant to the FILP. These special agencies are often called the Fiscal Investment and Loan agencies (FIL agencies) whose number totals 59 in 1996. They may be classified into five categories, as follows:

1. Special accounts—9: National Hospital, National School, National Forestry, etc.;
2. Government financial institutions—10: Japan Development Bank, Housing Loan Corporation, People's Finance Corporation, etc;.
3. Public corporations—34: Japan Highway Public Corporation, Japan Railway Construction Corporation, The Pension Welfare Service Public Corporation, etc.;
4. Special companies—5: Kansai International Airport Co., Power Development Co., Crossing Road on the Tokyo Bay Co., etc.;
5. Local Government—1.

These groupings are a bit different from those before the privatization of the Japanese National Railways in 1987. Before 1987, the scope of public corporations was limited to the Japanese National Railways. The remainder (e.g. *kodan, jigyodan*) are included in 'Other public corporations'. Now two categories are combined into one—public corporations. Special companies, including Japan Air Lines Co. at that time, were previously listed as 'Others,' with foundations (*kikin*) and associations (*kyokai*).

The FILP funds are used through these agencies to promote specific policy targets. What are the specific objectives of the allocation of FILP funds? According to an official classification of the MOF, the objectives are grouped into 12 categories with special reference to specific policy targets.

1. housing;
2. water supply, sewers, and other environmental facilities;
3. social welfare;
4. education;
5. small and medium-scale businesses;
6. agriculture, forestry, and fisheries;
7. national land preservation and disaster reconstruction;
8. roads;
9. transportation and telecommunications;
10. regional development;
11. industries and technology;
12. international trade and economic cooperation.

The following three categories contain four objectives which are often employed as a broader classification:

(I) areas that improve the quality of life (1–6);
(II) areas that preserve the nation's infrastructure (7–10);
(III) areas that promote industrial development and foreign trade (11–12).

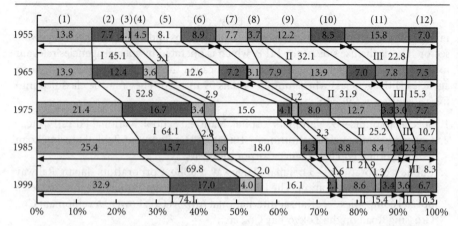

FIGURE 12.4. *Trends of the relative share in the policy objectives of FILP, selected years*

Notes: 1. Figures are computed as a percentage of general FILP
2. For each item: (1) housing, (2) water supply, sewers and other environmental facilities; (3) social welfare; (4) education; (5) small and medium-scale business; (6) agriculture, forestry and fisheries; (7) national land preservation and disaster reconstruction; (8) roads; (9) transportation and telecommunications; (10) regional development; (11) industry and technology; (12) international trade and economic cooperation

Percentage distribution in selected years after 1955 for the three categories, I, II, and III, are depicted in Figure 12.4. Broadly speaking, the relative share of category I has constantly increased, while those of categories II and III have continued to decrease for forty years. Indeed, category I has increased from 45.1 per cent in 1955 to 74.1 per cent in 1999. Categories II and III have decreased in importance since 1955. In particular, the remarkable increases are observed in housing and water supply, sewers and other environmental facilities, in contrast to the sharp declines of agriculture, forestry and fisheries, and industries and technology.

Let us shift our attention to explore the primary policy objectives in recent years. First, the most important target in the FILP has been housing, in which the funds are used to make loans for the construction of private housing. In fact, housing had a 32.9 per cent share of FILP funds in 1999. In order to enhance the quality of houses, several special measures have been taken; for instance, the basic amount of loans for housing construction has increased, the maximum floor space for a house applicable for the mitigated interest rates has expanded from 165m² to 175m², and so on. Secondly, with regard to the improvement of social welfare, the construction of nursing home and health facilities for the elderly has been promoted, as well as that of hospitals, clinics, and other facilities, by enlarging the size of loans to the Social Welfare and Medical Care Corporation. Also, the educational loan programme has been expanded at the Japan Scholarly Foundation and the People's Finance Corporation.

Thirdly, great emphasis has been placed on the construction of social infrastructure. Urban renewal projects have been promoted by the Housing and Urban Development Corporation to construct the high-quality housing units. In the field of private-sector infrastructure projects, the Japan Development Bank has played a vital role in enhancing the transport capacities of urban railways, improving other urban infrastructure, and promoting the development of information-related infrastructure. With regard to airports and railways, a large amount of the FILP funds have been allotted to the Special Account for Airport Improvement to extend new runways in local airports, as well as in the Tokyo International Airport at Haneda, and to the Japan Railway Construction Corporation and the Teito Rapid Transit authority in order to build new city lines and subways lines. Equally, the funds have been used to construct major roads by the Japan Highway Corporation, Metropolitan Expressway Public Corporation and so on in connection with the eighth road construction plan.

Fourthly, it is also important to facilitate the funding of small and medium-sized businesses by allocating the FILP funds to the People's Finance Corporation (PF), the Small Business Finance Corporation (SBC), and the Environmental Sanitation Business Corporation (ESB), etc. Such a loan programme was closely tied to the anti-recession measures after the collapse of the bubble in the 1990s to stimulate stagnant business activities. Furthermore, a new loan programme to support the business innovations for small and medium-sized enterprises has been established by the loans of the Japan Development Bank. This aspect of the FILP scheme is designed to reform the structural problems of the Japanese economy, such as the de-industrialization of domestic industries. Lastly, a substantial amount of loan funds have been allocated to the Export–Import Bank to promote the import of manufactured goods and to the Overseas Economic Cooperation Fund (OECF) to meet the demand for overseas investment.

In addition to the general use of the FILP described above, the FILP extended its function to a new scheme of portfolio investment. Although the FILP has as a basic principle the management of the funds on a comprehensive basis except postal life insurance, several agencies gradually began to be eager to administer their own funds, financed by themselves in the form of savings and pensions in order to gain a higher amount of interest than they would were they to remain within the FILP. Thus, three agencies—the Postal Savings Special Account, the Pension Welfare Service Public Corporation, and the Postal Life Insurance Welfare Corporation—were permitted to make portfolio investment by using a part of their own fund in fiscal 1987 in an attempt to combat financial liberalization. Since then, the FILP has been divided into two parts; one is the general FILP, the other is concerned with portfolio investment activity. The fund allocated for portfolio investment has increased sharply from an initial amount of ¥2,000 billion to ¥13,550 billion in fiscal 1999; that is, 6.8 fold over 12 years.

How do they make portfolio investment? In fiscal 1997, 46.1 per cent of the total amount was allotted to the purchase of national bonds, 11.7 per cent to bank and corporate bonds, 9.8 per cent to local public bonds, 7.7 per cent to foreign bonds and 5.3 per cent to public corporation bonds. The remaining 3.1 per cent is put into their own savings account, and 16.3 per cent is entrusted to the trust banks that are responsible for making portfolio investment instead of the three agencies listed above (see

MOF 1998, pp. 18–19). Evidently, the goal of managing the funds is restricted to fixed-interest bonds in order to secure a certain level of gain from the safety invested assets, reflecting the basic nature of the FILP funds mentioned above.

HISTORICAL BACKGROUND OF THE FILP

Pre-war Period

The FILP was established in 1953, the year after Japan regained its independence. The idea of the FILP as established was unprecedented, but its historical basis dates from the Meiji era, from the postal savings system in 1875 (see Johnson 1978, ch. 8). The Postal Bureau of the Ministry of Home Affairs operated a system enabling the general public to deposit money in savings accounts at post offices.[4] This scheme was part of a government campaign to raise funds and stimulate the economy. The savings collected at the post offices were controlled by the MOF in the *Yokinbu*.[5] The *Yokinbu*, which is the predecessor to the FILP, was merely one of the government's special accounts.

Before the twentieth century, postal savings were used only to secure national bonds. In 1907, the functions of the *Yokinbu* were expanded to include: loans to the *general and special accounts*, collateral for local bonds and for special bank bonds. The *Yokinbu* continued to increase in size, particularly around the time of the two world wars when the fund grew enormously. Using these expanded funds, the government began to make grants and loans to munitions companies and key industries, such as iron and steel.

Of special interest was the sharp increase in postal savings during the 1930s. Small savers (e.g. farmers, workers, and the owners of small enterprises) tended to put their money into postal savings accounts for two reasons. They feared defaults by private banks in the great depression after the panic of 1927. The other reason was the patriotic appeal to cooperate with wartime national policies. The increase in postal savings occurred in spite of interest rates being lower than the private sector.

In 1944, government pension funds were added to postal savings in the government fund. These new funds were from employee pension funds which were established to provide old age, disability, and death insurance for workers.

Apart from postal savings and pensions, another important development was the emergence of special banks. These banks were charged with promoting economic development and include: the Kangyo Bank of Japan (1897); the Hokkaido Development Bank (1899); and the Industrial Bank of Japan (1902). Of the three, the Industrial Bank of Japan (IJB) played the largest role.

---

[4] Later, in 1881, the Postal Bureau was transferred to the newly established Ministry of Agriculture and Commerce. In 1885, the bureau itself became the Ministry of Communications (the predecessor of the present Ministry of Posts and Telecommunications).

[5] *Yokinbu* in this context means post office deposits account.

The IJB was franchised by the special law of March 1900. Its major purpose was to meet the strong demand for long-term capital needed by joint-stock companies. This demand was related to the proliferation of joint-stock companies around the time of the Russo–Japanese War (1904–5). The IJB generated revenue by selling its government guaranteed bonds at home and abroad and played an important role in the financing of Japan's industrial development.

Similarly, other special banks had the same purpose and function as the IJB. For example, the 1906 bond issue of the Kangyo Bank of Japan was purchased by the *Yokinbu*, and special loans were made to help the less-developed Tohoku area (the northern part of Honshu) when a bad harvest caused financial difficulties.

Post-war Reforms

During the American occupation (1945–52), a variety of post-war reforms were instituted in political, economic, and social spheres by the Supreme Commander for the Allied Powers (SCAP), as argued in Chapter 1. Government investment and loan programmes were subject to crucial changes (see, for a comprehensive discussion, Patrick 1970; Patrick and Rosovsky 1976, ch. 1).

Most important for economic recovery was the Reconstruction Finance Bank (RFB). The RFB was established as a department within the IJB and in the following year became an independent special legal entity. The major task of the RFB was to make loans to industries essential for economic reconstruction[6]—coal, fertilizers, electric power, iron and steel—using funds obtained by selling RFB bonds to the Bank of Japan (BOJ). Strong inflationary pressure was built up by the extensive money creation, and it resulted in a tremendous price hike which was labelled the 'RBG inflation'.[7]

Inflation was finally halted as part of the Dodge Plan reforms, which were adopted by Joseph M. Dodge, an advisor to the SCAP, in 1949.[8] The Dodge Plan prohibited the RFB from issuing bonds, and three years later the RFB was dissolved. In 1952, the RFB was absorbed by the Japan Development Bank (JDB). The IJB, from which the RFB emerged, was transformed into an ordinary long-term credit bank for the industry at the request of the SCAP in 1948. The nature and functions of the IJB and the RFB were quite controversial among the American advisors to the SCAP.

During the occupation period, US aid was also very important. Until 1949, when Dodge first came to Japan, the USA provided Japan with about $1.2 billion worth of commodities purchased in America with Government and Relief in Occupied Area (GARIOA) and Economic Rehabilitation in Occupied Area (EROA) funds. These

---

[6] On the basis of the 'weighted (priority) production policy' (*keisha seisan hoshiki*), several basic industries were chosen for loans intensively for the purpose of concentrating the recovery efforts in capital investments.

[7] The consumers' price level, computed on the basis of 1934–36 prices, was 48 times higher in 1946, 191 times higher in 1947 and 230 times higher in 1950.

[8] The most famous policy he took was the balanced budget to cover all budgets in the government sector. For a comprehensive discussion concerning the Dodge Plan, see Yamamura 1967, ch. 2.

commodities were sold by the Japanese government and the yen proceeds were deposited in the Foreign Trade Fund Special Account.

Dodge renewed this special account for the US Aid Counterpart Fund in 1949, mainly because the US government wanted to know how its aid was used and how its money was being spent. Dodge and the SCAP were irritated upon learning that the Japanese government used this aid to finance the RFB and thus induce inflation. This Counterpart Fund was maintained until 1953 and thereafter was renamed the Industrial Investment Special Account. This account is now a part of the FILP (see Figure 12.2) and is supplied with direct appropriations from the *general account*.

The SCAP instituted several financial innovations. Among these were the creation of the Export Bank of Japan and the JDB in 1950 and 1951. The SCAP recognized the importance of providing long-term credit to exporters of heavy industrial equipment for export expansion. This meant that banks would contribute to Japan's earning more foreign currency. Dodge agreed to establish a special bank to promote Japan's exports subject to the following restrictions: it should not compete with private banks, and the government was to supply the capital instead of issuing bonds or borrowing. Based upon these ideas, the Export Bank of Japan Law was passed by the Diet in 1950, and the Japan Export Bank began business with an authorized capital of ¥15 billion, which was provided by both the *general account* and the US Aid Counterpart Fund. Although Dodge wanted a private-dominated bank, the law specified that the president of the bank was to be appointed by the Prime Minister and that the bank was to operate under the supervision of the MOF. When the Occupation ended in 1952, the government renamed the bank as the Export–Import Bank of Japan (EIBJ).

The JDB was created in 1951 to supply long-term, low-interest loans for domestic economic reconstruction and industrial development. In the initial planning stages, the Japanese government had ambitious plans for the bank,[9] but the SCAP considered the idea as a renamed RFB and a renewal of an inflationary policy. When established, the JDB was not allowed to issue bonds, borrow funds, or grant loans to cover a borrower's current expenses. Furthermore, the entire initial capitalization of ¥10 billion was to come from the Counterpart Fund. At the outset, the SCAP thought that the old RFB or the old Industrial Bank could not be revived, but the JDB expanded rapidly from this modest start. In fact, it enlarged its capital beyond the small amount from the Counterpart Fund that the SCAP had authorized.

While the various post-war reforms proceeded, the *Yokinbu* began to be revised. The MOF had complained about the restrictions on the uses of the *Yokinbu* and wanted the restrictions removed. Dodge approved the government's desire to open up the *Yokinbu* completely to government use. In 1951, the *Yokinbu* was abolished and replaced with a new special account called the Trust Fund Bureau. This account combined postal savings, several pension funds, and other trust funds. The use of such

---

[9] Finance Minister Ikeda Hayato proposed that the funds for the new bank should come from the *Yokinbu*, direct appropriations, counterpart funds, and recovered funds from the RFC. In addition, it was said that the new bank should have the authority to issue its own bonds.

funds was broadened to cover loans to special legal entities and to allow use of the funds as collateral for bond issues.

Regarding the reform of trust funds, attention should be paid to the increase of special legal entities.[10] Since the trust funds were available to special legal entities, those that already existed began to make use of the funds immediately. At the same time, many new entities were established to meet the country's urgent needs, for example electric power, regional development, housing, and the financing of small and medium-sized enterprises. In response to these needs, government financial institutions have begun to be established since 1950. Likewise, several other financial institutions (i.e. the PF, Housing Loan Corporation (HL), Agriculture, Forestry and Fisheries Finance Corporation (AFF), and SBC were also created around the time of the reform in trust funds in 1951. These institutions included two government banks and ten public finance corporations as listed in Table 12.2, but among them Medical Care Facilities Financing Corporation was repealed in fiscal 1985. Also, such public corporations and agencies as the Nippon Telegraph and Telephone Public Corporation and the Electric Power Development Co. were established as a result of the flexible use of trust funds in the 1950s.

In the ongoing process of administrative reform, the Diet approved the following three mergers in 1999: (i) EIBJ and OECF, (ii) JDB and Hokkaido-Tohuku Development Finance Corporation (HTD), and (iii) PF and ESB, each of which has started as new financial institutions of the Japan Bank for International Cooperation (JBIC) for the Development Bank of Japan (DBJ) and the People-Livelihood Finance Corporation from January 2000.

FUNCTIONS AND OBJECTIVES OF GOVERNMENT FINANCIAL INSTITUTIONS

The Development of Government Financial Institutions

Government financial institutions have been the most important agency in the operation of the FILP and we should pay special attention to an analysis of how they have developed since its birth in the FILP. As was mentioned previously, the FILP was created in 1953. This creation reflected the great demand for funds, coupled with the increase of public corporations to spend or lend them. Mainly, there were two purposes: one was to control government investments and loans more effectively on a comprehensive basis, and the other was to augment the funds of the Trust Fund Bureau, which were large but not large enough to meet the urgent demands of economic development. Several things were done to make sure the purposes of trust funds were met. First, the funds of the postal life insurance system held in trust, as distinct from the postal savings, were included in the FILP. Secondly, the old Counterpart Fund was abolished and replaced by a new Industrial Investment Special

---

[10] The term 'special legal entities' is similar to public corporations, used in the section on non-financial public enterprises below.

TABLE 12.2. *Government financial institutions, 1995*

Name	Year of establishment	Control	Number of employees in 1995
Government Banks (2)			
Export–Import Bank of Japan (EIBJ)	1950	MOF	557
Japan Development Bank (DBJ)	1951	MOF	1,102
Public finance corporations (10)			
People's Finance Corp. (PF)	1949	MOF	4,808
Housing Loan Corp. (HL)	1950	MOF	1,146
Agriculture, Forestry and Fisheries Finance Corp. (AFF)	1953	MOF, MAFF	940
Small Business Finance Corp. (SBF)	1953	MOF, MITI	1,760
Hokkaido-Tohoku Development Corp. (HTD)	1956	HDA, MOF, NLA	288
Japan Finance Corp. for Municipal Enterprises (JFM)	1957	MOF, MOHA	83
Small Business Credit Insurance Corp. (SBC)	1958	MOF, MITI	412
Medical Care Facilities Financing Corp. (MCF)	1960	MOF, MOHW	183
Environmental Sanitation Business Financing Corp. (ESB)	1967	MOF, MOHW	56
Okinawa Development Finance Corp. (ODF)	1972	MOF, ODA	228
Others			
Overseas Economic Cooperation Fund (OEC)	1961	EPA	327
Post Offices (PO)	1876	MOPT	24,590*

Notes:
[1] Year given is actual year of establishment, not Diet authorization.
[2] Abbreviations: MOF: Ministry of Finance; MAFF: Ministry of Agriculture, Forestry and Fisheries; MITI: Ministry of International Trade and Industry; HDA: Hokkaido Development Agency; NLA: National Land Agency; MOHA: Ministry of Home Affairs; MOHW: Ministry of Health and Welfare; ODA: Okinawa Development Agency; EPA: Economic Planning Agency; MOPT: Ministry of Posts and Telecommunications.
[3] The asterisk indicates the number of Post Offices in March, 1981.
[4] MCF was repealed in 1985. Number of employees is as of 1981.

Account. Thirdly, receipts from government-guaranteed bonds and borrowings were also allowed to be employed.

The credit programmes of government financial institutions are all included in the FILP. What is the importance of the activities of government financial institutions relative to the FILP as a whole? The relative shares of government institutions in total funds of the FILP showed an increasing trend until the 1980s—that is, 35.5 per cent in 1953, 38.5 per cent in 1960, 46.1 per cent in 1970 and 53.2 per cent in 1980—but since then its share began to decrease—42.0 per cent in 1990 and 43.0 per cent in 1999.

This indicates that government financing has expanded its role in the functioning of the nation's economy and financial markets for a long time. Returning to Table 12.2, it can be noted that only half the government financial institutions were in existence before 1953 when the FILP was created. The remaining institutions were successively established since then. In retrospect, it is certainly true that government financial institutions have played a crucial role in the allocation of funds to important government priority areas.

In the first half of the 1950s, the initial target of economic policy was economic reconstruction and independence, and primary concerns were with special fund allocation to key industries; that is coal, electric power, iron and steel, etc. Throughout the 1960s and until the first half of the 1970s, the Japanese economy continued to grow rapidly and finally reached the economic level of Western countries. Government financing was devoted to a variety of policy targets: promotion of heavy chemical industries, construction of infrastructures, technological development, social welfare, etc. Reflecting great demand for both government and private financing, government financial institutions were able to perform their role very well in cooperation with private financial institutions. This was so at least until the outbreak of the first oil crisis.

Since the mid-1970s, however, government financial institutions have begun to compete with private financial institutions in the provision of the funds needed by the nation's economy. The main reason for this is that the private sector demand for funds has sharply decreased, reflecting the slowdown of the Japanese economy. In particular, a great deal of criticism has been directed to inefficient uses of public funds through the FILP, as we will argue later.

Forms of Government Financial Instruments

In Japan, the credit assistance of government financial institutions is primarily in three forms: (i) direct loan; (ii) guarantee loan; and (iii) loan insurance. Direct loans are the most important instrument, and almost all activities of government financing are accomplished in the form of direct loans. By contrast, the other two forms are merely additional at the present state of government credit assistance.

Direct loans are related to the functioning of all government agencies as listed in Table 12.2. Loans are usually made on a long-term and low-interest basis to achieve special policy goals. A loan guarantee is the action of attaching a government guarantee to a loan contracted in the private sector. In other words, it occurs when a government financial agency enters into a firm commitment to use public funds if necessary to repay a lender upon default by the borrower. In Japan, this form is still not very highly developed.[11] However, the JDB sometimes guaranteed the obligation when private

---

[11] This is in sharp contrast to the cases of the USA and Canada. See: US Government 1983 and Economic Council of Canada 1982.

enterprises borrow money from foreign banks or issue debentures in overseas capital markets. Similarly, EIBJ, PF and the ODF guarantee loans in some cases.

The third form—loan insurance—is a type of guarantee in which a government agency operates a programme of pooled risks through the use of insurance premiums to secure a lender against default by a borrower. In Japan, the function of insuring loans is performed only by the SBC. When public financial institutions make loans to small businesses which have trouble finding adequate financing in private markets, loan insurance covers possible cases of default to lenders.

No doubt, the major task of credit assistance has been performed in the form of direct loans. Direct loans can be classified into two categories according to the basic nature of the loan. One is 'project financing', and the other is 'credit-gap-financing'.

'Project finance' is related to loans for big projects which are associated with risk. For instance, energy, space, and resource development are the typical cases in this category. In these cases, private financial institutions find some difficulty in making substantial loans on a profitable basis. Since these projects are of great importance to the nation's economy, the government has good reasons for assisting and promoting their financing. Among government agencies EIBJ, JDB and HTD in particular play a role in carrying out 'project financing'.

The second category of direct loans is made to close a credit gap. It occurs when certain loan applications are rejected in private financial markets because of poor collateral and creditworthiness. There are a number of individual borrowers in such specific areas as housing, low-productivity industries (e.g. agriculture), smaller business, etc., who are eligible for direct loans. In these cases loans are characterized by financial risk so to speak. HL, AFF, and SBF make private loans to fill a credit gap specific to particular borrowers.

It must be stressed that an element of subsidy is involved in all forms of government financial instruments. Government assistance is given on terms and conditions more favourable than those available in private financial markets. A subsidy is provided, in general, by lowering the levels of risk and of the interest rate. The government accepts risks that lenders in private markets are unwilling to bear or would bear only at higher interest rates than the government charges. Secondly, government financial assistance provides interest rates lower than those payable in private capital markets. The gap is made up by interest subsidies, which reduce the cost of borrowing to the recipient.

Table 12.3 shows these interest subsidies from the *general account* of the national budget after fiscal 1983. They amount to around the level of ¥1,200–1,600 billion for these years. Although the relative share in the FILP has steadily declined from 8.1 per cent to 3.1 per cent, its absolute amount is substantially high. The highest share of them is occupied now by HL; that is, 32.0 per cent in fiscal 1995.

Objectives and Sectoral Aspects

Broadly speaking, government intervenes in financial markets to achieve three major objectives: resource allocation, income distribution and social progress, and economic

TABLE 12.3. *Interest subsidies from the general account to the FILP, 1983–99 (¥ billion)*

Fiscal year	FILP (1)	Interest subsidies	
		Amount (2)	(2)/(1)
1983	20,702.9	1,677.7	8.1
1984	21,106.6	1,623.6	7.7
1985	20,858.0	1,651.9	7.9
1986	22,155.1	1,406.4	6.3
1987	23,731.3	1,239.8	5.2
1988	25,344.0	1,240.4	4.8
1989	26,340.5	1,229.7	4.7
1990	27,622.4	1,177.5	4.3
1991	29,105.6	1,218.9	4.2
1992	32,262.2	1,251.2	3.9
1993	36,595.6	1,272.1	3.5
1994	39,408.2	1,346.3	3.4
1995	40,533.7	1,325.1	3.3
1996	42,126.5	1,317.0	3.1
1997	39,327.1	1,398.0	3.5
1998	36,659.2	1,311.7	3.6
1999	39,238.9	1,359.8	3.5

Source: The MOF data.

Note: The concept of subsidies is including a broader scope of transfers, grant-in-aid, etc. The FILP is only limited to the general type except portfolio investment.

development. In the pursuit of the first goal, government attempts to allocate the resources existing in the economy to the best possible utilization from a nation's point of view. Over the longer term, it tries to increase the total stock of resources available to promote economic and social development. Secondly, government aims to achieve a more equitable personal and regional distribution of the nation's wealth. Lastly, government works to reach the third objective by promoting growth of output and employment in relation to specific industrial sectors and regions. In practice, these objectives are interrelated, not incompatible, and government often pursues all three simultaneously with the same instruments.

In working towards these goals, the government can in general play either a corrective or a stimulative role in financial markets. The corrective role must be designed to overcome the market imperfections that hinder the achievement of its economic and social objectives, while the stimulative role is required to bring about certain fundamental changes in the way the economy operates. In general, Japan's government has played a very positive role in both a corrective and stimulative fashion, aiming at specific targets.

When government financial institutions participate in certain markets, they have usually been in pursuit, directly or indirectly, of the broader objectives of fostering economic and social development and restructuring the nation's industry. Some examples may help to clarify the problem. The primary purposes of government involvement in small business or farm finance is to respond directly to the concerns of businessmen and farmers facing financing troubles, but at the same time the government usually bears in mind the much broader goal of contributing to the development of a healthy small business or the agriculture sector of the economy. Likewise, government intervenes in the field of housing finance with two different aims: to directly stimulate housing construction and to assist low-income families from the standpoint of social welfare.

These examples indicate that government financial institutions have always aimed at assisting specific sectors of the economy. These sectors may be broadly grouped according to the six major purposes that guide the government's financial programme:

1. general;
2. business;
3. agriculture;
4. housing;
5. regional development;
6. export.

In theory the distribution of government financial aid among economic sectors appears clear and precise, but in practice it is difficult to break down the amounts of investments and loans by sectors. For example, certain government agencies and programmes provide assistance to several sectors at the same time. Recipients, such as enterprises, can obtain financing from an assistance programme for business and, if applicable, from another programme assisting exports and regional development.

First, general assistance is represented by the government's multi-purpose financial programme which directs investments and loans to several sectors simultaneously. The DBJ and PF are typical cases of this category, which covers almost all forms of financial assistance to business, exports, regional development, etc.

Secondly, government financial institutions contribute significantly to the growth of industrial and commercial business and to the maintenance of a major source of jobs and income. Business assistance has been instrumental in achieving the major economic and social objectives in Japan. Since Japan's economy abounds in small and medium-sized firms, business finance is particularly important to keep their financing healthy. Financial instruments are not only limited to direct loans, but include a form of loan insurance in the field of business finance. Government intervenes through agencies like the SBF, the SBC, the MCF, and the ESB specifically to fill the credit gap in business finance. More precisely, government financial institutions lend to business for many years to offset an inadequate supply of term loans in private markets. Consequently, they try to encourage projects that the private sector does not consider profitable but that may benefit society as a whole.

The third category of government programmes is farm assistance, which has been entrusted to the AFF. Agriculture has long been a matter of concern for the Japanese people and government. Farming is indeed an economic activity, but it is also a way of life. Thus, interest in agricultural finance cannot be merely related to its economic dimension. Farming has always been a risky industry, because output depends upon many factors beyond the control of farmers, say, natural disasters, price fluctuations, etc. Therefore, farming has not generally been considered as a business on the same level as other business ventures. Private lenders and investors have often been reluctant to supply funds to this sector through private financial markets. Consequently, government finds good reasons to assist the financing of the agriculture sector. In Japan, the necessity of agricultural assistance has always been greatly emphasized and backed by strong political pressure, despite the fact that the importance of agriculture has continued to decline in the economy as a whole.[12]

Fourthly, housing poses a crucial problem in Japan, reflecting the very limited amount of open space and the high land prices. There has been a strong demand for housing throughout the post-war era in Japan, particularly in the Tokyo and Osaka areas. Even today, the quality of dwellings remains low and in some sense shabby,[13] although it is said that dwellings can be supplied sufficiently in quantitative terms. In view of its economic and social significance, the housing sector holds a high priority among the government's policy options. In private financial markets, housing loans were difficult to develop mainly because they had to cover terms as long as 20 or 30 years or more. In general, private financial institutions in Japan were reluctant to provide housing financing to individual borrowers. Mortgage loans and mortgage insurances have still not been developed as financial instruments of the government, and the government has to rely on direct loans through the HL, which is the only government agency in the field of housing finance. Direct loans are supplied to individual borrowers at interest rates,[14] although there is a certain income limit for eligibility. However, the position concerning housing loans changed completely after the financial and interest liberalization of the late 1980s. Private financial institutions have positively participated into the housing loan markets, reflecting the shrinkage of lending activities with good profits. Now the housing loans become one of the attractive markets in which private financial institutions can offer more favourable interest rates than those in the HL. The loans of the HL have been paid back before the end of the term of repayment and replaced by private housing loans to a substantial degree.

Fifthly, the government has a number of credit programmes to promote regional development. In the post-war period, Japan's economy has grown very rapidly, but with an unbalanced development across the various regions. Thus, the government devised instruments to channel financial funds to underdeveloped regional areas. For

---

[12] The distribution of seats in both the Upper and the Lower Houses of the Diet is weighted in favour of the agricultural areas.

[13] It used to be widely believed that the Japanese people are 'workaholics' living in 'rabbit hutches'.

[14] HL used to be obliged by law to make loans at the special interest rate of 5.5 per cent.

this purpose, HTD, ODF and JDB were created to make direct loans in relation to the economic and social development of specific regions, such as Hokkaido, Tohoku, and Okinawa, and to provide financial support to local governments. Needless to say, other government assistance which has already been classified under the headings of general and business is, to a greater or lesser extent, also related to the purpose of regional development.

Finally, attention was paid to export finance. The government credit offered to Japan's exporters was essentially an extension of government assistance to business. The promotion of exports had been one of the most important targets as a strategy to reconstruct the Japanese economy. Thus, government assistance to the export sectors had traditionally been stressed, and the EIBJ was established before other government agencies specifically for this purpose. Exporters usually face competition in international markets from foreign firms that often benefit from the financial support of their own governments. To compete with foreign counterparts, Japan's exporters required government assistance programmes that complemented the services offered by financial institutions in the private sector. Private financial institutions alone cannot provide sufficient support to enhance the export industry, because the risks taken by the partners in international transactions are generally great. Therefore, the government was requested to support the export sector in order to improve the current-account balance and to expand strategic industries. In Japan, the financial instrument that the government used to achieve these aims was the supply of direct loans rather than the use of credit insurance. In addition to providing export finance that benefits domestic producers, the government usually supports direct investment by specific Japanese industries overseas, and particularly big projects in foreign countries.

In addition to the six major types of government assistance, we might add 'others' to the list. They consist of government programmes related to medical care or the preservation of environmental quality. The government channelled its funds to such specific areas through ESB.

How have government funds been allocated so far to each sector as defined above in government financial institutions? It would be desirable to show the past trend for each category (e.g. business, agriculture, export etc.), but disaggregated data are not available on the basis of this sectoral movement. Thus, we shall shift our attention to the relative importance of primary policy objectives in the broader scope of FILP as a whole. Generally speaking, primary policy objectives are classified into three major categories with several sub-items as follows:

Category I: Improvement of national life
1. housing;
2. water supply, sewers and other environmental facilities;
3. social welfare;
4. education;
5. small and medium-sized business;
6. agriculture, forestry, and fisheries.

Category II: Social infrastructure
 7. national land preservation and disaster reconstruction;
 8. roads;
 9. transportation and telecommunication;
10. regional development.

Category III: Industry and trade promotion
11. industries and technology;
12. international trade and economic cooperation.

Figure12.4 depicts the relative shares of such categories by government lending activity for selected years. A few features must be pointed out. First, of greatest importance is the sharp rise of category I whose share has constantly increased relative to the total amount of government lending, starting from 45.1 per cent in 1955 to 74.1 per cent in 1999. Interestingly enough, two-thirds of government lending in the FILP is now occupied by this category. Great emphasis is placed on the increasing expansion of housing from 13.8 per cent to 32.9 per cent during the period under consideration; there are two main factors that can explain this phenomenon. One is that top priority in economic and social policies has been given to housing construction. The other is the fact that government occasionally increases the amount of housing loans as a device for stimulating domestic demand.

Secondly, by contrast, the importance of category III has sharply decreased since 1955 from 22.8 per cent to merely 10.3 per cent in 1999, apparently because of the recent development of private financial institutions. Third, category II has also reduced its share appreciably but to a lesser degree, which means that the government has consistently stressed social infrastructure.

RECENT ISSUES OF THE FILP

Cooperative or Competitive
In principle, the government credit programme has favoured 'strategic' or 'target' private industries over others. The FIL agencies, in particular JDB, has played a key part in aiding selected industries to expand. JDB loans to selected borrowers were designated to support investments judged to be more in the public interest than others. Government lending, especially from major FIL agencies, such as JDB, PF, and SBF, usually provided indications to commercial banks as to which industries or enterprises were designated for preferential treatment. As a result of these loans, it becomes easier for the favoured borrowers to seek further loans from private financial institutions, and thus the loans serve as a guarantee for private financing.

For instance, the role of JDB is a good example of a typical government credit programme. Its role is to foster industrial development and economic and social progress while conforming to the concept of a selective industrial development policy. The past performance of the JDB's lending has changed greatly. For 20 years starting from 1955, the two principal customers were the ocean shipping and the electric utilities industries (the relative shares were 32 per cent and 45 per cent each in 1955). Together with urban and regional development (warehouses, shopping centres, truck terminals), these four categories received over three-quarters of all the JDB's loans. On the contrary, since 1972 the emphasis in the JDB lending programme has shifted notably. The quality of life (including pollution prevention) has become an important concern. Thus, urban and regional development, and the quality of life dominated JDB lending in the 1970s. The share represented by energy loans (for oil refining and storage, energy conservation projects, nuclear power) increased after a long decline, mainly reflecting the oil crisis. To put it simply, the bulk of the post-1972 lending programme was for infrastructure and improvements in the quality of life. Such a tendency has continued to accelerate.

No doubt, the FILP has played an important role in achieving special policy objectives, but its function should be thought of as complementary to private financial activities. Both private and government financing have been cooperative, rather than competitive. In spite of the success of the FILP in the process of economic growth and development, its recent performance has begun to be criticized by private financial institutions. In particular, government financial institutions find it difficult to diminish the size and scope of loans and investments in response to the decrease in demand in the nation's economy while a large amount of interest subsidies has continued to be paid for a long time. It is widely pointed out that government financing became competitive after the 1980s, rather than cooperative and complementary with private financial institutions.

In spite of the fact that the FILP has been instrumental in accelerating Japan's economic growth and development, its recent performance has been criticized, especially from private financial institutions. It is difficult for government financial institutions to decrease the size and scope of loans and investments in response to the decreased demand in the nation's economy. Since the mid-1970s, as stressed above, the role of government financing seems to be competitive, rather than cooperative and complementary with the working of private financial institutions. In connection with the change of its role, it would be better to clarify the recent expansion of government financing. This is evident from Figure 12.5. First of all, note the two circles in the middle of the figure, which indicate the increased size of the nation's economy in terms of nominal GDP from 1970 to 1980 and from 1970 to 1990, respectively. These circles give us a sort of reference point to be compared with the growing size of government and private financial activities.

Next, two skewed octagons are drawn, depending upon the multiple of each of the indicators to cover the past two decades. Obviously, the figures are skewed towards the government sector on the sides of both fund sources and supply. This reflects the fact that the increase in the size of government financial institutions is much larger than that of private financial institutions during the period under consideration. For example, postal savings were 8.0 times higher in 1980 and 17.6 times higher in 1990 than in 1970, while the financial sources of all banks in the private sector were only 3.7 and

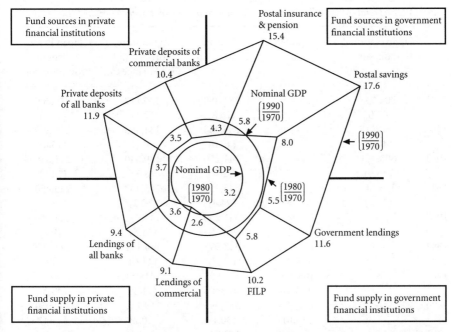

FIGURE 12.5. *Development of government financial institutions realtive to GDP and private financial institutions*

Source: Bank of Japan, *Annual Economic Statistics* 1990 and 1995; MOF

Note: Each figure indicates the multiple of 1980 and 1990 relative to the bench year of 1970. The solid lines depict the ratio of each indicator from 1970 to 1980 and that from 1970 to 1990 respectively

11.9 times higher, respectively. The same holds true also on the lending side when comparing one sector with another. Thus, it is clear that the government has increasingly expanded its relative size in the national economy and the financial markets.

Given such an expanded size relative to GDP and private financial activities, the criticism has mainly derived from the complaints of inefficiency in the operation of public funds through the FILP. It is, however, difficult to measure the efficiency of the government credit programmes. Some doubts have been raised with respect to the efficiency of the FIL agencies, doubts which are related to the rapid expansion of the government share in financial markets. In the private sector, profitability is the generally recognized criterion of efficiency. This criterion cannot be applied to the FIL agencies, mainly because the objectives they pursue lead them to operate in areas that the private sector has not considered profitable. Thus, their activities are not comparable with those of private financial institutions. No measure seems to be accurate, but it may be possible to observe indirectly the recent inefficiencies in government financial institutions.

TABLE 12.4. *Trends of subsidies from the general account to major agencies in the FILP (¥ billion)*

	Japan National Railroads	JR Liquidation Co.	Housing Finance Co.	Agriculture, Forestry and Fish Finance Co.	Japan Private School Promotion Fund
1983	704,537 (42.0)	—	281,450 (16.8)	130,172 (7.8)	277,000 (16.5)
1984	650,347 (40.1)	—	286,250 (17.6)	134,965 (8.3)	243,850 (15.0)
1985	603,991 (36.6)	—	341,250 (20.7)	139,840 (8.5)	243,850 (14.8)
1986	376,743 (26.8)	—	343,250 (24.4)	143,432 (10.2)	243,850 (17.3)
1987	—	186,997 (15.1)	343,250 (27.7)	143,732 (11.6)	244,350 (19.7)
1988	—	178,614 (14.4)	343,995 (27.7)	144,141 (11.6)	245,350 (19.8)
1989	—	165,880 (13.5)	353,995 (28.8)	141,751 (11.5)	248,650 (20.2)
1990	—	153,375 (13.0)	353,995 (30.1)	119,751 (10.2)	252,050 (21.4)
1991	—	100,400 (8.2)	373,995 (30.7)	120,851 (9.9)	255,950 (21.0)
1992	—	92,400 (7.4)	393,995 (31.5)	118,321 (9.5)	260,150 (20.8)
1993	—	85,000 (6.7)	404,500 (31.8)	108,125 (8.5)	265,550 (20.9)
1994	—	76,200 (5.7)	404,500 (30.0)	100,835 (7.5)	273,350 (20.3)
1995	—	63,500 (4.8)	410,900 (30.9)	100,727 (7.6)	280,350 (28.6)
1996	—	53,600 (4.1)	427,400 (32.5)	99,297 (7.5)	—
1997	—	40,100 (2.9)	440,000 (31.5)	98,635 (7.1)	0
1998	—	0	410,000 (31.3)	96,175 (7.3)	329,929 (25.2)
1999	—	—	435,000 (32.0)	87,723 (6.4)	338,031 (24.8)

Source: Tabulated from the MOF data.

Notes: Figures in parentheses are those as a percentage of total amount (see Table 12.3, column (2)).

We can observe efficiency in relation to the size of the funds obtained from the *general account*. Following this approach, Table 12.4 shows which of the FIL agencies depend on financial aid in terms of subsidies from the *general account* of the national government. Particular attention should be paid to the five largest cases of FIL agencies. First of all, the Japan National Railroads (JNR) are worth noting. In the early 1980s, their subsidies from the *general account* were enormous due to the enlargement of inefficient management in the JNR. Obviously, this triggered the privatization in 1987 in which the JNR was replaced by the JR Liquidation company. Subsidies began to diminish sharply. Secondly, for HL, the amount of subsidies from the *general account* which are in the form of interest subsidies has expanded tremendously. HL had to make loans to individual borrowers on preferential terms at an interest rate of 5.5 per cent for a long time. As a consequence, the HL's interest subsidies shared in total, say, more than 30 per cent in the 1990s. Thirdly, the AFF also provides assistance to the agriculture sector at interest rates sensibly below market rates whose interest subsidy this has substantially occupied. The AFF's share has substantially dropped, reflecting the decline of its relative importance in the Japanese economy. Lastly, the Japan Private School Promotion Fund has kept a substantial share of interest payments from the *general account* whose share has greatly increased.

The recent trends of such financial aid can lead to criticism of the efficiency of the operations of the government financial agencies, because this aid is financed by taxes. Whether or not such tax-financed interest payments should continue is now in question from a standpoint of efficiency in policy options. If such subsidies financed by taxes should be reduced or abolished, the government lending rate might have to be increased in order to decrease the gap between them and market rates.

Another indicator of efficiency is the amount of carry-forward and unused funds at the ends of fiscal years 1973–97, as shown in Table 12.5.[15] The ratios of carry-forward to the FILP are in the range of 10–17 per cent each year, implying that the allotted amount of public funds at the initial budget cannot fully be used within the relevant years. Furthermore, an amount of disuse has occurred every year, although its relative size is much smaller than that of carry-forward. Particular attention should be paid to a huge amount of disuse in fiscal 1995.

In order to explore this problem in detail, Table 12.6 indicates the levels of unused funds associated with the top ten cases of disuse caused by the FIL agencies. Of special importance is the disused ratio of HL and AFF relative to actual lending of the FILP: 55.4 and 66.6 per cent respectively. It is astonishing to learn that more than half of these allocated public funds cannot effectively be used for the initial target. Moreover, as compared with actual lending, the unused funds in HL are large enough to be worth noting. In fact, they occupy 61.0 per cent of the total disused amount.

---

[15] Of course, an unused amount might be the result of economizing the initially allotted funds. In this sense, it means the efficient indicator to the used funds. Given the current state of bureaucratic functioning, however, it would be difficult to anticipate the effect of the efficient use of funds.

TABLE 12.5. *Carry-forward and disuse of the FILP, 1973–97*

Fiscal year	FILP	Carry-forward		Disuse	
		Amount (2)	(2)/(1)	Amount (3)	(3)/(1)
1973	8,913.9	1,519.3	17.0	149.5	1.7
1974	10,648.6	1,550.3	14.6	75.7	0.7
1975	12,256.1	1,705.9	13.9	104.8	0.9
1976	13,095.2	1,886.5	14.4	165.1	1.3
1977	15,812.5	2,649.3	16.8	531.3	3.4
1978	18,190.5	3,241.8	17.8	1,546.5	8.5
1979	20,127.1	2,945.6	14.6	728.4	3.6
1980	21,202.3	3,119.0	14.7	152.9	0.7
1981	22,742.4	3,219.0	14.2	205.8	0.9
1982	24,055.3	3,354.7	13.9	229.7	1.0
1983	24,279.0	3,394.2	14.0	221.7	0.9
1984	24,346.1	3,570.0	14.7	1,346.4	5.5
1985	24,441.3	3,836.6	15.7	378.6	1.5
1986	26,063.9	4,143.3	15.9	655.0	2.5
1987	32,396.8	4,989.5	15.4	686.9	2.1
1988	35,174.8	3,999.7	11.4	675.8	1.9
1989	37,477.7	3,790.6	10.1	449.0	1.2
1990	39,831.3	3,851.9	9.7	245.6	0.6
1991	42,867.2	3,965.6	9.3	857.7	2.0
1992	50,693.1	5,554.5	11.0	595.8	1.2
1993	60,103.7	7,290.7	12.1	2,073.6	3.5
1994	59,422.3	7,112.1	12.0	1,566.1	2.6
1995	59,236.9	9,661.7	16.3	10,128.9	17.1
1996	58,777.4	8,918.8	15.2	3,254.6	5.5
1997	61,854.1	8,093.8	13.0	6,085.1	9.8

Source: The MOF data.

Notes: The figure of FILP is the sum of the amount at the initial budget, supplementary amounts, and carry-overs from previous fiscal years.

Given such circumstances, private financial institutions often complain about the inefficient performance of government agencies in a competitive environment with the government. These private institutions advocate the withdrawal of the FILP from areas that are considered the dominion of the private sector.

Special Problems of Postal Savings
Over the years, postal savings have posed serious problems to the functioning of financial markets and monetary policy in Japan. Broadly speaking, there are two points worth mentioning here. The first is the marked increase in the postal savings share in

TABLE 12.6. *Disuse of the FILP agencies: fiscal 1995*

Name	FILP (billion) (1)	Disuse (billion) (2)	$\frac{(2)}{(1)}$(%)	Percentage distribution
Housing Loan Corporation	11,149.5	6,179.2	55.4	61.0
People's Finance Corporation	3,250.0	250.0	7.7	2.5
Small Business Finance Corporation	2,571.1	920.0	35.8	9.1
Environmental Sanitation Business Corporation	385.7	139.7	36.2	1.4
Agriculture, Forest and Fish Corporation	425.0	283.0	66.6	2.8
Japan Development Bank	2,069.2	265.0	12.7	2.6
Export–Import Bank of Japan	1,546.5	310.0	20.0	3.1
Housing and Urban Development Corporation	1,620.6	250.0	15.4	2.5
Pension Welfare Service Public Corporation	4,586.8	779.6	17.0	7.7
Local Governments	15,140.2	155.6	1.0	1.5
Others	16,532.3	596.8	3.6	5.8
	59,236.9	10,128.9	17.1	100.0

Source: Tabulated from Ministry of Finance Statistics Monthly, vol. 31, July 1996, pp. 42–43.

the total amount of personal savings. As can be seen in Table 12.7, their percentage distribution rose by 20 per cent in 1980, compared with 14.2 per cent in 1973. This is explained as follows: 'The outstanding balance of postal savings exceeded 60 trillion yen, about three times the deposits held by Banque National de Paris, the largest bank in the world.'[16] Such a relative share increased up to 22.3 per cent in 1996. More importance should be paid to the ratio of the postal savings to private deposits and savings in a narrower sense of personal savings excluding insurance. Its share has constantly expanded from 20.4 per cent in 1973 to 35.7 per cent in 1997. Now it ought to be noted that more than one-third of private deposits and savings in the private sector are occupied by the postal savings that were essentially independent of financial markets.

As a result of the sharp rise, the postal savings are beginning to compete with private financial institutions. Why have the postal savings increased so rapidly in recent years? The postal savings system as a government institution has a number of advantages over its private counterparts. For instance, there are more than 23,000 post offices throughout the country to collect money from individual savers: private financial institutions have branch offices totalling 13,500.[17] Furthermore, interest on postal

[16] Federation of Bankers Association of Japan, 1982, p. 9.
[17] This figure covers the total number of branch offices in all banks and mutual loan and savings banks.

TABLE 12.7. *Share of postal savings in total personal savings, 1973–97*

Fiscal year	Personal savings outstanding (¥ billion) (1)	Deposits and savings (¥ billion) (2)	Postal savings (¥ billion) (3)	(3)/(1) (%)	(3)/(2) (%)
1973	108,228.7	75,540.1	15,376.5	14.2	20.4
1974	128,907.7	89,963.3	19,431.1	15.1	21.6
1975	154,614.5	106,471.8	24,566.1	15.9	23.1
1976	180,580.0	123,658.8	30,524.8	16.9	24.7
1977	210,232.9	142,953.0	37,726.4	17.9	26.4
1978	241,982.7	164,747.4	44,996.2	18.6	27.3
1979	274,288.3	185,506.8	51,911.6	18.9	28.0
1980	307,825.9	207,872.4	61,954.3	20.1	29.8
1981	343,652.3	231,411.0	69,567.6	20.2	30.1
1982	380,879.4	252,520.5	78,102.6	20.5	30.9
1983	420,209.9	272,241.8	86,298.2	20.5	31.7
1984	437,406.0	294,236.0	94,042.1	21.5	32.0
1985	479,111.2	318,005.4	102,997.9	21.5	32.4
1986	527,412.4	340,163.6	110,395.2	20.9	32.5
1987	582,005.1	365,895.0	117,390.8	20.2	32.1
1988	641,574.3	393,788.5	125,869.1	19.6	32.0
1989	710,506.5	436,083.5	134,572.3	18.9	30.9
1990	759,207.5	468,845.4	136,280.4	18.0	29.1
1991	800,917.9	505,011.4	155,600.7	19.4	30.8
1992	842,197.7	528,070.4	170,090.6	20.2	32.2
1993	884,512.1	554,969.0	183,534.8	20.7	33.1
1994	927,831.7	587,245.9	197,590.2	21.3	33.6
1995	1,182,950.8	613,343.5	213,437.5	21.9	34.8
1996	1,201,211.4	639,709.8	224,887.2	18.7	35.2
1997	1,227,120.8	674,135.3	240,546.0	19.6	35.7

Source: The Bank of Japan, *Annual Economic Statistics*, 1982, 1995, and 1998.

savings was completely tax exempt until 1989, although the total amount invested cannot exceed the legal limit of several millions, for example the figure was ¥3 million in 1987.[18] Likewise, the post office can offer depositors an attractive service called *Teigaku Chokin*, a deposit account that can be cancelled any time after six months and kept for up to ten years at gradually increasing rates of interest on a compound basis.

A second problem posed by the expanded size of postal savings was the difficulty in the efficient operation of monetary policy. Relevant authorities are divided with respect to the establishment of interest rates. Generally speaking, changes in lending rates charged by private financial institutions are related to changes in the official dis-

---

[18] For a more expanded discussion, see Ishi, 1993, ch. 8.

count rate charged by the BOJ. Until the mid-1980s before the launch of financial liberalization, the interest rates charged by private institutions were legally controlled by the Policy Board of the BOJ. By contrast, postal savings interest rates were formally fixed by the Cabinet upon the recommendation of the MOPT. Problems result because of this two-tier determination of the structure of interest rates. In order to protect its depositors' income, the MOPT has often been reluctant to reduce postal savings interest rates. During periods of declining interest rates, the cuts in postal savings rates has come after the rate changes decreed by the BOJ. In general, the BOJ cannot take the initiative of cutting discount rates until the MOPT approves the reduction of postal savings interest rates. Thus the lack of coordination between the BOJ Policy Board and the MOPT results in the inefficient operation of monetary policy. As a result, during periods of declining interest rates, the cut in postal savings rates has frequently been decided too late. Before the MOPT approves a reduction of postal savings rates, the BOJ cannot, in general, take the initiative by cutting the discount rate, and this hinders its efficient operation as a monetary instrument.

In January 1981, the Cabinet established an Advisory Council to the Prime Minister and requested it to study measures to solve the problems caused by the expansion in postal savings. This council presented its report in August 1981, and basically supported the views of private financial institutions. As a result, the government confirmed its favourable attitude towards the introduction of a new system: that is unified determination of the interest rates and the modification of the *Teigaku Chokin*. Although no action has been taken in this matter by the government for a long time, chiefly because of political pressures, an agreement between the MOF and MOPT was made in determining the interest rate of *Teigaku Chokin* in June 1989 in relation to interest rates for 3-year private deposits or the coupon rate of 10-year national bonds. The following formula was introduced:

> When the yield curve is positive, it should be equal to the interest rates of 3-year private time deposits × about 0.95.
> When the yield curve is negative, it should depend on the coupon rate of 10-year national bonds—about 0.5 per cent.

In addition to the establishment of such a rule in determining the interest rates of postal savings, it has been decided to base the interest rates on funds related to the FILP on the market interest rates, mainly reflecting that the FILP have to adjust to the liberalization of interest rates. When postal savings and pension funds are deposited in the Trust Fund Bureau that serves as an intermediary for the FILP, the deposit rate is based on the coupon rate of 10-year national bonds with the range of a 0–0.2 per cent premium. Similarly, when the Trust Fund Bureau lends such funds to the FIL agencies, the same rate is used without any premium. Thus, it is noteworthy that both deposit and lending rates by FILP are determined in line with market interest rates.

How Should we Evaluate the Role of FILP?

It is difficult to assess the role of FILP quantitatively in relation to predictions of its future development. As far as I know, no one has attempted to measure or assess its contribution to Japan's economic growth in quantitative terms, and the evidence so far produced in situations where probable effects might be expected is unconvincing. To sum up the foregoing discussion in this chapter, two points are worth noting as lessons from the Japanese experience.

To begin with, the past record of government financing, including both the pre-war period and the post-war high-growth decades (the 1950s and 1960s), was in many respects excellent. It was a good idea to design the *Yokinbu* and the FILP in order to control public funds on a comprehensive basis. In a historical perspective, they were easily financed by a variety of pension funds (e.g. employees' pension, national pension, etc.) and by postal savings. Excess savings in the personal sector were successfully channelled through the government's financial intermediary to the corporate business sector. Such public funds were invested and loans made effectively, with relatively lower interest rates, to specific industrial sectors, such as heavy-chemical industries, to achieve national goals and promote the national interest during the pre-war years and the earlier period of post-war Japan. For these years, this government financial institution performed very well, undertaking a complementary, not competitive, role of private financial institutions in the nation's financial markets.

Particular attention should be paid to the important role that the postal savings system has played in the raising of funds in Japan, despite the fact that criticism is now being levelled against the aggressive policy adopted by the MOPT in its efforts to compete with private financial institutions. As a matter of fact, the postal savings have worked very well, collecting deposits from individual savers, including low income-earners in regional areas. It is worth noting that some developing countries are interested in inspecting the Japanese system of postal savings from a standpoint of policy instruments for economic development. Backed by a well-organized system for accumulating financial resources, the FILP and government financial institutions worked effectively to foster economic growth in pre- and post-war Japan. Cooperative relations with private financial institutions were prevalent in the long period of rapid economic growth. In terms of both lending and collecting funds, government and private financing coexisted efficiently. In retrospect, emphasis should be placed on the significant role of the FILP and the system of postal savings in Japan.

As another point, however, we must look at the other side of the coin. Merits are often converted into demerits when preconditions change. After the two oil crises, the Japanese economy entered a period of modest growth and experienced decreasing opportunities for loans and investments in financial markets.

Given the change of environment, government financial institutions are now competing with the counterparts of the private sector, in both lending and collecting activities. There is a widespread view, especially on the private side, that government financial activity should gradually withdraw from this area which is considered the prerogative of private financial institutions. Moreover, the situations have been worsened by the collapse of the bubble economy in the 1990s. This implies that the size and the scope of the FIL agencies—of two banks and five public finance corporations —are essentially too large, compared to the diminished demand for their services as a

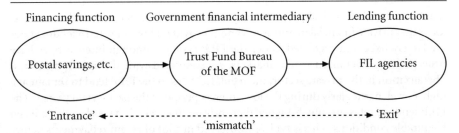

FIGURE 12.6. *Unconnected financial flow between financing and lending functions*

financial intermediary. In recent years reducing the number of finance corporations from eight to five has proved to be successful, because movements towards 'administrative reform' were strongly supported by the general public. Considering the strong resistance within the bureaucracy to any reduction in the size of the bureaucratic machinery, further reform of the government financial agencies in the near future seems highly improbable.

It is evident that the state of the FILP at the end of the 1990s poses a problem for its continuance as a financial intermediary. Figure 12.6 offers a schematic chart to clarify the mismatch between 'entrance' and 'exit' in the mechanism of FILP. At the entrance of the FILP system, postal savings, postal life insurance, and public pension contributions are collected as public funds by the Trust Fund Bureau of the MOF, which acts as an intermediary agency. In turn, such funds are lent to the FIL agencies through the Trust Fund Bureau. The problem is that both financial and lending functions are completely unconnected with each other.

On the entrance side, postal savings have typically continued to expand for a long time, as shown in Table 12.7. Indeed, while private bank deposits have recently been increasing at most by 2–3 per cent, postal savings have shown robust growth rates of 7–8 per cent every year. The reason behind this sharp rise is very clear. Facing the nation's unstable financial system after the post-bubble period, worried private savers shifted their money from private institutions to the post offices, which are backed by the government. Although higher interest rates of postal savings than their private counterpart have been amended recently, the postal savings system is still maintaining a number of advantages in collecting money from savers. For example, the post offices are not eligible for any form of taxes, such as corporate and property taxes. Any large internal subsidies are considered to be generated by interrelated business inside the post offices, on the basis of economies of scale and scope, in which office space and workers are hired alongside other services like mailing and postal insurance. Separated from lending activity, the postal offices have always intensified only the collection of money with special bonus in favour of saving collector's efforts, neglecting the demand side of public funds.

On the other hand, a big problem also occurred at the exit side of FILP, reflecting the process of interest liberalization and globalization in both domestic and overseas markets. The FILP basically has the target of making long-term, fixed low-interest loans that private financial institutions cannot provide. Thus, long-term lending rates are largely fixed and regulated under the FILP system, although interest rates have been partially liberalized in the markets. As compared with the speed of interest liberalization in the private sector, the regulated rates in the FILP tend to remain at a higher level, particularly during the low-interest period of the past several years.[19] The FILP lending rates are much higher than private ones which have sharply reduced favourable conditions. This is typically observed in a lot of recent repayments before the due period in the case of the HL, which were replaced by private lending. HL accumulated a huge amount of such repayment which it had borrowed from the Trust Fund Bureau on higher lending rates in the past. Thus, the government must support HL by increasing interest subsidies from the *general account*, as noted above.

To make the matter worse, the demand for funds has been stagnant to a great degree in recent years. Most of the FIL agencies are suffering from a shortage of lending opportunities in the sluggish state of the Japanese economy. No doubt, they are losing their competitive position in the markets, reflecting a higher level of regulated interest rates. This is the reason why interest subsidies and disuse have virtually increased, as indicated in Tables 12.4 and 12.5. The FIL agencies should be thoroughly reconstructed, reducing their scope and scale, in parallel with the overall restructure of special legal entities under the slogan of administrative reform.

A New Scheme of FILP

As described above, the present FILP poses a number of problems to be solved. No doubt, a symbolic issue related to the current state of FILP is an enormous expansion of postal savings that in turn cannot be fully utilized effectively by the FIL agencies for the nation's benefit. No private bank is big enough to compete with the post office system by itself, nor does it have the full credit and backing of the government behind it. This is the reason why private financial institutions fail to collect deposits in the private sector even if the interest rates of postal savings have been lowered to some extent. It is widely pointed out that the existence of the postal savings system itself now impinges on the profitable opportunities of private financial institutions. A number of proposals have been made by a variety of groups, including government committees, for reform of the FILP. In any case, there has been some pressure to reform the FILP on a comprehensive basis in line with the changing structure of Japan's economy.

Continuous discussion for achieving such a reform plan has been made by the sub-committee members of the Trust Fund Bureau Committee, a Prime Minister's Inquiry Body. As a result, a new scheme is being considered towards a desirable reform package for the future.

---

[19] Since September 1995, the official discount rate of the BOJ has been keeping a record-breaking low level of 0.5 per cent to stimulate monetary policy. Linked with this official rate, long-term prime lending rate was reduced to 2.6 per cent at the end of 1995, while the government lending rate of the FILP remained at 3.14 per cent.

First of all, the comprehensive scheme for controlling public funds on a unified basis should be repealed. Public funds collected through the channel of postal savings and various public pensions will be separated from the FILP framework and in turn they have to be made loans in the form of portfolio investments in the financial markets.

Secondly, the Trust Fund Bureau should accordingly be changed into a new one which is financed from two sources: (i) the FILP bonds issued in the financial markets and (ii) deposits from the reserves of special accounts. Stated differently, the FILP might mainly finance the lending funds by floating its own bonds (FILP bonds), rather than being dependent on postal savings, public pensions, and so on.

Thirdly, special legal entities, such as the FIL agencies, including government financial institutions, should also have to seek their own independent financial sources for their lending activities. Perhaps there would be several alternative cases for this purpose. For instance, each of the FIL agencies could issue their own bonds in the financial markets, depending upon the marketable test of fund raising. However, not all these agencies will be eligible to use this channel of marketable test because only a few agencies, such as DBJ or JBIC, are permitted to adopt the market-orientation of floating bonds. In the case of weak FIL agencies with poorer managerial performance, they will have to issue general government-guaranteed bonds, rather than their own bonds, in the markets. Also, agencies might be able to collect the necessary funds from a new Trust Fund Bureau or Industrial Investment Special Account in the form of loan or capital investment respectively. No doubt, all special legal entitites will be expected to manage their lending activities more efficiently, following market mechanism, with less resort to the government.

Finally, the postal savings system should be fully privatized, splitting the total number of post offices into more than ten regional districts, although it has been decided politically that they should take the form of a public corporation from fiscal 2001 under the ongoing administrative reform movement. Also, public pensions should be allowed to lend its own funds under self-management.

13

The Budgetary Behaviour of Local Governments and Intergovernmental Grant Policies

The basic aim in this chapter is to clarify intergovernmental fiscal relations in Japan. Particular attention is paid to the impact of various types of central government grants on local government budgets. This is an important issue in a nation like Japan, where the fiscal system is strongly centralized. First, a brief outline is given to clarify the Japanese system of local public finance as a preliminary consideration. Secondly, an empirical model is constructed to express the local fiscal behaviour under the current grant policies, following attempts developed in the USA. Thirdly, the estimates from this model are calculated using Japanese data, and some policy questions are examined. The main empirical conclusions that are drawn from the Japanese experience are much more plausible than those in the US case. This implies that the control of central government via various grant policies is more dominant in Japan.[1]

BASIC TRAITS OF THE CENTRALIZED FISCAL SYSTEM

Two-tier System and Poor Local Autonomy

In many countries, considerable attention has been paid in the field of intergovernmental fiscal relations to the interdependence between central and local governments from both an administrative and a financial point of view. Whether the fiscal system is centralized or decentralized, the central government can more or less influence the behaviour of local governments by various instruments in its budget. If a strong central government controls the local governments too rigorously in determining the level and nature of their fiscal activities, the extent of 'local autonomy' (that is, the ability of local governments to act independently of the central government) would be greatly impaired. This is the case in a nation like Japan, which has a centralized fiscal system.

In every country the public sector is stratified into more than one level of government, each one having some responsibilities for a particular set of public sector functions. In Japan, the main levels of government are the national government, the prefectural governments, and the municipal governments (the last two are usually called the local governments). That is to say, the local government has a two-tier system of local public finance (see, for a more comprehensive discussion, Ishi 1993,

---

[1] This chapter draws substantially on Ishi 1985.

ch. 14). The total number of prefectures is 47, which with one exception (that is, the forfeiture and return of the Okinawa islands after the Second World War) has not changed since the pre-war period. The number of municipalities, on the other hand, at 3,229 on 1 January 2000, has been reduced substantially from 10,520 in 1945. This reduction has been caused by the merger of cities, towns, and villages. In this study, the term 'local government' is used only for prefectures, but in quantitative terms all the fiscal activities of the municipal governments are considered to be included in those of the appropriate prefectural governments.

It is widely acknowledged that Japan is a highly centralized unitary nation. The national government controls very strictly almost all the activities of the local governments.[2] There are in particular two reasons for the dominant role of the national government. For one, no clear division of governmental functions exists between central and local governments. The other is that the local governments tend to get poorer access to tax sources in the allocation between each level of government. In the first point, it is noted that the division of governmental functions is too intricate to establish the share of responsibility among governments at the three levels. Although each level of government officially shares responsibility in many fields of government fiscal activities, excluding defence and other similar services, the national government tends to exercise very stringent controls over all the activities of the lower levels of government. Even if some activities are considered to be appropriate for local governments to undertake, they cannot be performed independently of the national government. A number of examples are typically found in the case of schools, roads, social welfare programmes, etc. Generally speaking, conditional grants are the major measures by which the national government can intervene in the decision-making process of local governments.

Intergovernmental Fiscal Transfers
As regards the second point, poorer financial resources at the local level are compensated by intergovernmental fiscal transfers between the national and local governments. In other words, these levels of government are mutually linked by grants from the higher to the lower levels. The dependence of the local governments on the national government has frequently been enhanced by grant policies.

Grants in Japan are of two broad types: unconditional and conditional. Unconditional grants are simply lump-sum transfers from central to local governments, called tax-sharing grants (*Chiho-Kofuzei*) under the local tax allocation system. This is a scheme of equalization payment (that is, tax-sharing grants) from the national government, depending upon the gap between basic fiscal needs and the capacity of

---

[2] For a decade or so, the movement of local finance reform has been precipitated towards decentralization in Japan. It is widely acknowledged that the current centralized system controls the behaviour of local governments too strongly and impairs local autonomy to a great extent. Greater importance is placed upon clarifying the division of the expenditure function between the national and local governments, and mitigating conditional grants in order to strengthen local power from both administrative and financial standpoints.

each local government. In 2000 financial sources for the fiscal equalization pro-gramme are earmarked from a certain percentage of specific national taxes: 32 per cent from the individual tax and alcohol taxes and 35.8 per cent from the corporate tax. In addition, 25 per cent of tobacco tax and 24 per cent of consumption tax (Japan's VAT) are included in the tax-sharing sources under the unconditional grant system. This equalization programme is obviously a sort of unconditional grant, but it is also quite frequently used by the national government to influence local government activities.

Conditional grants, on the other hand, are those which are tied in some way to the behaviour of the recipient government. They are usually given on the condition that the recipient government would match a certain proportion of them with their own expenditures. Furthermore, they are tied to specific types of expenditure (for example, education, road or harbour construction, etc.) rather than being available for general expenditure. These matching grants are known as specific purpose grants (*Kokko-Shishutsukin*).

These two types of intergovernmental grants are an essential element in the finan-cial structure of the poorer prefectures and municipalities in Japan. According to the figures for fiscal 1999 (MOHA 2000) the share of unconditional grants to the total rev-enue of the prefectural and municipal governments was 23.6 per cent, whereas that of conditional grants was 14.9 per cent. In contrast to a substantial share of intergovern-mental grants, both conditional and unconditional, the local tax revenues were only 39.9 per cent of the total financial resources.[3]

The Scope of the Problem

The major purpose in this paper is to analyse the impact of various types of inter-governmental grants on the local government budgets in quantitative terms. Some empirical estimates are used to identify the current dependence of local governments on the higher level of government via grant policies, using Japanese data. The object-ive of this analysis is limited to the scope of the fiscal behaviour of prefectural governments, excluding the municipal governments, mainly for two reasons. For one, the most important issues at present pertain to grants from the national government to the prefectural governments. The other is to simplify the analysis. Hereafter, the term local government will be employed to carry the specific meaning of prefecture.

This analysis is closely related to past attempts to explain one or more types of local government expenditure. In earlier periods, most empirical studies have used a one-equation multiple-regression model to express per capita local expenditure as a function of selected independent variables, employing cross-sectional data (for example, see Brazer 1959; Hirsch 1959; Hansen 1965). The selection of variables was often made on an ad hoc assumption; little attention was paid to the fact that different kinds of grants affected local government behaviour in different ways.

---

[3] The counterpart figures in fiscal 1982 are 17.6 per cent in the share of unconditional grant, 21.2 per cent in that of conditional grant and 35.7 per cent in that of local taxes. Briefly, for the past 15 years the relative reliance on local own fiscal sources with greater freedom has been increased.

Later, a movement gradually began to encourage the inclusion in empirical analysis of some of the concepts of social welfare analysis when modelling for the tax-expenditure decision of local governments (for a more expanded discussion, see Henderson 1968). A number of models have been developed to derive a more thorough understanding of the budgetary behaviour of local governments and, in particular, the way in which they are influenced by intergovernmental grants.

Following the past studies, a model is first constructed to express the local fiscal behaviour and to predict the way that tax-expenditure decisions respond to different types of grants. Using available data, this model is then estimated and the empirical results derived from these estimates are used to examine some policy questions. Major concerns for these policy questions will be with the following points: for example, what is likely to be the response of local governments to the grant policy of national government; what types of fiscal arrangements should be devised to increase the extent of local autonomy; what is the effect of removing the intervention of national government by grants; and so on. It is to be expected that the Japanese experience will produce unique observations, distinct from foreign cases in the field.

A MODEL FOR EMPIRICAL ESTIMATION

Formulation of Major Variables

The first thing to be done is to construct a basic model for estimation. Although there are several alternatives available to us, the basic model is usually the quadratic social welfare function which was developed by Gramlich and others (see Gramlich 1969; Galper *et al.* 1973; Gramlich and Galper 1973). Needless to say, it is impossible to employ the Gramlich model itself for the purpose here, because its construction is based on the US federal fiscal system. Some changes therefore have to be made to adapt it to the Japanese system with special reference to the availability of data, but basically the fundamental framework of the model remains unchanged.

To begin with, a community welfare function must be specifically formulated. It is postulated here that the elected representatives of local government units make many decisions on behalf of the residents of their communities. Attention is directed to four main factors from which the members of a community derive satisfaction: (i) social capital services; (ii) government current services; (iii) private disposable incomes; (iv) budget surplus of local governments.

The model incorporates an optimization procedure for the decision-makers at the local level similar to that used in the development of consumer–demand functions for households. It is assumed that the main objective of the local representatives is to determine the level of the above-mentioned variables (i)–(iv) that maximizes the welfare of their community subject to the budget constraints. Thus we can safely assume that the larger the values of these variables, the higher the welfare level of the local residents.

Social capital services The first objective of local budgetary policy is to increase the level of social capital services, which are financed by capital expenditures made by the local governments. Capital expenditure is divided into two parts: (i) expenditure mandated by conditional or categorical grants on a matching basis, I_M, and (ii) locally initiated discretionary expenditures, I_1. The first implies the subsidized activities of local governments, and the second the non-subsidized (that is, discretionary) activities. Total capital expenditure (grants plus purchases) can be defined as the sum of mandated and discretionary expenditure,

$$I = I_1 + I_M. \tag{13.1}$$

Conceptually, mandated expenditure is determined by its relevant conditional grant and matching rate as follows:

$$I_M = \frac{G_M}{m_M} \tag{13.2}$$

The utility of local decision-makers, whether they are government officials or private households, is then assumed to depend upon the level, Q_1, of social capital services. Thus

$$Q_1 = I_1 + \alpha I_M, \qquad 0 < \alpha \le 1, \tag{13.3}$$

where α is the adjustment coefficient to express the gap that allows for a differential utility from I_M as opposed to I_1. In the case of $\alpha = 1$, both can be considered perfect substitutes because they lead to the same utility level. However, a more general case is when α is less than unity, judging from the intervention of national government in the local decision-making process through the mandated character of conditional grants. Thus, I_M would add less utility than would I_1, and both must be only partially substitutable.

Government current services The second budgetary objective is concerned with the increase of services financed from government current expenditures, which are classified into the following subcategories: (i) social welfare services; (ii) education services; and (iii) general administration services. In each category, total expenditure $E^i(i = 1, 2, 3)$ equals the sum of mandated $E^i_M(i = 1, 2, 3)$ and discretionary $E^i_1(i = 1, 2, 3)$ expenditures:

$$E^i = E^i_1 + E^i_M \tag{13.4}$$

It is impossible to solve equation (13.4) directly from the statistical sources, because of data limitation. Therefore, some procedure must be evolved to distinguish each of the components in equation (13.4). In particular, discretionary expenditures cannot be computed straightforwardly on the basis of available data. We begin with the derivation of E^i_M, using the amount of conditional grant G^i_M and matching rates m^i_M (for detailed information, see Appendix 1).

Similar to equation (13.2), we can obtain:

$$E_M^i = \frac{G_M^i}{m_M^i} \tag{13.5}$$

Next, E_1^i is derived from equations (13.4) and (13.5); thus

$$E_1^i = E^i - \frac{G_M^i}{m_M^i} \tag{13.6}$$

In so doing, it is easy to calculate E^i directly from the data sources available to us.

Three types of current expenditure are assumed in order to determine the welfare level of the community in terms of the utility function. Each category of current services, Q_2, Q_3, Q_4, is formulated as follows:

$$Q_2 = E_1^1 + \beta_1 E_M^1, \quad Q_3 = E_1^2 + \beta_2 E_M^2, \quad Q_4 = E_1^3 + \beta_3 E_M^3, \qquad 0 < \beta_i \leq 1 \tag{13.7}$$

where β_i is the corresponding adjustment coefficient to that defined in equation (13.3), and is assumed to measure a sort of utility weight in mandated expenditures as compared with discretionary expenditures at the community welfare level.

Private disposable incomes Thirdly, the objective of higher private disposable incomes plays an important role in increasing the utility of local decision-makers. Private disposable income, Y_d, at the prefectural level can be defined by:

$$Y_d = Y - T_1 - T^x \tag{13.8}$$

where Y is prefectural pre-tax income, and T_1 and T^x are discretionary and non-discretionary local taxes, each at the prefectural level (that is, both the national and the municipal taxes are excluded).[4]

Since Japan is a unitary country under a centralized fiscal system, the tax systems of local governments throughout the country are more or less the same. In every local government, the same tax base and rates must be used to impose local taxes, based on the legislation of the Local Tax Law (Yonehara 1981). This is in sharp contrast to a federal system in which state taxes differ from one state to another. The Local Tax Law, however, allows local governments to adopt discretionary power over some minor taxes. Although the scope is limited, local governments can have some independent influence on budgetary allocation by using a discretionary portion of local taxes.

The community is then assumed to operate as if the utility, Q_5, associated with the objective of private disposable incomes, is a function of

---

[4] In the Japanese local tax system, we can observe the non-listed tax as a type of discretionary tax. It is not listed in the Local Tax Law and can be levied relatively freely by local governments in relation to a special need with the approval of MOHA. Typical examples are the nuclear fuel tax on nuclear power plants, the tax on a second house, the gravel collection tax and so on.

$$Q_5 = Y - T_1 - T^x \tag{13.9}$$

where increases in pre-tax incomes and a cut in taxes lead to a higher level of utility.

Fiscal surplus Lastly, decision-makers at the local level are assumed to gain satisfaction from larger amounts of fiscal surplus. Given the current situation of Japan's intergovernmental relations, increases beyond a certain level in fiscal deficits (for example, in terms of the proportion of debt service charges in total tax revenues) would induce a substantial degree of intervention from the national government. This being the case, the welfare level of a community, as defined here, is anticipated to be reduced to a considerable extent.

It is assumed that fiscal surplus S can also be defined as the sum of discretionary surplus S_1 and non-discretionary surplus S^x:

$$S = T_1 - I_1 - \sum_{i=1}^{3} E_1^i + S^x, \tag{13.10}$$

and S^x can be written as

$$S^x = T^x + G_M + \sum_{i=1}^{3} G_M^i + R - I_M - \sum_{i=1}^{3} E_M^i, \tag{13.11}$$

where a new variable R represents unconditional grants (that is, tax-sharing grants).

In practice, the discretionary expenditures are not necessarily financed out of discretionary taxes. Thus, it may not be clear what is implied by S_1 and S^x. It is necessary, therefore, to distinguish conceptually the discretionary fiscal surplus from the non-discretionary one in this model.

Let us denote by Q_6 the fiscal surplus term in the utility function. From equations (13.10) and (13.11), Q_6 is given in a simpler notation:

$$Q_6 = S = S^x + S_1$$
$$= T^x + G_M + \sum_{i=1}^{3} G_M^i + R + T_1 - I - \sum_{i=1}^{3} E^i. \tag{13.12}$$

Maximization of Community Welfare

After formulating six kinds of variables, the next step is to examine the process of local government behaviour through the optimization procedure. Mathematically, an attempt is made to maximize the preference function,

$$U = U(Q_1, Q_2, Q_3, Q_4, Q_5, Q_6), \tag{13.13}$$

subject to a budget constraint, S, which has already been defined in equation (13.12).

We must specify the preference function for our procedure. It is assumed below that this is specified in the form of a utility function made up of quadratic terms, as has frequently been employed previously. The function has the six objectives mentioned above, and constant coefficients a_{ij} for $i = 1, \ldots, 6, j = 1, 2$:

$$U = \sum_{i=1}^{6} \left(a_{i1}Q_i - \frac{a_{i2}}{2}Q_i^2 \right), \tag{13.14}$$

$$Q_1 = I_1 + \alpha I_M, \; Q_2 = E_1^1 + \beta_1 E_M^1, \; Q_3 = E_1^2 + \beta_2 E_M^2,$$

$$Q_4 = E_1^3 + \beta_1 E_M^3, \; Q_5 = Y - T_1 - T^x, \; Q_6 = S.$$

In this model, the local government is assumed to maximize the level of U, subject to its budget constraint S, by operating the controllable policy instruments on a discretionary basis. The model incorporates five discretionary variables $(I_1, E_1^1, E_1^2, E_1^3,$ and $-T_1)$ as policy instruments.

The optimization procedure is the method of Lagrange multipliers (see details in Appendix 2), which leads to a set of estimating equations that explain how discretionary variables respond to independent expenditures. Needless to say, the composition of independent variables comprises both conditional and unconditional grants, as well as the non-discretionary nature of local taxes, and private incomes; that is,

$$\left\{ \begin{array}{l} I_1 = b_{10} + b_{11}I_M + b_{12}E_M^1 + b_{13}E_M^2 + b_{14}E_M^3 + b_{15}(Y - T^x) + b_{16}S^x \\ E_1^1 = b_{20} + b_{21}I_M + b_{22}E_M^1 + b_{23}E_M^2 + b_{24}E_M^3 + b_{25}(Y - T^x) + b_{26}S^x \\ E_1^2 = b_{30} + b_{31}I_M + b_{32}E_M^1 + b_{33}E_M^2 + b_{34}E_M^3 + b_{35}(Y - T^x) + b_{36}S^x \\ E_1^3 = b_{40} + b_{41}I_M + b_{42}E_M^1 + b_{43}E_M^2 + b_{44}E_M^3 + b_{45}(Y - T^x) + b_{46}S^x \\ -T_1 = b_{50} + b_{51}I_M + b_{52}E_M^1 + b_{53}E_M^2 + b_{54}E_M^3 + b_{55}(Y - T^x) + b_{56}S^x \\ S = b_{60} + b_{61}I_M + b_{62}E_M^1 + b_{63}E_M^2 + b_{64}E_M^3 + b_{65}(Y - T^x) + b_{66}S^x \end{array} \right\} \tag{13.15}$$

In what follows, an attempt is made to measure the constant coefficients $b_{ij}(i = 1, \ldots, 6; j = 0, \ldots, 6)$ in estimating equations (13.15), by using empirical data. The main objectives of estimating the model are to clarify the impact of grants from central government on spending, taxes, and surplus of local governments. Empirical results derived from these estimates are then used to judge how the local sector responds to various types of central aid, and other non-discretionary variables.

EMPIRICAL RESULTS AND POLICY IMPLICATIONS

Estimating the Model

The model is estimated with annual budgetary and economic observations from 47 prefectures in Japan. The necessary data first had to be prepared on a prefectural basis for the present estimation.

Four budgetary variables are derived from the following expenditure items, which are disaggregated by function (*source*: MOHA 1984):

I   the total expenditure on social capital services—*public works*;
E^1 the expenditure on social welfare services—*current spending portions of social welfare and social security, health and sanitation, and labour relations*;
E^2 the expenditure on education services—those of *education*;
E^3 general administration services expenditure—the residual obtained when the above three items are subtracted from total expenditures.

TABLE 13.1. *Matching rates of mandated expenditures at the local level*

Social capital	Social Welfare	Education	General administration
0.5331	0.7540	0.5047	0.6560

Note: Figures are simple averages of both 1977 and 1978. The method of calculation is given in Appendix 1.

Next, these expenditures of various types must be disaggregated into two components: discretionary and mandated expenditures. As was stated earlier, social capital services alone can be obtained as disaggregated components in a straightforward way from the original source. The three cases of government current services, however, must be derived indirectly from equations (13.5) and (13.6). To do so, matching rates are required and these are shown in Table 13.1.

Private disposable incomes are easily computed by subtracting two taxes (T_1 and T^x) from the total prefectural incomes. The basic data for this can be collected from the 47 prefectures (EPA 1980–81). Likewise, the fiscal surplus of local governments is determined simply by adding a new item of unconditional grants to all variables described above.

The model defined by equations (13.15) is estimated with the pooled cross-sectional data for the period 1977–78.[5] For each year there are data relevant to 47 prefectures, and so the total number of samples gives us 94 figures. All variables are expressed in real terms by using deflators of government capital formation, consumption expenditures, and GDP based on the national accounts concept. Furthermore, they are defined as per capita variables, that is they are divided by the prefectural population. Therefore, it is implied that the utility function (13.14) is that for the average resident of a prefecture.

Major Fact Findings

Table 13.2 displays final estimates in terms of the b_{ij} coefficients in equations (13.15). It provides empirical results of how local fiscal authorities respond to central grants, assuming that they incorporate an optimization procedure of local preference function. Basically, the major concern is whether the response behaviour of local government is likely to be complementary, substitutional, or independent of the fiscal action of central government mainly through grant expenditures. The coefficients in Table 13.2 give the impact effect on the non-discretionary variables initiated by the national government.

[5] Data should be updated or added to cover more recent periods. Since past studies are used, the period for estimation remains untouched.

TABLE 13.2. *Results of empirical estimates. Coefficients of the non-discretionary variables.* $E_1^1 E_1^2 E_1^3 -T_1$

Discretionary variables	Non-discretionary variables						Dummy 1977 = 1 1978 = 0
	I_M	E_M^1	E_M^2	E_M^3	$Y - T^x$	S^x	
I_1	0.0597	−0.1865	−0.2583	0.5640	−0.0064	0.1675	−2,795.6
$r^2 = 0.593$	(1.63)	(−2.20)	(−1.89)	(3.43)	(−1.88)	(4.18)	(−4.22)
E_1^1	−0.0333	−0.2465	0.1014	0.4401	0.0055	0.3124	1,308.9
$r^2 = 0.839$	(−1.55)	(−4.97)	(1.27)	(1.58)	(2.76)	(13.36)	(3.39)
E_1^2	0.0645	−0.0223	0.2110	2.0254	−0.0012	0.1486	−2,647.2
$r^2 = 0.796$	(2.76)	(−0.41)	(2.42)	(0.24)	(−0.58)	(5.82)	(−6.28)
E_1^3	0.2405	0.2120	−0.2277	0.0235	0.0128	0.5077	1,738.3
$r^2 = 0.616$	(3.27)	(1.25)	(−0.83)	(0.07)	(1.88)	(6.33)	(1.31)
$-T_1$	0.0096	0.0228	−0.0109	−0.0623	−0.0034	−0.0142	−62.4
$r^2 = 0.656$	(1.52)	(1.55)	(−0.46)	(−2.19)	(−5.85)	(−2.05)	(−0.55)
S	−0.3410	0.2205	0.1845	−0.9906	−0.0072	−0.1219	2,458.1
$r^2 = 0.697$	(−3.93)	(1.10)	(0.57)	(−2.54)	(−0.89)	(−1.29)	(1.57)

Note: r^2 is a determinant coefficient adjusted for degrees of freedom, and the numbers in parentheses are t-values. I = social capital; E^1 = social welfare; E^2 = education; E^3 = general administration; T = local tax; S = fiscal surplus; M = mandated; 1 = discretionary; x = non-discretionary.

The major findings may be summarized by the following five points. First, the most outstanding feature is the positive effect of S^x in all expenditure cases. Since S^x includes unconditional grants, the increase of S^x provides the local governments with a substantial amount of guaranteed budgetary revenue. The greater the guaranteed revenue in the budgetary policy, the more room there is for the local authorities to exercise their discretionary judgement. Thus, discretionary expenditures and tax reductions tend to increase in response to the increases in S^x.

Secondly, the response of non-aided activities (I_1 and E_1^i) to aided activities (I_M and E_M^i) in each category should be noted. If the coefficients for the mandated grant expenditures (that is, for the latter cases) show positive signs, both types of activity in the same category would have complementary relations with each other. Stated differently, an increase in central grants will immediately increase discretionary expenditures by I_M and E_M^i. On the other hand, if the above-mentioned coefficients are negative, the mandated expenditures would have substitution effects on the discretionary spending at the local level.

For instance, there are positive relations in the cases of social capital and education services, whereas social welfare services have negative relations (look at the diagonal of the coefficient matrix in Table 13.2). These facts imply that an increase in discretionary expenditures on social capital and education services would be induced by a counter-increase in centrally mandated expenditures in terms of grants, whereas a decline in discretionary social welfare spending would be reflected as an increase in grant expenditures from the national government. Thus social capital and education can be argued to be central government initiated activities, which the local authorities merely follow. On the other hand, the non-aided social services of the local governments are being replaced by aided activities initiated by the national government.

There is no significant result in the case of general administration services. Since these include different services of various types (from commerce and industry to police, etc.), both complementary and substitutional effects as stated above might be cancelled out. In addition, the control of central government has been weak for general administrative services.

Thirdly, let us investigate how mandated grant expenditures affect other categories of discretionary expenditures (observe the coefficients $b_{ij}(i \neq j)$ of the matrix). There are two effects, depending on a minus or a plus sign, which is termed the displacement or the stimulative effect. In the case of the displacement effect, which is observed between social capital and social welfare services (b_{21} and b_{12}), grant expenditure from the national government tends to reduce the degree of discretionary spending at the local level.

By contrast, general government services have a stimulative effect on both social capital and social welfare services (b_{14} and b_{24}). A rise in grant levels will stimulate the increase of local discretionary expenditure in these fields. Moreover, some results of estimation, which in certain cases are statistically significant, can be found in Table 13.2, but it is difficult to find a concrete explanation for them being the result of a stimulative or a displacement effect.

Fourthly, the coefficients for $Y - T^x$ indicate a positive response of the two discretionary expenditures (social welfare and general administration) and of the tax increases (that is, a decrease in $-T^x$). This indicates that people at the local community level tend to expect a higher level of public services, such as social welfare, as the local income rises. At the same time, local governments will be inclined to increase discretionally a certain portion of local taxes.

On the other hand, an increase in $Y - T^x$ is likely to decrease discretionary expenditures on social capital services. It is suggested from this finding that priority will be given to agricultural and developing areas with a lower income level when allotting the financial sources of social capital to each region.

Lastly, attention should be given to the relation between fiscal surplus S and non-discretionary expenditures in Table 13.2 (see the row of coefficients b_6 ($j = 1, \ldots, 6$) of the matrix). Significant estimates can be observed only for the coefficients of mandated grant expenditures on social capital and on general government services. Both aided activities tend to induce a decline in S, which would be easier to compensate for in these cases by the flotation of local bonds.[6]

---

[6] As in most unitary nations, local borrowing is strictly regulated in Japan. In particular, the debt permit system of the MOHA reinforces central control, but it has recently tended to be less strict in the movement of local decentralization.

Policy Implications

The prime aim here has been to assess the role of grants from the national government and other factors in influencing the budgetary behaviour of local governments. Basically this study relied upon the Gramlich model, which was developed for large cities in the USA under a decentralized fiscal system, and applied it to the Japanese situation. The main empirical conclusions that are drawn from the Japanese data are much more plausible than those in the US case, although almost the same model is used for the empirical procedures. This reflects the fact that the control of central government via various grant policies has been more dominant in Japan.

The results derived from the above analysis appear to have been expected at the outset. The institutional comparison between Japan and the USA in terms of intergovernmental fiscal relations would make the difference in the empirical results easier to understand. In the USA, local governments are endowed with discretionary powers to accomplish their fiscal activities under the federal system, to the extent that their counterparts in Japan could not stand comparison with them. This is obvious from the following facts for US cities: there are big differentials of public services (such as social welfare programmes and the wages of government officials, etc.) in each local area, reflecting the different levels of local discretionary expenditure. In a similar way, local taxes can be individually determined, in terms both of tax bases and of rates, by the initiatives of local governments. This is not the case in a centralized system. Also, local bonds can be deliberately issued by local governments without any restriction. These facts indicate that the US local governments are allowed much more in the way of independent revenue sources thus decreasing the scope of central government to influence them.

Note should also be taken of the difference between the USA and Japan in the basic nature of intergovernmental grants. Generally speaking, both countries have more or less the same categories of grants, although there are no open-end matching grants in Japan. At the practical level of performance, the control and intervention from the central government seems to be more stringent in Japan. For example, the central government is in a position to determine the volume not only of 'mandated' expenditure supported by matching grants, but also of 'discretionary' expenditure of the recipient governments. This would imply that the activity of the lower government is controlled by the upper government in conjunction with the execution of the grant policies.

Based upon these analytical results, considerable attempts should be made to alter the present structure of intergovernmental fiscal relations towards a more decentralized system, in which local governments can achieve their own targets more deliberately supported by the general types of grants. Conditional grants on a matching basis should be converted into block grants in unconditional terms for the purpose of strengthening the extent of local autonomy, which is considered to be most desirable at present.[7]

---

[7] Even if we attempt to make an estimate by using updated data, our conclusion would remain the same. The present state of central control is still predominant in central–local fiscal relations.

APPENDIX 1. ESTIMATES OF MATCHING RATES IN CONDITIONAL GRANTS

When government current services are divided into mandated and discretionary components, matching rates are a key element, as indicated in equations (13.4), (13.5), and (13.6). Since these rates cannot be obtained in a straightforward way from any statistics, we have no alternative but to estimate them.

The basic procedure is as follows, using Hojokin Binran (Statistics of Governmental Grants) published by the Budget Bureau at the MOF. Two fiscal years, 1977 and 1978, are used for this estimation.

1. Each category of grant expenditure from the national government has a code number of eleven digits to distinguish one grant from another; for example, by economic function, by ministry, by spending objectives, by recipient, and so on. The amounts of categorical grants (conditional) and the entire mandated expenditure (the sum of grants and the correspondent share from local governments on a matching basis) are collected by approximately 2,000 grant items in the *general account* of national government each year.

2. According to the code number by economic function, current services are distinguished from capital services as follows:

Code	Expenditure items	Classification in this paper
1	current purchases of goods and services	
4	current subsidies	current services
6	transfers	
2	capital expenditures for goods and services	capital services
5	equity investment and lending	

3. Government current services are divided into three categories, coded by spending objectives:

Code	Expenditure items	Classification in this paper
082	relief for the poor	
083	social welfare	(1) social welfare services
085	unemployment relief	
086	sanitation	
071	school and education	(2) education services
072	other education	
all other numbers		(3) general administration services

4. When the necessary code numbers for the purpose are found, all the items of the current services are grouped with both (1) the amount of grants and (2) the amount of the whole mandated expenditure. Matching rates are calculated from the ratio of (1) to (2).

Table 13.1 is constructed using the results of these procedures. Each rate implies a uniform average of matching rates on a nationwide scale. It is applied to equation

(13.4) in the text, in which mandated expenditures G_M^i are derived from the prefectural data for each region. It has to be assumed that all local governments have the same matching rates, but this is not true in reality. Depending upon the level of economic development of the regions, preferential rates are often applied by the central government to specific local areas. In this study, however, the differentials are neglected in the application of matching rates.

APPENDIX 2. MAXIMIZATION OF COMMUNITY WELFARE FUNCTION

It is assumed that a utility function is made up of quadratic terms in the six objectives, as was mentioned in the text:

$$U = U(Q_1, Q_2, Q_3, Q_4, Q_5, Q_6)$$

$$= \sum_{i=1}^{6} \left(a_{i1} Q_i - \frac{a_{i2}}{2} Q_i^2 \right), \qquad a_{i2} > 0 (i = 1, \ldots, 6)$$

(Aa)

$$Q_1 = I_1 + \alpha I_M, \qquad Q_2 = E_1^1 + \beta_1 E_M^1, \qquad Q_3 = E_1^2 + \beta_2 E_M^2,$$
$$Q_4 = E_1^3 + \beta_3 E_M^3, \qquad Q_5 = Y - T_1 - T^x, \qquad Q_6 = S.$$

Subject to the budget constraint,

$$S = S^x + T_1 - I_1 - \sum_{i=1}^{3} E_1^i,$$

(Ab)

the community welfare, as defined above, is maximized by using the Lagrange multiplier method.

First, the Lagrange expression is formed,

$$F(I_1, E_1^1, E_1^2, E_1^3, -T_1, S, \mu) = \sum_{i=1}^{6} \left(a_{i1} Q_i - \frac{a_{i2}}{2} Q_i^2 \right) + \mu \left(S - S^x - T_1 + I_1 + \sum_{i=1}^{3} E_1^i \right)$$

(Ac)

where μ is an unknown Lagrangian multiplier.

Next, the first-order partial derivatives are set to be equal to zero:

$$\left\{ \begin{array}{llll} \dfrac{\partial F}{\partial I_1} = 0, & \dfrac{\partial F}{\partial E_1^1} = 0, & \dfrac{\partial F}{\partial E_1^2} = 0, & \dfrac{\partial F}{\partial E_1^3} = 0, \\[3mm] \dfrac{\partial F}{\partial (-T_1)} = 0, & \dfrac{\partial F}{\partial S} = 0, & \dfrac{\partial F}{\partial \mu} = 0, & \end{array} \right.$$

(A1)

Which are the conditions for a critical point.

Since the coefficients of the second-order partial derivatives of the function F are negative, a maximum, subject to the budget constraint, is indeed ensured. To obtain equations (13.15) in the text, we need a further procedure as follows. A system of equations is derived from rewriting properties in equation (A1) in more detail.

$$
\left.
\begin{aligned}
\frac{\partial F}{\partial I_1} &= a_{11} - a_{12}(I_1 + \alpha I_M) + \mu = 0, \\[8pt]
\frac{\partial F}{\partial E_1^1} &= a_{21} - a_{22}(E_1^1 + \beta_1 E_M^1) + \mu = 0, \\[8pt]
\frac{\partial F}{\partial E_1^2} &= a_{31} - a_{32}(E_1^2 + \beta_2 E_M^2) + \mu = 0, \\[8pt]
\frac{\partial F}{\partial E_1^3} &= a_{41} - a_{42}(E_1^3 + \beta_3 E_M^3) + \mu = 0, \\[8pt]
\frac{\partial F}{\partial (-T_1)} &= a_{51} - a_{52}(Y - T_1 - T^X) + \mu = 0, \\[8pt]
\frac{\partial F}{\partial \mu} &= S - S^X - T_1 + I_1 + \sum_{i=1}^{3} E_1^i = 0.
\end{aligned}
\right\}
$$

(A2)

$$
\frac{\partial F}{\partial S} = a_{61} - a_{62}S + \mu = 0.
$$

(A3)

Substituting equation (A3) into equations (A2), and rearranging terms, the first-order conditions for a maximum are expressed in matrix form:

$$
\begin{bmatrix}
-a_{12} & 0 & 0 & 0 & 0 & a_{62} \\
0 & -a_{22} & 0 & 0 & 0 & a_{62} \\
0 & 0 & -a_{32} & 0 & 0 & a_{62} \\
0 & 0 & 0 & -a_{32} & 0 & a_{62} \\
1 & 1 & 1 & 1 & 1 & a_{62}
\end{bmatrix}
\begin{bmatrix}
I_1 \\ E_1^1 \\ E_1^2 \\ E_1^3 \\ -T_1 \\ S
\end{bmatrix}
=
\begin{bmatrix}
-a_{11} + a_{61} + a_{12}\alpha I_M \\
-a_{21} + a_{61} + a_{22}\beta_1 E_M^1 \\
-a_{31} + a_{61} + a_{32}\beta_2 E_M^2 \\
-a_{41} + a_{61} + a_{42}\beta_3 E_M^3 \\
-a_{51} + a_{61} + a_{52}(Y - T^x)
\end{bmatrix}
$$

(A4)

Call the square matrix on the left-hand side A, and note that $a_{i2} > 0 (i = 1, \ldots, 6)$, then

$$
|A| = -a_{12}a_{22}a_{32}a_{42}a_{52}a_{62}\left(\frac{1}{a_{12}} + \frac{1}{a_{22}} + \frac{1}{a_{32}} + \frac{1}{a_{42}} + \frac{1}{a_{52}} + \frac{1}{a_{62}}\right) \neq 0.
$$

(Ad)

Thus, the inverse matrix A^{-1} can be found. By multiplying both sides of equation (A4) on the left with A^{-1}, we have the following formula:

$$\begin{bmatrix} I_1 \\ E_1^1 \\ E_1^2 \\ E_1^3 \\ -T_1 \\ S \end{bmatrix} = B \begin{bmatrix} \alpha I_M \\ \beta_1 E_M^1 \\ \beta_2 E_M^2 \\ \beta_3 E_M^3 \\ Y - T^x \\ S^x \\ 1 \end{bmatrix} \qquad (A5)$$

Where $B = (b_{ij})(i = 1, \ldots, 6; j = 1, \ldots, 7)$ is a proper matrix. This gives a basic foundation to use the estimating system (13.15) in the text.

Conclusion

In order to conclude the discussion developed in this book, it is necessary to point out the major issues and stress any relevance to be derived from the preceding chapters. In a word, we have to seek what kind of lessons can be derived from the Japanese experience, particularly for the developing countries of the world. Japan is the first country in Asia to catch up with the leading Western powers, and it seems that there are a number of positive lessons that the Japanese economy can offer. Indeed, it is widely acknowledged that the process of growth experienced by post-war Japan in the 1950s and 1960s can be regarded as a success story, and one in which the government played an important role in promoting unprecedented economic growth. There are several features which should be stressed regarding the interaction between the impressive performance of the Japanese economy and a well-organized government (see Ishi 1999a).

First, it was very fortunate that Japan was occupied by the Americans after the Second World War and was forced, under pressure from the occupational authority of SCAP, to thoroughly complete a number of structural reforms which freed socio-economic institutions from the established system. Four major economic reforms in the package of the occupation policies (i.e. land reform, renewed labour union movement, Zaibatsu dissolution and anti-monopoly legislation) greatly contributed to the establishment of a fundamental base for Japan's later growth. How could these striking reforms have been achieved with no apparent difficulty in terms of social disorder during the occupation period? Many people in the world have raised such a question. Interestingly enough, the occupation was considered the greatest social experiment attempted by the Americans, rather than a punishment for the defeat in the War. The Japanese people were compelled to follow occupation policy and to accept the result. Furthermore, since Japan was completely devastated and in a state of chaos, the need for tremendous sacrifices through reform was accepted by all. As evidenced from land reform and Zaibatsu dissolution, the forcible adjustment caused by structural reform took the form of transferring economic power from a small minority to a large majority of Japanese who responded favourably. In the process, the previous owners of wealth and wielders of power could not sustain their vested interests as they were under attack economically, socially, and politically. This was a very important factor —unique to Japan—and instrumental in the successful completion of this drastic experiment. No doubt, these sweeping structural reforms in the economy were advantageous, enabling the Japanese government to take optimal growth strategies from an initial stable condition. This is in sharp contrast to other Asian countries and countries in transition that are suffering from fiscal and external imbalances, uneven income distribution, incessant inflationary pressure, or external debt burdens.

Secondly, gradualism rather than shock-therapy was predominant in the decision-making process of policy formation. The anti-inflationary measures taken by the

Dodge plan were the only one exceptional case of shock-therapy, for other policy measures were made through a relatively gradual adjustment throughout the post-war period. For instance, tariffs were lowered step by step while import quotas were widened gradually. Foreign exchange transactions were restricted first on the current account and later on capital account transactions, and afterwards they were removed one after another. While import protection was gradually lifted, the government targeted certain industries for growth in view of an import substitution strategy and provided them with many favourable subsidies or loans during the earlier post-war period. Thereafter, the government gradually phased out these favourable conditions over a number of years, and attempted to strengthen their competitiveness in the world market. Japan's successful attempt with the formation of an import substitution industry may be in stark contrast to the unsuccessful experiences of many other developing countries in view of an import substitution strategy. In addition, the government encouraged export growth successfully by introducing special tax measures or making favourable loans to large-scale enterprises. Thus, the emphasis should be placed on a government-led industrial policy and a gradual approach to liberalizing and deregulating the markets in Japan. The speed of policy change and economic reform is obviously an important issue—consider the shock-therapy disorders in the context of continuing radical economic transformation in the former Soviet Union and Eastern Europe. The Japanese experience seems to suggest that if these countries had taken a more gradual approach to economic reform, the severe economic collapse experienced by many might have been avoided.

Thirdly, macroeconomic policies performed very well in encouraging rapid economic growth in collaboration with private sector activities. The national government had operated fiscal policy until 1965 under the balanced budget principle, and as a result no inflationary impetus was caused by fiscal deficits. This neutral fiscal position was very important in that it was not forced to generate rampant inflation seen in many other developing countries. Likewise, annual tax reductions played a vital role in encouraging private businesses by refunding the benefits of economic growth to the private sector, restricting the expansion of government in promoting the efficient performance of the market. Tax reductions were closely linked to tax incentives in order to achieve specific policy targets, in particular capital accumulation, savings increases, export promotion and so on, although this was undertaken at the sacrifice of equitable tax burdens among various income earners. In one sense, these policy actions in view of both balanced budget and tax cuts might be interpreted as a passive role being played by the government to support the strong movement of private sector activities. By contrast, a more active role was played by monetary policy in adjusting for macroeconomic fundamentals in the Japanese economy. In the 1950s and 1960s a continuous low-interest policy was taken by the monetary authority to stimulate private investment, which was further reinforced by favourable government loans via the FILP. In an overheated economy, in which the reduction of foreign reserves was always a threat, tight monetary policy was initiated by the BOJ at the right time in order to mitigate inflationary pressure and to stop foreign reserves being reduced. This is the success story of government-led mini-recessions in the process of post-war economic growth in order that a better growth performance could be sustained over a long period of time.

Lastly, and most importantly, we should note the debate over government intervention versus free market policies when assessing the performance of Japan's growth-oriented policy in the early post-war period. One of the remarkable features of this post-war government performance was widely believed to be a sort of government intervention into the market via the unconventional instrument of administrative guidance, rather than the adoption of orthodox macroeconomic policies. Generally speaking, in many developing and transitional economies whose markets are still incipient and immature, a market-based growth policy cannot be used effectively. Needless to say, such markets should be fostered in a proper fashion by the government to guide market development and correct market failure. This was true in the earlier post-war period of Japan. According to such a 'Japan model', a number of East Asian countries, such as Korea, have successfully intervened in the markets to achieve higher growth and better economic performance than other countries with a market-based strategy. Consequently, we might be able to place a greater importance on government intervention, at least in the early stages of a growing market economy, and observe not distortive, but productive, government intervention. Related to the gradualist approach, the Japanese style of government intervention seems to have more advantages than the IMF-supported programmes, in which the IMF pushes for rapid adjustment on all fronts of the market economy, such as price liberalization and privatization of government-owned enterprises. These adjustments that the East European transition countries pursued under the IMF programmes inevitably led to accompanying socioeconomic turmoil. If Japan had not grown swiftly in the 1950s and 1960s, it might have been bombarded with IMF missions that would have recommended the adoption of more market-based strategies, unlike its own interventionist approach. Consequently, Japan's rapid growth gave it a sort of arrogant belief that the normal rules of market economies did not apply.

The argument developed above obviously describes a great success story which the Japanese had experienced in the past. Such a brilliant history has completely disappeared now. No doubt, attention should be turned to the recent agonies of the Japanese economy after the collapse of the bubble phenomenon in the 1990s. The heady days of higher economic growth have been radically changed in the Japanese economy, and it pulled hesitantly away from its three-year standstill. Real growth rates of GDP were only 0.4 per cent in 1992, 0.5 per cent in 1993, 0.6 per cent in 1994. However, certain recovery signs began to show themselves in the next two years, and real growth rates of GDP rose to 3.0 per cent in 1995, and 4.4 per cent in 1996. Despite such higher growth rates, nobody seem to believe that they would be able to return to a level of more than 3 per cent in the near future. What is worse, real growth rates for 1997 and 1998 turned into minus growth rates: −0.1 per cent in 1997 and −1.9 per cent in 1998, mainly reflecting the sudden slump caused by a combination of tax increases, in light of the hike of the consumption tax (VAT) rate, and the financial crises in other Asian countries. The stock market in Japan has remained stagnant, and the real estate market is still feeble as a result of the collapsing bubble. The Japanese economy has managed to achieve 0.5 per cent real growth rate in 1999, despite minus growth in the two previous years.

Generally speaking, such pessimistic predictions about the Japanese economy seem to be closely tied with certain negative lessons regarding the shortcomings of both an inefficient decision-making process in public sector and regulated private markets that Japan has steadily fostered throughout the whole post-war period. No effective policy action has been taken by the government to solve any serious economic problems in recent years, and the situation is getting worse as a number of scandals emerge from financial and security companies. The Japanese government may act to stimulate aggregate demand, but no promising prospect can be expected in order to repeat such a Keynesian type of fiscal expansionary policy. In the last eight or nine years of the twentieth century, the government has employed too many fiscal stimuli to buoy up the economy in the light of increased public investment, but this has merely produced poorer results, leaving a huge level of fiscal deficit behind. No doubt, structural problems in the Japanese economy must be resolved if genuine economic recovery is to be achieved and higher growth rates recovered in the future. One of the best candidates for this aim appears to be a large scale deregulation programme to enable new industries to respond to that demand.

The Hashimoto cabinet was making a great effort to tackle six structural reforms for 1996–97: economic, administrative, fiscal, financial, social security, and education. However, it has yet to produce any meaningful results. In Japan, policy measures and institutions have remained untouched for a long time, even after their original objectives were completed in the economy. Since there are both strong vested interests and a persistent resistance on the part of bureaucrats against a reformist approach, it is almost impossible to repeal these kinds of entrenched policy stances which take on a life of their own once given. Typical examples are the postal savings system, government financial institutions, agricultural subsidies, public work projects, and so on.

Government involvement in the economy under the triangle of the ruling party, big business, and the central bureaucracy, has been recently criticized for its creation of opportunities for inefficiency and rent-seeking in the policy-making process. Such government involvement which was previously deemed efficient has turned out to be extremely unproductive today and no longer leads to the positive results seen in the previous days of the rapid growth process. Once the Japanese economy achieved its successful economic performance based on an interventionist approach, the pitfalls involved in this approach came to the forefront all at once.

We wish we could analyse the post-success story with negative lessons described above in this book, but it is beyond the scope of my writing, mainly because time is so limited and policy arguments are still immature with poorer data access at the present time. Perhaps we will try to study in detail all the stories of the post-bubble period as a future task.

References

Abeglen, James C. (ed.) (1970) *Business Strategies for Japan*, Sophia University, Tokyo.

Ackevli, *et al.* (1998) *Structural Change in Japan*, International Monetary Fund, Washington, DC.

Ackley, G. and H. Ishi (1976) 'Fiscal, Monetary and Other Related Policies', in H. T. Patrick and H. Rosovsky (eds.), *Asia's New Giant: How the Japanese Economy Works*, The Brookings Institution, Washington, DC.

The Advisory Group on Economic Structural Adjustment for International Harmony (1986) *The Report Submitted to the Prime Minister, Mr. Yasuhiro Nakasone.*

Allen, G. C. (1965) *Japan's Economic Expansion*, Oxford University Press, Oxford.

—— (1979) 'Government Intervention in the Economy of Japan', in P. Mannder (ed.), *Government Intervention in the Developed Economy*, Croom Helm, London.

—— (1981) *The Japanese Economy*, Weidenfeld and Nicolson, London.

Angel, Robert C. (1991) *Explaining Economic Policy Failure—Japan in the 1969–1971 International Monetary Crisis*, Columbia University Press, N.Y.

Balassa, B. and M. Noland (1988) *Japan in the World Economy*, Institute for International Economics, Washington, DC.

Bank of Japan (1966) *Hundred-year Statistics of the Japanese Economy.*

—— (1973) *The Bank of Japan: Its Organization and Monetary Policies.*

—— (1976) *Japan and the World: A Comparison by Economic and Financial Statistics.*

—— (1981) *Japan and the World: A Comparison by Economic and Financial Statistics.*

—— (1991) *Economic Statistics Annual*, Statistics Department.

Bayoumi, T. and Collyns, C. (eds.) (2000) *Post-Bubble Blue: How Japan Responded to Asset Price Collapse*, International Monetary Fund, Washington, DC.

Boltho, A. (1975) *Japan, An Economic Survey 1953–1973*, Oxford University Press, Oxford.

Brazer, H. E. (1959) 'City Expenditures in the United States', op-66 NBER.

Brown, E. C. (1956) 'Fiscal Policies in the "Thirties": A Reappraisal', *American Economic Review*, December.

Buchanan, J. M. (1958) *Public Principles of Public Debt*, Richard D. Irwin, Homewood, IL.

Chancellor, E. C. (1999) *Devil Take the Hindmost: A History of Financial Speculation*, Gillen Aitken Associates Ltd., London.

Daiwa Research Institute (1996) *Long-term Prediction on the Expansion of Fiscal Deficits and the Japanese Economy*, November 5.

de Larosiére, Jacques (1986) 'The Growth of Public Debt and the Need for Fiscal Discipline', in Barnard P. Herber (ed.), *Public Finance and Public Debt*, Detroit: Wayne State University Press.

Denison, E. and W. K. Chung (1976) *How Japan's Economy Grew So Fast*, The Brookings Institution, Washington, DC.

Domar, E. D. (1944) 'The Burden of the Debt and the National Income', *American Economic Review*, December.

East Asian Ministerial Meeting on Caring Societies (1996) *The Japanese Experience in Social Security*, December 5.

Economic Council (1991) *Report of the Year 2010 Committee* (Abstract), Economic Planning Agency, Tokyo.

Economic Council of Canada (1982) *Intervention and Efficiency*, Ottawa.

Economic Planning Agency (1965) *White Paper on National Income.*

—— (1972) *Annual Report on National Income Statistics.*

—— (1975) *Economic Survey of Japan*, 1974/75.

—— (1980) (1981) *Annual Report of Prefectural Income Statistics.*

—— (1995) *Keizai Yoran* (Summary of Economic Data).

—— (1996) *Implications of the National Burden Ratio and Its Future Prediction* (in Japanese).

—— (annual) *Annual Report on National Accounts.*

Economic Research Institute, EPA (1995) *Economic Analysis* (in Japanese), Vol. 139, May 1995.

El-Agrra, Ali. M. (1988) *Japan's Trade Friction*, Macmillan, London.

Federation of Bankers Association of Japan (1982) *Banking System in Japan*, Tokyo.

Feldman, R. A. (1986) *Japanese Financial Markets*, MIT Press, Cambridge, MA.

Filippini, C. (1994) *The Italian and Japanese Economies in the '80s*, EGEA, Milan.

Funaba, Masatomi (1996) *Government and Regions in Japan*, Kobe University of Commerce, Monograph, Vol. 55.

Galenson, W. and K. Odaka (1976) 'The Japanese Labor Market', in H. T. Patrick and H. Rosovsky (eds.) *Asia's New Giant: How the Japanese Economy Works*, The Brookings Institution, Washington, DC.

Galper, H., E. Gramlich, C. Scott, and H. Wignjowijoto (1973) 'A Model of Central City Fiscal Behavior', *Issues in Urban Public Finance*, Editions Cujas, Paris.

General Agreement of Tariffs and Trade (1958) *Basic Instruments and Selected Documents*, Vol. 3, Text of the General Agreement, Geneva.

Gramlich, E. M. (1969) 'State and Local Government and Their Budget Constraint', *International Economic Review*, June.

—— and H. Galper (1973) 'State and Local Behavior and Federal Grant Policy', *Brookings Papers on Economic Activity*, Vol. 1, pp. 15–65.

Group of Ten (1995) *Saving, Investment and Real Interest Rates—A Study for the Ministers and Governors prepared by the Deputies*, October.

Hansen, N. H. (1965) 'The Structure and Determinants of Local Public Investment Expenditures', *Review of Economics and Statistics*, May.

Hart, A. G. (1961) *Money, Debt and Economic Activity*, 3rd. edn., Englewood Cliffs, NJ.

Henderson, J. M. (1968) 'Local Government Expenditures: A Social Welfare Analysis', *Review of Economics and Statistics*, May.

Hhagemann, R. P. and C. John (1995) 'The Fiscal Stance in Sweden: A Generational Accounting Perspective', *IMF Working Paper*, November.

Hirsch, W. Z. (1959) 'Expenditure Implications of Metropolitan Growth and Consolidation', *Review of Economics and Statistics*, August.

Hollerman, Leon (1988) *Japan Disincorporated—The Economic Liberalization Process*, Hoover Institution Press, Stanford.

Horioka, C. Y. (1996) 'Is Japan's Household Saving Rate Really High?' *ISER Reprint Series* no. 246, Osaka University, Osaka.

—— (1997) 'A Cointegration Analysis of the Impact of the Age Structure of the Population on the Household Saving Rate', *Review of Economics Statistics*, August, pp. 511–16.

—— (1999) 'Japan's Public Pension System: What's Wrong with It and How to Fix It', *Japan and the World Economy*, April.

—— and W. Watanabe (1997) 'Why Do People Save? A Micro-Analysis of Motives for Household Saving in Japan', *Economic Journal*, May.

—— *et al.* (1996) 'Do the Aged Dissave in Japan? Evidence from Micro Data', Discussion paper no.402, ISER, Osaka University, Osaka.

Horne, James (1985) *Japan's Financial Markets: Conflict and Consensus in Policymaking*, George Allen & Unwin, New York.

Huber, Thomas M. (1994) *Strategic Economy in Japan*, Westview Press, Boulder.

Inoguchi, T. and D. Okimoto (1988) *The Political Economy of Japan, Vol. 2, The Changing International Context*, Stanford University Press, Stanford.

Institute of Fiscal and Monetary Policy (1993) *The Mechanism and Economic Effects of Asset Price Fluctuations*, MOF, Tokyo.

International Monetary Fund (1996) *World Economic Outlook*, May.

Ishi, H. (1968) 'The Income Elasticity of the Tax Yield in Japan', *Hitotsubashi Journal of Economics*, Vol. 9, No. 1, June.

—— (1973) 'Cyclical Behavior of Government Receipts and Expenditures: A Case Study of Postwar Japan', *Hitotsubashi Journal of Economics*, Vol. 14, June.

—— (1976) 'A Note on Demand Management Policies in 1974–75', in H. Kanamori (ed.), *Recent Development of Japanese Economy and Its Differences from Western Advanced Economies*, Japan Economic Research Centre, September.

—— (1982a) 'Causes and Cures of Tax Shortfalls', *Economic Eye*, Vol. 3, No. 2, September.

—— (1982b) 'Financial Institutions and Markets in Japan', in M. T. Skully (ed.), *Financial Institution and Markets in the Far East*, Macmillan, London.

—— (1983) 'The Role of Government Financial Institutions', *Public Enterprises*, Vol. 4, No. 1, International Center for Public Finance, United Nations.

—— (1985) 'The Budgetary Behavior of Local Governments and Intergovernmental Grant Policies: A Case Study for Japan', *Government and Policy*, Vol. 3.

—— (1986a) 'Overview of Fiscal Deficits in Japan with Special Reference to Fiscal Policy Debate', *Hitotsubashi Journal of Economics*, Vol. 27, No. 3, December.

—— (1986b) 'The Government Credit Program and Public Enterprises', in T. Shibata (ed.), *Public Finance in Japan*, University of Tokyo Press, Tokyo.

—— (1990) 'Taxation and Public Debt in a Growing Economy: The Japanese Experience', *Hitotsubashi Journal of Economics*, Vol. 31, No. 1, June.

—— (1993) *The Japanese Tax System*, 2nd edn, Oxford University Press, Oxford.

—— (1994a) 'The Incentives for Export Promotion in Japan, 1953–1964', in R. A. Musgrave, C. H. Chang, and J. Riew (eds.), *Taxation and Economic Development Among Pacific Asian Countries*, Westview Press, Boulder, CO.

—— (1994b) 'Japan's Economic Development after 1973: Structural Changes and Economic Policies', in C. Filippini (ed.), *The Italian and Japanese Economies in the 1980s*, Bocconi University, EGEA.

—— (1995a) 'Trends in the Allocation of Public Expenditures in Light of Human Resource Development—Overview in Japan', Paper presented to the Asian Development Bank Symposium, July.

—— (1995b) 'Rigidity and Inefficiency in Public Works Appropriations: Controversy in Reforming the Budgeting Process in 1994', *Journal of Japanese Studies*, Vol. 21, No. 2.

Ishi, H. (1996a) 'Budgets and Budgetary Process in Japan', *Hitotsubashi Journal of Economics*, Vol. 37, No. 1, June.

—— (ed.) (1996b) *The White Paper on Fiscal Structural Reform* (in Japanese), Toyo Keizai Shinpo, Tokyo.

—— (1999a) 'Macroeconomic Fundamentals of Postwar Economic Growth in Japan—A Great Success and Recent Frustration—Lessons in Asian Economics', *Journal of Asian Economics*, vol. 10, pp. 247–61.

—— (1999b) 'The Role of Government in the Postwar Growth Process of Japan', *Journal of Asian Economics*, vol. 10, pp. 65–90.

Ito, Takatoshi (1992) *The Japanese Economy*, MIT Press, Cambridge, MA.

—— (1996) 'Japan and the Asian Economies: A "Miracle" in Transition', *Brookings Papers on Economic Activity*, Vol. 2.

Johnson, Chalmers (1978) *Japan's Public Policy Companies*, American Enterprise Institute, Washington, DC.

Johnson, P. and J. Falkingham (1992) *Aging and Economic Welfare*, SAGE Publications, London.

Kawagoe, Toshihiko (1993) 'Land Reform in Postwar Japan', in J. Teranishi and Y. Kosai (eds.), *The Japanese Experience of Economic Reforms*, St. Martin Press, New York.

Kawasaki, Kenichi (1996) 'The High Japanese Saving Ratio—Will it really decline rapidly?' EPA, Economic Research Institute, Discussion paper no.63.

Kindleberger, Charles P. (1991) 'Bubbles', in J. Eatwell, M. Milgate, and P. Newman (eds.), *The World of Economics*, Macmillan, London.

Kita, N. *et al.* (1997) *Regional Development and the Government Role in Japan* (in Japanese), Nihon Keizai Hyoron-sha, Tokyo.

Komine, Takao (1993) 'The Role of Economic Planning in Japan', in J. Teranishi and Y. Kosai (eds.), *The Japanese Experience of Economic Reforms*, St. Martin Press, New York.

Komiya, R. (1975) 'Economic Planning in Japan', *Challenge*, May/June.

—— and M. Suda (1991) *Japan's Foreign Exchange Policy 1971–82*, Allen & Urwin, N. Sydney.

Kosai, Y. and Y. Ogino (1984) *The Contemporary Japanese Economy*, Macmillan, London.

Kotlikoff, Lawrence (1992) *Generational Accounting*, Free Press, New York.

Krause, L. and S. Sekiguchi (1976) 'Japan and the World Economy', in H. T. Patrick and H. Rosovsky (eds.), *Asia's New Giant: How the Japanese Economy Works*, The Brookings Institution, Washington, DC.

Kuroda, M. (1993) 'Price and Goods Control in the Japanese Postwar Inflationary Period', in J. Teranishi and Y. Kosai (eds.), *The Japanese Experience of Economic Reforms*, St. Martin's Press, New York.

Lerner, A. P. (1948) 'The Burden of the National Debt', in *Income, Employment and Public Policy: Essays in Honor of A. H. Hansen*, W. W. Norton & Co., New York.

Lewis, W. Jr. (1962) *Federal Fiscal Policy in the Postwar Recessions*, The Brookings Institution, Washington, DC.

Lincoln, E. J. (1989) *Japan: Facing Economic Maturity*, The Brookings Institutions, Washington, DC.

—— (1998) 'Japan's Financial Problems', *Brookings Papers on Economic Activity*, Vol. 2.

Lockwood, W. W. (ed.) (1965) *The State and Economic Enterprise in Japan*, Princeton University Press, Princeton.

Mackinnon, R. I. and K. Ohno (1997) *Dollar and Yen*, The MIT Press, Cambridge MA.

Matsushiro, Kazuo (1970) 'Industrial Concentration and Profit Rates' (in Japanese), *Sanken Ronshu*, Kansai Gakuin Daigaku, March.

Matsuura, Katsumi (1994) 'Width Distribution Before and After the Collapse of the Bubble Economy' (in Japanese), Discussion Paper no.1994–15, Institute for Post and Telecommunication.

McMillan, C. J. (1985) *The Japanese Industrial System*, 2nd edn, Walter de Gruyter, Berlin.

Minami, R. (1986) *The Economic Development of Japan*, Macmillan, London.

Ministry of Finance (MOF) (1949) *Monthly Report of Fiscal-Monetary Statistics* (Zaisei Kinyu Tokei Geppo), August.

—— (1962) *Fiscal Statistics* (Zaisei Tokei).

—— (1978) *The Financial History of Japan: The Occupation Period 1945–52*, Vol. 19 (Statistical Data), Tokyo Keizai Shimposha.

—— (1995) *The Japanese Budget in Brief*.

—— (1996, 1998, 1999) *FILP Report*.

—— (1997) *Social Security Data*.

Ministry of Health and Welfare (MOMW) (1996) *Annual Report on Health and Welfare 1994–1995*, March.

—— (1999) *White Paper on Pensions: How to Construct the Pension System for the 21st Century* (in Japanese), Institute of Social Insurance, Tokyo.

Ministry of Home Affairs (MOHA) (1995) *New Gold Plan*, Health and Welfare Bureau for the Elderly.

—— (1966–2000) *Summary of Local Finance* (Chiho Zaisei Yoran), Tokyo.

Ministry of International Trade and Industry (MITI) (1996) *On Maintaining Economic Vitality and the State of Government Finance*, Mimeo, November 5.

Mitchell, Wisley C. (1951) *What Happens during Business Cycles*, NBER, New York.

Mizouchi, T. (1970) *Personal Saving and Consumption in Postwar Japan*, Kinokuniya, Tokyo.

Moriguchi, C. (1989a) 'Economic Structural Adjustments and Macroeconomic Balance of Japan', *Rivista Internazionale di Science Econmiche e Commerciali*, Vol. 36, No. 2, February.

—— (1989b) 'Driving Forces of Economic Structural Change: The Case of Japan in the Last Decade', in W. Krelle (ed.), *The Future of the World Economy*, Springer-Verlag, IIASA.

—— (1991) 'The Japanese Economy and Economic Structural Adjustments', *Economic Studies Quarterly*, Vol. 42, No. 2, March.

Morris, J. ed. (1991) *Japan and the Global Economy, Issues and Trends in the 1990s*, Routledge, London & New York.

Mourdoukoutas, P. (1993) *Japan's Turn—The Interchange in Economic Leadership*, University Press of America, Lauham.

Murakami, T. (1987) 'The Japanese Model of Political Economy', in K. Yamamura and Y. Yasuba (eds.), *The Political Economy of Japan*, Vol. 1, Stanford University Press, Stanford.

Myrdale, G. (1939) 'Fiscal Policy in the Business Cycle', *American Economic Review, Papers and Proceedings*, March.

Nagano, Atsushi (1988) 'Japan', in Pechman (ed.), *World Tax Reform*, The Brookings Institution, Wasington, DC.

Nakamura, Takafusa (1981) *The Postwar Japanese Economy*, University of Tokyo Press, Tokyo.

Nikkeiren (1982) *Report of Committee on Labor Problems* (in Japanese), Tokyo.

Nishibe, S. (1987) 'The Mob Approach to Tax Reform', *Japan Echo*, Vol. 14, No. 2.

Nishimura, Yoshimasa (ed.) (1993) *Reconstruction and Growth of Fiscal-Monetary Policies* (in Japanese), MOF Printing Bureau, Tokyo.

Noguchi, Yukio (1983) 'Problems of Public Pensions in Japan', *Hitotsubashi Journal of Economics*, Vol. 24.

Noguchi, Yukio (1986) 'The Public Sector in the National Economy', in T. Shibata (ed.), *Public Finance in Japan*, University of Tokyo Press, Tokyo.

—— (1987*a*) 'Public Finance', in K. Yamamura and Y. Yasuba (eds.), *The Political Economy of Japan*, Stanford University Press, Stanford.

—— (1987*b*) 'Tax Reform—The Missing Rationale', *Japan Echo*, Vol. 65, No. 1.

OECD (1972*a*) *Labor Force Statistics 1959–1970*, Paris.

—— (1972*b*) *The Industrial Policy of Japan*, Paris.

—— (1972*c*) *Monetary Policy in Japan*, December.

—— (1994) *Environmental Performance Review: Japan*, Paris.

—— (1995), (1998), (1999) *Economic Outlook*, December 1995, June 1998, December 1999.

—— (1997) *Aging in OECD Countries: A Status Report*.

—— (1999) *Economic Surveys Japan*, November, Paris.

Office of Management and Budget (1986) *Budget of the US Government*, US Government Printing Office, Washington, DC.

Ohkawa, K. (1974) *National Income: Estimates of Long-term Economic Statistics of Japan since 1968*, Tokyo Keizai Shinposha, Tokyo.

Ohkawa, K. and H. Rosovsky (1973) *Japanese Economic Growth*, Stanford University Press, Stanford.

Okimoto, Daniel I. (1989) *Between MITI and the Market*, Stanford University Press, Stanford.

Okita, Saburo and Takahashi, Takeo (1971) 'International Aspects of Planning in Japan', *Economic Planning and Macroeconomic Policy*, Japan Economic Research Center.

Okun, Arthur M. (1971) *Rules and Roles for Fiscal and Monetary Policy*, Brookings Reprint 222.

—— and Nancy Teeters (1970) 'The Full Employment Surplus Revisited', *Brookings Paper on Economic Activity*, Vol. 1.

Ono, A. (1994) *Labor Economics* (in Japanese), Toyo Keizai Shinposha, Tokyo.

Ott, Attiat F. (1993) *Public Sector Budgets: A Comparative Study*, Edward Elgar, Hants.

Patrick, H. T. (1970) 'The Phoenix Risen from the Ashes: Postwar Japan', in J. B. Crowley (eds.), *Modern East Asia: Essays in Interpretation*, Harcourt Brace and World, New York.

—— (ed.) (1980) *Japan's High Technology Industries*, University of Tokyo Press, Tokyo.

—— and H. Rosovsky (1976) *Asia's New Giant: How the Japanese Economy Works*, The Brookings Institution, Washington, DC.

—— and R. Tachi (1986) *Japan and the United States Today*, Center on Japanese Economy and Business, Columbia Univ., New York.

Pechman, J. A. and Kaizuka, K. (1976) 'Taxation', in H. Rosovsky and H. T. Patrick (eds.), *Asia's New Giant: How the Japanese Economy Works*, The Brookings Institute, Washington, DC.

Pepper, T., M. E. Janow, and J. W. Wheeles (1985) *The Competition Dealing with Japan*, Praeger, New York.

Reischauer, E. O. (1977) *The Japanese*, Harvard University Press, Cambridge, MA.

Rosenbluth, F. M. (1989) *Financial Politics in Contemporary Japan*, Cornell University Press, Ithaca.

Sanchez-Ugate, F. (1987) 'Rationality of Income Tax Incentives in Developing Countries—A Supply-Side Look', in V. P. Gandi (ed.), *Supply-Side Tax Policy: Its Relevance to Developing Countries*, IMF, Washington, DC.

Sato, K. (ed.) (1999) *The Transformation of the Japanese Economy*, M. E. Sharpe, New York.

Schmiegelow, Michele (ed.) (1986) *Japan's Response to Crisis and Change in the World Economy*, M. E. Sharpe, Inc., New York.

Shibata, Tokue (ed.) (1993) *Japan's Public Sector*, University of Tokyo Press, Tokyo.

Shimizu, Y. (1992) 'Problems in Japanese Financial System in Early 1990s', *Hitotsubashi Journal of Commerce and Management*, Vol. 27, September.

Shinohara, M. (1964) 'Factors in Japan's Economic Growth', *Hitotsubashi Journal of Commerce and Management*, February.

—— (1970) 'Causes and Patterns of Postwar Growth', *The Developing Economies*, December.

—— (1982) *Industrial Growth, Trade and Dynamic Patterns in the Japanese Economy*, University of Tokyo Press.

Social Insurance Agency (1996) *Outline of Social Insurance in Japan*, Tokyo.

Sumitomo Bank (1988) 'Business Expansion Induced by Sustained Domestic Demand' (in Japanese), *Economic Monthly Report*, July/August.

Suzuki, Y. (ed.) (1987) *The Japanese Financial System*, Clarendon Press, Oxford.

Suzumura, Kotaro (1996) 'Industrial Policy in Developing Market Economies', in E. Malinvaud, and A. K. Sen (eds.), *Developing Strategy and the Market Economy*, Clarendon, Oxford.

Tachi, R. (ed.) (1995), (1996), (1998) *Data Book on Public Finance* (in Japanese), Ohkura Zaimu Kyokai, Tokyo.

Tachibanaki, T. (1996) *Public Policies and the Japanese Economy*, Macmillan, London.

Tajika, E. and Y. Yui (1996) 'Public Policies and Capital Accumulation: Japan at the Dawn of Economic Growth', *Hitotsubashi Journal of Economics*, Vol. 37, No. 2, December.

Takayama, Noriyuki (1992) *The Greying of Japan: An Economic Perspective on Public Pensions*, Kinokuniya, Tokyo.

—— (1998) *The Morning After in Japan*, Maruzen, Tokyo.

Takenaka, H. (1992) *The Japanese Economy*, University of Michigan Press, Ann Arbor.

Tanaka, Kakuei (1972) *Building a New Japan: A Plan for Remodeling the Japanese Archipelago*, Tokyo.

Tax Advisory Commission (1960) *The First Tax Report*, December.

Teranishi, Juro (1994) 'Japan's Way', *Economic Policy*, December.

—— and Y. Kosai (eds.) (1993) *The Japanese Experience of Economic Reforms*, St. Martin's Press, New York.

Thorn, R. S. (1987) *The Rising Yen*, Institute of Southeast Asia Studies, Singapore.

Trevor, M. (1987) *The Internationalization of Japanese Business*, Compus/Westview, Frankfurt.

Trezise, Philip H. and Yukio Suzuki (1976) 'Politics, Government and Economic Growth in Japan', in H. T. Patrick and H. Rosovsky (eds.) *Asia's New Giant: How the Japanese Economy Works*, The Brookings Institution, Washington, DC.

Tsuru, S. (1993) *Japan's Capitalism*, Cambridge University Press, Cambridge.

United Nations (1985) *World Population Prospects*, Department of Economic and Social Affairs, Population Studies, No. 85, New York.

US Government (1983) *The Budgets for Fiscal Year 1984 Special Analysis D.F.*, GPO, Washington, DC.

Viner, A. (1987) *Inside Japan's Financial Markets*, The Economist Publications, London.

Wiseman, J. (1984) 'Public Debt and Public Policy: An Evaluation of Recent History', Paper submitted to the 40th Congress of IIPF.

Yamamura, K. (1967) *Economic Policy in Postwar Japan*, University of California Press, Berkeley and Los Angeles.

—— (ed.) (1982) *Policy and Trade Issues of the Japanese Economy*, University of Tokyo Press, Tokyo.

Yamamura, K. and Y. Yasuba (1987) *The Political Economy of Japan, Vol. 1, The Domestic Transformation*, Stanford University Press, Stanford.

Yashiro, N. (1987) 'Japan's Fiscal Policy—An International Comparison', *Japanese Economic Studies*, 61, Fall.

Yovehara, J. (1981) *Local Public Finance in Japan*, Australian National University Press, Canberra.

Yoshikawa, H. and T. Okazaki (1993) 'Postwar Hypso-Inflation and the Dodge Plan, 1945–90: An Overview', in T. Teranishi and Y. Kosai (eds.), *The Japanese Experience of Economic Reforms*, St. Martin's Press, New York.

Yuzawa, T. (1994) *Japanese Business Success*, Routledge, London & New York.

Name Index

Subject Index

administrative guidance   2, 40
administrative reform, Rincho   143–5
ageing
  demographic changes   227–31
  nursing care for elderly   257–61
aggregate demand (1955–73)   30–4, 36
agriculture
  support by government financial institutions
    297, 302
  Uruguay Round   222
  see also land reform; Ministry of Agriculture,
    Forestry and Fisheries
Agriculture, Forestry and Fish Finance Co. (AFF)
  302, 303
airports   287
Annual Report of National Account (EPA)   203,
  204, 209
anti-monopoly legislation, occupation policies
  15
anti-recession policies (1975)   59
asset prices
  speculation and bubble economy   75, 80, 85–6
  see also land prices; stock prices
assets, non-performing (post-bubble recession)
  82, 88–9

balance-of-payments
  export promotion   266–7
  foreign exchange reserves   268
  limitations on growth (1955–73)   38–9
  see also current account deficit
balanced budget   329
  budget orthodoxy   126–30, 162–3
  countercyclical policies (1953–65)   156–78
  see also budget; fiscal consolidation; fiscal
    deficits; government
Bank for International Settlements (BIS)   89–90
Bank of Japan (BOJ)   19, 20, 289, 329
  bubble economy   78–9, 81
  budgetary process   116
  discount rate policy (1973–74)   57, 59
  interest rates   306–7
banks
  aggressive expansionism and bubble economy
    80, 81–2
  capital injection in post-bubble recession
    90–2
  Jusen problem   84
  nationalization   95–6
  see also specific names of banks

Basic Law for Environmental Pollution Control
  49
Black Monday   76
Board of Audit   117
bonds
  attempt to avoid issuance   141
  bond dependency   123–5
  construction bonds   104, 130, 180–1
  deficit-covering bonds   130, 148, 152, 197
  national bonds   103–4, 160, 180–1
  Yokinbu   288, 289, 290, 308
bubble economy   1, 11, 73–81
  consequences of collapse   82–98
  definition   74–6
  discount rate   78–9, 81
  and fiscal consolidation   190–3
  tax revenue   191–3
budget
  balanced budget   126–30, 156–78, 162–3,
    329
  budgetary process   110–17
    local government   117–18
  countercyclical policies   156–78
  cyclical patterns of surplus and deficit
    159–60, 162–70, 172–5, 177
  expansionary policies   59, 134–5
  general account   106–7
  government sector in System of National
    Accounts   107–10
  Local Public Finance Programme   105–6
  national budget   103–5
  overview of system   101–3
  process of formulation and tax revenue sources
    186
  see also Dodge Plan; fiscal consolidation; fiscal
    deficits; *general account*; Keynesian fiscal
    policies; special accounts
Budget Bureau   224, 226
business cycles
  (1951–75)   31, 39
  (1953–65)   156–9
  apparent end of   80–1
  countercyclical policies   59, 60, 130–1,
    156–78
  patterns of fiscal surplus and deficit
    159–65
  policy-induced (1955–73)   40–4
  recession and expansionary fiscal policies
    130–1
  see also growth